TRIBES AND THE STATE IN LIBYA AND IRAQ

ALISON PARGETER

Tribes and the State in Libya and Iraq

From the Nationalist Era to the New Order

OXFORD
UNIVERSITY PRESS

Oxford University Press is a department of the
University of Oxford. It furthers the University's objective
of excellence in research, scholarship, and education
by publishing worldwide.

Oxford   New York

Auckland   Cape Town   Dar es Salaam   Hong Kong   Karachi
Kuala Lumpur   Madrid   Melbourne   Mexico City   Nairobi
New Delhi   Shanghai   Taipei   Toronto

With offices in

Argentina   Austria   Brazil   Chile   Czech Republic   France   Greece
Guatemala   Hungary   Italy   Japan   Poland   Portugal   Singapore
South Korea   Switzerland   Thailand   Turkey   Ukraine   Vietnam

Oxford is a registered trade mark of Oxford University Press
in the UK and certain other countries.

Published in the United States of America by
Oxford University Press
198 Madison Avenue, New York, NY 10016

Copyright © Alison Pargeter 2023

All rights reserved. No part of this publication may be reproduced,
stored in a retrieval system, or transmitted, in any form or by any means,
without the prior permission in writing of Oxford University Press,
or as expressly permitted by law, by license, or under terms agreed with
the appropriate reproduction rights organization. Inquiries concerning
reproduction outside the scope of the above should be sent to the
Rights Department, Oxford University Press, at the address above.

You must not circulate this work in any other form
and you must impose this same condition on any acquirer.

Library of Congress Cataloging-in-Publication Data is available
Alison Pargeter.
Tribes and the State in Libya and Iraq: From the Nationalist Era
to the New Order.
ISBN: 9780197769430

Printed in the United Kingdom on acid-free paper
by Bell & Bain Ltd, Glasgow

CONTENTS

Foreword	vii
Introduction	1

SECTION I
LIBYA

1. From Palace to Revolution: Tribes and the Coming to Power of the Nationalist State	15
2. Tribes and Qadhafi's Revolutionary Toolbox: From Khout Al-Jed to Social Control	41
3. Tribes, Revolution and Revenge	67
4. Tribes and the Post-2014 Order	103

SECTION II
IRAQ

5. Tribes and the Iraqi Republic	137
6. Tribes and the Ba'athist State	157
7. Tribes, Occupation and Shi'ite Iraq	191
8. Tribes and Mobilisation: Politics, Power and Protests	223
Conclusion	255

Notes	263
Bibliography	297
Index	311

v

.

FOREWORD

This book is the culmination of research carried out between 2019 and 2022 that was generously funded by the Smith Richardson Foundation. I would like to give special thanks to Marin Strmecki for his continued support of my research, as well as for his patience in the face of repeated delays caused by the Covid pandemic. The global shutdown posed major challenges for the project, especially in relation to carrying out fieldwork. However, much of the research for this book is based on interviews conducted with tribal sheikhs, notables and tribesmen in Libya and Iraq, as well as in the diaspora. It is also drawn from interviews carried out with Libyan and Iraqi officials, former officials, politicians, academics and journalists. I would like to thank all the respondents who kindly gave their time and insights and who helped shed light on what is a complex and often opaque topic. Their kindness, frankness and willingness to share their expertise and experiences has been invaluable, especially given the limited scholarship on the subject matter. While I cannot list all by name, particular thanks go to a number of individuals who were especially generous with their time, expertise and first-hand knowledge of the subject matter. They include Sheikh Sami al-Majoun, Sheikh Takleef al-Minshed, Naji Sultan al-Zuhairi, Sheikh Adnan al-Danbous, Sheikh Jawad al-Assad, Ammar al-Ameri, Abdulsalam Jalloud, Sheikh al-Senussi Buheleq, Sheikh Mabrouk Buamid, Sheikh Mohamed Omar Benjdiriya, Sheikh Abdulhameed al-Kezza, Sharif al-Abbar, Abduljawad Badeen. This book would not have been possible without them and I am extremely grateful. I

FOREWORD

would also like to thank Professor Jon Hill at King's College London for his support in carrying out this project.

This book is dedicated to the late Professor George Joffé, who was an inspiration, mentor and friend. His deep knowledge of the Middle East, passion for the region and generosity in sharing his wisdom and expertise with me and many others made him a truly remarkable man, scholar and friend. He is sorely missed.

INTRODUCTION

The seismic events that have shaken the Arab world over the past two decades have changed the landscape of the Middle East. One notable shift has been the emergence of a host of sub-state and quasi-state entities, ranging from tribes, militias, religious groups and other currents that mobilise on identity. Nowhere is this more apparent than in Libya and Iraq, where the state has either receded (Iraq), or been swallowed up altogether (Libya). In both states, the sudden overturning of centralised and authoritarian nationalist regimes that had been in power for decades opened the door to a host of competing subnational actors and forces, who took advantage of the chaos that followed regime change. These forces moved into the foreground and have continued to vie for dominance and control ever since.

Not least of these forces is the tribe. After decades living in the shadow of the revolutionary nationalist state, tribes in both Libya and Iraq have taken advantage of the fracturing and fragmentation that accompanied regime collapse to play a more expansive role in the political and security arenas. Tribes, which formed a key part of the ruling polity at independence in both states, have a presence in both national and local power structures; have forged mutually beneficial relationships with key powerbrokers; and in some instances have become key security providers in their own areas. Yet despite their increased role and visibility, tribes and tribal influence remain poorly understood. This lack of understanding has its roots partly in the inadequate study of the tribe in these countries outside of the anthropological field, especially during the nationalist period. Although

TRIBES AND THE STATE IN LIBYA AND IRAQ

tribes are the oldest, most enduring and most controversial social entities in the Middle East,[1] they have been paid scant attention in the modern literature on both states.

There are several reasons for this neglect. Firstly, there has long been much anti- and post-colonial unease about examining a politico-social unit associated with colonialism and Orientalism, and that came to be linked in some academic departments with 'political incorrectness'.[2] The US military's embedding of anthropologists and social scientists in its military operations in Iraq and Afghanistan during the 2000s aggravated this discomfort. Thus, although in recent years there has been an increased propensity to engage with the tribe as an analytical unit of study, doing so still provokes questions, especially in the region, about motive, intent and value-judgement. Furthermore, there is still a detectable embarrassment and dismissiveness about the tribe among some parts of the elite in both states, attachment to kinship relations seemingly prompting uncomfortable questions regarding the role and nature of modernity in the Arab world.

Secondly, in line with the progressive discourse they espoused, nationalist rules in Libya and Iraq sought to bury or conceal the tribe, relegating it to the social sphere and deeming its study taboo. While Muammar Qadhafi and Saddam Hussein may have employed tribal symbolism in a more direct fashion from the 1980s and 1990s, neither opened up real space for scholarship on the issue. Carrying out empirical research of any nature under these repressive regimes was challenging enough, but working on the tribe carried additional risks both for researcher and respondents, as Husken testifies in his impressive study of tribes in the borderland of Egypt and Libya.[3]

Thirdly and more importantly, there has been a lack of critical engagement with nationalist and modernist notions of political development and social progress. The view of the tribe as a pre- or even anti-modern unit that is antithetical to the linear progress of the modern state and that will weaken and disintegrate over time has often held sway. Assumptions that modernisation, urbanisation and mass education policies would diminish tribalism and attachment to tribal identity served to push tribes and tribalism further off the research agenda.

Thus, while there are studies that have addressed the role of the tribe in both states under the monarchy and prior to it, literature on

INTRODUCTION

the tribes during the Arab nationalist period is almost non-existent and focuses almost exclusively on the regimes, the voice of the tribes being all but absent. Most scholarship on the Qadhafi period in Libya brushes over the tribe, reiterating the same broad generalisations about how Qadhafi manipulated tribes and relied on particular tribal groupings to buttress his regime. It is also drawn largely from a handful of sources that are lacking solid empirical basis.[4] There is almost a 'set history' of the tribe under Qadhafi that is retold repeatedly and in which the voice of both tribe and regime is absent. There is a tendency too to ascribe exceptional power to the regime, with suggestions that Qadhafi 'shaped tribal identity', or that he 're-tribalised society',[5] as if it were in his gift to manipulate social structures in such a profound way. Some scholars have gone as far as to assert that the regime's efforts at 'mobilising tribal support and exploiting communal division' led to tribal identity remaining 'unbroken'.[6] These kinds of arguments give the impression that the tribe had little real cultural or social embeddedness in Libya, nor any life outside the regime. As this book will argue, such portrayals do not take sufficient account of tribal agency, which was certainly compromised by living in the shadow of the revolutionary state, but was not absent altogether. Rather, Qadhafi's relationship with the tribe was always far more complex and nuanced than this set history would suggest, with there being a greater bargain between ruler and ruled than is often portrayed.

Some works on the Qadhafi period have engaged with the tribe in a more nuanced fashion. Obeidi has shown how despite the regime's nationalist and modernist ideology, tribes continued to play a significant role in forming identities in Libya, and remained 'instruments of the socialisation process'.[7] Davis's 1998 anthropological study of the Zuwiya tribe demonstrates how at the local level, tribal agency and kinship politics were able to co-exist with the revolutionary regime in what was more of a bargaining process between ruler and ruled.[8] However, central to Davis's thesis is the idea that, as a result of the particularities of its colonial experience, Libyan society has a 'deeply entrenched image of statelessness' and an aversion to statehood. Davis sees this statelessness as being bounded in kinship relations and reflected through Qadhafi's personal philosophy and promotion of the

3

TRIBES AND THE STATE IN LIBYA AND IRAQ

'stateless state'.[9] Anderson also ascribes Libya the characteristic of 'statelessness', assigning it to its colonial history and arguing that the 'ethos of the tribe in Qadhafi's ideology', and the role of 'hinterland culture' in the regime's political ideology, including the emphasis on equality, the aversion to hierarchy, the social complexity associated with urban life and the disregard of territorial boundaries, struck a 'responsive chord in the Libyan psyche' reflecting a continued scepticism in the modern state.[10]

Aside from the contestable description of Qadhafi's Libya as 'stateless'—traditional state structures may have been weak but they were not completely absent—Anderson deals with the tribe as a static entity and an ahistorical concept that has not changed in over a century.[11] The characteristics cited are more akin to the Bedouin tribes of old, while there is no attempt to understand the differences and variations both within and among Libyan tribes. As this book will demonstrate, tribes are not monolithic or collective political actors. Moreover, they do not necessarily reject or even seek to obstruct the modern state.

While there has been considerably greater scholarly attention on Iraqi tribes over the years, the role of kinship relations during the nationalist period is still poorly understood and lacking sound empirical evidence. Tribes are often afforded little more than a cursory mention in the literature, reflecting the fact that the historiography of modern Iraq has remained heavily focused on the Ba'athist regime. Although scholars have alluded to the importance of kinship relations, especially as tools for social control,[12] there is a tendency to oversimplify the relationship between tribes and regime. Moreover, as in Libya, Iraqi tribes have been portrayed as little more than instruments to be manipulated by an omnipotent dictator, who has it in his power to 'de-tribalise' or 're-tribalise' society at will. Such assumptions belie the fact that while undoubtedly authoritarian, both Qadhafi and Hussein were forced to deal with social realities that they couldn't ignore or fully control.

Furthermore, those studies that have engaged with the tribe in Ba'athist Iraq have tended to focus on the regime's promotion of tribal sheikhs and tribal values after the Shi'ite and Kurdish uprising of 1991, leaning heavily on Baram's formative 1997 article which frames this

INTRODUCTION

shift as a rehabilitation of 'neo-tribal values' engineered by the regime.[13] While certainly insightful, Baram still presents the tribe as a largely passive actor whose influence is predicated on its relationship to the body politic only. As with other works that address this shift, power arrangements and activity are attributed almost exclusively to the state, ignoring the fact that tribes have a life and history of their own, no matter how dependent on the state they might be. This book will show that tribal agency was more important in Iraq during this period than is often understood, and that relations between tribe and state were more complex than is often portrayed.

Given the lack of attention afforded to the tribes during the nationalist period, their sudden visibility following the toppling of the Qadhafi and Ba'athist regimes in 2011 and 2003, respectively, came as a surprise. Yet when tribes emerged out of the chaos that accompanied regime change and began to assert themselves along with the collection of other sub-state entites, it became glaringly apparent that tribes were still critical components within both societies and were going to play an important role in the new [dis]order. As such, this coming to the fore prompted a renewed interest in the study of the tribe in both states. This is especially true for Iraq. However, much of the empirical work carried out on Iraqi tribes after 2003 has been written through a counter-terrorism lens, and while this by no means reduces its value, the focus is limited and is almost exclusively on the country's Sunni tribes. The Shi'ite tribes of Iraq's central and southern governorates have been all but overlooked despite their interconnectedness with the Shi'ite ruling establishment and the *Marja'iya* (supreme Shi'ite religious authority). In the case of Libya, the tribes have still received limited attention, with observations about the tribe generally folded into broader discussions about sub-state entities in the post-2011 landscape.

This lack of emphasis, despite tribes' obvious importance, is perhaps unsurprising. The changed research landscape may have catapulted the tribe into the open, but studying tribes and tribal dynamics remains challenging. Tribes are notoriously elusive and defy classification. They are units of social organisation bounded by their own traditions, social codes and localities, yet at the same time they are able to wield influence both nationally and locally in the political, security and

TRIBES AND THE STATE IN LIBYA AND IRAQ

economic spheres. Tribes are able to deploy tribal agency and exert power, yet they do so in seemingly intangible ways. Part of this intangibility is due to their fluid nature and their pragmatic flexibility, characteristics not shared by some of the other components operating inside the power vacuums that opened up with regime change. As one revolutionary commander and member of a prominent tribe in eastern Libya remarked, 'There is nothing in the tribe that is absolute.'[14]

It is this lack of absolutes that makes tribes all the more difficult to define, and there have long been heated debates in academia about what constitutes a tribe. The term 'tribe' has been used by academics across disciplines (history, anthropology, political science, sociology, human geography) to describe so many different kinds of groups or social formations that it is virtually impossible to produce a single, all-encompassing definition.[15] Furthermore, theorists have long been divided over a conception of the tribe as a concrete local structure or an abstract or symbolic construct.[16] Some scholars have gone as far as to deny that tribes even exist as concrete local structures, viewing them as little more than a 'state of mind' or 'social constructs with a problematic history'.[17] While kinship may be imagined, and may contain symbolic or constructed elements that do not rely solely on blood lineage, many Iraqis and Libyans consider tribes to be concrete local structures that have meaning and that are more tangible components of their lives than some of the literature suggests. As Husken rightly observes, 'Tribe and kinship are essential parts of the way people view the world and how they form their identity, and are central to their practices.'[18] Tribes are fluid and flexible, but for those in them, they are concrete at the same time.

Yet this does not belie the challenges in identifying patterns of tribal behaviour. Not only do tribes differ in Libya and Iraq, there are key divergences between tribes in different areas of each country, and within tribes themselves. Patterns among tribes or clans or even sections of tribes in one locality are routinely contradicted by patterns and behaviours in another. In Libya, the picture is complicated further by the ethnic dimensions in the south and parts of the west of the country, but also by the fact that in some instances there is a crossover between town and tribe, particularly in the west. In places such as Zawiya, Misrata, Zintan and Tarhouna, for example, the identity of

6

INTRODUCTION

various sub-clans has fused with their locality, with tribes referred to as the Zawiya tribes, the Zintani tribes and so forth. In the east and south of the country, meanwhile, tribes tend to be more cohesive and are more clearly bounded within their own territorial area. The large Cyrenaican tribes such as the al-Awaqir, al-Obediat and Barassa for example have a distinct tribal identity that is arguably more pronounced than in areas such as Misrata or Zawiya, and also have their own traditions and dynamics linked to the particular historical experience of eastern Libya.

In Iraq, the tribal tapestry is even more complex. This is partly due to ethnic and sectarian factors, as well as differences in tribal structure. While broadly speaking, the Sunni tribes are concentrated primarily in the western governorates and the Shi'ite tribes in the south and centre, there are also mixed Sunni-Shi'ite tribes that display different levels of cohesion. There are also Kurdish tribes in the north, as well as Turkoman tribes and tribes belonging to other minorities, which have different characteristics. In addition, the tribes of the centre and south have a history that is embedded in agriculture and feudalism, with agricultural settlement resulting in some sheikhs becoming agents of the state, while those in the western governorates lived a more Bedouin existence. Although times have changed, these factors have conditioned the way in which tribes have evolved in different parts of the country.

It is wrong to generalise therefore, as tribes are not uniform, nor do they act as cohesive units capable of taking unified political action or stances. Tribes change and adapt according to the prevailing political, security and social circumstances. As Lacher observes, the notion of 'tribe' does not imply an 'age-old, unchanging social structure', with tribes having 'always evolved along with changing economic or military conditions and as a result of their interaction with states'.[19] The tribes of Libya and Iraq today are not the same entities they were when the nationalist regimes took power. Yet there has been a tendency in some of the literature that has emerged since the collapse of both regimes to continue to deal with them as unchanging static bodies that have not evolved in generations. Some of the literature on post-2011 Libya has pigeonholed tribes as part of an imagined 'periphery', echoing Ibn Khaldoun's cyclical theory in which the

7

TRIBES AND THE STATE IN LIBYA AND IRAQ

Bedouin periphery takes over the urban centre, becomes urbanised and is subsequently displaced by the next wave of Bedouin interlopers.[20] There has been a tendency to relegate Libyan tribes to a 'hinterland' that is in competition with or in opposition to an urbanised and more ideological centre.[21] While there are doubtless fault lines between the more urbanised-Islamist forces that emerged after Qadhafi's demise and the more traditional tribal elites and forces, one cannot make such neat distinctions. As Cherstich observes, tribal identity is still deemed important in Libya's urban centres.[22]

Tribes in Iraq are also often associated with the hinterland and there is an assumption in some of the literature that tribes are still 'mostly found in the rural areas and not in the main cities'.[23] Although Jabar's theory of 'cultural tribalism' and 'social tribalism' acknowledges that forms of tribal ethos or tribal culture are present among migrants to Iraq's large urban centres, he denies the existence of any form of tribal organisation in these urban centres binding these groups together.[24] Yet, in both Libya and Iraq, the borders between hinterland and urban centres were blurred long ago, with tribes and tribal structures having spilled over into the main cities. As a result, parts of these tribes became urbanised or semi-urbanised themselves. This didn't only mean that migrants held on to tribal customs and culture, but they remained part of concrete tribal structures and formed part of a new urbanised tribal elite. It is precisely these urbanised tribal elements and sheikhs that provide the tribes with political weight and influence. Many of today's sheikhs are professionals—doctors, lawyers, university lecturers, military officers—who are part of the urban elites of their own societies, but who see no contradiction between this and their tribal role. The tribesman is no longer solely part of the hinterland.

Furthermore, tribal identity is multifaceted. There is still a tendency in the literature to separate out identities as though being part of a tribe precludes inhabiting other identities simultaneously. Assertions that the post-Qadhafi period resulted in a 'return' to premodern or pre-national identities such as the tribe are misplaced. One shouldn't confuse a rendering visible of the tribe with a 'return' to a form and mode of being that has never gone away. Rather, the tribesman can be a proud member of his tribe but also have a strong sense

INTRODUCTION

of national identity; the two are not mutually exclusive. Being part of a tribe doesn't prevent the adoption of other worldviews. Zeidal argues that after 2003, tribes failed to 'offer an alternative to the prevailing ideologies of sectarianism, political Islam, Iraqi nationalism, and even liberalism', while Harling considers tribal identity as a 'social trend' akin to Islamism, nationalism and communism.[25] Yet tribal identity does not necessarily impede the embracing of such ideologies, and sheikhs and tribesmen can also be nationalists, Islamists, revolutionaries, members of political parties and ideological currents. As this book will demonstrate, tribes are far more diffuse and flexible than often portrayed.

Furthermore, much of the literature on tribes in Libya and Iraq—both old and new—is confined within the strong state-weak tribe paradigm, with tribal resurgence explained as a response to state weakness.[26] Dealing with the tribe as the negation of the state fails to appreciate the nuances and complexities of state-tribe relationships, as well as the fact that tribes are organic components of these societies that have co-existed with the state—weak or strong—over generations. As Genat has remarked with regards to Iraq, but whose comments could apply equally to Libya, 'Literature on tribes in Iraq is scant and often falls prey to simplistic binary approaches to state-society relations.'[27] As this book will show, tribes generally prefer stability and seek to work within the confines of the state rather than against it. Indeed, the main argument this book puts forward is that tribes in their various permeations cannot be relegated to the hinterland or be associated with pre-modern identities and modes of social organisation that are in contradiction to the state. Tribes continue to form a core component of these societies and have withstood the repeated onslaughts of the past decades, proving able to adapt and remain relevant. This is not to overplay their role; tribes are one component among many that are operating in the public space and their importance should not be exaggerated. However, this book is an attempt to uncover the history and role of the tribe and its relationship to the state in Libya and Iraq from the nationalist regimes until today.

This pairing of countries offers useful parallels and divergences. Both countries were tribal at the time of state formation and tribes

9

TRIBES AND THE STATE IN LIBYA AND IRAQ

formed key components of the ruling elites under the monarchies. Both states experienced the coming to power of authoritarian Arab nationalist military regimes that ruptured existing political and social structures and employed an anti-tribal rhetoric while simultaneously co-opting and using tribes as political tools. After decades of nationalist rule, both experienced abrupt regime change through the intervention of foreign forces (to varying degrees), and as the state fragmented, tribes moved into the power vacuums that opened up. Yet there are notable sectarian and ethnic variations in the two countries, as well as differing colonial experiences and divergent levels of development and political culture. As a consequence, tribes in each state have evolved differently, with Iraqi tribes becoming notably more diffuse than many of their Libyan counterparts. However, in both states, tribes have come to play key roles in the fraught and violent transitions that emerged out of regime change, and there are striking parallels in the way they operate and respond to the state.

The book is divided into two sections, one on Libya and the other on Iraq, and argues that despite their primary function as units of social organisation, tribes have been able to exercise tribal agency to impact the political and security trajectory of both states. In so doing, the book has tried to cover a broad range of issues across both states. Due to the unwieldy nature of the subject matter, it inevitably focuses on certain tribes and geographical areas more than others. The Kurdish tribes of Iraq and the southern tribes of Libya are glaring omissions but are beyond the scope of this work, which does not pretend to be a comprehensive account of tribes and tribal politics during this period. Moreover, although the book touches on the Sunni tribes of Iraq, the main focus is on the Shi'ite tribes of the centre and south, which have received almost no scholarly attention in the contemporary period.

The first section covers the role of the tribe in Libya from the coming to power of the Qadhafi regime in 1969. It shows how despite the dismissive rhetoric employed by the regime, Qadhafi crafted a web of tribal alliances to underpin and buttress his rule. It also shows how the tribes responded to these overtures, exercising tribal agency and entering into a succession of bargains with the regime. This section goes on to examine the events of 2011, showing

INTRODUCTION

how tribes responded to the uprising and the events that unfolded after it. In so doing, it looks at how tribes situated themselves in the new political and security environment, and how and in what ways tribes were able to exercise influence. This section also focuses on relations between tribes and the new powerbrokers who came to dominate post-Qadhafi Libya. From Islamist political forces to revolutionary and militant Islamist groups, including ISIS, to the self-styled Libyan National Army (LNA) of Khalifa Haftar, it looks at how tribes engaged and bargained with these new actors in order to further their interests and objectives.

The second section of the book covers Iraq. Starting from the coming to power of the Republican state in 1958, it traces how tribes dealt with and responded to a succession of nationalist Republican regimes that dismissed tribes as backwards relics of the past and that set about trying to dismantle tribal structures. It goes on to analyse the experiences of the tribe under Ba'athist rule between 1968 and 2003, showing how tribes were emasculated and shattered by the Ba'athist state, but were nevertheless able to deploy a degree of tribal power, especially in the latter years. This second section also analyses the response of the tribes to the invasion and occupation of Iraq in 2003, and assesses how tribes responded to the new political order. It goes on to demonstrate how tribes were able to influence the political and security arenas, albeit often in intangible ways. Concentrating particularly on the Shi'ite tribes, it shows how tribes succeeded in mobilising in both the political and security realms, and how their unique relationship with the *Marja'iya* impacted upon these dynamics.

As such, the book will show how and why tribes are still important sub-state actors in both Libya and Iraq, and show that while they may have altered in shape and structure, they remain important components of both societies.

SECTION I

LIBYA

1

FROM PALACE TO REVOLUTION

TRIBES AND THE COMING TO POWER
OF THE NATIONALIST STATE

Tribalism is hated, surely by all as a principle. It is a social phenomenon in every backward society... When a society enters a stage of social advancement, it will gradually get rid of this social phenomenon.

Muammar Qadhafi[1]

The revolutionary has to deal with reality in order to change it.

Abdulsalam Jalloud[2]

On 1 September 1969, 27-year-old Muammar Mohamed Abu Minyar Qadhafi and a group of young revolutionaries seized power in a bloodless military coup. Inspired by the Arab nationalism of Egyptian President Jamal Abdulnasser, who had overthrown the monarchy in Egypt a decade and a half earlier, these young revolutionaries sought to overturn the old order and build a radical new regime that could replace Libya's creaking monarchy. In line with the Arab nationalist ideas of the time, they sought to do away with tribal, ethnic and sectarian loyalties—which they viewed as backwards and reactionary—and to replace them with allegiance to the modern 'Arab nation'. The Arab nationalist lexicon despised and disparaged such

15

TRIBES AND THE STATE IN LIBYA AND IRAQ

loyalties, and by the 1950s, it had already become decidedly unfashionable in many parts of the Arab world, especially among the elite, to profess a tribal or sectarian identity.[3]

To these young ideologues, King Idris al-Senussi, who came to power at independence in 1951, represented the antithesis of their Arab nationalist ideals. They viewed the ageing Idris, who prior to becoming king had been first the leader of the Senussi religious order and then the Emir of Cyrenaica,[4] as an anachronism and a stooge of colonialist powers. The monarchy's willingness to host British and American military air bases on Libyan soil was considered a violation of sovereignty, while its reluctance to join other Arab states in sending forces to fight against Israel in 1967 was a betrayal of the Arab cause. These fervent young nationalists also condemned the monarchy as a 'reactionary, backward and decadent regime', accusing it in their Proclamation of the Republic, issued on 1 September 1969, of facilitating 'bribery, intercession, favouritism, treason and treachery'.[5] Idris had ruled mainly through powerful families and notables, who peopled his Royal Diwan, many of them hailing from the large tribes of the east, such as the Barassa, the al-Obediat and the al-Awaqir, which formed the foundations of the king's power. Politics was a matter of family, factional, tribal and parochial interests, with prime ministers selected for their regional origins and loyalties, and with cabinet appointments following a rough and ready principle of tribal balance.[6]

This system was buttressed by patronage and corruption. As one account from 1964 described, 'The direct effects of such a strong tribal system upon Benghazi's life can be seen in many fields. Top personnel often become wealthy and prosperous even if they stay in power for a short time, and also take full advantage of employing their relatives and supporters in key posts without any regard to their qualifications. Most Cyrenaicans emphasise the name of the tribe they belong to especially if it is a strong tribe and enough of its people are in power. This situation does not apply to intellectuals, who are still few.'[7] For Qadhafi and his fellow revolutionaries, who came from predominantly modest backgrounds, this reliance on tribal sheikhs and notables flew in the face of their progressive nationalist vision, and they associated tribalism with backwardness, colonialism and corruption. As Qadhafi proclaimed while addressing students at Tripoli

FROM PALACE TO REVOLUTION

University on 2 January 1970, 'Tribalism is hated, surely by all as a principle. It is a social phenomenon in every backward society as you know. When a society enters a stage of social advancement, it will gradually get rid of this social phenomenon.'[8]

Yet for all the iconoclasm of the new regime and despite its attempts to create a new state and society, it quickly became apparent that tribes were an essential component of Libyan culture and society that could not be dismissed or done away with. Rather, they would continue to play a part in the country's political life, albeit behind the scenes. Qadhafi came to realise soon enough that ideology was not going to be sufficient to guarantee the survival of his revolutionary nationalist state and that by binding certain tribes to his regime and manipulating the country's tribal tapestry, he could shore up his rule and give it social and political depth. Tribes became, therefore, a key component of Qadhafi's revolutionary toolbox, and were built into the social contract upon which he relied during the four decades of his rule.

Despite the important role played by tribes under the Qadhafi regime, as Wehrey has observed, 'Tribalism in Libya has long remained an enigma, shrouded by the country's decades of isolation and the paucity of serious scholarship on the topic.'[9] As noted in the introduction, there are very few studies that deal with the tribe under Qadhafi, and those that do touch on the topic are often confined to the realm of theory and supposition.[10] As a result, a narrative has developed within the scholarship that does not necessarily reflect the reality on the ground or paint an accurate picture of the relationship between tribes and Qadhafi's Jamahiriyah (state of the masses). This narrative holds that Qadhafi's revolution represented the triumph of lowly, underprivileged tribes over powerful wealthy tribes associated with the monarchy; that Qadhafi deliberately marginalised and alienated these eastern tribes, replacing them with a new modernising elite unfettered by tribal affiliation; that Qadhafi 'revived' or 'revitalised' tribalism in the late 1980s and 1990s to compensate for state failure or state weakness; that the tool he used to 're-tribalise' society at this time was the Social People's Leaderships; and that attachment to the tribe in Libya stems from the country's weak bureaucracy and a 'natural' aversion to statehood.[11]

17

TRIBES AND THE STATE IN LIBYA AND IRAQ

While there are doubtless elements of truth in all these arguments, the reality of Qadhafi's relationship with Libya's tribes was always far more complex and nuanced than these neat arrangements suggest. Furthermore, Libyan tribes were not monolithic or passive actors but were multifaceted bodies that changed with time and that used tribal agency to enter into bargains with the regime. Doubtless, this relationship was unequal and was weighted far more heavily towards the state, but there was a relationship between ruler and ruled nonetheless. Despite all the ideological fervour and the heavy reliance on repression, Qadhafi could not travel far without the tribes. He still had to navigate his way through what was a complex and ever shifting web of kinship networks and alliances which, as he very quickly discovered, could either facilitate or frustrate his rule.

'The Sons of the Country's Tribes'

Despite his desire to forge a modern state that would transcend tribal and regional divisions, Qadhafi grew up steeped in tribal tradition and tribal values. The son of an illiterate goat herder from a small village named Jehenam (Hell)—so called because of the unbearable heat in the summer months[12]—that is located outside of Sirte in central Libya, Qadhafi grew up in a tent-dwelling community in the desert. His family came from a small and uninfluential tribe, the Qadhadhfah, one of the murabitun tribes—those that claim special religious significance and in some instances claim a direct link to the prophet.[13] The Qadhadhfah's Libyan origins are in Ghayran in the western mountains. It is here, on the Abu Ghaylan Mountain, that Sidi Omar Qadhaf al-Dam, a murabit (holy man) from whom the tribe is said to have descended, is buried. Some accounts suggest that Qadhafi used to refer to Ghayran as the 'mother country', and to have erected a sign in white bricks on the Abu Ghaylan Mountain reading, 'Gharyan is the motherland'.[14]

While tribal histories are often constructed and imbued with myth and legend, the Qadhadhfah are believed to have migrated away from Gharyan in the seventeenth century, some of its members settling in the harsh deserts of the Sirte plains and others ending up in Sebha in the south. Qadhafi's ancestors, who belong to the small Qahous

18

FROM PALACE TO REVOLUTION

branch of the tribe, were among those who relocated to Sirte. Forced to survive in challenging conditions, these families held fast to tribal traditions and to the often crafted stories of their own tribal history. Qadhafi recalled in a 1972 magazine interview, 'Kinship and descent are important matters in the tribe, because they determine one's identity. Every individual must have an identity, and ours is Qadhadhfah. I remember the people of the village speaking about Qadhaf al-Dam, the holy man, from whom the tribe is descended. As impressed upon my mind, Qadhaf al-Dam was a horseman, a murabit and wali salah [a saint]. The idea of chivalry was nourished by the old people in the village.'[15] Notably, from the 1980s, Qadhafi—known for his theatrical displays—would ride into stadia to preside over mass political celebrations wearing tribal attire and astride a white horse, while billboards routinely depicted Qadhafi on horseback.

Yet despite the tales of chivalry, the Qadhadhfah were a weak and uninfluential tribe, always in the shadow of other, more powerful tribal groupings, especially the large Awlad Suleiman tribe, with whom the Qadhadhfah had joined forces under the *Saff al-Fawqi*, a tribal alliance established to oppose Ottoman rule. This alliance was led by the Awlad Suleiman, whose leading house had held the sheikhdom since the eighteenth century and supplied all the governors of Sebha during the monarchy.[16] As a young man, Qadhafi was able to lean on this historical alliance to get out of trouble. While in secondary school in Sebha, Qadhafi fell foul of the bey of Fezzan, Mohamed Saif al-Nasser, who was infuriated by the young Qadhafi's nascent political activism that included organising protests, giving speeches denouncing the 'lax morals' of Libya's ruling elite, and on one occasion, leading a band of pupils as they smashed in the windows of a hotel serving alcohol. However, he was saved the worst of the bey's wrath thanks to the intervention of his uncle, Mohamed Qadhaf al-Dam, who had close links to the Saif al-Nasser family. It was through these links that members of the Qadhadhfah had been recruited into the Sebha mobile police force over the years.[17] Yet his uncle's intervention wasn't sufficient to prevent Qadhafi from later being expelled from his school for his outspokenness, forcing him to continue his studies in Misrata.

It was at the military academy in Benghazi, however, where Qadhafi and some of his fellow school friends had enrolled as recruits

TRIBES AND THE STATE IN LIBYA AND IRAQ

with a view to staging a military coup, that he began conspiring in earnest to bring down the monarchy. These recruits referred to themselves as the Free Unionist Officers, and contrived, in conjunction with civilian 'revolutionaries', to bring down the king. The young cadets were part of a new generation who had benefitted from the opening up of the education sector after independence and who were ripe for the Arab nationalist ideas that had taken hold in the region during the 1950s and 1960s. This generation had come of age during a time of great social upheaval. The discovery of oil in 1959 and the development of the country's energy industry catapulted Libya from being one of the poorest countries in the world to becoming an oil-rich state almost overnight. Between 1958 and 1964, GDP rose from £52 million to over £332 million, and by 1969, Libya was one of the world's major exporting states.[18] This oil boom was accompanied by mass rural-to-urban migration. Between 1954 and 1964, the population of Tripoli grew by 64 per cent from 130,000 to 213,000, while Benghazi's doubled from 70,000 to 137,000.[19] These new migrants often ended up living in fetid suburban shanty towns, the rural-to-urban relocation disrupting their traditional social ties.[20] This did not mean that these social bonds were cut completely; although tribal structures were certainly disrupted, families and extended families tended to move together, resulting in neighbourhoods or areas in the towns being dominated by particular tribes or clans. More often than not, these tribal lines were clearly delineated, especially in the east, where rural migrants congregated in loose families to create mini-townships within the city.[21] This urbanisation did not spell the end of tribal affiliations, but brought about their transfiguration.[22]

The oil boom also saw newly settled underdeveloped and impoverished communities rubbing up against the burgeoning wealth of a small but new urban elite and administrative class who were benefitting from the energy industry. In some areas, this wealth gap was particularly stark. Despite the riches that had poured into some Benghazi neighbourhoods with their newly built homes occupied by the new elite and foreign oil workers, by the early 1960s, the 17,000 residents of the Sabri shanty town (which had absorbed almost a quarter of Benghazi's population growth) comprised 'a primitive and

20

FROM PALACE TO REVOLUTION

miserable society living on the lowest margins of human subsistence'.[23] According to an account from 1962, these residents suffered dirt, mud and rain in the winter, and 'millions of flies living on the dirt and sewage found all over the place', in summer.[24] Sabri lacked public transport, electricity, health services, schools, clean water and other basic amenities, while most of the housing was made of wooden or metal huts or traditional tents. This juxtaposition bred new resentments not harboured in the past against the country's traditional leaders into which Qadhafi and his fellow plotters could tap.[25] By the end of the 1960s, the monarchy had all but run its course, and despite the many vested interests, the country was ripe for change. There was no major resistance to the overturn of the old order therefore, and to what was to be the dawn of a new nationalist era that was going to prioritise loyalty to the state over tribal and regional identities.

As noted above, this military coup, dubbed by its instigators as the al-Fateh revolution, has often been portrayed in the literature as a triumph of disenfranchised members of lowly tribes from the oases of the interior who wanted to turn the tables against the rich and powerful tribes that had held sway under the monarchy.[26] Such assumptions need revisiting. It is certainly true that, like Qadhafi, many of the Free Unionist Officers who seized power with him came largely from the lower social strata of society. Many of the seventy or so young recruits who joined the plot were born in oases in the interior and were the children of nomads or lowly cultivators.[27] Others were from the lower classes of the coastal towns and cities and many—although by no means all—came from small and uninfluential tribes. Likewise, the Revolutionary Command Council (RCC), the twelve-member body established after the coup to serve as the highest executive ruling power and hand-picked by Qadhafi from among the Free Unionist Officers, comprised individuals who mostly came from the lower or middle classes and who were brought up in the desert oases or poor immigrant neighbourhoods of the towns. As for tribal background, while Qadhafi and some other RCC members came from small and uninfluential tribes that were limited in geographic spread, including Abu Bakr Younis Jaber, who was from the Majabra tribe, Abdulsalam Jalloud, who was from the Magarha tribe, and Khweildi Humaidi, who was from the Mahameed, two of its members hailed from large and influential eastern tribes. Mohamed al-

21

TRIBES AND THE STATE IN LIBYA AND IRAQ

Magariaf came from the Magharba tribe that is concentrated in western Cyrenaica, while Mohamed Najm was from the al-Awaqir, one of the largest tribes in the east and closely associated with the monarchy. Others had no tribal affiliation at all. This included Omar al-Mehishi, who came from a distinguished Misratan family and whose father had been a provincial administrator during the monarchy. While most hailed from less fortunate backgrounds and areas, the RCC was more of a mixed bunch than is often portrayed, and its members were drawn from across the country, from large and small tribes, with some professing no tribal affiliation at all.

Table 1

Name	Tribe	Place of Birth	Region
Muammar Qadhafi	Qadhadhfah	Sirte	Centre
Abdulsalam Jalloud	Magarha	Wadi Shatti	South
Bashir Huwaidi	Ashraf Waddan[28]	Waddan oasis	South
Abdulmonem al-Houni	—	Janzour	West
Mohamed Najm	Al-Awaqir	Benghazi	East
Awadh Hamza	—	Qaminis (Misratan origin)	East
Mohamed al-Magariaf	Magharba	Ajdabiya	East
Abu Bakr Younis Jaber	Majabra	—	East
Khweildi Humaidi	Mahameed	Zawiya	West
Mustafa Kharrubi	Al-Belaza	Zawiya	West
Mukhtar al-Gherwy	none	Tripoli (Old City)	West
Omar al-Mehishi	none	Misrata	West

Source: While difficult to identify exactly which tribes some RCC members came from, this list was drawn up by Moncef Ouanes, although it appears here with some corrections.[29]

Moreover, those who carried out the coup were not deliberately seeking to marginalise those tribes that had formed the backbone of the monarchy. In fact, while they were plotting, they had been des-

FROM PALACE TO REVOLUTION

perate to win over recruits from the large tribes, including those associated with the old order. Qadhafi's once right-hand man, Abdulsalam Jalloud, recounts, 'The problem we faced when choosing [Free] officers was that in the most tribal areas, there were no recruits. When we asked officers to bring recruits from their own areas to the military college, they said they had to consult with their fathers. We didn't know what to do. The biggest gain for us was that officers from the al-Obeidat tribe and [Mohamed] al-Magariaf [from the Magharba] joined us. We told them, "Don't consult your fathers."'[30] Indeed, the revolutionaries were not thinking in terms of taking power in order to exact revenge against certain tribes. As Jalloud remarked, the revolution was about overturning the notables and tribal elites who had associated themselves with the monarchy rather than seeking vengeance against the tribes from which they hailed.

Moreover, despite their Arab nationalist ideals, the RCC members considered themselves to be 'the sons of the country's tribes', a term Qadhafi regularly used to refer to himself and his fellow revolutionaries. In his account of the days leading up to the 1 September coup that was published in the Libyan media in 1969, he declared, 'We did not fear the tribes because we all represent them from top to bottom. We are the sons of those tribes… We are the sons of the villages, cities, and countryside and represent the Libyan people with its tribes, cities, villages, nobility and true heritage'.[31] While these young revolutionaries may have viewed themselves as modern progressives who were not constrained by sub-state and pre-modern identities, as this comment reflects, they emerged out of what was still a profoundly tribal society, and were well aware of their tribal roots. Abdullah Othman, Qadhafi's cousin and prominent member of the former regime explained, 'Tribe and affiliation to region were part of the culture of this new elite. Tribes and the surrounding villages looked at the regime that came to power in 1969 as representing them. They found in it their culture and saw in it elements of themselves. They had more common ground with Qadhafi than they did with the [pro-] Idris elite city dwellers'.[32] The revolution appealed precisely to the semi-Bedouins and inhabitants of the shanty towns and poor neighbourhoods around the urban centres, where tribes had moved in en masse. It was from these areas that some of the regime's most ardent

TRIBES AND THE STATE IN LIBYA AND IRAQ

supporters were drawn, prompting some urban Libyans to complain right until the end of Qadhafi's rule that the country had been ruined by 'ignorant Bedouins' who were in control.[33]

Yet, it wasn't only the poor who rallied to the revolution. Even in the east—the core of the monarchy's support base—the revolution found support among those who belonged to wealthy influential kinship networks and the tribal elite.[34] As Husken observes, 'These men became part of Qadhafi's revolution without touching the traditional status of their families. On the contrary, these families combined both realms (revolution and tradition) in order to ensure and perpetuate their political and societal influence'.[35] One former judge and senior member of the regime recounted how a few days before the coup, he returned from a trip abroad and was shocked to discover a group of his colleagues in Benghazi University who had 'jumped on the bandwagon of the revolution despite the fact that until a few months before, they were some of the biggest supporters of the monarchy'.[36] Some of these colleagues, he added, 'had even been co-operating with the monarchy's intelligence services'.[37] As such, there were recruits and supporters of the revolution drawn from among prominent tribes, including the large tribes of the east that had formed the bedrock of the monarchy's support base.

That some members of those tribes associated with the monarchy should have seen something for themselves in this revolution is unsurprising. The sclerosis of the monarchy was such that it was barely able to function, and people wanted change. Fathi al-Deeb, President Nasser's special envoy to Libya, described how the tribes were open to the new order, explaining, 'Popular support is limitless from workers, from young men and women, as well as from teachers, public sector workers, national political elements and most tribes, including the Barassa, which is the only armed tribe that was one of the main pillars of support for the King.'[38] Likewise, Egyptian author Mustafa Nabil wrote how the Barassa tribe not only handed in their weapons, they also told the RCC that they were willing to supply their tribesmen to fight alongside the revolutionaries.[39] While being part of the Arab nationalist vanguard, both al-Deeb and Nabil had their reasons for wanting to paint the new regime in the best light possible, there was no serious attempt by any of the tribes to stand in

FROM PALACE TO REVOLUTION

the way of the revolution. As Jalloud commented, 'What proves that the tribes were weak at the time of the monarchy was that the Al-Fateh [1969] revolution was bloodless and the tribes that the King relied upon didn't resist at all.'[40]

This lack of resistance also reflects the fact that tribes are not monolithic beings that act in unison. They comprise different houses and clans that pull in different directions and that have different levels of status and wealth. While some tribes were associated with the monarchy, this did not mean that all houses in the tribe were wealthy or shared in the prestige. Social stratification existed within tribes as well as within the wider society. Thus, while the 1969 coup may have brought forward a new class of young modernisers, who may have spouted progressive ideas, they still belonged to the traditional society out of which they had emerged. These young revolutionary cadres did not come out of a social or political vacuum; some were the sons, grandsons and nephews of men and tribal leaders who had been involved in politics under the monarchy.[41] In fact, the RCC appointed like-minded, pro-revolutionary individuals from the large eastern tribes in their new governance structures. This included Abdulati al-Obeidi, who was appointed as a minister in the first civilian government. Al-Obeidi came from the al-Obeidat tribe and his father-in-law, Hamid al-Obeidi, had served as defence minister during the monarchy and was the son of a powerful al-Obeidat sheikh. This new band of revolutionaries were not, as some have argued, simply modernising administrators without tribal affiliation who took over and replaced tribal sheikhs.[42]

Dismantling the Old

Despite their tribal roots and their desire to present themselves as the sons of tribes, Qadhafi and his fellow revolutionaries aspired nevertheless to move beyond kinship relations and to build a modern state that was not reliant on tribes or tribal loyalties. They sought a completely fresh start that would wipe the slate clean and save the nation from itself and its outmoded ways, freeing the masses from their 'chains' and creating an egalitarian society that was not built on cronyism or nepotism. This was no small feat. They were operating in an underde-

TRIBES AND THE STATE IN LIBYA AND IRAQ

veloped society that had limited political tradition and culture, and that had yet to develop a concrete sense of national identity. Libya's three regions—whose main population centres were separated by the country's uncompromising geography—had been bolted together at independence, and local and regional identity was still strong. Furthermore, the country boasted little to none of the political activism that had spread in many other states of the region. From the Communists, to the Ba'athists, the Nasserites, the Muslim Brotherhood and to trades unions and other civil currents, Libya was largely devoid of such movements which, if they existed at all, were embryonic.

The new revolutionaries looked to Arab nationalism therefore to remedy these ills and to try to bring society together in the name of one people, one nation. In line with this ideology, they presented an idealised image of themselves and of a society that was modern, progressive and unfettered by 'backwards' and 'reactionary' sub-state loyalties. Qadhafi told a group of students at Tripoli University on 2 January 1970, 'Tribalism used to exist in a specific place and tribalism existed in the tents and tribesmen responded quickly to the call of their leaders and sheikhs when there was a conflict. But now in Libya, when you go to any place, you don't find tribes like this because children went to school and the rest of them went to the armed forces'.[43] The following year he gave a speech in Sabratha in which he denounced tribal sheikhs linked to the monarchy as 'schemers' and 'exploiters', noting, 'We don't have tribal sheikhs, we don't have advisors'.[44]

They also took concrete steps to move against the elites who had underpinned the monarchy, purging the state of individuals and elites including those from prominent tribes. Yet the purge was hardly draconian. King Idris was sentenced to death by the newly established People's Court, but was outside the country so the sentence was passed in absentia. Members of the royal family, the royal diwan, the cabinet and parliament—many of whom were also leaders or senior figures within the most influential tribes—were arrested and tried. Those closest to the king received prison sentences or were placed under house arrest, although many were released after a few years. Abdulhameed al-Abbar, for example, who was head of the Senate of the Libyan parliament after independence and a sheikh of the most

26

FROM PALACE TO REVOLUTION

prominent house of the al-Awaqir tribe, was imprisoned for six months and then placed under house arrest.[45] Other officials, including governors, mayors and deputy mayors, most of whom hailed from prominent tribes, were forced out of their jobs, although many were provided with severance settlements.[46] The leaders of the Cyrenaican Defence Force (CYDF)—a regional constabulary that outstripped the Libyan armed forces in men and material, and that served as a kind of Praetorian Guard for the king—were put under internment for several years, but the rank and file were absorbed into the army. The police were brought under military command and while senior police officers were arrested, lower-ranking members were disarmed.

This was no wholesale purge of the large eastern tribes, therefore, but more a weeding out of individuals from tribes who were directly associated with the monarchy. It was these emblems of the past that the regime wanted to bring down. As Sheikh Mohamed Aujail Hasnawi of the Hasawna tribe describes, 'In the beginning, in terms of sheikhs and notables, Qadhafi changed the old symbols associated with the monarchy. It wasn't appropriate for these symbols to remain.'[47] This was more about removing certain sheikhs and notables from positions of power in the state therefore than it was about targeting or curtailing the tribes from which they hailed.

However, the new regime took steps to halt the formal role of the tribe in political life. It cancelled the counsellor system whereby each major tribe had a counsellor, appointed by Royal Decree, who received a salary from the state and who served as an intermediary between his tribe and the government.[48] The RCC also embarked upon changes to land ownership laws that impacted upon the tribes. Prior to 1969, tribes were permitted to register land in their name and to form committees to resolve property disputes over tribal land.[49] In 1970, the RCC passed two laws aimed at shaking up land ownership. The first—Law 142 of 1970 on Tribal Lands and Wells—ruled that the state would take over all unregistered lands and wells used by one or more tribe in accordance with prevailing customs.[50] The law also revoked all land registrations that were based on decisions made by the tribal disputes committee during the time of the monarchy. This law has been cited repeatedly in the literature as representing a pointed and deliberate attack by the new revolutionar-

TRIBES AND THE STATE IN LIBYA AND IRAQ

ies on tribes and tribal power.[51] However, as far as the RCC were concerned, this law was primarily about putting an end to the chaotic land policies that had persisted under the monarchy and that often resulted in conflict. A 1969 report by the UN Food and Agriculture Organisation highlights the chaos, noting, 'Legal rights of possessors and of the state on tribal property are still vague. Even the Land Registration offices in Benghazi stated that only possessors of tribal land have the right to usufruct, the Barce Office considered the tribal land collectively owned by the tribes residing on it'.[52] As a study published in 1969 put it, tribal land ownership was 'a source of endless and sometimes bitter disputes on land and water rights between both tribes and members of the same tribe'.[53]

According to Jalloud, the RCC introduced the Tribal Lands and Wells law precisely to put an end to these kinds of tribal conflicts, explaining, 'From our own experience of tribal competition, it was the conflicts over water, wells and land that led us to come up with the tribal land and wells law. We announced that the land is common property and that tribes could benefit from it whether by shepherding or agriculture. It was a deliberate policy to stop the competition, the conflict among tribes over tribal land'.[54] Moreover, the legislation was in line with the egalitarian socialist orientation of the new regime and stipulated clearly that the law was meant to ensure 'fairness' and guarantee that one group of citizens in an area did not 'obtain use to the exclusion of another'. This principle of just distribution was reinforced through Law 123 of 1970, which ruled that seized land should be divided up into productive agricultural units and reallocated to those who were 'lacking the means of a dignified life'.[55]

Furthermore, these changes had little tangible impact on the ground where the tribes were concerned. Law 142 ruled that tribes who were using the tribal land and wells could continue to do so, and that compensation for 'necessary or beneficial expenses incurred' was payable if the persons concerned did not continue to make use of the land and wells, although in practice this compensation was rarely paid. In reality, therefore, the regime confiscated unregistered and mainly unproductive land held collectively by tribes, which it redistributed to individuals, albeit often individuals who were part of the same tribes that had controlled the land before. The agricultural

28

FROM PALACE TO REVOLUTION

project established at Wadi al-Mardoom in Bani Walid in western Libya was a case in point. Although initially, the land confiscated for this project was redistributed without consideration for who had owned the land previously, it soon came to be distributed among members of tribes who had previously owned it, while the selection of new beneficiaries was delegated to the tribes themselves.[56] As such, the law did not elicit any rebellion or revolt by the large tribes despite it being introduced at a time when the new regime was only starting to establish its authority. As Jalloud remarked, 'There was no resistance to that law. Although some expressed dissatisfaction at it, even tribal notables were sick and tired of the tribal conflicts. The law that we introduced was us doing a surgical operation while the king, being weak, could not take such a drastic measure.'[57] In any case, as the regime became increasingly radical and focused around the ideas and personal philosophy of Qadhafi, it introduced Law 38 of 1977, which invalidated all land ownership in the country regardless of whether it had been registered or who it belonged to. What appeared on the surface therefore to be a law aimed at undermining tribal power had little real impact. As Libyan commentator Mousa Rumaila has observed, 'Qadhafi talked more than he took action. That law was just for show. He never intended to enact that law because he knew his power came from the tribes.'[58]

Some scholars have also pointed to the RCC's redrawing of administrative boundaries soon after taking control as further evidence of its attack against tribal power.[59] This boundary shift is cited repeatedly as evidence of the regime's early attack against tribes. Yet, once again, this shift did not impact tribes in the way it has sometimes been portrayed in the literature. It is true that Law 62 of 1970, which was replaced by Law 130 of 1972, created new administrative borders, which unlike the time of the monarchy did not follow tribal boundaries. In reality, this was not aimed at tribes and the way the new boundaries were drawn had little tangible impact upon the tribes themselves. Jalloud was explicit on this point, explaining, 'We divided Libya into governorates and municipalities. The law wasn't against tribes... This local government law wasn't to weaken tribes. It was because we wanted decisions to be taken locally and not centrally. We had to weaken the centre and strengthen the peripheries.

TRIBES AND THE STATE IN LIBYA AND IRAQ

The law didn't affect tribes whatsoever, and it wasn't aimed against them.'[60] Sheikh Mohamed Aujail Hasnawi of the Hasawna tribe took a similar view, asserting, 'The reason why Qadhafi changed the boundaries was nothing to do with the tribe. It was to bring about a big leap in Libya's development.'[61]

Thus, while the RCC may have moved against prominent sheikhs and notables who were part of the monarchy, it did not make any serious move to undercut or dismantle the tribes. In many instances, local tribal elements who had held positions under the king lost their formal roles, but continued to engage in dispute mediation and other local services for their communities. As Husken rightly observes, from the outset, tribal politics and the local production of order continued, albeit in the shadow of the revolutionary state and institutions and disciples.[62]

Tribal Engagement

While Qadhafi may have come to power employing an anti-tribal discourse, and seeking to bring down the old tribal elite right from the start, the regime was also mindful that it could not ignore the tribes. Qadhafi fully understood the weight and influence of kinship relations and structures, and thus had no choice but to reach out to tribal elites in order to widen his support base and to shore up the fledgling regime. This regime may have viewed itself as an articulation of a new modernised order, but it could not leapfrog over society. Despite the urbanisation and modernisation that had been ongoing as a result of the oil boom, tribes and tribalism still formed an integral social institution for most Libyans. The intelligentsia were still limited in number, and for the most part, had not cut off with their tribal roots. A survey carried out in 1973 in the western town of Zawiya found that out of 319 local residents, 71.4 per cent considered themselves either 'very attached' or 'attached' to their tribe, with 9.4 per cent considering themselves to be 'somewhat attached'.[63] Indeed, Libya did not have a large politicised middle class or a national historical narrative that would create the conditions for immediate consensus for his revolutionary ideas.[64] While Qadhafi sought to engage in a radical shake-up of the political and economic system, therefore, he was well aware

30

FROM PALACE TO REVOLUTION

that, even if he had wanted, he could not go against the social fabric of the country. What emerged therefore was a schizophrenic policy that oscillated between denigrating tribalism while simultaneously trying to lure in the tribes and their sheikhs.

The new regime opted therefore to bring the tribes in, albeit in a low-key fashion. Jalloud commented how, after the coup, 'We declared in media and cultural outlets the need to move on from a tribal society to a national society. We fought against the tribe in the media, in cultural events. Some sheikhs didn't like that. But we never clashed with them. The meaning of our call wasn't to fight them but to bring them in so they could help build a national state... Tribes are very brave. The tribesman can die for water but he doesn't understand the meaning of dying for a national cause.'[65]

As such, the new regime paid attention to the tribes and chose to engage them from the start. In September 1969, RCC member Adam Hawas asked al-Deeb to write him a speech with which he could address a meeting of the al-Obeidat tribe in the Jebel Akhdar (Green Mountains) in the east.[66] In April 1970, Qadhafi addressed a crowd in al-Baida, portraying himself as a defender of the rights of honourable tribesmen against the corrupt practices of the monarchy that he accused of having tried to silence the tribes that were calling for their rights regarding land and oil.[67] Qadhafi declared, 'The monarchy's policy insulted al-Baida because a large section of the budget didn't go to factories and farms or to the service of people or of al-Baida... In fact it didn't go to al-Baida or for services or for the people of al-Baida and wasn't in the interests of the tribes that live around al-Baida. It was used to build palaces for deputies, ministers and American experts.'[68] RCC officials continued to meet with sheikhs and tribal leaders. This included Jalloud, who had a reputation for being especially averse to tribalism and tribal practices. As he explained, 'Even me, I met tribes, as the revolutionary has to deal with reality in order to change it. All of Libya is tribal. I met with the young and afterwards, we would meet the sheikhs, a large number of sheikhs, and we spoke to them. We had to recognise this reality. If we ignored it, we wouldn't be able to change it.'[69]

In his efforts to mobilise the population in the service of the new order, Qadhafi also wove tribal narratives of jihad against invading forces into his anti-imperialist discourse. The new regime had made anti-imperialism a key tenet of its revolutionary state and moved quickly to nationalise the oil sector, to close down foreign air bases and to expel Italian settlers, 20,000 of whom were forced out of the country on 7 October 1970, a date that was to be celebrated every year as the 'Day of Revenge'. Such policies chimed well with large swathes of the population, including the tribes, who were traditionally hostile to outside forces and who sent delegations and telegrams of support to the new regime praising its efforts to curb foreign influence in the country.[70] Many tribes prided themselves on the battles they had fought against invading forces over the centuries, with their heroic struggles against the Ottomans and the Italians crafted into the myths and legends they had built around themselves. Jihad against foreign invaders is intrinsically linked with the historical experience in Libya, and the tribes were at the very heart of this experience. Qadhafi not only constructed a narrative about his own tribe and its exploits against Italian colonisers, but also lauded the tribes for their role in the jihad against the Italians and the Ottomans.[71] As Sharif al-Abbar, of the al-Awaqir tribe commented, 'Qadhafi never insulted the tribe. He respected the tribe and he opened the door fully for the tribe to be praised and for its jihad [against the Italian colonisers] to be proclaimed.'[72] Right from the early years of his rule, therefore, Qadhafi employed Libya's historical experience to legitimise himself and ingratiate himself with a wider audience.

He also looked to kinship as a source of protection and as a means of shoring up his new regime. Immediately after taking power, he encouraged his own tribesmen to join the military and promoted junior Qadhadhfah officers, often to sensitive posts. Those young Qadhadhfah who were directed to the military colleges graduated in record time, and after just six months of training were awarded the rank of second lieutenant.[73] He also encouraged and facilitated members of the Qadhadhfah to transfer from the police, of which many had been members during the monarchy, to the armed forces.[74] In addition, Qadhafi called on other RCC members to encourage their relatives to join the military too. Al-Magariaf complied to the point where he was bringing in so many of his fellow tribesmen that Qadhafi is alleged to have asked jokingly whether he was intending to stage a

FROM PALACE TO REVOLUTION

coup against him. Jalloud was less enthusiastic. When he objected to the idea, insisting that the revolution was meant to be for all and not based on tribal affiliation, Qadhafi allegedly went behind his back and reached out to other members of the Magarha, such as Abdullah al-Senussi, who went on to become Qadhafi's intelligence chief and his brother-in-law.[75] Although much has been made in the literature of Jalloud's tribal links, according to other senior members of the regime, it wasn't he who engineered the pragmatic alliance that was to develop between the Magarha and Qadhadhfah.[76] Yet Jalloud's being part of the RCC clearly helped cement the links between his tribe and the regime. Many Magarha joined the regime's security apparatus. Several Magarha officers were appointed to leading positions in the army, while members of the tribe were selected to head up several economic institutions after they were nationalised.[77] Through both Jalloud and Abdullah al-Senussi, the tribe was able to play an outsized role compared to larger tribes that did not have the same connections.

However, in order to secure itself the new regime knew that it also needed to bring in other tribes from beyond the RCC, including those in the east. One early link came through Qadhafi's marriage in 1970 to Safiya Farkash, a nurse from al-Baida, who came from the Barassa tribe and whose uncle had been the head of an important military unit during Idris's rule. Although it isn't clear whether this union was a deliberate attempt to forge a kinship alliance or simply a love match, it secured a link between Qadhafi and a Cyrenaican tribe that had been one of the main supporters of the former regime. Qadhafi also drew in individuals from the large eastern tribes and made them part of his ruling elite. This included from tribes that had been associated with the monarchy, especially the al-Obeidat. Abdulfattah Younis al-Obeidi, Embarak al-Shamakh, Ibrahim Bakkar and Suleiman Mahmoud al-Obeidi, who all came from the large al-Obeidat tribe, became prominent members of his regime. He also drew in Tayib al-Safi from the Menfa tribe, which was the tribe of famed Libyan resistance hero Omar al-Mukhtar. Through these connections, and by relying on certain figures, Qadhafi was able, in Abdullah Othman's words, 'to break the wall of the east'.[78] Othman also commented that 'Qadhafi focused his attentions on the al-Obeidat, as it is a very large

TRIBES AND THE STATE IN LIBYA AND IRAQ

and pacific tribe and it resides in an area that was insecure for him, and not guaranteed either. He needed an un-rebellious group of people. Especially if you had members of the Free Officers who belonged to that tribe, such as Abdulfatah Younis, Suleiman Mahmoud and Ibrahim Bakkar. So he could access this tribe easily through them'.[79]

Qadhafi went further and opened channels to rehabilitate certain tribal sheikhs who had been powerful under the monarchy. This included Sheikh Abdulhameed al-Abbar (the former head of the senate) and Sheikh Abdulsalam al-Kezza, both of whom were prominent sheikhs of the large al-Awaqir tribe. Both were influential historical figures in the al-Awaqir due to their role in the resistance against the Italian colonisers. Al-Abbar, who was imprisoned in 1969 and then put under house arrest by the new regime, was particularly important, as he came from dominant al-Abbar house within the tribe. After 1975, Qadhafi started to bring both al-Abbar and al-Kezza closer to him and began to re-engage and rehabilitate them.[80] After both died, new figures from the al-Abbar and Kezza houses of the tribe were brought into the regime, and as al-Awaqir member Sharif al-Abbar remarked, 'It was necessary for the new sheikhs to give their loyalty to Qadhafi... He chose them from the same symbolic family.'[81] Similarly, as Kamila Othman of the Warshefana tribe described, 'Qadhafi used the same people who were very powerful during the time of the king. He pushed some families away during the first years of his rule, but later he used them and they became powerful again.'[82]

Right from the early years of his rule, therefore, Qadhafi may have spouted an anti-tribal discourse, but he never moved against the tribes per se; rather he sought to engage tribal sheikhs and leaders in order to garner support for his regime. However, as his rule progressed and as he focused more power on himself, moulding the state to his unique ideas and philosophy, he came to articulate a view that accepted tribes as a social construct but which disassociated them from the political realm. In October 1975, he declared, 'Tribalism must be reduced, because tribal struggles and clan spirit corrupt the democratic experience.'[83] This was in line with his general suspicion of organised political activity. The regime banned political parties in 1972, making membership of such punishable by death. In fact, this

FROM PALACE TO REVOLUTION

was not a break with the past; the monarchy had prohibited political parties, claiming they exacerbated internal instability and from 1952, all candidates for election had to be government nominees. Qadhafi therefore was articulating a general suspicion of political parties and organised political activism outside of the confines of his regime.

Qadhafi was even more explicit in his famous *Green Book*, the first part of which was published in 1975. This publication laid out Qadhafi's unique philosophy for Libya and served as a kind of blueprint for the state he was to go on to establish.[84] Divided into three parts—political, economic and social—this short treatise mentions the word 'tribe' no fewer than seventy-three times. Most strikingly, Qadhafi dismisses tribes, along with political parties, classes and sects, as 'dictatorial instruments of rule' that have 'plundered the sovereignty of the masses and monopolised politics and authority for themselves'.[85] He also asserts that 'tribal allegiance weakens national loyalty', and that 'a political structure is corrupted if it becomes subservient to the sectarian social structure of the family, tribe, or sect and adopts its characteristics'.[86]

Qadhafi is clear in *The Green Book* that tribes should have no role or place in the political arena. This does not mean that he rejected the tribe as a social institution. While condemning the tribe for being dictatorial, *The Green Book* simultaneously lauds it for its social role and refers to it as a 'natural social "umbrella" for social security'. He also describes the nation as 'an enlarged tribe'. Qadhafi employed a rhetoric therefore that rejected the tribe as a political actor, aside from its historical role as defender against foreign invaders, but extolled its virtues as a social organiser. As he declared, 'You will realise that the tribe is a social structure, a natural social formation that should be respected and viewed as sacred. We should maintain it in our social life and not drag it into the political realm. Politics is politics; social things are social things'.[87]

However, Qadhafi's engagement with the tribes was to deepen, especially after 1975, when the regime was shaken to the core by an attempted coup d'état carried out by some of those who were closest to him. In the summer of 1975, Qadhafi was stunned when RCC member Omar al-Mehishi turned against him and plotted his downfall. This wasn't the first rebellion he had faced. In 1969, Defence

TRIBES AND THE STATE IN LIBYA AND IRAQ

Minister in the first government, Lieutenant Colonel Adam Hawaz, and Interior Minister in the same government, Mousa Ahmed, along with a number of supporters, had tried to stage a revolt. Although they were dealt with swiftly with both men tried in military court, the pushback against the regime prompted a feeling of insecurity. This insecurity worsened in 1970, when civilian and military elements in Sebha came together under the leadership of Ghaith Abdulmajid Saif al-Nasr, from the famed Saif al-Nasr family, to attempt a counter-revolution. Many of those involved were officers from the Zuwiya tribe in the south, although this was also swiftly put down.

However, it was the plotted rebellion in the summer of 1975 that hit Qadhafi particularly hard. The root of this rebellion lay in the internal bickering that had characterised the RCC after its coming to power. Qadhafi and his cohorts were a small group of inexperienced and unworldly individuals who, for all their Arab nationalist rhetoric, had little solid vision or knowledge of how to run a country. It wasn't long therefore before the squabbles erupted. Moreover, it became clear early on that this was to be Qadhafi's project, and as he sought to impose his authority over the new state he agitated some of his fellow revolutionaries. This included Omar al-Mehishi, who had been fiercely loyal to Qadhafi with whom he had been at school, but who was becoming increasingly angered at Qadhafi's attempts at concentrating power in his own hands. Al-Mehishi, along with some thirty officers from his hometown of Misrata who were part of the Republican Guard that had been established to protect the revolution and Qadhafi personally, began to plot a coup. Other RCC members, Awadh Hamza and Bashir Huwaidi, as well as Abdulmonem al-Houni, are also rumoured to have been in on the scheme. Although al-Mehishi, who fled to Tunisia, denied he had been plotting anything other than to warn Qadhafi to change his ways,[88] for Qadhafi, this looked very much like an attempted coup d'état engineered by one of his most trusted companions.

Qadhafi retaliated hard, executing twenty-one Misratan officers suspected of involvement in the plot. However, he clearly saw this as more than a betrayal by al-Mehishi and a group of followers. For Qadhafi, this was a betrayal by Misrata, and he took measures against the city that amounted to a form of collective punishment. Adopting

36

FROM PALACE TO REVOLUTION

a mentality that bore the marks of a tribal outlook and that was not far removed from tribal practices, Qadhafi treated Misrata not as a collection of individuals, but as a town of families and tribes that bore collective responsibility for their actions. He boycotted the city, and according to Nasser al-Hassouni, the former co-ordinator of the Revolutionary Committees in Benghazi, didn't visit for over ten years.[89] Jalloud described how after the coup, 'Qadhafi ignored Misrata and ignored the people of Misrata. He looked at them as traitors.'[90] He also tried to prevent the Libyan Iron and Steel Company (LISCO) from being established in Misrata. When the contract to establish the plant was being signed, he had sought to shift its location to another town, only relenting when Jalloud convinced him not to do so.[91]

Playing on tribal sensibilities, Qadhafi also began to foster attention on the nearby town of Bani Walid, the home of the Warfalla tribe. This was of particular significance given that Misrata and Bani Walid had long had an antagonistic relationship, dating back to the 1920s. It was at this time that the leader of Misrata, Ramadan al-Suwayhili, was killed while staging a surprise attack against the Warfalla in Bani Walid. The two towns remained rivals thereafter. Qadhafi deliberately fanned the flames of division by going to Bani Walid after the al-Mehishi affair to make a speech, bringing supporters from Sebha and Sirte (both towns with a strong Qadhadhfah presence) to Bani Walid for the occasion, along with members of the Magarha tribe. The former dean of the post-graduate studies centre in Tripoli, Saleh Ibrahim, who is from Bani Walid, described Qadhafi's move as his way of telling Misrata, 'I can use my own cities and tribes against you.'[92]

It is true that, aside from the execution of the actual plotters, this collective revenge was not especially severe and was more a case of Qadhafi's snubbing the town to make an example of it rather than any large-scale retribution. Moreover, he did not strip all Misratans from his regime. However, his actions stuck in the collective consciousness of many Libyans, who saw in it evidence of Qadhafi's willingness to play with tribal and regional sensibilities in order to consolidate his control.

More importantly, following al-Mehishi's aborted coup, Qadhafi turned more concertedly to his own tribe as a means of self-protec-

TRIBES AND THE STATE IN LIBYA AND IRAQ

tion. This episode made him realise that he needed to 'rely directly on tribal loyalty to protect himself and to guarantee control and power'.[93] Or, as Saleh Ibrahim described, 'After the al-Mehishi affair, he went back to history. He understood he had been dreaming and that the reality [of ruling] was completely different'.[94] This episode woke Qadhafi up to the realities of realpolitik. As Othman commented, 'Muammar used to like Misrata a lot. He studied there. Most of his friends prior to 1969 were from Misrata. After al-Mehishi's conspiracy, Qadhafi realised the importance of tribal elements. If those elements are used against you negatively, it is possible to use them for yourself positively'.[95]

Qadhafi therefore began making changes to shore himself up against further such rebellions. After 1975, he brought more of his relatives into the Republican Guard and into the most sensitive posts in the security and intelligence apparatus. Jalloud recounts how Qadhafi dismantled the Free Officers at this time, saying, 'We need new officers, new people who feel we have done them a favour.'[96] Jalloud also noted how Qadhafi ordered the education authorities to start forging certificates for his relatives so that they could get into military colleges and schools more easily.[97] He also started demanding to have sight of lists of all applicants to military schools and colleges, insisting that each application included details of the individual's parents and tribe, enabling him to decide personally on who should and shouldn't be admitted, a practice he continued until the end of his rule.[98] Jalloud also observed that, 'After the Misrata conspiracy… Qadhafi lost trust in Libyans and returned to his tribe. He began implementing a coup that lasted until the 1980s. He set up brigades and appointed officers from the Qadhadhfah as commanders. He weakened the army and established military units and took full control of the guards and security forces. For eight years, he built forces that were controlled by his relatives, as well as some officers from the Warfalla and Magarha.'[99] Among those Qadhadhfah at the heart of his regime were Khalifa H'neish (house of Awlad Omar), Masoud Abdulhafiz (house of Khatra), Ahmed Qadhaf al-Dam (house of Qahous), Hassan Ishkal, Barani Ishkal (house of Awlad Omar) and Ahmed Ibrahim (house of Qahous). As such, Qadhafi retreated into tribalism and kinship in order to shield his regime from further shocks.

38

FROM PALACE TO REVOLUTION

This wrapping himself in the protective layers of kinship coincided with Qadhafi's efforts to mould the Libyan state around his idiosyncratic personal philosophy. In 1977, Qadhafi proclaimed the launch of his Jamahiriyah, which was supposed to embody direct democracy and 'people power'. Under this system, all Libyans were meant to share in governing through participation in a complex hierarchy of people's committees and congresses, where decisions would be agreed at the grass-roots level and fed up the chain of command until they could be implemented by the General People's Congress (parliament) and General People's Committee (government). In reality, this hierarchical tangle of committees and congresses was little more than a façade. As Bruce St John observes, Qadhafi claimed to have created a unique model of direct democracy, based on an intricate system of congresses and committees, in which power rested in the hands of the people but in reality, he constructed 'two parallel sectors of power, a people's sector in the form of the direct democracy system and a revolutionary sector, consisting of himself, the remaining members of the RCC, and Free Unionist Officers and the revolutionary committees'.[100] The Revolutionary Committees, a paralegal security force set up in the late 1970s and tasked with defending the revolution and enforcing Qadhafi's utopian vision, became particularly potent, unleashing terror on the population. The top posts in the Revolutionary Committees went to Qadhafi's relatives, including Mohamed al-Mahjdoub, who was the real power behind the movement.

If the Qadhadhfah made up the first circle of protection around the regime, the Warfalla, the Magarha, the Awlad Suleiman and the Hasawna followed close behind. It was these tribes, along with the Qadhadhfah, who populated Qadhafi's security brigades and who, from the 1980s onwards, began to overshadow the army, which after its routing in Chad came increasingly to resemble an old boys club, with officers far outnumbering soldiers. These security brigades were responsible for Qadhafi's personal security and were almost exclusively headed by members of the Qadhadhfah, although some were led by the Magarha. These brigades included the Mohamed al-Magariaf Brigade in Bab al-Aziziya that was headed by Barani Ishkal, the Saidi brigade that was located in Sirte and that was headed

39

TRIBES AND THE STATE IN LIBYA AND IRAQ

by Qadhafi's cousin, Sayid Qadhaf al-Dam, and the Hussein Juwaifi Brigade in Shahat, headed by Qadhafi's nephew Abdulkader Said Qadhafi.[101] These security brigades were mainly filled with soldiers from Bedouin tribes that were loyal to the Qadhadhfah and were supplied with the best weapons and training.[102]

Qadhafi had made himself the centre around which others from trusted tribes orbited, in a system where kinship relations formed the building blocks of power. Qadhafi, who had declared tribes to be backwards, had now wrapped himself in a protective layer of tribesmen from his and other loyal tribes. He had also proved willing to engage and accommodate other tribes, including in the east. Arguments suggesting that Qadhafi made great efforts to eliminate tribal loyalties and attachments during the early years of his rule[103] are, therefore, exaggerated. As Qadhafi was to prove throughout the decades that he remained in power, he understood tribal traditions and practices, and was willing and able to harness them to his needs. He may have dismissed tribes in his discourse as backwards and reactionary, but he was fully cognisant of the influence they muster. As Sheikh al-Senussi Buheleq of the Zuwiya tribe remarked, 'Qadhafi was a tribal man. His problem was that he filled his head with empty theories.'[104]

2

TRIBES AND QADHAFI'S REVOLUTIONARY TOOLBOX

FROM KHOUT AL-JED TO SOCIAL CONTROL

The social deterrent is stronger than any civil law or city police force.

Muammar Qadhafi

While Qadhafi used kinship relations to his advantage in the first years of his rule, it was in the late 1970s and 1980s that he came to rely on tribal alliances in a more direct fashion. This occurred at a time when Qadhafi was investing more power in himself, further centralising the state, and bending the country to his will and to his unique vision. He was also becoming increasingly alert to the fact that, despite his efforts, his ideology had no organic social roots and was not sufficient to motivate or rally the people in the cause of his revolutionary state. Most Libyans were proving indifferent to the new regime's political experiment and were not engaging with his attempts to install 'people's democracy'. Attendance at the Basic People's Congresses—local forums established in 1976 in which all Libyans were supposed to participate and discuss issues related to their local areas—was pitiful, and corruption was already seeping in. Old forms of social organisation had not dissipated, and the masses were reluctant to mobilise.

TRIBES AND THE STATE IN LIBYA AND IRAQ

Instead, the Jamahiriyah system was already lending itself to manipulation by traditional social forces, which were proving able to use local governance structures to their advantage. Outside of the large urban centres, where the population was more mixed, the largest tribes dominated local institutions such as the Basic People's Congresses and People's Committees. Elections to these bodies were often a source of friction. In his study of tribes in Ajdabiya, John Davis describes in detail the competition and tussle for power between the Zuwiya and Magharba tribes as they sought to dominate the 1978–9 elections to the People's Committees (local council) of their area. These local institutions enabled tribes to access resources and jobs. As Sheikh Mohamed Omar Benjdiriya of the Warfalla tribe describes, 'Tribes benefitted hugely from the Jamahiriyah system. They used it to their advantage and through the people's congresses could make their own demands, such as including hospitals, clinics, jobs, roads and tarmacking in the budgets they proposed.'[1]

That tribes were able to manipulate this system frustrated Qadhafi, who in October 1975 issued a stern warning against tribal affiliation being used as a basis for election, which was done through a process known as 'tasayid', whereby people had to raise their hands publicly to vote. Qadhafi warned, 'Tribalism has to disappear', telling Libyans they didn't 'deserve democracy'.[2] Yet, while still displaying a public aversion to tribalism, Qadhafi turned to the tribes at this time in such a way that surprised even those who were closest to him. He began to play heavily on historical tribal concepts to construct and weave a web of tribal alliances that would consolidate his regime and provide it with greater depth and geographical spread. At the same time, he began to manipulate tribes, playing one off against another, fomenting agitation and drawing on old tribal rivalries to maintain a tribal equilibrium to ensure that no tribe could become overly powerful. In this way, he succeeded in creating two key myths around himself: firstly that he embodied tribal tradition and genealogical knowledge, and secondly that he was a 'master manipulator' of the tribal landscape. These myths served to further consolidate his power and charisma.

Qadhafi also intervened inside the tribes themselves, fostering alternative centres of power inside them by bringing up loyal tribesmen who could bypass and in some instance dwarf the traditional

TRIBES AND QADHAFI'S REVOLUTIONARY TOOLBOX

sheikhs in the service of his Jamahiriyah. As the decades progressed and as the regime came under greater pressure, including internationally, where it was now dubbed a 'pariah state', Qadhafi leaned further on the tribes as a means of enforcing social conformity and control. This included in his struggle against the Islamist opposition during the 1990s, a time when his revolutionary ideology had worn especially thin and his dream of mobilising the masses had been shattered. For Qadhafi, the tribes were an organic social antidote to the challenge of political Islam and he instrumentalised them to this end. As such, this revolutionary nationalist, who had come to power dismissing tribes and sheikhs and demanding their exclusion from the political arena, ended up using them as a key component of his revolutionary toolkit and being far more in tune with the tribal sheikhs than is often portrayed.

For the most part, the tribes were willing to comply. While scholars have tended to pit the state against the tribe in a binary relationship that categorises the state as 'modern' and the tribe as 'backwards', this relationship has always been more complex, with accommodation and mutual benefit playing a larger role than is sometimes implied. In Qadhafi's Jamahiriyah, tribes were not working in opposition to the state, but in many instances were working with it and buttressing it. This does not mean that there weren't opponents of the regime from within the tribes, or that within such a repressive environment, the tribes had free rein. However, there was a social contract between ruler and ruled, and contrary to the common perception that Qadhafi only looked to the tribes in a more concerted and formal way in the latter decades of his rule, tribes formed a key component of Qadhafi's nationalist regime right from the start. Moreover, the tribe was not an adversary of modernisation and change. It proved willing not only to open itself to the new revolutionary state, but to transmogrify and be woven into the very fabric of the regime.

'Khout Al-Jed'

'Khout al-jed' translates literally as 'brothers of the grandfathers' and is a widely understood concept in Libya. It refers to tribal alliances

43

TRIBES AND THE STATE IN LIBYA AND IRAQ

born out of blood, in which tribes share a common ancestor, or alliances born out of historical events in which tribes came together in the face of a common enemy. By employing khout al-jed, with all its elasticity, Qadhafi drew on history to tap deeper into the country's tribal fabric, especially in western and southern Libya, to provide his revolutionary vision with the necessary underpinnings.

One of the most important tribal alliances through which this concept was formally revived was that between the Qadhadhfah and the Warfalla, the latter of which had filled the ranks of the Free Officers and was already a key provider of military and security personnel. The Warfalla, which comprises fifty-two clans,[3] is one of the largest tribes in Libya, and as noted in Chapter 1, was part of the Suff al-Fawqi, which along with the Qadhadhfah also included the Awlad Suleiman, the Hasawna and other smaller tribes. Following the al-Mehishi affair, Qadhafi opted to formally revive and deepen this alliance with the Warfalla by declaring khout al-jed with the tribe. He attended a formal ceremony in Bani Walid at which the sheikhs of the two tribes signed a statement confirming their alliance. While this act came as a surprise to many given that Qadhafi had come to power on the ticket of Arab nationalism, what was even more shocking to some was that this seemingly outmoded, pre-modern act was broadcast live on Libyan television. Jalloud, with his reputation for being an arch nationalist, recounted his shock at seeing the footage, 'I contacted him and told him that to give orders to the tribes to create this fictitious alliance was one thing, but to actually attend in person and for the agreement to be handed to him in this way was something else.'[4] In another account, Jalloud recalled how he told Qadhafi after the incident, 'Oh Muammar, are you a sheikh of a tribe? You attended the meeting. They broadcast the communiqué while you were sitting there. These are tribes!'[5]

Yet Qadhafi had seen the advantages such an alliance offered, and sought to extend the khout al-jed principle by entrusting two of his senior officials and relatives, Khalifa H'neish and Omar Ishkal, to construct a new web of tribal alliances, binding other smaller tribes and clans to his own tribe. In this way, he could compensate for the limited size and influence of the Qadhadhfah and seek protection through alliance building. The semi-literate H'neish, who like Qadhafi was

44

TRIBES AND QADHAFI'S REVOLUTIONARY TOOLBOX

brought up in a poor family in the plains of Sirte, was a member of the Qadhadhfah tribe but from the Awlad Omar branch. He was one of the first to join the Libyan army when it was established at independence, prompting former foreign minister Abdulrahman Shalgam to describe him as being brought up 'between the tribe and the army'.[6] Shalgam also described, 'He was aware he came from a small tribe that moved among the valleys and around the large tribes that had land and sheep; he didn't understand the concept of a nation'.[7]

H'neish was entrusted by Qadhafi to cultivate tribal alliances in what Shalgam has described as a plan to expand the Qadhadhfah's 'social association' with all Libyans, referring to H'neish as someone who 'became a genealogist swimming in the history of the Libyan tribes'.[8] H'neish travelled around western Libya visiting different towns and areas, including Gharyan, Misrata, Tarhouna and Warshefana, seeking out evidence of old tribal linkages to reactivate. These places comprise mainly small tribes whose unity and identity is forged around the towns and areas in which they are located. Libyan commentator Mousa Rumaila recounted how, during the 1980s, H'neish and his family had turned up in his village near Zintan in western Libya and stayed for three months, getting to know everyone and learning about their families and about what conflicts and differences were dividing people.[9] In this way H'neish was able to dig up evidence of old linkages, whether spurious or real, to cement alliances between clans and tribes. As Kamila Othman described, 'Qadhafi was trying to find roots for his tribe everywhere in Libya. If there were common names in the tribes' history, this translated to, "You are part of Qadhadhfah and you are with us."'[10] Shalgam described how, from the mid-1970s, Qadhafi used tribal linkages 'in a very deliberate and programmed way, weaving the ropes that would pull the vehicle of power that only he would ride'.[11] He also commented that 'Muammar played on history, names and places to bring tribes from different parts of Libya to join his tribe. So many people from the east and the west and the south raced to join the Qadhadhfah tribe in the pursuit of power and wealth. Muammar used to encourage it and he received the tribal notables who used to come to him with historical documents proving their affiliation to Qadhadhfah'.[12] Although these tribes came under

TRIBES AND THE STATE IN LIBYA AND IRAQ

pressure from H'neish to sign these alliances, there were plenty of individuals, clans and tribes who were ready to respond to his attempts to forge linkages that were often tenuous at best.[13] This included the small Qahsat tribe. H'neish and former justice minister Mohamed Belqassim Zwai are said to have worked with Abdulmajid al-Qa'ud, who held various senior posts in the regime, to sell the idea that given the similarity in the sound of the names, the Qahsat were brothers of the Qahous branch of the Qadhadhfah.[14]

In another illuminating incident that took place in the late 1970s, an alliance was struck between the Qadhadhfah and the Nawayal tribe, which is concentrated in the Jumail area of western Libya. The basis for this alliance was the discovery of an ancestor in the Qadhadhfah named Ben Nayal. This ancestor and the similarity in the names 'Nawayal' and 'Ben Nayal' was seized upon by both tribes as evidence of their shared origin, and a whole history was constructed about how the Nawayal tribe was a branch of the Qadhadhfah that had broken away centuries earlier.[15] Former higher education minister Dr Aqeel Hussein Aqeel recounted how Baghdadi Mahmoudi, who went on to become General Secretary of the General People's Committee (prime minister) in 2006 and who was part of the Nawayal tribe, used to tell him about Qadhafi's plans to link the two tribes. Aqeel recalls, 'Baghdadi talked to me all the time about the family Qadhafi wanted to link him to. He had no relation to that family whatsoever. Baghdadi always whispered to me cautiously that Qadhafi wanted to connect the Qadhadhfah with the Nawayal tribe'.[16] Once this shared connection had been 'confirmed', a Qadhadhfah delegation from Sirte and Sebha visited the Nawayal in Jumail to officially proclaim the old tribal union. Not everyone from the tribe was comfortable about this artificial alliance. Mahmoudi's father, a prominent member of the Nawayal who had worked for the monarchy, refused to sign the document confirming the alliance, telling Mahmoudi's brother, 'How can I sign this when I know my roots are from the Magarha tribe?'[17] However, he also told Mahmoudi and his brother that they should feel free to sign in order to avoid danger. In the event, Mahmoudi's brother, Ahmed, signed the agreement, cementing the fictitious alliance, news of which was published in the state media. The ridiculousness of the pairing drew the derision of

TRIBES AND QADHAFI'S REVOLUTIONARY TOOLBOX

some, including a poet from the Nawayal—Ahmed Nuwairi—who composed a verse about the agreement as follows:

> My brothers made new brothers.
> Allah is one.
> When they met, none of them recognised each other.[18]

Yet despite both tribes being fully aware of the artificiality of the process, it was this linking of the two tribes through the elasticity of the khout al-jed tradition that enabled Mahmoudi to rise to prominence and to serve as a vehicle through which members of the Nawayal could access benefits. Indeed, all sorts of transactions were taking place at this time, as sheikhs rushed to bind themselves to the regime, deploying tribal agency to promote and secure their interests through access to posts and privilege. This is not to suggest that all tribes behaved the same way; there were particular tribes that through khout al-jed had a special connection to the regime. However most had no objection to working with the authoritarian nationalist state, while for Qadhafi, these alliances were a way to bind tribes to his own and to bring them into the fold of the regime where they would serve as his subordinates.

'Master Manipulator'

While Qadhafi revived tribal alliances as a means of fortifying his power, he also began to tamper in internal tribal mechanisms, shifting the balance of power within them and neutralising the sheikhs. He did so by bringing up loyal regime elements from inside the tribe. By virtue of their link to the regime, these figures had access to power, money and status, and came therefore to serve as alternative foci of power to the sheikhs and traditional tribal leaderships. These individuals often ended up in competition with the traditional sheikhs and leadership structures of their tribe. Libya's oldest surviving political prisoner, Saleh al-Ghazail Senussi of the Zuwiya tribe, observed, 'Qadhafi chose the worst people in the tribe. He started giving them money and jobs, and he marginalised the old leadership… He tried to bring new faces. In this way, he started breaking up the body of the tribe. People followed those who were prominent, so the old sheikhs

47

were frightened... and they could see others taking their role bit by bit.'[19] Qadhafi shattered the Saif al-Nasr family's dominance of the Awlad Suleiman tribe, for example, by promoting the Zadma family, which came to replace the Saif al-Nasr family as the dominant power within the tribe. As Sheikh Mohamed Aujail Hasnawi, the Sheikh of the Hasawna tribe, described, 'Qadhafi inevitably promoted those inside the tribe who satisfied him.'[20] Jalloud described this process too, although he was less complimentary about who Qadhafi chose to promote. He explained how Qadhafi used to 'break into the tribes by paying bribes to influential figures within them,' and how he would 'promote the riffraff of the tribes so they became the masters. He never changed the sheikhs of the tribes, but he leapt over them. Those riffraff became stronger than the sheikhs themselves.'[21] These loyal figures became almost like de facto sheikhs, serving as the intermediaries between their tribesmen and the regime. This did not mean that the traditional sheikhs disappeared; they continued to have status and to wield respect among their tribesmen. However, they were weakened by Qadhafi's meddling.

By ensuring there were strong and faithful elements who commanded a following inside the tribe, Qadhafi could feel secure about leaving the tribes to run their own areas and to police themselves. Sharif al-Abbar explains, 'In the al-Awaqir areas, such as Qaminis, Rajma, al-Abiar, Tocra, Suluq, Qadhafi never imposed someone from outside upon them. The Revolutionary Committees, the security were the sons of the tribe. They were the ones who elected, voted and ran the areas. Qadhafi never imposed someone on these areas. For example, in Sulouq, 80 per cent of the inhabitants were al-Awaqir and everything remained in their hands.'[22] This was of enormous importance to the tribes, whose predominant preoccupation had always been to run their own affairs without outside interference, including from the state. By giving tribes space in this way and not making the mistake of trying to impose outsiders, Qadhafi exhibited an acute awareness of tribal sensitivities and the dangers that would ensue should he try to do otherwise.

However, Qadhafi was careful to maintain a tribal balance and to ensure that no tribe became overly empowered. He did so by pitting one tribe against another, stirring up trouble between tribes, towns and areas, often reviving old tribal antagonisms that had lain dormant

TRIBES AND QADHAFI'S REVOLUTIONARY TOOLBOX

for years. An internal document written by the opposition group the National Front for the Salvation of Libya (NFSL) during Qadhafi's rule observed, 'Qadhafi was very keen on playing on contradictions, differences and conflicts between tribes. He worked to implant fitna and create new differences among tribes, especially those that were dangerous to him.'[23] Given that this assertion came from the opposition, it is likely to be somewhat exaggerated. Yet Qadhafi certainly took steps to agitate the tribes, including whipping up the al-Awaqir tribe against Misrata. Large numbers of Misratans had migrated to and settled in Benghazi over generations, and those who originated from Misrata controlled much of the business and wealth in the city. They lived mainly in the central neighbourhoods, in some instances making up almost half the population. In 1976, Qadhafi is said to have told a gathering of sheikhs during a meeting in Sulouq, 'Benghazi belongs to the al-Awaqir. How have you left it to the Arabs [tribes] of Misrata, who are outsiders?'[24] In a similar vein, he played upon the competition between the Magharba and the Zuwiya tribes in the eastern town of Ajdabiya. As Sheikh al-Senussi Buheleq of the Zuwiya tribe explained, 'He tried hard to kindle friction between the Magharba and Zuwiya. For example, he told the Zuwiya, how can you accept having someone from the Magharba as mayor for Ajdabiya? You are the majority!'[25] Buheleq went on to note, 'He implicated tribes in conflicts they weren't party to. He burdened the tribe with things they weren't responsible for.'[26]

Qadhafi also stirred trouble when he called on the Jawazi tribe to return to Libya. The Jawazi were expelled to Egypt from Benghazi in 1817, following a massacre of thousands of their tribesmen by the Karamanli dynasty in conjunction with the al-Awaqir tribe, the latter of whom sought revenge for the fact that around 1811, the Jawazi had put members of the al-Awaqir under siege in the Murabit of Sidi Khrbish, where many starved to death.[27] The al-Awaqir, who had allied themselves to the Karamanli authorities, helped push the Jawazi out of Cyrenaica, becoming the dominant tribe in and around Benghazi as a result. A Jawazi poet wrote the following lines at the time of the tribe's expulsion:

We bid farewell to you now Cyrenaica
But we shall come back –

TRIBES AND THE STATE IN LIBYA AND IRAQ

God willing
We will never forget who expelled us
The Turkish ruler –
With him was al-Awaqir.[28]

Qadhafi encouraged the Jawazi to return to Libya and gave them 5,000 housing units in the east, as well as control of the fruit and vegetable market in Benghazi, in a move perceived as a deliberate attempt to aggravate and weaken the al-Awaqir.[29] As Mehdi al-Bargathi, defence minister in the Government of National Accord (GNA), explained, 'When Qadhafi brought the Jawazi in, they played their role. They strengthened themselves through Qadhafi and Qadhafi empowered himself through them. They are a weak tribe and were vulnerable to being used.'[30]

Even those tribes that were closest to him found themselves at the receiving end of Qadhafi's meddling. The regime adeptly exploited intercommunal rifts including over land, stirring up recurrent conflicts, which sometimes led to confrontations with knives and daggers between tribes, which were resolved by neutral tribes acting as mediators.[31] In the early 1970s, Qadhafi began building 600 housing units for the Mashashiya tribe on land that Magarha considered to be its own. Despite being khout al-jed with the Mashashiya, the policy irritated the Magarha, prompting hundreds of young Magarhans to go out one night with tractors and bulldozers and to destroy the units. Jalloud described the 'sigh of relief' from both tribes once the destruction had occurred, as this put an end to the dispute and conflict was averted. He noted, 'They are our brothers. We are simple people.'[32]

In the 1980s, Qadhafi agitated the Magarha again when he started supplying weapons to the Hasawna tribe, a move that prompted Jalloud's brother, Omar, to go to Qadhafi and accuse him of using the Hasawna against the Magarha, threatening that the tribe would emigrate if the situation continued.[33] The following day, Qadhafi sent the head of military police, Khaeri Khalid, to Sebha to collect the weapons from the Hasawna, putting an end to 'the biggest fitna [strife] between the two tribes'.[34] While Qadhafi may not have completely trusted the Magarha, allegedly having been warned by his father neither to make enemies of them nor to bring them too close, he was careful not to antagonise them too much. Yet he stepped in when he felt the need to

50

TRIBES AND QADHAFI'S REVOLUTIONARY TOOLBOX

do so, including when the Magarha tried to strike alliances with other tribes. At the end of the 1980s, for example, the Magarha agreed to have khout al-jed with Zintan. When Qadhafi learned of the alliance, he sent H'neish and other senior figures in the regime to threaten them, warning them that their alliance was 'against the revolution'.[35] He also intervened when the Magarha sought to strike an alliance with the Ferjan as a means of balancing out the Qadhadhfah's alliance with the Warfalla, and put the brakes on it.[36]

Some of the administrative changes introduced by the regime also upset the tribal equilibrium in certain areas. This included his decision to merge the Basic People's Congresses of Zintan and Rajban into a single Basic People's Congress. In its first session, which was broadcast live on television, a fight broke out over whether to name the congress after Zintan or Rajban. This move was perceived by some as a deliberate attempt on Qadhafi's part to disturb the historical alliance between the tribes of Zintan and Rajban and to get the two to 'crush each other'.[37]

It isn't always clear whether these antagonisms were deliberately fashioned by Qadhafi or whether they were the result of his haphazard and chaotic approach. They are certainly reflective of the enormity of the challenges of ruling a society so strongly demarcated along tribal lines. However, a narrative evolved during Qadhafi's time in power that made him out to be not just a manipulator but a master manipulator, capable of bending the country's kinship networks to his will. Both his supporters and detractors alike frequently alluded to his superior powers in this respect, seeing his handiwork behind almost every tribal conflict. This was an image that Qadhafi fostered as a means of mythologising himself. He was always at pains to demonstrate his deep genealogical knowledge and would routinely try to impress upon others his familiarity with the history of their particular tribe or house. His speeches were also replete with references to old tribal conflicts and battles. All this came within his efforts to present himself as the all-knowing patriarch and the charismatic 'brother leader' who could communicate with his people. Qadhafi used tribal history therefore to construct a myth around himself that would sit alongside the other myths he had created as a means of elevating his status, including that he was a world-class intellectual and thinker,

51

TRIBES AND THE STATE IN LIBYA AND IRAQ

that he was the foremost revolutionary among revolutionaries and that he was more pious and devout than the political Islamists he was trying to suppress. Thus Qadhafi wove a web of tribal narratives as a bid to present himself as 'sheikh of all sheikhs', capable of manipulating the country's tribal tapestry to his needs.

The Second Betrayal

However, the tribe was to trip Qadhafi up again. If the al-Mehishi affair of 1975 had dealt Qadhafi a bitter blow, an attempted plot by a group of military officers from the Warfalla tribe, uncovered in 1993, was to prove equally devastating. This betrayal came at a time when the regime was under immense strain. Qadhafi's mission to export his revolutionary Jamahiriyah beyond the confines of Libya was coming home to roost and Libya had been branded internationally as a 'pariah state'. The adventurous foreign policy he had adopted after coming power, including his involvement in international terrorism, had prompted the US to impose unilateral sanctions on Libya in 1986. In the same year, the US launched bombing raids on Tripoli and Benghazi in retaliation for Libya's suspected role in a terrorist attack on a German nightclub used by American servicemen. Things became even more difficult for the regime in 1992 when the UN enforced an air and arms embargo, as well as a ban on the export of oil equipment to Libya, in retaliation for Qadhafi's refusal to hand over the two suspects in the 1988 bombing of flight PanAm 103 over Lockerbie.

The sanctions meant that Libyans—already subjected to the chaotic and often unfathomable policymaking of the regime—were cut off from the world. They were also forced to struggle even harder to access basic goods and services, something that was already challenging given the years of economic mismanagement made worse by the global fall in oil prices in the late 1980s. By the early 1990s, Qadhafi's distributive state was creaking at the seams, while disillusion was growing at the regime's brutality and its arbitrary decision-making. As early as 1986, the regime was feeling the pressure. Jalloud recalled his and Qadhafi's attending a revolutionary celebration in Ras Lanuf to which only a handful of people had turned up, prompting Jalloud

TRIBES AND QADHAFI'S REVOLUTIONARY TOOLBOX

to recall, 'I realised then that the revolution had lost its people. In fact, the people had turned their backs on the revolution.'[38] The following day, he and Qadhafi lunched with leaders of the Awlad Suleiman tribe in Harawa, where a five-year-old girl told them that she hadn't eaten an apple in five years, after which one of the sheikhs declared, 'Muammar and Abdulsalam, if we told you that 10 or 15 per cent of Libyans are with you, we would be lying to you. Be careful.'[39] By the start of the 1990s, therefore, the challenges were stacking up and the regime was starting to look vulnerable. This situation prompted a group of Warfallan military officers from Bani Walid, who were led by Muftah Ghroum, to plot a coup against Qadhafi. Aware that in order to succeed, they would need to expand their network, the plotters reached out to the exiled NFSL and asked it to connect them to other officers. Although the Warfallans succeeded in recruiting a handful of officers from other tribes, their attempt to expand proved fatal, as in the process, news of the plot reached Qadhafi's intelligence chief, Abdullah al-Senussi, and those involved were rounded up and arrested.[40]

Although the plot was averted, Qadhafi was so distraught at this betrayal that, three days later, he went to Jalloud, hugged him, and told him that his revolutionary ideas had triumphed and that his own tribal policy had collapsed.[41] Two notables from the Qadhadhfah who were present seized upon the occasion and suddenly shouted, 'Magarha are khout al-jed [with Qadhadhfah], not Warfalla!' to which Jalloud told them to shut up.[42] This second betrayal was all the more unsettling for Qadhafi, as it came from inside one of the tribes that was khout al-jed with his own and that had enjoyed special privilege and position, particularly after the al-Mehishi affair. Assertions that the plot had been fuelled by grievances among the educated of Bani Walid, who believed the town had not been sufficiently rewarded with government posts, are unconvincing.[43] The Warfalla, by virtue of their size and loyalty to the regime, as well as their tribal alliance with the Qadhadhfah, held posts throughout the state. One leading Warfalla sheikh described how there was a 'very well-balanced quota of Warfallans in all state bodies. They were influential in the decision-making process.'[44] Warfallans were in control of many university bodies, and held senior posts in the military too. Prior to the 1993 coup, out of the 4,823 officers in the army, 2,900 were from the Warfalla.[45] Moreover, what happened in 1993 cannot be categorised as a tribal rebellion; it was an attempted coup plotted by a small group of military officers who believed that the regime was already on the point of collapse.[46]

Once the plot was uncovered, Jalloud and others cautioned Qadhafi against retaliating in the same uncompromising way he had responded to Misrata in 1975. The Warfalla were equally concerned that Qadhafi would punish the whole tribe for the actions of the few and sought to contain the situation. Warfalla member Saleh Ibrahim recalled impressing upon Qadhafi that he should implement the law against the plotters but not to 'use the coup against the Warfalla, like what happened against Misrata after al-Mehishi'.[47] Sheikh Benjdiriya described, 'Eighty-one very influential figures from the Warfalla in Bani Walid, headed by Education Minister Mohamed Matouq, took the decision to not react. These eighty-one wanted to prove that these officers had acted as individuals and it was not the act of the tribe. The fault was of the individuals, not the fault of the tribe. This was especially the case when these individuals came on TV and confessed that they had links to the CIA. Warfalla and tribal tradition hates foreign intervention or foreign meddling'.[48] Rumours that the plotters had met with the CIA through their connections to the NFSL made it easier for the tribe to separate itself from its sons, also enabling the regime to mete out its punishment against them rather than the tribe as a whole.

Yet while Qadhafi did not go as far as to unleash mass retribution on Bani Walid or the Warfalla as a whole, he deployed tribal traditions in his response. Rather than punish the tribe en masse—something that would have been impossible given its size and influence—he played on tribal norms and forced the Warfalla to dispose of its own sons. This was not an easy process. The tribe's leadership initially refused to comply, and it wasn't until 1997 that the eight ringleaders were executed by regime loyalists from the tribe. Although this incident pitted families inside Bani Walid against each other, Qadhafi succeeded in making it look as though the Warfalla had rooted out the traitors within, avoiding a potentially more serious rebellion that could have occurred had he killed the ringleaders himself. As

TRIBES AND QADHAFI'S REVOLUTIONARY TOOLBOX

Dr Buamid, Sheikh of the Warshefana tribes, observed, 'Qadhafi used tribal tradition to his advantage and allowed the tribe to finish them off. If he had killed them himself, the Warfalla would have sought revenge from the Qadhadhfah'.[49] Similarly, Sheikh Benjdiriya described Qadhafi as a 'very cunning' politician who didn't want Warfalla as his enemy, meaning that he punished some individuals and 'never punished the tribe as a whole'.[50] Sheikh Benjdiriya continued, 'He used members of the tribe to execute them. They brought my uncle to his neighbourhood and executed him there. The tribe didn't react because if it did, it would have instigated infighting within Warfalla itself. The wise men accepted the de facto reality in order to avoid the worst'.[51]

However, in line with tribal norms, Qadhafi punished not only the plotters but their families too, depriving them of education and salaries, getting loyal members of the Warfalla to bulldoze their houses, and forcing them to relocate to different areas of Libya, including the western mountains. He also replaced some security and military commanders who had belonged to the families of the plotters with individuals who hailed from other families or clans of the tribe.[52] He ordered that an annual cap be placed on the number of Warfallans who could be recruited as officers in the army.[53] In this way, Qadhafi did not exclude or sideline the tribe, but rather curtailed it and punished it in a way that made it an example to others. As Sheikh Benjdiriya commented, 'Qadhafi didn't seek at that time to marginalise Warfalla, but he realised the danger of strengthening them.'[54]

Qadhafi also made a point of courting and bringing in other tribes and areas. As one Bani Walid resident recalled, 'Qadhafi visited our neighbours—the Wershafana, Zliten, Tarhouna—demanding that they punish Bani Walid as traitors and spies.'[55] As if to hammer the point home, on one occasion, he visited nearby al-Sadadah, which is located just outside of Bani Walid's boundary, but refused to cross into Warfalla territory. A delegation of sheikhs from Bani Walid went to al-Sadadah to meet him where they begged him to come to their territory, with one sheikh pleading, 'We call upon the Brother Leader to visit us house by house. He can enter every house of ours safely.'[56] According to one sheikh, the regime also put Bani Walid under economic siege, depriving it of money, construction and roads.[57] It should be noted, however, that there was little money, construction or investment being directed into any region during this period when sanctions were biting hard, and such assertions may reflect a narrative that has evolved, especially after 2011, with Bani Walid residents seeking to distance themselves from the Qadhafi regime for fear of reprisals. While Qadhafi may have felt betrayed by this plot, and while he needed to make an example of those involved, he was shrewd enough to understand he could not abandon his reliance on what was one of the largest tribes in Libya and one that still formed part of the backbone of his security apparatus and continued to have khout al-jed with the Qadhadhfah.

Tools of Legitimacy

Qadhafi may have declared 'Down with the tribe!' to Jalloud after the discovery of the Bani Walid plot, but the 1993 conspiracy did not result in his shunning the tribe as an instrument of rule. Tribes may have proved imperfect instruments upon which to rely, but the revolutionary ideals on which the regime had based itself had not permeated to the masses. Libyans were not rallying to the cry of the revolutionary Jamahiriyah; most were indifferent at best. There was also growing resentment at the hardships brought about by sanctions and international isolation, which some Libyans believed to have been self-inflicted. With elements of society becoming increasingly restive, Qadhafi needed a way to keep the base under control. While he had crafted a multi-layered security apparatus comprising many different brigades and forces, he needed a more organic form of engagement with the masses to keep control of the social sphere. The tribe was the only real glue holding society together. Unlike in other authoritarian nationalist states such as Iraq or Egypt, where different political, religious and social currents had developed, such as Communism, political Islam including that articulated through the Muslim Brotherhood, Nasserism, Ba'athism and trades unions, there was no real equivalent in Libya. Although some of these currents had started to emerge in Libya prior to the 1969 coup, they were quashed almost immediately by the regime, which refused to tolerate any political activity outside of the framework of the state, making mem-

TRIBES AND QADHAFI'S REVOLUTIONARY TOOLBOX

bership of a political party punishable by death and forcing what existed of these currents underground. The tribe was therefore the sole form of social organisation. As Sheikh Benjdiriya put it, 'The tribe is the reference and people orbit around it. The tribes feed the hungry, the tribes bring justice for you; tribes are an authentic component of the Libyan man's life'.[58] Libyan scholar Zahi Mogherbi argues that the development of civil society during this period was hampered by prevailing cultural and social attitudes and behaviours, with family and tribal affiliation still dominating patterns of interaction and with primordial not civil loyalties and connections determining and guiding individual attitudes and actions.[59] Qadhafi had no choice therefore but to harness the tribe in a more overt fashion, it being the best social structure through which to 'embrace individuals and control their political paths'.[60]

Qadhafi began to lean into the tribes in a more vigorous fashion, amplifying tribal symbols and values and using the tribes as a source of legitimacy and social control. This does not mean that Qadhafi 'revitalised tribalism' or 're-tribalised society', as has been suggested in some of the literature.[61] While he may have been a manipulator of tribes, it was never within Qadhafi's grasp to initiate such enormous social change. Rather, Qadhafi opted to deal with the realities of the society he was trying to rule, pulling back the lid and allowing what was already present greater visibility. To this end, the regime started to open up more space for the outward manifestation of tribal traditions and values. Although unlike other nationalist leaders of his day, Qadhafi was never shy about meeting sheikhs publicly, the 1990s saw a more overt elevation of tribal symbolism. This went as far as Qadhafi's promoting the idea that the Qadhadhfah were ashraf (descended from the Prophet). While Qadhafi had always maintained that his tribe was of noble origin, he began actively seeking out connections to prove a direct linkage to the Prophet as a means of acquiring both tribal and religious validation. Qadhafi made a particular play of this alleged linkage while attending the Arab Summit in Baghdad in 1990, claiming a direct connection between his own tribe and the Ahl al-Beit (family of the Prophet) through the figure of the seventh Shi'ite imam, Mousa al-Kadhem, whose shrine is in Baghdad. Qadhafi asserted that as the Qadhadhfah were also known as Awlad Mousa

57

TRIBES AND THE STATE IN LIBYA AND IRAQ

(the sons of Mousa), they must have been related to the imam. In typically theatrical fashion, he walked in late to one of the summit sessions and announced that he had been delayed because he had been visiting the shrine of his forefather.[62] This concocted holy linkage was a recurring theme throughout the remainder of his rule.

At home, meanwhile, Qadhafi started making a major play of visiting large tribal gatherings and celebrations, which were broadcast on state media. At these events, tribes would welcome, glorify and reaffirm their allegiance to him and his revolution.[63] Abdullah Othman observed, 'When they imposed sanctions in 1992, Muammar started going to mass gatherings outside Tripoli. He went to villages and tribes to reproduce legitimacy. This is the human pool that gave him legitimacy in the first place. Why not return to it?'[64] There was a notable shift in the discourse of some of the state press too and articles started appearing, especially in *al-Shams* newspaper, lauding the tribe and its role in national security, as well as its importance in Islamic history.[65] The regime also began promoting the establishment of tribal associations and clubs, encouraging the youth to become engaged in their activities. Analyst Mohamed Ben Taha observes, 'In 1992, Qadhafi established tribal associations inside the big towns including Tripoli, Benghazi, Misrata and Zawiya. The aim was to resist the embargo that was imposed on Libya, and to prove to the world that he had popular legitimacy. These associations had a role in the social, cultural and political scene.'[66] The social sphere was filled therefore with activities that confirmed that tribes were still strong and cohesive.[67]

It was also at this time that banners started appearing on fenced-off pieces of land inside the towns proclaiming the existence of the gathering of one tribal association or another. This was a reflection of the decades of rural-to-urban migration that had seen kinship relations and tribal values implanted in the main urban centres. While there had been a huge influx of rural-to-urban migration after the discovery of oil, these flows continued during the early decades of Qadhafi's rule, with many taking advantage of the new housing units that were erected at this time. In some towns, incomers dwarfed the local population. Gharyan is a case in point. Between 1973 and 1995, the number of inhabitants of the Gharyan region who lived in towns increased from 14.8 per cent to 66 per cent.[68] Many of the newcom-

TRIBES AND QADHAFI'S REVOLUTIONARY TOOLBOX

ers were from tribal areas and were members of Bedouin tribes including the Akara, Saba'a, Salaamla, Ja'afara and al-Harrarat, who moved into Gharyan town from the surrounding countryside. Their position inside the town was strengthened by the fact that members of these tribes belonged to the Sahban Brigade, a security force set up by Qadhafi at the start of the 1980s and led mainly by members of the Magarha tribe.[69] Like many other security brigades at this time, the Sahban Brigade established its own investments and shops—known as the Sahbane shops—next to its headquarters at the southern entrance to the town, and also took control of the Jandouba and Upper Western Mountain agricultural projects. Through this brigade, and through their numerical superiority, these one-time Bedouin tribesmen became the majority in the town, and in the mid-1990s, took over all the secretariats [local governance bodies] that used to be in the hands of Gharyan's local inhabitants.'[70] In this way, tribal culture and values continued to be replicated inside towns, albeit with an urbanised slant.

Tribes were also given greater space to permeate the state, local governance and administrative structures providing tribes and tribesmen with access to funds and jobs. Tribal affiliation was always a key component in local governance structures—this being a function of the fact that certain tribes dominated certain areas. Even in Benghazi, tribal affiliation was the most important factor in determining appointees to the People's Committees in 1990.[71] However, the tribes were given increasingly free rein to dominate these local structures. When the Shabiya (province) system was introduced in 1995, tribal representatives in each area would agree upon how to divide up the posts. As Libyan academic Mustafa Attir describes, 'They would decide, education or health is the share of this tribe or that tribe. Each tribe would choose which of its members would occupy the post.'[72] Once appointed, post holders began employing their relatives to the point where schools had more staff on their rolls than pupils, and where officials had given so many positions to their relatives that turning up for work was rendered optional.[73] In this way, the state became increasingly hostage to the family or tribe of its senior employees. A 1997 report by the General Authority of Labour Forces observed, 'Many of the national general companies employ elements who are

TRIBES AND THE STATE IN LIBYA AND IRAQ

relatives or members of the same tribes as the officials running these companies. In one company, the number of employees was 368. Of those, 245 were from the clan or tribe of the secretary of its committee.'[74] According to Sheikh Benjdiriya, in one year during the 1990s, the small town of Ben Jawad, east of Sirte, was given 50 million dinars in its annual budget, 45 million dinars of which was siphoned off by influential figures from local tribes, leaving only 5 million dinars for the municipality.[75] Benjdiriya observed, 'Qadhafi knew that and didn't mind. At this time—the 1990s—Qadhafi was very keen on buying loyalty… Qadhafi never punished a corrupt person so long as they maintained security and stability in their own area.'[76] This was part of the social bargain that Qadhafi had struck with the tribes in order to secure their loyalty to the Jamahiriyah.

During the 1990s, the tribe was brought to the fore, therefore, and rendered more visible as Qadhafi began acting more in tune with his own society in order to enhance his legitimacy and validate his regime. The 1990s also saw Qadhafi turn to the tribes to help him enforce social control. This was especially important in light of the growing challenge of Islamism, including militant Islamism, that was pressurising regimes across the region. Neighbouring Algeria had become embroiled in a bloody civil war between militant Islamist groups and the military-backed regime, while Egypt and Tunisia were grappling with their own Islamist opposition and Sudan was ruled by a military officer who had seized power in a coup through the backing of Hassan al-Turabi's National Islamic Front. While Qadhafi's complete intolerance of any organised political activity outside the state meant that Islamist movements had not been able to gain the same foothold inside Libya as they had done elsewhere in the region, the Islamist current has established a presence nonetheless. Young Libyans had left Libya to join the jihad in Afghanistan in the 1980s and had returned keen to topple the regime. This included those who went on to form the Libyan Islamic Fighting Group (LIFG). Although the LIFG leadership struggled to get back into the country after its members left Afganistan, it had succeeded in recruiting a cohort of Libyans who aspired to topple the 'infidel pharaonic regime'. It, along with other small and nascent Islamist groups and networks that were operating in the shadows at this time,

TRIBES AND QADHAFI'S REVOLUTIONARY TOOLBOX

including the Libyan branch of the Muslim Brotherhood, posed a challenge to Qadhafi. After uncovering an LIFG network in the mid-1990s, the regime unleashed the forces of repression, placing parts of eastern Libya under siege and engaging in a guerrilla war in the Green Mountains.

Yet although Qadhafi relied predominantly on repression to eliminate this threat, he augmented it by instrumentalising kinship networks to contain and neutralise the problem socially, turning the tribes into more ardent social enforcers. He did so through the Social People's Leaderships (SPL), which were set up across the country and brought together in a national organisation in 1996 to serve as 'a leading national umbrella' of all forces within Libya. The members of these committees were billed as 'respected natural leaders' of local communities and would choose a group of co-ordinators, from whom a general co-ordinator would be selected to represent the area at the Shabiya level.[77] There was also an overall general co-ordinator at the national level.[78] The committees were tasked with spreading revolutionary culture, resolving local conflicts, and 'countering corruption, deviation and attempts at treasonable conspiracy'.[79] Or, as Qadhafi put it himself in 1997, 'Members of this institution will be individuals whose words are listened to. If they say to the people, "come out into the street", the people will come out into the street. And if they say, "go home", they will go home, exactly like the father who tells his family to leave or enter the house, or to come here, and the family obeys him'.[80]

The literature had tended to portray the SPLs as a formalisation of the role of the tribe in the political arena, often assuming that loyal tribal chiefs were appointed to head the committees in the service of the state.[81] The heads of the SPLs are often referred to as tribal sheikhs. The SPLs have also been cited as evidence of Qadhafi's coming full circle in his approach to tribes and tribalism, or of his perpetuating and revitalising tribes.[82] Such assertions are not reflective of the whole picture. Rather than enabling or formalising the role of tribal leaders, the SPLs were more a means by which Qadhafi enforced control over traditional tribal leaderships and rather than using them to revitalise tribes, used the SPLs to further foster alternative centres of power inside the tribe in order to better curb and contain them. In the words of Sheikh Hasnawi, Qadhafi used the SPLs to 'dwarf the sheikhs'.[83]

61

TRIBES AND THE STATE IN LIBYA AND IRAQ

While Qadhafi described the SPLs as a 'natural product of Libyan society',[84] he decided who should be appointed as co-ordinators. Many of those appointed were former army officers, including Free Officers. They included individuals such as former Free Officer, Ali al-Faitouri, who was appointed as co-ordinator for Bani Walid. Al-Faitouri proved a loyal servant of the regime, perceived by residents of Bani Walid as responsible for the collective punishment that was meted out to the families of the 1993 Bani Walid plotters.[85] Mehdi al-Arabi, another former Free Officer, was chosen as co-ordinator in Zawiya. As for the General Co-ordinators, these were also military men, including Qadhafi's cousin, Sayid Qadhaf al-Dam. According to Shalgam, al-Dam was chosen as the regime didn't know what other job to give him![86] Mohamed Yousef al-Magariaf, who went on to head the General National Congress (GNC) after the 2011 revolution, explained how Qadhafi chose mostly senior military officers to take on the role of SPL co-ordinator in most shabiyas.[87] Sheikh Abdulrahim Alburki, a spokesperson for the Tarhouna tribes, described meanwhile, 'We didn't choose our leaders. We had guidance, and aspects that we had to consider when choosing tribal representatives. It was social and political. Yousef Buhalaq was a candidate for the Social People's Leadership of Jefara. He had political and social weight. Qadhafi used to know these figures either directly or indirectly, so he appointed him in that social leadership.'[88]

Appointees to the SPLs were not generally the sheikhs of tribes, therefore, or even the tribes' traditional leaders, but were largely loyal pro-regime elements from within the tribes. In this way, Qadhafi used the SPLs to bypass the traditional leadership and create new foci inside tribes by appointing figures whose loyalty was guaranteed. This was Qadhafi's way of taking power away from the traditional sheikhs, with appointees from inside the tribe being tasked with communicating the regime's directions and instructions in return for financial benefits. These appointees became representatives of the regime inside their tribes more than they were representatives of their tribes for the regime, their being to defend the political system.[89] Sheikh Mohamed Aujail Hasnawi painted a similar picture, 'There was a social leadership in my region... Qadhafi appointed the general co-ordinators, two or three people who had

TRIBES AND QADHAFI'S REVOLUTIONARY TOOLBOX

no weight socially or tribally and who had no power on the ground... He told these figures, "You take priority in leading despite the fact that you don't have a strong base." From my own experience, the strong tribes of my area were never given the job of heading that social leadership.'[90] He continued, 'I believe that when Qadhafi formed the SPLs he wanted to undermine the power of the tribe. As evidence of that, he brought non-tribal figures and gave them the reins. What Qadhafi wanted to achieve out of this body was... to neutralise the tribe so it wouldn't get out of control.'[91] Abdullah Othman described how Qadhafi used the co-ordinators of the SPLs: 'If I am a marginalised person in the tribe and you choose me and give me a senior post, the tribe will support me fully despite it not being fully convinced. The tribe will seek to achieve its interests through me. Because I, as Qadhafi, am interested in creating a new social formula, I will seek to strengthen the tribe by bringing in elements who are loyal to me and not to the traditional sheikhs. And the clientele economy will help me to do that.'[92]

The power of the SPLs derived from their relationship to Qadhafi therefore and the tribe could not go beyond the SPL appointees, who acted as gatekeepers and with whom they always had to consult.[93] This did not mean that the sheikhs or the traditional leadership were marginalised altogether. Rather the tribes of the eastern region, and to a lesser extent those of the western region, 'maintained tribal figures who were capable of exerting influence inside the tribe away from the Social People's Leaderships. Members of the tribe would follow their orders.'[94] The traditional sheikhs may have been weakened and dwarfed by these regime loyalists, but they maintained a degree of status and respect among their tribesmen, who knew who the 'authentic' sheikhs were. Furthermore, as an institution, the SPLs were never particularly powerful. In theory, they came above other state institutions, including the People's Committees and Congresses. Yet, in reality, up until the 2000s, they were more symbolic bodies that provided an additional layer of monitoring and security for the regime at a time when it felt vulnerable.

In 1997, Qadhafi tried to extend this layer of monitoring through the introduction of a 'Charter of Honour'. This charter, which was signed by tribal leaders, was essentially a collective punishment con-

TRIBES AND THE STATE IN LIBYA AND IRAQ

tract, stipulating that a criminal's family or tribe could be stripped of civil rights and social services for failing to denounce a member's involvement in acts of subversion, violence, tribal fanaticism, possession of weapons and membership of an armed terrorist group, as well as being accomplices of criminals and 'apostates'.[95] This charter was meant to further pressurise tribal leaders to ensure that their sons did not go astray. Qadhafi had already employed the spirit of this charter in the way he dealt with the families of the Warfalla officers involved in the 1993 plot. He had also invoked the same concept of collective punishment in his speeches around this time, telling the masses in Bani Walid in September 1995, for example, 'The spies, traitors and lackeys should not be able to live among you or to constitute a fifth column for the benefit of the forces of the enemies. You have set an example which ought to be followed—to condemn treason, then to encircle treason and to finally destroy the nest of treason.'[96] Similarly, when addressing the tribes of Zintan one year earlier, he had proclaimed, 'When traitors are discovered within a tribe, the Libyan people automatically consider the whole tribe as traitors; they disdain it and humiliate it. Such a tribe should defend its honour; it should, from within, look for treason, detect it and contain it and disown any of its clans which are involved in treason and say to the Libyan people: we are not traitors, we have washed our hands of such-and-such a clan which has traitors.'[97]

A similar mindset was evident in the way in which Qadhafi punished the Hasawna tribe after it had failed to denounce one of its members who had been involved in an assassination attempt against him in November 1996. LIFG member Abdulmonem Salim Khalifa Hasnawi, known as Abu Talha al-Libbi, who was from the Hasawna tribe (and killed by the Libyan National Army in 2019), threw a grenade against Qadhafi in Braq al-Shatti, north of Sebha, although it failed to detonate. After the incident, Qadhafi accused the tribe of involvement in the attack and put the al-Gurda neighbourhood of Sebha, where large numbers of the tribe were concentrated, under siege.[98] The regime proceeded to suspended all Hasawna tribesmen who worked as officials in the administration or as officers in the military. This resulted in what Sheikh Mohamed Aujail Hasnawi described as 'a period of tension between the tribe and Qadhafi', which lasted

64

TRIBES AND QADHAFI'S REVOLUTIONARY TOOLBOX

until Qadhafi accepted the tribe's insistence that it had not been involved in the assassination attempt.[99] Sheikh Hasnawi described how he met with Qadhafi years later and how he had acknowledged that an injustice had been done to the tribe, blaming his military commander in the south, Masoud Abdulhafiz, who was from the Qadhadhfah tribe, for having frozen the Hasawna's posts in the state. Afterwards, however, 'The tribe and Muammar's relations went back to normal. When he came to visit the south, which he often did, he was very keen on meeting the Hasawna. And the Hasawna returned to taking part in all state bodies'.[100]

Even before the tribes were made to sign Qadhafi's Charter of Honour therefore, he had foisted upon them the role of containing and taming their sons. This role was especially useful to the regime in its attempts to contain and deal with youth who had become part of Islamist opposition currents. Nasser al-Hassouni, the former head of the Revolutionary Committees in Benghazi, explained how, whenever an Islamist prisoner was to be released, the regime would bring the sheikh of his tribe who had to give guarantees before he could be freed.[101] Al-Hassouni explains, 'The reason for doing that was to embarrass you and make it as though the sheikh was doing you a favour.'[102] He added, 'If someone from a tribe did something against the regime, Qadhafi was very keen that he should be confronted by someone from the same tribe.'[103] Notably, in his collection of short stories, *Escape to Hell*, Qadhafi declared, 'The social deterrent is stronger than any civil law or city police force.'[104]

During the 1990s therefore, Qadhafi saw the tribes as an organic part of society that he could use to strengthen his regime, foisting upon them the role of social enforcers. As his rule progressed, Qadhafi not only wove tribes into the fabric of his revolutionary state, but mobilised tribal agency to full advantage. This Bedouin from the desert may have come to power with a dream of creating a new country that would catapult Libya beyond tribal, regional or even national boundaries, but he ended up relying on old social units that proved to be more solid and dependable than his revolutionary ideals.

3

TRIBES, REVOLUTION AND REVENGE

Libyans may wear a suit and tie, but it doesn't change their mentality. Revenge in the Arab mind never dies.

Sheikh Mohamed Omar Benjdiriya[1]

The tribal structure in Libya is such that the tribes worry about their own members. Tribes fear reactions, fear revenge.

Juma al-Ma'arafi[2]

If Libyans felt aggrieved at the state of affairs during the 1990s, grievances at the regime's failure to deliver reached new heights in the 2000s. These grievances were all the more bitter given the optimism that had accompanied the lifting of international sanctions in 1999. Qadhafi's decision, of the same year, to hand over the Lockerbie suspects for trial in the Netherlands, followed by his willingness to cooperate in the War on Terror and his agreeing to abandon the country's WMD programmes in 2003, had seen Libya re-accepted into the international fold. This shedding of the country's pariah status had prompted the regime to adopt the language of reform, and it promised far-reaching political and economic transformation. Finally, it looked as though more normative forms of governance and state organisation might prevail. Yet, as the 2000s progressed, it became increasingly apparent that reform was only ever going to be cosmetic—a veneer aimed at portraying a new image of Libya to the

67

TRIBES AND THE STATE IN LIBYA AND IRAQ

world. When the Arab Spring exploded therefore, with protests erupting in neighbouring Tunisia and Egypt, Libya was ripe for change. On 17 February 2011, Libyans came out in the streets of Benghazi and called for regime change. Yet this was not to be a broad-based revolution with any clear ideological underpinnings. The uprisings were initiated mainly by urban, middle-class professionals, who may have raised slogans calling for democracy and the rule of law, but who had not articulated any vision beyond a shared desire to bring down Qadhafi. However, the protests spread quickly across the east and found echoes in parts of the west.

This turning of the tide against the regime placed Libya's tribes in a dilemma and they found themselves caught between the regime on one side and the growing popular revolt on the other. Tribes prefer stability and order and are not naturally revolutionary entities. Being loose units of social organisation, they generally shy away from taking independent collective political action or stances, especially those that involve confrontation and risk. In the interests of self-preservation, therefore, the tribes were hesitant to commit themselves and preferred to remain in the background, allowing their members freedom of choice as to whether to join the uprisings or not. Even those tribes in the east, where the uprisings took hold with remarkable speed, were not uniformly quick to embroil themselves in such momentous events. This didn't mean the tribes played no part in the 2011 events; it was the tribes that gave the uprisings in the east both weight and depth, and their refusal to heed Qadhafi's call for help was pivotal in how the revolution unfolded.

Once Qadhafi was toppled, tribes, along with other components, were inevitably catapulted into the power vacuum that opened up with the fall of the central authority. This new visibility of the tribes prompted some scholars to argue that the end of the Qadhafi regime saw Libyans return to pre-national forms of identity, including that of the tribe, with assertions that tribal identity suddenly became an 'all-encompassing characteristic, defining an individual's loyalty and political views'.[3] Such assertions are exaggerated and overly simplistic; they also fall back on the old trope of linear notions of development. Libyans didn't 'return' to an attachment to tribal identity. Rather, the events of 2011 revealed what Qadhafi had tried so hard to hide, namely that Libya was still a tribal society and four decades of education,

68

TRIBES, REVOLUTION AND REVENGE

urbanisation and modernisation—albeit Qadhafi's unique version of such—had not eroded kinship alliances. As Mogherbi observed in 2012, 'Tribal influence permeates all aspects of social life in Libya… Libya is still a tribal society and tribal structures are evident throughout the country.'[4] While kinship may have been less pronounced in Libya's main urban centres, state-societal relations still revolved in large part around tribal structures, and Libyans clearly had no difficulty in adopting multiple identities simultaneously.

It was unsurprising, then, that once the lid of repression had been lifted, tribes, along with other components, sought to assert themselves as they navigated the new (dis)order. That this disorder proved so fragmented was equally unsurprising. While the way in which the revolution unfolded, with town after town, or community after community, rising up against the regime, and others standing by it, may have been a contributory factor towards the disintegration, what emerged after 2011 was more a reflection of the fact that local and tribal identities were still strong and continued to permeate and shape people's worldview. However, it wasn't long before the tribes found themselves sidelined by more urbanised and often ideologically driven forces that had emerged as the country's new masters and who were reaping the spoils of the Arab Spring. Not that this situation was clear cut. As the country unravelled, the tribes' response to the new reality was as varied and fluid as everything else that was evolving. In the mosaic of competing forces, it was often difficult to ascertain what was attributable to the tribe and what to other actors and components. This was even more challenging in the west of the country given the crossover between town and tribe, which made the post-2011 local order even more opaque. Nevertheless, for many tribes, the post-Qadhafi period was proving challenging and they felt themselves to be either excluded or increasingly outmanoeuvred by new forces that sought to wipe the slate clean and to call on history in the service of clearing out all vestiges of the former regime.

Towards Revolt

On 17 February, protestors came out into the streets of Benghazi for what had been dubbed a 'Day of Rage' against the regime. This date

TRIBES AND THE STATE IN LIBYA AND IRAQ

had been selected as it was five years to the day that fourteen Libyans had been killed when the regime opened fire on popular protests that erupted in the city after Italian MP Roberto Calderoli proclaimed his intention to print T-shirts bearing reproductions of the Danish cartoon of the Prophet Mohamed. Although the size of the 2011 uprisings and the speed with which they spread came as a shock to the regime, it had been bracing itself for trouble. Following President Zinabedinne Ben Ali's overthrow in Tunisia in January 2011, calls appeared on social media encouraging Libyans to take to the streets. In the same month, thousands of Libyans staged sit-ins in empty and half-built housing projects across the country to protest against housing shortages.[5] This was a reflection of the fact that one decade on from Libya's return to the international fold, for most Libyans, there was little tangible improvement in their lot. The economic opportunities brought about by rehabilitation had been swallowed up by those in the upper echelons of the regime, and by Qadhafi's children in particular. As they had come of age, Qadhafi's offspring had carved up the country, each creating their own fiefdoms and running vast business empires across a dizzying array of sectors. They, along with senior officials, came to be known colloquially as 'the fat cats'. Shalgam describes in his memoirs how Qadhafi's sons, their cousins and some senior officials could routinely be found calculating the amount of commission and backhanders they would get from various deals and contracts.[6] While this narrow elite got richer and as corruption expanded, most Libyans continued to experience deprivation and hardship. To add insult to injury, Qadhafi's children also ran roughshod over the population and over senior officials. Baghdadi Mahmoudi complained to Shalgam that his time as prime minister was spent servicing the needs of Qadhafi's children, who routinely insulted him, with Moatassim Qadhafi once throwing a mobile telephone at him when he hadn't responded to his demands for money.[7] Qadhafi's children had become so out of control that they created further dysfunction in the state and its institutions.[8]

If the promised economic reforms were turning out to be a mirage, the longed-for political changes were proving equally elusive. Saif al-Islam, who spearheaded the so-called reformist current, had embarked upon a host of projects including drawing up a constitu-

TRIBES, REVOLUTION AND REVENGE

tion; instigating an 'independent' media; luring back dissidents from abroad; and launching a major 'reform and repent' de-radicalisation initiative for Islamist militants. Although a significant number of intellectuals and middle-class Libyans engaged with these initiatives, viewing them as the best hope of change in an otherwise bleak environment, it gradually became apparent that this reformist push was hot air. By the late 2000s, Saif al-Islam's projects had either dissolved or gone nowhere, while his efforts to de-radicalise militant Islamists and to lure back dissidents were simply ways of neutralising the opposition. It turned out that there were red lines that couldn't be crossed, one of which was Qadhafi and his Jamahiriyah system.

Qadhafi meanwhile seemed increasingly detached from day-to-day ruling and more focused on self-aggrandising projects such as presiding over mass conversions to Islam in Africa, where he dubbed himself 'King of Kings', and engaging in surreal televised debates with Western intellectuals such as Benjamin Barber and Antony Giddens. With Qadhafi seemingly distracted, and Saif al-Islam's political role expanding, it was looking increasing likely that son was being groomed to take over from father and that Libya was heading in a dynastic direction. One indication of this was that in 2009, Qadhafi arranged for Saif al-Islam to be offered the post of General Co-ordinator of the SPLs. Although the SPLs had had little real power since their inception, they came increasingly to the fore from the mid-2000s onwards, when Qadhafi involved them in a number of taboo files that had been opened by Saif al-Islam in the name of reform. This included using them as mediators in the case of the families of the 1996 Abu Sleem prison massacre in which hundreds of mainly Islamist prisoners from the east were executed extra-judicially.[9] The regime also continued to rely upon the SPLs and the tribe more widely as a means of containing the country's youth, who were still proving susceptible to Islamist ideology. Any sheikh or prominent figure who succeeded in bringing someone 'back to the straight path' would receive a reward, while those who didn't comply would find themselves insulted by Qadhafi and having benefits taken away.[10] Qadhafi also encouraged young people to join Social Youth Associations, explaining in 2005 that such associations would avoid the problem of 'lots of frustrated young people hanging

TRIBES AND THE STATE IN LIBYA AND IRAQ

around', and enable everyone to know who young people were related to, ensuring that if a youth committed a crime, it would reflect on their whole tribe.[11]

Saif al-Islam also turned to the tribe for support and promoted tribal youth associations, handing out cars, computers and loans to loyal members and declaring in April 2005, 'We do not have a history in political parties, but we have tribes and affiliations… Tribal, clannish or social affiliations are not shameful.'[12] Such assertions are somewhat curious given that Saif al-Islam had a reputation for putting his own tribe at one remove. His special advisor, Abdulmotaleb al-Houni, described how Saif al-Islam 'didn't like to be connected to his tribe… Apart from having guards, or officers or soldiers around him, the only member of the Qadhadhfa he linked himself to was Abdullah Othman.'[13] According to al-Houni, it was Saif al-Islam's 'hatred' for his tribe that prompted so many Qadhadhfa to support his brother Moatassim.[14] Moatassim was a military man and like his brother Khamis, had his own brigade that was afforded the best equipment and military kit. Both Moatassim and Khamis recruited mainly from loyal tribes that were in alliance with the Qadhadhfa. A member of the small al-Breiki tribe from the western mountains, which is the tribe of Qadhafi's mother Aisha Bint Abu Neran al-Breiki, explained how he and other members of his tribe were selected to join one of Khamis's elite units.[15] They were summoned to attend military training sessions overseen by Khalifa H'neish in Sirte, where they received artillery training.[16] Yet while Khamis and Moatassim depended on the same tribal alliances that had propped up their father's security apparatus, Saif al-Islam tried to break free from such tribal connections, presenting himself as a more 'modern' reformist figure. This put him on a collision course with the Qadhadhfa, who accused him of having 'killed assabiya' (group solidarity). Al-Houni described, 'The assassination attempt that Saif al-Islam was subjected to during the revolution was carried out by members of his tribe who never forgave him for his hatred towards the tribe and for his political behaviour.'[17]

By the time of the Arab Spring, therefore, an imbalance had evolved within the system Qadhafi had created. His sons were creating havoc, the hoped-for economic benefits had not materialised, and all hope of reform had dissipated. Libya looked more anachronistic than ever. It was little wonder then that once popular protest took

TRIBES, REVOLUTION AND REVENGE

hold in neighbouring Tunisia and Egypt, the regime began to steel itself for trouble.

Tribes and the Uprisings

When it became apparent that Libya was not immune from the effects of the Arab Spring and that a 'Day of Rage' was being planned, Qadhafi turned to the tribes to try to shore himself up in his hour of need. He was well aware that if he could keep the large tribes on side, his regime would be safe. As former revolutionary commander and analyst Abduljawad Badeen, from the al-Awaqir tribe, explained, 'Qadhafi tried feverishly to isolate the tribes from the revolution... In his attempt to abort the revolution he called on the tribes by name. "Where is al-Obeidat? Where is al-Awaqir?" He knew that this would be the only way to abort it.'[18] To this end, Qadhafi called on the sheikhs of the tribes to meet him in Tripoli and embarked upon a major mobilisation effort. Revolutionary Committees Co-ordinator in Benghazi, Nasser al-Hassouni, explained Qadhafi's thinking: 'The most important thing was that the tribe should use its influence to weaken the [planned] protests.'[19] Qadhafi dispatched his cousin Omar Ishkal, who was military ruler of Sirte, to meet with tribal representatives across the country. This included in the east, where he met with representatives from the large eastern tribes, but focused especially on the al-Awaqir and Jawazi, and on the eastern sections of the Warfalla and Qadhadhfa in Benghazi. Ishkal called on these tribal representatives to encourage their members to stay away from the planned protests and to attend counter-demonstrations in Benghazi instead. In the case of the al-Awaqir, he designated Brigadier Suleiman Ayad, an influential figure in the tribe who was also a Qadhafi loyalist, and told him to convince his fellow tribesmen not to join the protests.[20] In some instances, Qadhafi intervened personally to convince tribal sheikhs not to take part. Sheikh al-Senussi Buheleq of the Zuwiya tribe described how in 2011, Qadhafi had phoned him and offered to send him 'millions of dollars' for not taking part, noting, 'He contacted me because I was the sheikh.'[21]

The regime also organised for youth from tribes loyal to the regime to go to Benghazi to stage counter-demonstrations. Thousands of

TRIBES AND THE STATE IN LIBYA AND IRAQ

unarmed young people from the Qadhadhfah, Awlad Suleiman and Warfalla tribes, and who came mostly from Sirte and Sebha, were bused into Benghazi and other eastern towns to this end. Dubbed the 'Yellow Hats', these youth first went into the streets of Benghazi on the night of 16 February. However, they agitated the local population, refusing to listen to anyone other than their own sheikhs and officers and engaging in 'provocative behaviour', including dancing and singing in the streets, something that did not sit well with the conservative orientation of Benghazi residents.[22] In addition, the regime armed members of loyal tribes and formed military brigades out of the Warfalla, Tawergha, Riyayna, Reheibat, Mashashiya, Qawalish, Magarha and Qadhadhfah tribes, among others.[23] Despite the fact that many of those who took up arms on behalf of the regime were among the poorest in Libyan society—or the ragadi riyah (misfortunates)—they were willing to stake their future on the regime.

This arming of the tribes did not always run smoothly. Initially, the regime armed only those houses of the Qadhadhfah related directly to Qadhafi.[24] This caused consternation inside the tribe, with other houses complaining they were not being treated fairly and demanding weapons of their own. Such was the upset that Ishkal and Sayid Qadhaf al-Dam met with the Qadhadhfah elders to mediate, promising them senior positions in the state if they co-operated. Following this meeting, thousands of armed volunteers from the Qadhadhfah were sent to Tripoli and Sebha to protect the regime. Eyewitnesses in Sebha claimed to have seen members of the Qadhadhfah as young as 15 or 16 years old walking around armed with guns.[25]

Yet despite the regime's efforts to instrumentalise the tribe for its own defence, its endeavours proved insufficient to stem the tide of anger and the protests quickly gathered momentum. For the tribes in the east, the situation presented a major predicament. There has been a tendency in some of the literature to paint a picture of the eastern tribes joining the uprisings, while tribes in the west and south proved more divided, with some sticking by Qadhafi and others joining the revolution.[26] While it is true that those tribes most closely associated with the Qadhafi regime defended it most fiercely, such a neat division risks oversimplifying the way in which tribes react to major political upheaval. It also assumes a form of collective political action

74

TRIBES, REVOLUTION AND REVENGE

and agency that tribes do not possess, especially in such critical situations. In reality, the tribal response was far more complex and fragmented. In the interests of self-preservation, many tribes, including those in the east, proved hesitant about adopting a definitive stance one way or another, preferring to remain in the background. Even those tribes that had no love for the Qadhafi regime were reticent about taking a common position.

This reticence was related to a number of factors. Firstly, the events of 17 February were utterly overwhelming and like the regime, the tribes were thrown into confusion by what was unfolding. Secondly, tribes were afraid that if they joined the uprisings and the attempt to unseat Qadhafi failed, the regime would unleash its revenge upon them. As al-Houni described, 'When the revolution reared its head, there were towns, tribes and villages that didn't move to support it. This wasn't because they liked the regime, but they feared the tyranny they had experienced and the fire they had been subjected to.'[27] Thirdly, tribes prefer order and stability, and by nature are not revolutionary-minded.

Yet the tribes in the east did not want to stand against the protests either. Not only did they not want to end up on the wrong side of history, large numbers of their youth were already taking part. Indeed, many tribes had urbanised or semi-urbanised sections. The al-Awaqir for example stretch in a large arc around Benghazi but also spill over into neighbourhoods of the city itself. It was these urbanised elements who had been part of the administration and who had engaged with the state in some form or another, who joined the uprisings.[28] These elements had been involved in the politics and life of the city, albeit under the shadow of the regime, for decades. Many sheikhs were part of the professional classes and had held positions in the state. The same was true of the al-Obeidat in Derna, which also has urbanised components. The tribes were not separated from urban life and their members were as swept up in events as others. Thus the sheikhs did not want to stand against their own tribesmen. They were wary too, fearing that if they heeded the regime's call to stand against the protests, violence and killing would ensure, embroiling them in cycles of tribal revenge.[29] Furthermore, while tribal elites may have been reluctant revolutionaries, some were also

75

TRIBES AND THE STATE IN LIBYA AND IRAQ

seeking change. Although they had benefitted from their relations to the Qadhafi regime, many eastern tribes felt resentful that rather than treating them as partners in ruling, Qadhafi had subjugated them. As such, they weren't ready to stand against the uprisings in defence of the regime.

Many eastern tribes opted to remain ambivalent, therefore, adopting a more neutral position by allowing their members to decide whether to take part and shying away from taking any collective political stance. As former defence minister and member of the al-Awaqir tribe al-Bargathi explained, 'There was no specific tribal guidance. When we took part, we did so as individuals. February was spontaneous.'[30] This is in line with the fact that while tribes may wield power on the social level, they do not generally try to enforce any political line.[31] As a result, tribes found themselves split between those who joined the uprisings and those who had serious misgivings about what was unfolding. Even the al-Obeidat did not take a uniform stance towards the regime despite the defection of prominent regime personnel from among its own ranks. While the defections of Interior Minister Major General Abdulfatah Younis al-Obeidi and Commander of the Tobruk military region Suleiman Mahmoud al-Obeidi may have served as a green light to some members of their clans to join the uprisings, they neither represented nor triggered collective tribal action. Some prominent al-Obeidat members, including senior officials such as Abdulati al-Obeidi and Embarak al-Shamakh, stood with and defended the regime. The same was true of the al-Awaqir, with certain leading figures from the tribe standing by Qadhafi, including Saad al-Asfar, the General Secretary of the People's Committee of Benghazi shabiya, who fled to Egypt in February 2011, and Brigadier al-Senussi S al-Waziri, deputy secretary of the General People's Committee for Public Security in Benghazi, who described, 'At the start of the crisis, my cousins pressurised me to defect. I rejected their request and they turned their backs on me.'[32] Even some of the tribe's senior sheikhs were against the uprisings.[33] Moreover, as late as early March, the regime appears to have been unclear as to the al-Awaqir's stance. In a recording leaked to al-Jazeera, Saif al-Islam can be heard telling senior regime member, Tayib Safi, 'The al-Awaqir are crucial. If they join us, we are set.'[34] Safi responds, 'Their position is still with

76

TRIBES, REVOLUTION AND REVENGE

us. If we had both the al-Awaqir and the al-Obeidat tribes, we could shake the situation.'[35]

The Zuwiya tribe was also split between those who supported the revolution and those who did not. As Salah Ghazal Zuwiy explained, 'Tribes didn't move as tribes but as individuals... When the uprising took place and I came out in Benghazi against the regime, my cousins in Kufra and Tazerbo moved against the regime. The family revolted and others joined them. But not all my tribe joined the revolution. The tribe was divided. Some were with the revolution and some were against it'.[36] He also explained how the Zuwiya in Kufra issued a statement announcing they were joining the revolution and because the majority of the population in Kufra are Zuwiya, it looked like a 'tribal move', while those members of the Zuwiya who joined the uprisings in Ajdabiya did so more as part of a civil movement in which members of several tribes took part.[37]

While certain families or individuals, or even parts of tribes, may have issued statements declaring their allegiance one way or the other, these were largely personal decisions taken by individuals or houses and did not represent a singular tribal stance. This period was full of statements issued by individuals, families and sections of tribes. Academic Mohammed Bamyeh examined twenty-eight tribal declarations issued between 23 February and 9 March 2011 and found that the vast majority were issued in the name of specific sections or locations of a tribe, or spoke in the name of the tribe but proceeded to list its locations to implicitly exempt those residing elsewhere.[38] As Lacher observes, therefore, while individual notables and their networks appeared as actors in the uprisings, the events in Cyrenaica were not driven by the collective action of eastern tribes.[39]

This doesn't mean that the eastern tribes' role was inconsequential. While they may not have driven the events or spearheaded the protests, through their decision not to stand against the uprisings, the tribes gave the uprisings depth and momentum. They were what one revolutionary commander described as the 'social incubators' of the revolution.[40] Had the tribes bent to the regime's demands and stood against the protests, or had they tried to impress upon their tribesmen not to join in, the uprisings would have been stymied early on. Thus while not instigators or revolutionary actors, the eastern tribes played

TRIBES AND THE STATE IN LIBYA AND IRAQ

their part and were instrumental in the events that were to lead to Qadhafi's downfall.

Tribes in other parts of the country also faced a serious dilemma when the uprisings began. Even in Zintan, which was the first western town to rise up against the regime, the tribes were somewhat reluctant partners in events. In anticipation of the 'Day of Rage', the regime had called on the town's tribal sheikhs to convince their youth to mobilise and deploy to the east in support of the regime. While the town's sheikhs were meeting to discuss the issue on 16 February, a handful of local residents and one of the town's elders began protesting in the town's central square. They were joined by others and the protests started to grow. Such overt activism worried the tribe and, fearing the regime's response, elders urged caution against provoking repression.[41] Once again, the tribe feared being dragged into events it could not control and that could have fateful consequences for its members. Yet, the town's youth were insistent, leaving the tribe with little alternative but to offer support from behind. Zintani Imam, Sheikh Taher al-Judai, described, 'When the sheikhs of the tribes saw that the demonstrations were getting bigger, they started assisting and siding with the youth.'[42]

However, most tribes in the west and the south preferred to adopt a more neutral stance, fearing any action that might risk consequences for them or their members. Even those tribes traditionally allied to the regime were not prescriptive and allowed their members the freedom to choose what side they wanted to be on. Sheikh Hasnawi of the Hasawna tribe described, 'We gave individuals the freedom to do what they saw fit and not to do things in the name of the tribe. If they chose to go with February, this was their political choice and not the tribe's... The tribe's name shouldn't be used.'[43] The Warfalla followed the same path; Sheikh Benjdiriya described how Warfalla's tribal council opted to take a neutral stance and to give the freedom to individuals to decide whether or not to take part.[44] This decision was then disseminated to all Warfalla tribal councils across the country. Likewise, the Magarha opted not to take any particular line, wanting the tribe to be left out of things, allowing its members 'personal choice' as to whether to join the uprisings.[45] Thus while some parts of the Magarha joined the uprisings, including in Benghazi,

78

TRIBES, REVOLUTION AND REVENGE

Zawiya, Misrata, Zintan and Tripoli, among other areas, other sections of the tribe remained more neutral.

Many of these western and southern tribes preferred to hunker down in their own areas and in the interests of self-preservation, to wait to see what transpired. As the conflict progressed, and as rebel forces pushed through western Libya to reach Tripoli, many tribes tried to seal off their territory from the advancing forces. Sheikh Mabrouk Buamid of the Warshefana explained, 'The political role of the tribe is in the service of the state… Warshefana didn't take part in 2011 and were against [the events of] February. But we didn't join the other camp. When the revolutionaries came, we told them, "Don't enter Warshefana's territory." We did that in the name of the Warshefana tribe. But we allowed them the use of the coastal road. If we had been against the February events, these revolutionaries wouldn't have reached Tripoli.'[46] In Tarhouna, the tribes showed a similar preoccupation with keeping other forces out of the town, whether from the regime or from the rebel side. Sheikh al-Breiki described how after seventy or eighty people started protesting in the town, the local SPLs called on the regime to send them the names of the protestors so they could deal with them inside the town.[47] He elaborated, 'After we received the list, we told the authorities, "Thank you and we will do our job." We told them frankly, "We are with the security of Tarhouna, so don't bring any forces from outside the town." Many of the young responded positively to our plea at that time.'[48] Giuma al-Ma'arafi, who commanded Qadhafi's forces in Tarhouna at the time, commented, 'Because of our tribal structure, we didn't allow others to come in [to the town]. Tarhouna was with the revolutionaries, but we didn't let others come in.'[49]

NATO's entry into the conflict in March 2011 also posed particular dilemmas for the tribe. Given tribes' natural hostility towards outsiders, this international dimension created a new predicament for many and prompted some to feel as though they should stand with the regime. Sheikh Hasnawi commented, 'Whoever enters [Libya] illegally is an occupier. Some of us Hasawna took part in February and some of us resisted the NATO fighter jets… The important thing for us in the tribe is national sovereignty and the state.'[50] Abdullah Othman concurred that tribes stood more by the

TRIBES AND THE STATE IN LIBYA AND IRAQ

regime after 19 March because of the intervention of a foreign element.[51] Similarly, Sheikh Benjdiriya of the Warfalla noted, 'If NATO hadn't intervened in the war, tribes wouldn't have stood behind Qadhafi.'[52] This is not to suggest that these tribes adopted any formal collective position. Moreover, some of these explanations may have been made in hindsight and proved a useful excuse for some elements who backed the 'wrong side'. However, some sheikhs and tribesmen were more inclined to back the regime once NATO joined the conflict and to provide a safe haven for Qadhafi and senior regime figures until the very end.

The intervention of French intellectual Bernard-Henri Lévy, who went to Benghazi in February 2011 in support of the rebels, also caused consternation among some of the tribes. Sheikh Benjdiriya commented, 'The worst thing for us was that Lévy appeared with some tribal leaders in the east… These meetings made the opponents of Qadhafi stand with him.'[53] In April 2011, the National Transitional Council (NTC), a body set up by the rebels in the east to serve as a government in waiting, had hosted a meeting between Lévy and some tribal sheikhs in Benghazi that culminated in a statement appealing for national unity and condemning the Qadhafi regime.[54] This appeal was signed by what the NTC and Lévy described as sixty-one 'chiefs or representatives of all the tribes that make up Libya'.[55] Yet, in most instances, the signatories were not the heads of the tribes but were individuals or heads of certain sections of the tribe. Muftah Matouq al-Warfalli for example signed on behalf of the Warfalla despite only being the head of the Jamamla section of the tribe in Benghazi. Despite this, the NTC used the statement as evidence that it had tribal weight behind it. The regime retaliated in kind, convening a National Conference for the Sheikhs of Libya's Tribes in Tripoli on 11 May. The official media claimed that 2,000 tribes participated in the event. While this is a gross exaggeration, the event was attended by a large number of tribal sheikhs from across Libya, including the east. Those present condemned the NATO attacks, called for national unity and urged the rebels to disarm. Similar gatherings were to follow and the tribes became pawns in the conflict, with both sides trying to demonstrate that they had tribal backing.

Ultimately, the regime was unable to hold things together and with the help of foreign intervention, Tripoli fell into rebel hands in August

TRIBES, REVOLUTION AND REVENGE

2011. Two months later, Qadhafi was located in the deserts of Sirte and was subjected to a gruesome end, bringing four decades of rule to an end.

The New Powerhouses

Qadhafi's downfall and the collapse of the centralised regime left a gaping power vacuum and morass of disjointed forces that had risen up with little more in mind than bringing down the regime. Out of this chaos, Libya tried to set itself on a new path. The NTC—recognised internationally as Libya's ruling power—relocated from Benghazi to Tripoli and set about trying to govern the transition. It was challenged from the start by the fact that it represented little more than a loose collection of individuals deemed to represent their own areas who had been cobbled together in a time of crisis. More importantly, it was up against a host of armed groups and militias that had formed during the uprisings and that had no interest in relinquishing their weapons or newfound power. With the collapse of the army, these groups multiplied once the regime collapsed, assuming responsibility for the local order in their own areas where they established military councils, which became the new local centres of power. These victors of the revolution set about imposing their control and jostling for dominance in the new order. Indeed, it became apparent early on that the new Libya was to be built on 'revolutionary legitimacy' and that this same legitimacy was to be augmented by history and used by these new powers to crush and exclude those who got in their way.

The two main powerhouses in this revolutionary new order were Misrata and Zintan, which had emerged out of the ashes as the new masters of western Libya by virtue of the role they had played in defeating the regime. Although both Misrata and Zintan are sometimes referred to as tribes, the tribal tapestry of both is complex. Demographically, Misrata comprises different components including Karaghala,[56] those of Circassian origin, as well as an assortment of small Arab tribes, clans and sub-clans (l'hamat). In this melting pot, kinship is based more on alliances than it is on blood lineage. The city's inhabitants are woven together through these alliances. Misrata

81

TRIBES AND THE STATE IN LIBYA AND IRAQ

is also a financial powerhouse, known for its wealthy business families, such as the al-Dbeibahs, the Muntassars and the al-Suwayhilis, who were able to draw on their resources during and after the revolution to fund large, powerful revolutionary brigades. These brigades rose up solidly against the Qadhafi regime, having hounded out pro-regime elements in the city. These included members of the Maadan tribe, who lived in the city's suburbs, as well as members of the Warfalla and the Tawergha, who, fearing revenge for their perceived closeness to the former regime, left in their droves.[57] While Misrata is sometimes referred to as a tribe, it is more urban and less tribal in orientation than many other areas. Zintan by contrast is dominated by two main tribes—the Awlad Abul Hul and Awlad Dweib—the latter of which is a branch of the Magarha. Zintan also comprises other smaller tribal groupings. As with Misrata, the identity of the town has merged with tribal identity, with references to the 'Zintan tribe' or 'Zintan tribes'.

In Zintan, and to a lesser extent Misrata, as well as in other western towns, sheikhs and traditional tribal leaderships found themselves overwhelmed by the new revolutionary order. In Tarhouna, the tribes were at the mercy of revolutionary militias including the notorious al-Kaniat, which terrorised the town's population. Tribal sheikhs were also elbowed out in Zawiya, where hard-line Islamist forces had taken over. The main focus of power in Misrata meanwhile was its military council, which served as an umbrella for the commanders of the city's myriad armed groups. While certain tribal leaders and figures may have been members and even leaders of some of these armed forces, and while the distinctions between town, tribe and revolutionary forces are often blurred, it was the leaders of these revolutionary brigades who emerged strongest. The likes of Fathi Bashagha, Mahmoud Rajab and Saleh al-Badie, who headed unwieldy revolutionary brigades, became the new foci of local authority. The same pattern replicated itself in Zintan, where the military council became the de facto leading power. Although tribal sheikhs in Zintan came together after the collapse of the regime to divide up posts and portfolios in the local administration between the different tribal groupings,[58] the new powers in the town were largely unknowns who had cut their teeth on the battlefield. The head of the military council,

82

TRIBES, REVOLUTION AND REVENGE

Osama Juwaili, was a former teacher and state ministry employee, who had served briefly in the military under the former regime; brigade leader Abdullah Naker was a former television repairman who stationed himself in Tripoli; and another brigade leader, Mukhtar al-Akhdar, had been a wedding caterer.[59] While the tribes may have backed these individuals and while their tribesmen may have joined their militias, traditional tribal leaderships found themselves relegated to the sidelines as these new strongmen took charge. A similar pattern replicated itself in Zawiya, Nalut and other towns that had risen up against Qadhafi, while in Tripoli, a tangle of competing forces, many of them Islamist in orientation, took control. These new revolutionary powers treated the country as if it were a pie to be divided up, taking over key strategic sites and extending their areas of control. The revolutionaries also forced the hand of the country's embryonic governing authorities working on the premise that prowess on the battlefield should translate into government posts. Drawing up the first government, which was appointed in November 2011, was a masterclass in appeasement and bargaining, with the prime minister, Abdulrahman al-Keib—an unknown who was chosen as a compromise candidate—a hostage to the demands of competing revolutionary forces.[60] Zintan ended up with the defence ministry, while Misrata gained the interior, justice and finance ministries. While tribes are often associated in the literature with reaping the spoils, often caricatured as if this is their primary and overriding objective, it was these young, more urbanised revolutionaries rather than the traditional sheikhs and tribal leaderships who sought to extract all they could. In 2013, Zintan tribal council complained that the town's militias were risking escalation through their efforts to extend their power.

Furthermore, the revolutionaries used their newfound power to try to subjugate those elements they deemed tainted by their association with the past. This was particularly pronounced in the west and south of the country. While the east had fallen in a matter of days, the battle for the rest of the country had been more protracted, taking on the hue of a civil war. Once the regime collapsed, the victors unleashed a torrent of vengeance against those tribes and areas that had stood shoulder to shoulder with the regime or who had remained neutral in the 2011 events. Al-Houni observes, 'The revolutionaries

83

TRIBES AND THE STATE IN LIBYA AND IRAQ

who triumphed over the regime couldn't read the hesitant stance [taken by some tribes towards the revolution] and considered this hesitancy as a betrayal of the revolution. They dealt with these societal components with the mentality of the victor and the vanquished in such a way that shattered national unity.'[61] Indeed, they adopted a policy of communal revenge. This was particularly evident in Qadhafi's hometown of Sirte, where rebels who came mostly from Misrata went on the rampage, killing fighters and civilians alike, and looting and destroying property. One Sirte resident described at the time, 'They envy and hate us because Muammar is from here. But we are just civilians. The revolutionaries are coming here for revenge and destruction... We didn't resist in this neighbourhood so why did they destroy our homes?'[62] A revolutionary from the east complained that he couldn't dissuade the Misratan revolutionaries who had said it was time to treat the Qadhadhfah in the way that Qadhafi had treated them.[63] Misratans also wreaked revenge on the nearby town of Tawergha, which had stood with the regime including during its bloody siege on the city that lasted from February until May 2011. The attack was so ferocious that the town's 35,000 residents were forced to flee, after which Misartan forces set about looting, vandalising and burning down houses.[64]

Perhaps the most blatant example of communal revenge and score-settling occurred in 2012, when Misratan forces attacked Bani Walid and put the town under siege. Bani Walid had already been attacked when it fell to rebel forces, with Brigade 28, a force made up of revolutionary elements from the town including some Warfallans who had been involved in the 1993 coup plot, attacked property and individuals linked to the regime. After this episode, Bani Walid was put under the administration of forces chosen by the NTC, something that was fiercely rejected by the town, which turned to the Social Council of the Warfalla tribe to run the town. Meanwhile, hundreds of young men from Bani Walid were detained by revolutionary elements and held on the accusation that they were supporters of the former regime. A feeling of collective stigmatisation and humiliation soon descended on Bani Walid therefore. Tensions reached boiling point in September 2012, when Misratan revolutionaries surrounded the town and put it under siege, arguing that they were saving it from

TRIBES, REVOLUTION AND REVENGE

Qadhafi loyalists who were sheltering there.[65] They were assisted by the country's new ruling authorities, who were so beholden to their new masters that they sanctioned what amounted to tribal revenge by passing law number 7 of 2012, authorising the use of force against the town. One Libyan commentator observed at the time, 'I have never heard of a state imposing such a thing on a town… The authorities are dealing with Bani Walid as if it is a separate state.'[66] This ruling gave the Misratan revolutionaries political cover as they proceeded to shell and attack Bani Walid, leaving scores dead and injured, before they finally took it over at the end of October 2012. Notably, these revolutionaries appealed to history in their quest for vengeance, erecting pictures of Misratan leader Ramadan al-Suwayhili, who was killed by the Warfalla in Bani Walid in 1920 after staging a failed attack on the town. A member of the al-Rubaya tribe recounted hearing Faraj al-Suwayhili, the commander of the al-Suwayhili brigade, which had been involved taking over Bani Walid, commenting on the radio, 'Now we have returned!'[67] As Ouanes has observed, 'historical hatreds among tribes and regions were mobilised to rekindle conflict… some tribes deliberately dug up historical memory and brought its bloody elements back to life to use in the conflict.'[68]

Despite its revolutionary fervour, Zintan refused to support Misrata in its attack on Bani Walid. This reluctance was partly related to the competition for control that was developing between Zintan and Misrata, but was also linked to the fact that the Warfalla were khout al-jed with Zintan and thus would not support the attack against it. However, Zintan conducted revenge attacks of its own. During the summer of 2011, Zintani forces led assaults against the Mashashiya tribe (which was associated with the former regime) in al-Awaniya and Zawiyat al-Bagul in the Nafusa Mountains, with homes, shops and hospitals looted, and residents displaced. Zintan launched another attack against the Mashashiya in December 2011, bombing a residential area and killing local residents on the grounds that the tribe was the Qadhafi regime's 'fifth column'.[69] Revolutionary forces from Zawiya, meanwhile, attacked the Warshefana tribe in November 2011 on the claims that they were 'Qadhafi supporters', prompting members of the Warshefana tribe to protest in Tripoli. Sheikh Mabrouk Buamid of the Warshefana described in 2019, 'Warshefana

85

TRIBES AND THE STATE IN LIBYA AND IRAQ

has had seven wars since 2011. The militias in Tripoli took control of all the country's resources. They closed all the bank branches in Warshefana. They closed the university to put Warshefana under siege. They set 7,500 houses on fire'.[70]

Similar scenes unfolded in the south, where the picture was further complicated by the region's ethnic heterogeneity. Not only were the Qadhadhfah attacked in Sebha, fierce fighting erupted between the Awlad Suleiman and the Tebu, and between the Tebu and the Tuareg. The Awlad Suleiman and the Qadhadhfah also fought it out. The south became a vast struggle for control between competing armed groups.[71] The Magarha were also subjected to revenge attacks and paid for the alliance it had had with the former regime. As Sheikh Suleiman Buhulouma of the Magarha commented, 'The Magarha were subjected to abuse and oppression as a result of the events of the armed uprising against Qadhafi. When the new rulers took power, they worked to punish the members of the tribe because a limited number of leaders were working for the state during the time of the former regime, despite the fact that the tribe didn't adopt the positions of those leaders and didn't agree with Qadhafi's policies throughout his rule.'[72]

Large swathes of Libya splintered into a series of fights therefore between revolutionary elements on one side, and those tribes and areas that were associated with the former regime and that had provided the core of its security apparatus, on the other. As Badeen observed, the revolutionaries labelled certain tribes including the Warshefana, Nawayal, Sayan, Mashashiya and others as 'opponents' despite the fact that there were revolutionary elements among these tribes.[73] As Libyan journalist Hisham Shalawi observed, 'One of the gravest mistakes made by those who instigated the February revolution was the quick tendency to place entire tribes in western and southern Libya in the category of 'enemy of the revolution' and to blame them for the mistakes of the Qadhafi regime.'[74] This prompted mass flight of thousands of Libyans from these tribes and areas, who got out of the country while they could. This is not to suggest that the bloodletting and score-settling that took place was part of any coordinated effort. It was more a reflection of the fact that society was fractured along many different faultlines and the combination of

TRIBES, REVOLUTION AND REVENGE

history, geography and the violent overthrow of the Qadhafi regime had combined to create a potent mix. This situation left many tribes feeling deeply unsettled and marginalised. They also hated the chaos that had enveloped the country. Contrary to the cliché that posits the tribe in opposition to the state, tribes prefer order and the security of working within the confines of state structures, enabling them to strike their own bargains with the ruling power in order to best protect and serve their interests. This brave new Libya was turning into a nightmare and many of the tribes in the west and south felt as though they had been scapegoated and outmanoeuvred by other forces that had scant regard for tribal tradition.

Outmanoeuvred in the East

While the west descended into score settling and revenge, the east appeared, initially at least, to be more ordered and cohesive. This isn't to suggest that there were no acts of vengeance against elements linked to the former regime. On 19 February 2011, Saif al-Islam bemoaned the fact that members of his mother's tribe, the Barassa, had exacted revenge against members of the Qadhadhfah, describing, 'Relatives from my mother's side killed relatives from my father's side.'[75] In March 2011, meanwhile, a group of unarmed Qadhafi loyalists were discovered hiding in a school in Benghazi, and were executed on the spot.[76] Yet, the east did not experience the kind of identity-based killings and abductions that were commonplace in the west in the immediate aftermath of Qadhafi's fall. The future for the eastern region looked more promising therefore. This included for the tribes, which believed that they would be able to reap the benefits of the revolution and become partners in the new Libya.

This did not mean they sought to lead. Rather, they were happy to open space for the new forces that had thrown off the yoke of the past. These forces represented a loose collection of revolutionary elements focused around towns and neighbourhoods, who had pulled together to take up arms when the uprisings morphed into a conflict. They included defectors from the regime's armed forces, tribesmen and Islamist elements, some of whom had fought on the frontlines of various jihads, as well as large numbers who had been freed under

87

TRIBES AND THE STATE IN LIBYA AND IRAQ

Saif al-Islam's de-radicalisation initiatives in the 2000s or by the regime in a concession intended to appease the east during the conflict itself. Once the east was freed from the regime's shackles, the tribes were largely ready to welcome these revolutionary forces in their varying hues. As one member of the al-Awaqir tribe commented, 'The tribes were very happy in the beginning. They furnished the road with flowers for the revolutionaries. The tribes are *daraweesh* (simple people).'[77]

However, it wasn't long before the eastern tribes, along with the professional urban elite that had spearheaded the uprisings, found themselves sidelined and at the mercy of predominantly Islamist forces who wanted to take over both the state and the street. This is not to suggest that these Islamist forces, many of which came together in May 2011 to form the Revolutionary Brigades' Gathering under the leadership of Fawzi Bu Katef, were cohesive. They represented a mosaic of groups and forces of different ideological persuasions that imposed themselves on their own areas, relying on revolutionary legitimacy more than religious legitimacy to do so. As in the west, their leaders were relative unknowns and included the likes of Wissam Ben Hamid, a car mechanic; Ismail Salabi, the brother of Islamist scholar Dr Ali Salabi; Ahmed Majberi; and Ziyad Balam. Many of these figures belonged to the sizeable section of Benghazi society who originated from Misrata and who were known as 'gharabala' (westerners). As noted in Chapter 2, large numbers of Misratans had settled in the central neighbourhoods of Benghazi over the decades, their wealth and success becoming a source of grievance and resentment to more traditional and tribal elements in the city.

Many of these more ideologically driven elements had a hostile or negative perception of tribes. Islamist commander Mustafa Sarkasli remarked, 'By sidelining the sheikhs, the Libyan revolution sought to establish a citizen's state.'[78] These Islamist elements also presented themselves as more authentic and honourable alternatives to what they viewed as corrupt and reactionary tribal elements. They considered themselves to be the rightful inheritors of the revolution and frontline defenders against counter-revolutionary forces linked to the former regime, of which they viewed the tribes to be a part. These Islamist forces started flexing their muscles on this front early on. In

88

TRIBES, REVOLUTION AND REVENGE

August 2011, Abdulfatah Younis al-Obeidi, who, as the most senior defecting military officer, had been appointed to lead the Free Libya Armed Forces, was killed by an Islamist militia in shadowy circumstances. While al-Obeidi's killing came as a shock, Islamist forces had already expressed their objections to him given the role he had played in the regime's brutal campaigns to put down militant Islamist elements in the east in the 1990s. After al-Obeidi's appointment, several Islamist brigades refused to serve under his command, forcing the NTC to establish two parallel security structures, one for the army, headed by al-Obeidi, and the other for the various Islamist brigades that had emerged out of the 2011 uprisings. Suleiman Mahmoud al-Obeidi described how the Islamists had their own separate operations chamber and were already receiving weapons from foreign states.[79] Abdulfatah Younis al-Obeidi was so frustrated at being sidelined in this way that he had been intending to resign once the town of Brega had fallen to rebel forces.[80] However, he did not get the opportunity, as he was assassinated by elements of the Islamist Abu Obeida Ibn Jarrah Brigade. His killing set the tone for much of what was to come in the east. It also created uproar within the al-Obeidat tribe, who threatened to use the 1,000 tribesmen they had on the frontlines to hunt down his killers. Members of the tribe also staged daily protests in Benghazi at the NTC's failure to investigate his death properly, while there were strong suspicions that certain members of the NTC were implicated in the murder. Yet, by this point, Benghazi was falling increasingly into the hands of the Islamist forces and brigades that made up the Revolutionary Brigades' Gathering.

This dominance by Islamist forces did not preclude the tribes from retaining their own militias. Tribal forces took control in various parts of the east, while those suburbs of Benghazi that were dominated by particular tribes also fell into the hands of tribal forces that had sprung up during the uprisings. Some of these tribal militias took over key strategic sites that were located in their territory. Benina airport, which lies to the east of Benghazi and is in al-Awaqir territory, was taken over by the brigade of Ezzadine Wakwak, who was from the Baragatha, a branch of the al-Awaqir. The 204 Tank Battalion, stationed in the Qwayfiya suburb to the east of the city, was led by Mehdi al-Bargathi, also of the Baragatha, and comprised

89

TRIBES AND THE STATE IN LIBYA AND IRAQ

largely members of the al-Awaqir. Although al-Bargathi rejected the suggestion that his brigade was 'tribal', emphasising the force's professional character,[81] a senior member of the al-Awaqir tribe described, 'Brigade 204 tanks were part of the al-Awaqir. My relatives were proud that this brigade was ours; 80 per cent of it is al-Awaqir'.[82] Similarly, the Awlia' Aldam Brigade, led by Uyad al-Faysi, comprised mainly al-Awaqir, while the Hussein Juwaifi Brigade was made up mainly of members of the Barassa, and the al-Obeidat Revolutionaries were formed out of tribesmen of the al-Obeidat. The tribes also had some influence inside the Saiqa, or Special Forces, although Salafist elements were also strong, with the force divided between different components.

Yet while these forces may have been affiliated to various tribes by virtue of their commanders and members, this didn't make them official tribal forces or mean that their commanders represented their tribes. It didn't mean either that the sheikhs had any hierarchical control or authority over them. Rather, these forces were comprised mainly of individuals from a single tribe, were located in areas dominated by these same tribes, and as such enjoyed informal tribal support. However, it was the more ideologically motivated Islamist forces that came to have the upper hand. These forces were bent on becoming Benghazi's new security providers. Unlike those of a more extreme militant bent, who rejected the state as a Western construct that ran counter to Islam, these Islamist commanders wanted to work within the confines of state structures. More explicitly, they sought to take over and eclipse those forces that had linkages to the former regime. Fearing that their newfound power was at risk from counter-revolutionary elements, they refused any kind of reconstitution of the former regime's military and security apparatus, seeking instead to form the bedrock of security provision themselves. This desire to 'purify' the state chimed with the new powers in the capital, who also sought to sideline the military of the former regime and who bolstered this ragtag collection of forces by providing them with money, contracts and official recognition. This process of formalisation culminated in 2012 with the formation of the Libya Shield Brigades and the Supreme Security Committees (SSCs), which answered nominally at least to the ministries of defence and interior, but that continued to operate as independent forces both in the east and the west, as well as the south. Meanwhile, some of these more ideological forces and commanders were given an additional boost from the support they received from outside powers.

The new masters in the east were working hand in hand with the new masters in the west therefore to purge the state, sideline those linked to the former military and impose a new order. This closeness between these revolutionary commanders and the new powers in the capital troubled the tribes. According to one former Islamist commander, tribes were uncomfortable with the fact that the Islamist brigades in the east had given their 'absolute loyalty' to the new powers in Tripoli, with some viewing this as a new form of centralisation.[83] The tribes were craving security and stability, and were also becoming increasingly unsettled by a number of assassinations of those with links to the former regime that were gathering apace. The bid to formalise revolutionary forces that had established themselves to overturn the former regime was also difficult to fathom for some tribes. In the Qwayfiya area of Benghazi for example, many members of the Baragatha tribe didn't understand the need for camps and forces, believing the revolution to be over.[84] It was becoming increasingly apparent to the tribes therefore that while they believed the revolution had ended with the fall of Qadhafi, for these more ideological elements, it was still ongoing.

Furthermore, the tribes were concerned at the emergence and increasing boldness of more militant Islamist currents. On 7 June 2012, some of the most hardline of Islamist elements, including from Ansar al-Sharia, came together in Benghazi's Tahrir Square for the 'First Gathering to Support Islamic Sharia'.[85] Participants, who had timed the event ahead of Libya's first elections, erected tents and began waving black flags and giving impromptu speeches denouncing democracy and calling for nothing short of the implementation of sharia law. One participant told the local media that the aim of the gathering was to 'terrorise those who don't want the rule of Allah's sharia'.[86] What made the gathering all the more alarming for the eastern tribes was that many of the forces who attended had been endorsed by the new authorities in Tripoli. One attendee explained, 'All the brigades that took part in the forum belong to the defence

TRIBES AND THE STATE IN LIBYA AND IRAQ

and interior ministries'.[87] The tribes felt deeply disturbed by such manifestations of militancy. Bargathi remarked, 'There was a group of extremists; the tribes weren't comfortable with them... The Islamists don't distinguish between tribes or the status of the tribe. It isn't important for them if the person is from al-Awaqir or not. They target whoever they want to target'.[88]

In September 2012, Islamist militants opted for a particularly high-profile target. US Ambassador Chris Stevens was killed by militant Islamist elements that had stormed the US Mission in Benghazi. Many tribal leaders were outraged at his killing. More than 500 tribal leaders and elders gathered at a conference to denounce Stevens's death as 'shameful', condemning the government's reliance on militia groups, and the 'marginalisation' of the national security forces.[89] Sheikh al-Senussi Buheleq described, 'When they killed the American ambassador, I argued with them. I told them, "How could you kill a guest?" They accused me of being taghout [a false deity]. They attacked my house. I brought my tribe to protect me. Ahmed Abu Khattala was the first who attacked my house. He came with thirty-seven armed vehicles and we responded'.[90] The overturning of the old order by these ideologically driven revolutionary and Islamist forces left the eastern tribes feeling increasingly sidelined and disempowered, with some describing the 2011 revolution as an 'act of revenge' by the urbanised elite against tribal sections of society.[91]

Tribes and Politics

If the rise of these new revolutionary forces left the tribes feeling sidelined, developments on the political front were proving equally alienating. Urged on by international powers, Libya moved quickly to elections to a legislative power, the General National Congress (GNC), in July 2012. This was despite the fact that the country was awash with weapons, had no national security force and, more importantly, had no political culture or experience to speak of. Furthermore, in line with the revenge mentality that had come to predominate, the NTC sought to ensure that those with links to the former regime were excluded from the process. It did so by incorporating uncompromising criteria for those wishing to stand as candidates into the election law.

TRIBES, REVOLUTION AND REVENGE

The law ruled that candidates had to meet the standards set by NTC resolution 192 of 2011, which banned members of the former regime's security apparatus who had not defected early on in the revolution, as well as those in the administration, from nominating themselves. It also ruled out anyone with a professional or commercial relationship with any member of the Qadhafi family, anyone who had attained an academic qualification in the thought of Qadhafi or *The Green Book*, and any opposition figure abroad who had reconciled with the regime and taken up a position and many others. This law was a clear message to anyone connected to the Qadhafi regime, namely that they had no part to play in Libya's political future.

This ruling inevitably impacted those tribes that had been closely linked to the regime, and some, such as the Magarha, Qadhadhfah and Warfalla, disengaged completely with the electoral process. This served as another bitter blow to these tribes whose hopes for a post-revolution national reconciliation process had already been dashed. On 10 December 2011, the NTC had organised a first National Reconciliation Conference that was attended by the elders of Libya's main tribes. NTC head, Mustafa Abduljalil, struck a conciliatory note and declared that the NTC was ready to forgive those who had fought for the regime, declaring, 'In Libya we are able to absorb all. Libya is for all... Despite what the army of the oppressor did to our cities and our villages, our brothers who fought against the rebels as the army of Qaddafi, we are ready to forgive them... We are able to forgive and tolerate.'[92] One Tripoli resident noted the importance of taking a pro-active approach to reconciliation, commenting at the time, 'If we do not deal with these people now, then it will be the next generation from their tribes who will stand against us.'[93] The NTC's attempts to heal these rifts met with outrage from the revolutionaries and the issue of national reconciliation was swiftly buried. For those tribes associated with the former regime, it was becoming increasingly apparent that the collective scapegoating was going to persist and that the victors of the revolution were going to ensure they had no role in Libya's political future.

The way in which the country's transitional leaders went about shaping the election law alienated others too, especially in the east. The first draft allocated constituencies according to population

TRIBES AND THE STATE IN LIBYA AND IRAQ

weight rather than geographical area, resulting in the less populated east being allocated only 60 out of the 200 seats in the GNC (with 106 going to the west and 34 to the south). This incited fury in the east, prompting a group of federalists to close down the road between Tripoli and Benghazi at Wadi Ahmar in order to demand that the country's three regions be given an equal share of seats. The federalist movement had been swelling in the east and to a lesser extent in the south since the toppling of the regime and had been able to tap into the grievances that were mounting in these regions. Many easterners and southerners had hoped that the overturning of the political order would bring an end to the extreme centralisation that had characterised the past forty years, seeing 2011 as a chance to correct the regional imbalance. Yet, those in the east soon came to feel as though the revolution that had started in Benghazi was being 'snatched away' from them by the new powers in the west, who were upholding the former regime's centralisation tendencies. Al-Keib's first government, appointed by the NTC in November 2011, had been a case in point. Not only were Misrata and Zintan heavily represented, most key portfolios went to the west of the country, including defence, interior, justice and oil. Al-Keib and his deputy prime minister, Mustafa Abushagur, were also both from western Libya. This blatant promotion of western interests stirred up feelings among some in the east that the country's new powers were bent on supressing the eastern region altogether. Disgruntled members of the al-Awaqir and Magharba tribes held protests in Benghazi to object to the line-up.[94]

Such resentment fuelled support in the east for a federalist vision that was articulated by a group of activists, including a number of eastern tribal figures. In March 2012, these activists, who also comprised revolutionary commanders and political activists, came together for a large gathering in a disused soap factory in Benghazi to unilaterally declare the establishment of a Barqa region under the Barqa Transitional Council. These figures were not demanding secession but sought autonomy within a federal Libya based on the constitution of 1951, which laid down a federal system comprising three wilaya (provinces) and that had been abandoned in 1963. Although some notables from the large eastern tribes, including the al-Awaqir,

TRIBES, REVOLUTION AND REVENGE

Magharba and al-Obeidat, were a driving force in this federalist movement, this did not mean that these tribes supported federalism wholesale, or that one can even describe federalism as a 'tribal project'. It is certainly incorrect to depict the federalist project as a manifestation of the 'retribalisation' of Libyan society, as some scholars have done.[95] While the idea of returning to a system of governance that prevailed during what was a 'golden age' for some eastern tribal elites may have appealed to certain tribal elements in the east, the federalist project did not have widespread support inside these tribes, where there was still a strong attachment to the concept of national unity.

Furthermore, the federalist project had started out as an elitist project in the 1940s, conceived of and promoted by urbanised intellectuals who were influenced by European notions of statehood, and whose ideas at this time did not translate beyond a small section of the small elite.[96] The revival of this federalist ideal after 2011 was also driven primarily by urban intellectuals, including Dr Abu Bakr Bouaira and Sadique al-Gaithi al-Obeidi, and by some tribal activists. Again, their ideas did not travel far. They certainly failed to win over the revolutionaries and Islamists, although this was not for want of trying. Badeen recalled how federal activists from the Barassa, Magharba, al-Awaqir and al-Obeidat had tried and failed to convince members of the Revolutionaries Brigades' Gathering to join the movement. Although Badeen threw his weight behind them, going on to become a proponent of the federalist cause, his fellow revolutionary commanders were unconvinced. As he commented, 'Most of the Islamists couldn't see beyond the February revolution. They wanted to protect it. They feared that Qadhafi's men could penetrate this federalist movement. Plus, a large section of them were listening to the fatwas of [Grand Mufti] al-Gharianni and others in Dar al-Ifta.'[97] Ultraorthodox and particularly hardline in his views, al-Gharianni was explicit in his rejection of federalism. The federalists' efforts to give their movement force and additional clout through these revolutionary elements failed therefore.

Yet the movement also failed due to the limited support it had within the tribes. Most eastern tribes, including the al-Obeidat and al-Awaqir, were split between individuals or families who rallied behind the cause and those who opposed it. Badeen explained that out

TRIBES AND THE STATE IN LIBYA AND IRAQ

of the al-Awaqir's thirty-strong administrative committee, which comprises sheikhs from the three main branches of the tribe, 'Only eight sheikhs were openly and explicitly with us.'[98] He also noted, 'The federalist movement was spontaneous and supported out of personal conviction. But if an influential [tribal] figure joined the movement, then the house or clan that he was affiliated with may follow suit.'[99] Yet this wasn't guaranteed. Furthermore, some al-Awaqir sheikhs were overtly hostile to the project. One senior figure in the al-Awaqir encapsulated the views of some in the tribe when he remarked, 'Only the fools of Barqa demand the rights of Barqa,' noting that the tribe's historical sheikhs would not have supported such a project.[100] This division of opinion within the tribes is unsurprising given tribes' reluctance to adopt collective political decisions, preferring to maintain a flexibility that enables them to absorb and accommodate those of differing political stances. Badeen observed, 'Politically, each individual in the tribe has absolute freedom.'[101] It is this flexibility and lack of ideological fixedness that permits tribes to respond to shifting circumstances and environments, and to endure and hold together beyond political upheaval.

Thus while many proponents of federalism may have been tribesmen, the tribes did not rally behind the federalist project en masse. Moreover, federalism was roundly rejected in the west of the country, where the attempt was perceived as a bid to break the country apart. It was also rejected by many Islamist elements, including Dr Jamal Hiraysha, the founder of the Muslim Brotherhood's Justice and Construction Party (JCP), who declared, 'I am worried about what is happening in Benghazi… I call upon all Libyans and the revolutionaries to confront these people [federalists] and to stop them by all means and to stop them from spreading the culture of division and marginalisation among brothers in one country… there are no easterners or westerners in Libya, neither Fezzani, nor Amazighi, nor minorities, nor tribalism. All Libyans are equal in rights and duties.'[102] The federalist project was quashed almost as soon as it had announced itself, therefore, although it was to rear its head in a considerably more radical fashion in 2013 through the figure of Ibrahim Jedhran (see Chapter 4).

The federalists also failed to secure a change in the distribution of seats between the regions at the GNC elections. At the end of June

TRIBES, REVOLUTION AND REVENGE

2012, NTC head, Mustafa Abduljalil, declared that it was too late to alter the seat allocation, although in a sop to the federalists, two days before the polls, the NTC amended the 2011 draft constitutional declaration so that instead of the GNC appointing the body that would be tasked with drafting the constitution, it would now be directly elected by the people. However, other parts of the 2012 election law were proving contentious. This included the fact that only 80 of the 200 seats in the GNC were allocated to political parties, the remainder being set aside for independent candidates. Some of the new political parties that emerged on the scene feared that this allocation split would see the tribes take the lion's share of seats. Wasila al-Ashiq, the leader of the Al-Umma party, complained, 'We should not be voting for x or y, but candidates should join a party with clear political objectives... Otherwise, the larger tribes will gain all the seats and minorities such as the Berbers will be ignored.'[103] In the event, the tribes did not mobilise in a major way at the polls. Tribes, along with other components, were still scrambling to situate themselves in the new Libya, where events were moving fast. Moreover, revolutionary fervour was still strong and personality sometimes trumped other considerations. Thus while kinship played a part in voting patterns in some electoral constituencies, such as in Sebha, where some voters acknowledged that they had voted for candidates affiliated with or openly supported by their tribes,[104] this did not hold true across the board. In the Qwayfiya and Sidi Khalifa suburbs of Benghazi, for example, where the Baragatha and al-Awaqir are dominant, tribal candidates lost out to Saleh al-Jueuda, who took the seat for that constituency. Al-Jueuda, a well-known opposition figure during Qadhafi's time, who comes from Benghazi but is of Misratan origin, won the largest number of votes of any independent candidate in the elections.[105]

This did not mean that tribal considerations held no sway at all. Tribes in the east and the west held meetings before the polls to proclaim their support for the candidate affiliated to their tribe, while several candidates who lived in Tripoli and Benghazi stood in their towns or areas of origin in order to maximise support from their tribes.[106] Political parties also gave priority in each constituency to candidates who originated from that area. Even the Brotherhood

97

TRIBES AND THE STATE IN LIBYA AND IRAQ

acknowledged that it had fielded some of its candidates, who were known in their local area, as independents in the hopes of securing a greater number of seats.[107] Additionally, the National Forces Alliance (NFA), headed by Mahmoud Jibril, a former planning minister who defected at the time of the uprisings, relied heavily on local and tribal connections to secure victory. Although referred to as a political party, the NFA was a large coalition of factions and currents, brought together by Jibril's simple and direct message that revolved around getting the country back on its feet. It also served as a focal point for those who, having witnessed the coming to power of Islamist parties in Egypt and Tunisia, wanted to prevent an Islamist victory in Libya. Although Jibril did not campaign on a secular ticket, noting himself that the constitution should be based on sharia, he found support among those who wanted to avoid a Muslim Brotherhood victory.

However, much of Jibril's support relied upon kinship connections. Born in Benghazi, Jibril was from the Warfalla tribe, enabling him to attract backing from members of the tribe who were spread across the country. He also won support from those tribes with whom the Warfalla had khout al-jed, including tribes in Zintan. Despite their revolutionary credentials, the Zintanis were willing to back this former member of the Qadhafi regime on account of this tribal lineage, although this same lineage was to work against him in Misrata, where there was some hostility towards him on account of his tribal origin. Unlike many of his political rivals, Jibril made a special point of courting the tribes. He reached out beyond the main urban centres and travelled around the country meeting with tribal sheikhs and leaders, visiting thirty-six towns and villages in the very short campaign period. He told tribal leaders in the eastern town of Tobruq that if they supported him he would guarantee stability in the centre and flexibility in the margins.[108] In other words, he would not interfere with the tribes' freedom to run their own affairs.

Jibril's approach paid off; the NFA took 39 of the 80 seats reserved for political parties, while the JCP notched up just 17. More strikingly, the NFA took 714,769 votes, representing 48.14 per cent of the vote share, while the JCP took just 152,441, representing 10.27 per cent. Thus, while the tribes had not been a major force in these elections, they affected the outcome nevertheless, with con-

TRIBES, REVOLUTION AND REVENGE

sideration being given to personality, kinship and locality rather than political programmes or vision. As this election demonstrates, therefore, while tribes may be reticent to adopt a single political position or to put forward a specific candidate of their own, tribal power and weight can affect political outcomes in such a way as to serve the interests of the tribe. However, the new candidates to the GNC were soon to realise that their room for manoeuvre was to be tightly restricted. The new legislative body may have had electoral legitimacy, but it had no concrete power of its own. With the country still bereft of a national armed force, the GNC was at the mercy of the revolutionaries and militias that routinely pressurised and intimidated its members. Outraged revolutionaries stormed the GNC on countless occasions, such as in October 2012, when they objected to Prime Minister Ali Zidan's ministerial choices. So frequent were the protests by revolutionary elements that the GNC was forced at one point to hold its sessions in a tent outside of the building. Revolutionary militias also abducted ministers and MPs at whim, including Zidan himself, who was seized in October 2013 and held until he agreed to step down.

These revolutionary forces also invested energy in trying to ensure those linked to the former regime were excluded from the political process. While it would be wrong to assign any collective agency to these disparate revolutionary elements, that were each wedded to their own local area and embroiled in in-fighting and turf wars, they were united in their desire to wipe the slate clean. These efforts were to manifest themselves in their support for the drafting and passing of a draconian political isolation law banning those with links to the former regime from holding political office. This law, described by some revolutionary elements as 'the security valve of the revolution',[109] cast the net far and wide, prohibiting those with even the most tenuous associations with the regime. Many GNC members were deeply uncomfortable about the extreme nature of this law and what it would mean for national reconciliation prospects. However, they were subjected to intense intimidation such as on 5 March 2013, when 500 armed elements stormed a GNC meeting and took the twenty-six members who were present hostage, assaulting those who tried to flee.[110] The intimidation reached such a point that on 28 April,

200 armed revolutionaries, mainly from Misrata, surrounded the foreign ministry with pick-up trucks and banners calling for 'Azlam Qadhafi' (Qadhafi's men) to be purged from the ministry and demanding the political isolation law be passed. The following day the ministries of finance and justice came under attack, and an attempt was made on the ministry of interior. Faced with such a show of force and with the revolutionaries having all but brought the administration to a standstill, GNC members had little option but to pass the controversial law, despite the fact that it had the potential to force some of them out of their posts.

As the dust settled on the events of 2011 therefore, the country was ensnared in conflict and had fallen into the hands of a morass of competing revolutionary and Islamist forces that had succeeded in imposing their authority. In this environment, the tribes felt as though they had been pushed to the back. This is not to suggest they were inactive; the tribes had engaged where they could, especially through conflict mediation, where they came into their own. Wisemen's councils, comprising tribal sheikhs and elders, had emerged in almost every town. These councils sought to resolve disputes both locally and across the country, often being dispatched by the authorities in Tripoli to mediate in tribal conflicts in other areas. The Wisemen's council in Benghazi, for example, which comprised some 1,000 tribal figures, focused its efforts on reconciliation in the western region and on 'protecting the country from tribal wars and revenge'.[111] Such efforts increased and by 2013, they had started promoting themselves as 'incubators of dialogue and compromise'.[112]

Many of these tribal interventions were successful in so far as tribal mediators were able to open dialogue and broker settlements between conflicting parties. Yet, they often fell down at the implementation stage, not least because the authorities were unable to provide the military clout necessary to ensure the agreements were upheld and because the forces involved did not always hold to their word. Sheikh Abdulrahim Alburki observed, 'The armed groups tend not to comply with what they sign. This is unlike the tribes. When they [the tribes] sign an honour charter, they uphold it until the end... I am proud I work for the tribe rather than for ideology. The tribe is more ingrained and more rooted in the Libyan soil than ideology or any

TRIBES, REVOLUTION AND REVENGE

other thought.'[113] Moreover, while the tribes were content to play such a role, it was hardly the partnership they had hoped for and they were left feeling utterly dominated by the militias and revolutionary groups that were gaining in power and influence. The new authorities were proving utterly inept at reining in the revolutionaries, who were becoming increasingly entrenched in their own areas.

In a reflection of the degree of disillusion, leaders of over fifty tribes came together at a large tribal gathering in Zintan in July 2013 to condemn the situation. Zintan was willing to host such a gathering, as it was also feeling outmanoeuvred. Revolutionary forces from Misrata and Zawiya were increasingly making common cause with armed groups in Tripoli, and Zintan felt itself being squeezed out. At the gathering, tribal elders called for the dissolution of militias and brigades and also demanded the police and army be activated. They also condemned the GNC and the government, demanding their dissolution too. One participant lamented, 'We don't know why on earth they brought political parties [to govern]. They call for Allah and loot the Libyans.'[114] The tribes were crying out for order. As far as they were concerned, the revolution had turned toxic, and had either made an enemy of the tribes or left them feeling excluded. As Sharif al-Abbar remarked, 'The revolutionaries ignored the tribes... By the time they contacted the tribes and tried to establish relationships with them, it was too late.'[115]

4

TRIBES AND THE POST-2014 ORDER

I will not name each tribe individually, as we have become a single tribe.

Khalifa Haftar, January 2016[1]

Tribe will save Libya like the army saved Egypt.

Izzadine Wakwak, 2014[2]

While the years immediately following Qadhafi's downfall were marred by chaos and violence, the summer of 2014 catapulted the country to a whole new level of conflict. In the west of the country, those forces that had emerged victorious from the collapse of the regime battled it out for control among themselves, while in the east a new power struggle emerged after a retired military officer, Khalifa Haftar, embarked upon a campaign to take control of Benghazi. These separate yet interlinked conflicts were to ravage the country, with the south oscillating between the competing sides. With neither camp strong enough to defeat the other, Libya became trapped in a torturous war of attrition, aggravated by the intervention of foreign powers and a failed UN peace process, which sought repeatedly to impose so-called consensus governments from above.

For those tribes and areas associated with the former regime, these developments meant a continuation of the marginalisation they had experienced since 2011. The ongoing dominance of revolutionary forces in the west that were relentless in their efforts to purge the state meant that these tribes—including the Qadhadhfah, the Magarha and the Warfalla—stood largely apart from the conflict. National reconciliation was still a dim and distant prospect, meaning that thousands of their tribesmen and women would remain displaced, both externally and internally, with thousands more in arbitrary detention at the hands of militia forces, who were still able to act with impunity.

Other tribes seized upon this new phase in the transition in the hopes it would bring about some sort of recalibration in the path the country was taking. This was particularly the case in the east, where the Cyrenaican tribes had become increasingly frustrated at the chaos, dysfunction and violence that had enveloped Benghazi and beyond. Targeted assassinations and kidnappings had become near daily occurrences in Benghazi, while the tribes feared the Islamists' efforts to uproot society and traditional values in the interests of their rigid ideological objectives. When Haftar appeared on the scene, promising to rebuild the army, impose order and eliminate Islamist elements in Benghazi, these tribes saw a way out. To the tribes, Haftar, the military man, looked as though he could rebuild a strong state and provide the best chance of stability. Equally importantly, these tribes saw in Haftar a chance for the east to fight back against the dominance of Misrata and its Islamist allies. These powers that had taken over the capital clearly had no intention of ceding control or of breaking with the centralisation policies of the Qadhafi regime. Benghazi's dream of becoming the country's economic capital and of having a greater share in power and wealth looked to have gone up in smoke. Thus the tribes saw in Haftar a way to break the yoke of the Islamist forces that were dominating in the east and an opportunity to reassert some authority and control over their own domain while simultaneously kicking back against the dominance of forces in the west. This was their way to reclaim what they believed was their historical right. The eastern tribes threw their weight behind Haftar, therefore providing him with fighters and support, forging an alliance that was to have a major impact on Libya's trajectory.

Not that tribal support for Haftar was confined to the east. Some tribes in the west and in the south also proved willing to align themselves, albeit loosely, with Haftar's forces. These tribes had become increasingly frustrated with the hold that the axis of revolutionary

TRIBES AND THE POST-2014 ORDER

forces, led by Misrata, had over the country and over the west in particular. These forces were largely tone deaf to the tribes, their focus more on subjugating the country rather than bringing it together. Some of these tribes pushed back therefore. This included the Zintan tribes, which allied themselves with other western tribes, including those associated with the former regime, to try to wrestle power out of Misrata's hands. Meanwhile, other western tribes and towns stood firm, refusing to be dominated by the revolutionary current. This included Warshefana, Nawayal, Aujailat, Assaba, Surman and to a lesser extent, Tarhouna. As a result, Misrata and its allies failed to break into whole areas of the west, their power confined primarily to the capital, Zawiya and Misrata. This did not mean that these tribes or areas all supported Haftar but they certainly sought an alternative to the dominance of Misrata and its ideologically driven allies.

For many tribes, but particularly for tribes in the east, Haftar's message resonated therefore, and while they may have been wary of him and his personal ambitions, they looked to him to deliver them from the crisis. As one tribal sheikh from Warshefana commented, 'With the collapse of Qadhafi, we lost our national sovereignty and with the armed forces [LNA], we feel as if we retrieved part of this sovereignty.'[3] This is not to suggest that his relationship with the tribes was unproblematic. Even the large eastern tribes did not rally behind him wholesale, with different houses and branches pulling in different directions or, in some instances, refusing to give their support altogether. Moreover, those tribes living in more settled areas like Tobruk, which had remained in the hands of local tribes and families, were less in need of a rallying figure who could bring law and order than cities like Benghazi that were under the grip of ideologically driven forces. Moreover, tribes do not give their support unconditionally. As under Qadhafi, there was still a bargain to be had between Haftar and the tribes, and he had to work hard to contain crises and retain tribal support, especially following his failed attempt to seize control of the capital in April 2019.

Yet these difficulties did not diminish the fact that much of Haftar's power was predicated on tribal support and that the tribes provided him with a weight and depth he would not otherwise have had. Some analysts have dismissed this interpretation of events, downplaying the role of the tribes and arguing that Haftar's success in establishing primacy over the east was the result of a combination of foreign support, repression and his ability to use patronage to exploit weak and divided leadership.[4] While external support and repression, as well as Haftar's use of patronage, all played a role in his ascendency in the east, as did his ability to draw Salafist Madkhalist forces, which also formed an important component of his arsenal, such assertions belie the fact that the Cyrenaican tribes were perhaps the most important factor in his success. Without tribal support, Haftar would not have been able to build a force on the ground. Had the tribes been unwilling to back him and allow him space to operate, they could have blocked his way at the outset of his campaign. While tribal support for Haftar's Operation Dignity campaign may have been opportunistic and riven with fissures and frictions, it was through the tribes that Haftar was able to extend beyond his circle of retired military officers to become a major powerbroker in the east and also to find support in those parts of the west that were resistant to control by Misrata and its allies.

New Divisions

On 14 February 2014, the al-Arabiya television channel unexpectedly broadcast a recorded statement by Khalifa Haftar, who spoke in the name of the 'National Command of the Libyan Army'. Stumbling over his words and reading from an autocue, an uncomfortable-looking Haftar called for the implementation of a new roadmap that would correct the path of the revolution.[5] While insisting that he wasn't trying to stage a coup, he also demanded the suspension of the government and the General National Congress (GNC), the latter of which had just voted to extend its own mandate, prompting public protests. Although the air at this time was thick with rumours of conspiracies and coups, Haftar's surprise appearance was widely dismissed and even mocked, not only because of his wooden delivery, but also because of the limited power and military force at his disposal. Moreover, Haftar had already tried and failed to make his mark in post-revolutionary Libya. A onetime Free Officer who had seized

TRIBES AND THE POST-2014 ORDER

power with Qadhafi in 1969, before defecting from the regime during Libya's conflict with Chad in the 1980s, Haftar had returned from exile in the US at the time of the 2011 uprisings. He had aspired to lead rebel forces upon his return, but to his frustration, was overlooked in favour of Abdulfattah Younis al-Obeidi, and had to settle for the role of commander of Libya's ground forces instead. Once the Qadhafi regime fell, Haftar all but faded into the background.

Yet this television appearance did not come out of nowhere. Haftar had been working up a plan to try to re-establish the armed forces from as early as 2012, and to this end had been reaching out to various constituencies, including tribal sheikhs, across the country in a bid to bring them on board. He had forged particular links with military officers and notables in Tarhouna, a town known for its recruits to the military under the former regime, and also a centre for Haftar's own tribe, the Ferjan. Haftar had also reached out to notables and military figures in Bani Walid, Zintan and other towns. These efforts culminated in a meeting hosted by Haftar in Martyrs' Hall in Tripoli three days before his recorded television broadcast. This meeting brought together dozens of military officers, who like Haftar had been forcibly retired from the Libyan army by the GNC in 2013, and who came together to discuss Haftar's plan to establish a military council that would replace the GNC and take over ruling the country. However, the plan backfired and Haftar and his fellow officers were all referred to the military prosecutor by the GNC, prompting him to flee to the east of the country.

Yet while Haftar's 'stunt' was widely dismissed at the time, it turned out to be a defining moment in Libya's transition. Undeterred by the uncompromising response he had received in the west of the country, Haftar sought to try to 'correct the path of the revolution' from the east. On 16 May 2014, he unleashed his Operation Dignity campaign, proclaiming his mission to rid the country of terrorism and extremism. The operation kicked off with a round of attacks against bases belonging to Islamist forces in Benghazi. Although Haftar's forces were no match for their Islamist opponents at this point and were forced to withdraw, the ferocity of these sudden attacks sent shockwaves around the country and they were roundly condemned by the authorities in Tripoli, who accused Haftar of staging a coup against the 'revolutionaries'.

TRIBES AND THE STATE IN LIBYA AND IRAQ

While a long, extremely bloody battle was to unfold in Benghazi between Operation Dignity forces and their mainly Islamist opponents, the launch of Operation Dignity emboldened some forces in western Libya. Haftar's message clearly reverberated among a number of constituencies who felt a growing sense of unease at the dominance of the revolutionary current. The myriad of forces and armed groups that made up this current were not only forcing the hand of the elected powers in the capital, they were also embedding themselves ever deeper in their own areas. These forces were still acting with impunity, carrying out arrests, detentions, abductions and killings, their towns and areas littered with extrajudicial detention centres where many detainees were being held based on identity. The lawlessness was palpable, and many Libyans felt deeply troubled at the absence of any centralised force that could bring these unruly militias under control. Haftar's call to 'correct the path of the revolution' chimed well with some elements in the west and there were public demonstrations on 23 and 30 May in Tripoli and other towns in support of his operation.

Haftar's entreaty also had a special resonance for some forces in Zintan, who were finding themselves increasingly outmanoeuvred in the power struggle that had developed in western Libya between those forces that had emerged triumphant out of regime change. Despite having successfully imposed themselves at various strategic sites in the capital after Qadhafi's fall, Zintani forces were proving no match for Misrata and for more Islamically minded forces that were also present in Tripoli. While Zintan had been able to punch above its weight in the immediate aftermath of Qadhafi's collapse on account of the fact that its forces had captured Saif al-Islam Qadhafi, the town was now struggling to maintain its influence, and the friction with Misrata was growing steadily. Aligning themselves with Haftar appeared to be a vehicle whereby some of these forces might be able to tip the balance in their favour and claw back some of the power they had lost. Two days after the launch of Operation Dignity in Benghazi, therefore, the Qaqa, Madani and Sawaiq brigades—all from Zintan and all of whom had provided security for Haftar at his Tripoli meeting in February—declared themselves to be part of the Libyan National Army (LNA). They stormed the GNC, demanding

TRIBES AND THE POST-2014 ORDER

its dissolution. The resulting clashes left two dead and more than fifty wounded. Although the extent of the co-operation between Haftar and these Zintani brigades was not clear at this point, LNA spokesperson Mohamed al-Hijazi claimed responsibility for the attack and accused the GNC of supporting 'extremist Islamist entities', declaring the aim of the assault to have been to 'arrest these Islamist bodies that wear the cloak of politics'.[6] On 21 May, Haftar told a televised press conference that a judicial council should take over running the country and appoint an emergency civilian cabinet to oversee new elections. Three days later, he warned the GNC that if they tried to meet, its members would be considered 'a legitimate target for arrest'.[7]

Although this assault was quashed easily enough, the new boldness on the part of these Zintani forces, as well as their alignment with Haftar, was deeply troubling for the revolutionaries in the west. Equally unnerving was the large tribal conference that was convened on 25 May 2014 in al-Aziziya and that was hosted by the Warshefana tribe. This gathering was attended by some 2,000 sheikhs of the Warfalla, Magarha, Tarhouna, Mashashiya, Jumail, Aujailat, Sayan, Tuareg and Tebu tribes. These tribes, whose territory was spread across the west and many of which were associated with the former regime, were also feeling marginalised and were deeply disturbed at the dominance of the revolutionary current. Clearly galvanised by events in Benghazi, they came together to call for the dissolution of the GNC and the militias. Although there were disagreements between participants, including over the fact that some tribes wanted to re-instate the Qadhafi-era flag and national anthem, these tribal sheikhs and notables were united in their call for the return of the 'legitimate army, police and security agencies'.[8] Khalid Buamid, the spokesperson of the conference, declared, 'The Libyan army is made up of the sons of tribes and the tribes are the social base for everyone'.[9] In a final statement, these sheikhs also demanded the establishment of a Supreme Council of Tribes to take over governing until such a time as elections could be held and a constitution approved. The statement also called for an amnesty for all those who did not have blood on their hands and for full citizenship rights to be restored to all Libyans. This was a bold move on the part of the tribes and was one of the first clear articulations of political ambition on their part.

TRIBES AND THE STATE IN LIBYA AND IRAQ

Not used to intervening directly in this way given their role as units of social organisation and their preference for working from behind, the tribes capitalised on Haftar's actions in what was a desperate bid to assert themselves to try to puncture the hold that Misrata and its allies had over the country. Sheikh Mabrouk Buamid of the Warshefana tribe described how, at this meeting, 'We, the tribes of Libya, met in Warshefana and we decided to go against Misrata'.[10]

Although these western tribes were not sufficiently strong or united to be able to pose any serious challenge to the dominant forces in the west, this new assertiveness on their part, as well as the articulation by these tribes of objectives that tallied with those of Haftar, stoked concerns among the revolutionary camp. These concerns intensified with the June 2014 elections to the House of Representatives, which was meant to take over from the GNC. These polls served as a bitter blow to the revolutionaries and the Islamist camp, which lost out significantly to the civil current and to the federalists, who scored particularly well. For the Islamists in particular, these results signified what appeared to be a turning of the tide against them and they could feel power starting to slip away. This feeling was fuelled by the blows that were raining down on Islamist forces across the region, including the toppling of the Muslim Brotherhood-led government in Egypt and the edging out of the An-Nahda-led government in Tunisia. Meanwhile, the goodwill towards the revolutionary current that had accompanied the end of the Qadhafi era was dissipating fast, as the country was unravelling. Islamist forces and their Misratan allies were under enormous pressure therefore, and were feeling vulnerable.

Fearing that power was about to be snatched from them, these forces came together in July 2014 under the umbrella of Operation Libya Dawn. The aim of this loose coalition, of which Misrata formed the backbone, was to drive its Zintani opponents out of the capital and impose full control. On 13 July, Operation Libya Dawn forces launched attacks against strategic sites in Tripoli under the control of Zintani brigades, including Tripoli International Airport and the headquarters of the Islamic Call Society. Given its limited size and power, Zintan needed to find allies in this fight and looked to some of the western tribes who were antagonistic towards Misrata and the

110

TRIBES AND THE POST-2014 ORDER

revolutionary currents, most notably Warshefana. Zintan was in a somewhat anomalous position. On one hand, it was one of the winners of the 2011 events and was thus imbued with revolutionary legitimacy, yet on the other it had a traditional closeness to tribes and areas associated with the former regime, including having khout al-jed with the Warfalla and one of Zintan's tribes belonging to the Magarha. As noted in Chapter 3, this khout al-jed relationship was one of the reasons Zintan objected to Misrata's attack on Bani Walid in 2012. Furthermore, Zintan was not comfortable about Misrata's alliance with political Islamist forces and was ideologically at one remove from some of the armed groups operating in the new revolutionary axis. This is not to suggest that Zintan operated as a united force. Certain armed elements from the town were more revolutionary minded than others. However, it was not that surprising that in its hour of need, Zintan turned to the Warshefana for help. Equally importantly, Warshefana provided Zintan's access to the capital, its territory being located in between Zintan and Tripoli.

For its part, Warshefana proved willing to ally itself to Zintan in the interests of stemming Misratan influence. Sheikh Buamid of the Warshefana described, 'When Misrata and others wanted to crush Zintan we took the decision as Warshefana to stand with Zintan against Libya Dawn.'[11] He went on, 'We found Zintan more amenable to us than Misrata. Zintan's problem was that they are few. They couldn't do anything without the Warshefana.'[12] In return for joining the fight against Operation Libya Dawn, Warshefana demanded that Zintan release a number of detainees who had been arrested in 2011 for their links to the former regime.[13]

Despite coming together, these Zintani and Warshefanan forces were no match for Operation Libya Dawn, and by September 2014, they had been pushed back out of the capital. This was to mark the end of Zintan's power in the capital, its armed groups forced back into the western mountains. It also saw large numbers of Zintani residents of the capital flee their homes and neighbourhoods, adding to the growing numbers of internally displaced. By the end of September, Operation Libya Dawn had all but subjugated Warshefana as well. Although both forces tried to launch a counter-attack, they only got as far as retaking Warshefana's capital, al-Aziziya, in April 2015.

111

This 2014 conflict resulted therefore in the almost complete domination of Tripoli by revolutionary forces, led by Misrata. In other words, one set of victors of the revolution had successfully defeated and dislodged the other. Yet while this revolutionary axis stamped its control over Tripoli and the country's national institutions that were housed there, it was unable to impose its authority fully. Operation Libya Dawn remained divided, its component parts engaging in clashes as they vied for control and resources. Moreover, while it gave itself political cover through its reconstituting of the GNC, which appointed a government of its own, it had competition in the form of the House of Representatives, which had established itself in Tobruk and its own government in al-Baida. From now on, Libya was to have two competing governments and legislatures that were to engage in a major competition for control of the country's institutions and resources, effectively dividing the country. Furthermore, these revolutionary powers in the capital failed to bring in the tribes in the west, who could not stomach the dominance of Misrata and its allies, and who remained an obstacle to these forces' efforts to control the western region. For all their revolutionary power, these forces remained ringfenced and unable to extend their control. However, tribal sheikhs and notables continued to feel cowered and as though they had been pushed to the back.

Haftar and the Eastern Tribes

While the tribes in the west were to remain in the shadow of more revolutionary actors, the situation in the east unfolded differently and was to be shaped by the new relationship forged between Haftar and the eastern tribes. After fleeing to the east following his television appearance in February 2014, Haftar wasted no time in rallying support for his efforts to build an army. He not only called on former military officers and professionals, but also tapped into the eastern tribes. To this end, he started touring the east and the centre of the country, meeting with tribal sheikhs in a bid to win them over. He started off in Sirte, where he met with sheikhs and notables from the al-Madaan (who had fled Misrata in 2011) and Qadhadhfah tribes, as well as from his own tribe, the Ferjan. Haftar also met with sheikhs

TRIBES AND THE POST-2014 ORDER

of the al-Awaqir in Benghazi, and, in the second week of March 2014, hosted a large gathering at Qasr Libya in the Green Mountains that was attended by hundreds of sheikhs, notables and wisemen.[14] Abu Bakr Bu Nuwar al-Mismari, a notable from the al-Masameer tribe, explained how his tribe had pledged its support for Haftar, describing how Haftar had 'called upon tribal sheikhs and notables to pull their sons out from the militias and illegitimate armed groups', and how they had promised to provide Haftar with men and money.[15] Also in March, tribes in al-Baida agreed to hand over the al-Abraq airbase complete with weapons and equipment, with members of key tribes from the area attending the handover ceremony.

Haftar's efforts paid off and it wasn't long before he had the backing of prominent sheikhs from most eastern tribes. While the al-Awaqir were perhaps the most enthusiastic proponents of Operation Dignity, not least because the tribe is concentrated in and around Benghazi, where the operation was focused, other tribes also rallied round. As Sheikh al-Senussi Buheleq of the Zuwiya tribe recounted, 'I was among the first to embrace Haftar. His tribe is very small... so we supported him with tribes and men... Haftar didn't have an army with him; we made an army for him.'[16] Buheleq described how leading sheikhs from the eastern tribes had met in Haftar's house describing, 'Me and a group of leading tribal sheikhs went to Khalifa. The al-Awaqir were there, so were the al-Obeidat, Magharba, Hassa, Dersa, Barassa, Ubaid, Fawakhar, Menfa, al-Masameer and Majabra... We met him in his house and because he is a brave man and the son of a tribe, the tribesmen were happy to join him to fight terrorism.'[17] Likewise, Sheikh Salah Lattioush, the leading sheikh of the Magharba tribe, recalled how the tribes had 'welcomed Khalifa Haftar right from the start of the Dignity Operation. They stood next to him and supported him and they gave him every help until he succeeded in building the army for Libya. This all came because of the support of the Cyrenaican tribes.'[18]

This alliance was not without its ironies. Although Haftar was born in the eastern town of Ajdabiya, the fact that his tribe, the Ferjan, originate from Tarhouna means that in the eyes of many in the east, he is considered Gharabala (a westerner). Moreover, his tribe is both small and uninfluential, meaning that he had no tribal weight or history

113

behind him. He was first and foremost a military man and nationalist who had emerged out of the same nationalist military tradition as the likes of Qadhafi and his contemporaries. Haftar had never intended to confine himself to the east, his ambitions always stretching far wider in scope. On the surface, therefore, the tribes and Haftar did not appear natural allies. Yet their interests collided, both seeing the opportunity to forge a mutually beneficial relationship that would enable Haftar to build his army and the tribes to assert themselves in the east and to challenge the centralising tendencies of the west.

The willingness of these tribes to buy into Haftar's project was rooted in multiple factors. Foremost among them was that the tribes saw in Haftar a strong figure with military experience who could bring some order and stability to the chaos that had enveloped Benghazi. Mehdi al-Bergathi, the commander of 204 Tank Brigade, explained, 'The al-Awaqir with its different houses... in fact, all people supported Dignity. People looked at him as a military man with military expertise and as the only person able to bring an end to the complete chaos. Everyone wanted a solution.'[19] He continued, 'What pushed tribes towards Haftar were the slogans he employed about building the state and building the army... The tribe trusted Haftar blindly because he was a strong man who wanted to build the army and the state.'[20] Furthermore, as a nationalist and a military man who had emerged out of the same tradition as Qadhafi, Haftar represented a kind of continuity to the tribes. He was thus someone they felt they could do business with. Rather than working in opposition to the state, the tribes were crying out for a functioning authority with which they could engage and bargain so as to better get on with the business of managing their own affairs.

This did not mean that the tribes shared Haftar's almost ideological determination to root out Islamist elements. The tribes were not intrinsically hostile to the Islamists per se, not least because some of their own sons had joined the array of Islamist brigades and groups that were operating in the east. Yet, being flexible and pragmatic entities, the tribes did not appreciate the ideological rigidity of the Islamist camp or its desire to overturn traditional social structures and norms. The sheikhs were also uncomfortable with the Islamists' insistence that the revolution had to be taken to its ultimate conclusion.

TRIBES AND THE POST-2014 ORDER

For the tribes and sheikhs, the revolution had ended with Qadhafi's downfall and they feared the purging tendencies of the Islamist forces that were bent on turning over a completely new page in the country's history. The net in this respect appeared to be closing in with the almost daily assassinations and abductions that were being carried out by unknown extremist elements. The victims of these targeted killings were predominantly members or former members of the military and security apparatus, who were also the sons of tribes. The al-Obeidat especially had been well-represented in Qadhafi's military and felt particularly vulnerable.

The eastern tribes were also still frustrated at the co-operation between the Islamist brigades in Benghazi and the authorities in Tripoli. This co-operation came under the spotlight after 8 June 2013, a day that came to be dubbed 'Black Saturday' after the Libya Shield 1 Brigade opened fire on protestors who had amassed outside of its headquarters in the Qwayfiya area of Benghazi demanding the brigade's dissolution. The massacre left 40 dead and over 150 injured. The commander of the Libya Shield Brigade 1, prominent Islamist, Wissam Bin Hamid, tried to deflect the blame and accused youth from the al-Awaqir tribe who had been part of the protest for the violence. Bin Hamid claimed that the young al-Awaqir had attacked the Brigade's base after their tribal elders had left.[21] The commander of the Libya Shield Brigade 2, another Islamist, Mohamed Araibi, levelled the blame at Qadhafi loyalists.[22] What really irked the tribes in the east, however, was that although the defence minister, Yousef al-Mangoush, resigned in response to the massacre, other officials in the capital defended the Libya Shield Brigade 1, arguing that it was a legitimate entity that could not be dissolved.[23] Despite the authorities in Tripoli issuing instructions that the Libya Shield 1 brigade, along with other forces, should be brought more directly under the control of the defence ministry, nothing changed and these forces continued to have free rein. For the sheikhs, who were still feeling disoriented and weakened by the social upheaval wrought by the 2011 events, the fact that the new powers in the capital were working with and sanctioning these armed groups in the east was too much.

The tribes were a ripe constituency for Haftar therefore and were willing not only to allow him space to operate, but also to supply him

115

TRIBES AND THE STATE IN LIBYA AND IRAQ

with fighters to make up the rank and file of his Libyan National Army (LNA). As Sheikh Tayib Sharif, a leading sheikh in the al-Obeidat tribe, observed, 'The [Libyan National] Army wasn't built by the state. It is made out of Cyrenaican tribes. The Cyrenaican tribes are the incubators of the army and provide its strategic depth.'[24] Likewise, Sheikh Buheleq commented, 'We gave Haftar the power; we were his incubators. When Haftar came he had only 200 people with him and his opponents numbered 17,000 in Benghazi. What could he do with 200 soldiers? If it wasn't for the tribe he wouldn't have been able to take over a single police station.'[25] While this is somewhat of an exaggeration, the tribes viewed Haftar as a saviour of sorts—at least in the immediate term—and as their best hope of restoring the imbalance that had evolved in the east.

Inevitably, this tribal support was not uniform. While many houses and clans of these eastern tribes rushed to back Haftar, others remained unconvinced. All the main tribes had sections that refused, including the al-Obeidat and the al-Awaqir. Many al-Obediat sheikhs were deeply wary of Haftar and his Dignity Operation.[26] There were several reasons for their reticence. Firstly, the al-Obeidat had not forgotten the acrimony that developed between Haftar and Abdulfattah Younis al-Obeidi in 2011 when the latter was chosen to lead rebel forces.[27] Secondly, some al-Obeidat could not accept the idea that Haftar came from a small tribe whose main concentration was in western Libya, meaning that they did not view him as a befitting leader for the east. Lastly, many al-Obeidat considered the army as their domain. Having held key military posts under the Qadhafi regime, many prominent al-Obeidat were wary about Haftar, who seemed to be challenging them on home turf. While Sheikh Tayib Sharif and others stood behind Haftar, other al-Obeidat sheikhs did not. However, one member of the al-Obeidat explained that these sheikhs who do not support him do not express their opposition to Haftar publicly as they do not want to fracture the tribe, observing, 'If the general line of the tribe is one way, they don't want to rock the boat and upset the equilibrium.'[28]

In the main, therefore, the tribes pulled behind Haftar, and he was able to launch and sustain his Operation Dignity campaign thanks to the backing of the al-Awaqir, the al-Obeidat, the Barassa, the Zuwiya,

TRIBES AND THE POST-2014 ORDER

the Magharba and other smaller tribes that had a presence in the east and the south and that hoped that joining Haftar would not only bring stability and order, but that it would also enable them to regain some status and lost prestige. As Misratan journalist Tareq al-Qzeeri describes, 'For the tribes, the Dignity Operation was the gateway to restoring centrality, status and prestige.'[29] This was particularly the case for the al-Awaqir, some of whom felt that Benghazi was rightfully theirs and that it had been taken from them. Haftar is alleged to have played on this feeling, reportedly telling the al-Awaqir at the outset of Operation Dignity that Benghazi belonged to them, echoing similar sentiments expressed by Qadhafi to the al-Awaqir in the 1970s when he told them their city had been overrun by outsiders.[30] Regardless of the veracity of this assertion, the battle in Benghazi came to take on a narrative of a fight between the 'native inhabitants' of the city against 'outsiders'. These so-called 'outsiders' referred to those Benghazi residents whose origins lay in the west, and in Misrata especially, the latter of whom were labelled 'Masareet'. Strikingly, many prominent Islamist commanders who emerged during and after 2011 were of Misratan origin, including Wissam Bin Hamid, Ismail Salabi, Ziyad Ballam and Fawzi Bu Katif, among many others. In the narrative that emerged, these figures were painted as an extension of the powers in the west and as individuals whose loyalties did not lie with the east. This gave the conflict the hue of a fight between indigenous Benghazi residents who were defending their land against 'interlopers' from the west of the country. It was notable that this discourse targeted Misratans in particular. Those who originated from other areas of the west, or who came from tribes such as the Warfalla, were largely spared such hostility. As one member of the al-Awaqir tribe commented, 'Most revolutionary commanders came from Misrata. A few were from Benghazi. The majority are from Misrata. In Qadhafi's time, there was no difference between someone who was Awquri [from the al-Awaqir] and someone who was Misrati, but this was revived. The old sensitivities started reappearing. My brother started saying, "They caught a Misrati dog"'.[31]

This anti-Misratan sentiment was to evolve into something more akin to a witch hunt after Haftar widened out his Operation Dignity campaign and orchestrated a popular uprising in Benghazi in October

117

TRIBES AND THE STATE IN LIBYA AND IRAQ

2014. Despite launching in May 2014, the LNA was struggling to make headway, while many of its Islamist opponents had grouped together in June 2014 under the umbrella of the Benghazi Revolutionaries Shura Council, which comprised a hotchpotch of armed factions including those of a more militant bent, such as Ansar al-Sharia. These Islamist forces were proving difficult to dislodge. Aware that he needed to bolster his forces, Haftar succeeded in October 2014 in bringing in the powerful 204 Tank Brigade, headed by Mehdi al-Bargathi, who had remained neutral during the early part of the campaign. Haftar also looked to Benghazi's youth, calling on them to rise up and take control of their neighbourhoods. Bargathi described, 'I told Haftar, we need legitimacy. Otherwise we will drown in blood… Benghazi was clouded by flags of Ansar al-Sharia and Islamists, and we agreed on arming the youth of Benghazi to protect us.'[32] In what was dubbed 'Operation Snake Bite', so-called Awakening Councils were unleashed in various Benghazi neighbourhoods including Buhdima, Sertiya, Assalam and Majouri. Some of these youth went on the rampage and set fire to the homes and businesses of commanders linked to the Benghazi Revolutionaries Shura Council. They also hounded entire families out of their neighbourhoods, with accusations that they targeted families whose names clearly denoted their Misratan origins, such as the Suwaid, Kershini and Ikreem.[33] Thousands fled the city during this period, many seeking refuge in the west of the country. As one Benghazi revolutionary commented, these youth 'went beyond the call of duty. They started scratching at old wounds.'[34]

While the numbers involved in such activities were limited, the involvement of local residents who blockaded their neighbourhoods helped turn the tide of the conflict, and by mid-2017, the LNA had all but taken control of Benghazi, opening the way for Haftar to stamp his dominance over the eastern region. While it is true that his power grew through his incorporating Salafist Madkhalist brigades into the LNA and through the foreign backing he received both in terms of material and moral support, it was his alliance with the tribes that gave him a solid grounding in the east and that enabled him to assert his primacy over Benghazi and beyond.

118

TRIBES AND THE POST-2014 ORDER

Expanding Control

Haftar's domination of Benghazi left the country effectively divided, with a Misratan-led camp dominating in the west and an LNA-led camp dominating in the east. Not that either camp was cohesive; both were riven with factions and rivalries, especially in the west. By this time, there was a new government in Tripoli. At the end of 2015, the UN had succeeded in bringing representatives of the two opposing camps together in Skhirat, Morocco to sign a political agreement. This deal resulted in the establishment of what was meant to be a consensus executive comprising a Presidency Council and a Government of National Accord (GNA), which installed itself in the capital in spring 2016. Despite the optimism that accompanied this new start, these new ruling powers failed at the first hurdle and were unable to acquire proper legitimacy or buy-in among all the warring camps. Like their precedessors, they were unable to control the array of armed groups on the ground, while the east quickly disengaged with the process, the House of Representatives refusing to approve the political agreement and its representatives in the Presidency Council withdrawing.

The country remained split therefore between two camps. Yet Haftar's ambitions always extended beyond eastern Libya, and he had been pushing to extend his power both southwards and westwards. In the south, he had worked through various tribes, including some Tebu elements, as a means of consolidating his power, bringing them under the LNA umbrella. While the loyalty of these southern elements oscillated, Haftar had secured loose control over some parts of the south. However, it was through the Magharba tribe that he was to secure what was arguably his greatest coup, using his relationship to the tribe to take over the ports of the Oil Crescent. These ports account for the majority of Libya's oil exports, meaning that whoever controls them controls a major part of Libya's purse strings.

These export terminals had long been a source of friction and conflict, much of it centred around the figure of Ibrahim Jedhran, the commander of the Petroleum Facilities Guard (PFG)—Central Branch and a member of the Magharba tribe. The tribe stretches from Nawfalia to Ajdabiya in the east and its territory includes the Oil

Crescent ports. A federalist, Jedhran, who had headed the politburo of the Cyrenaican Transitional Council, had blockaded the oil ports in the summer of 2013 to demand that a greater share of oil revenues generated in the east be channelled into what he and his followers described as their 'marginalised land'.[35] Jedhran's demands had resonated with certain constituencies in the east and the Oil Crescent, and many rallied behind him and his demands, including a significant number of youth from the Magharba tribe who formed the majority of the central branch of the PFG. Jedhran also won the backing of some prominent tribal sheikhs, particularly those who were pro-federalist, such as Sheikh Abdulhameed al-Kezza of the al-Awaqir. He was supported too by whole sections of the al-Obeidat. These tribal elements considered Jedhran to be defending the interests of the east against the centralising tendencies of the capital.

Set against this, other elements, including leading sheikhs from his own tribe, felt decidedly uncomfortable about what amounted to Jedhran's holding the country to ransom in the service of his demands. These elements included the Magharba's general sheikh, Sheikh Saleh al-Atyush, who explained how the tribe had held a meeting on 10 December 2013 attended by 4,000 to 5,000 members of the Magharba, as well as all of its sheikhs, to try to persuade Jedhran to lift the blockade. Al-Atyush recalled, 'We agreed with Jedhran during that meeting that he would allow the export of oil. He asked us to give him until 15 December and declared before the sheikhs of the tribe that he would open the ports on that agreed day.'[36] Al-Atyush duly told the media that the ports would re-open on 15 December, declaring, 'Oil is for all Libyans and only the state has the right to manage it.'[37] Yet, Jedhran reneged on the deal, prompting al-Atyush to bemoan, 'He violated the agreement and made a mockery of us. He broke the covenant that he proclaimed in front of 5,000 men.'[38] The tribal leadership responded by threatening to publicly disown Jedhran.[39] This was a radical step on the Magharba's part, as lifting tribal cover means that the individual can be killed without tribal revenge being exacted for their death.

Yet by this point, Jedhran, like other revolutionary commanders at this time, had become such a force in his own right that he ignored the tribe and continued the blockade, going as far as to strike a deal

TRIBES AND THE POST-2014 ORDER

to sell oil independently of the state. Although the vessel that had set sail from Sidra port with the oil cargo was intercepted by the US Navy, this illegal deal was the last straw for the authorities in Tripoli, who dispatched Misratan forces towards Sidra port and sites in Sirte and issued a decision (Decision 42) ruling that a military force be established to 'liberate the ports'. While most forces in the east rejected this call, some eastern brigades heeded it and began fighting Jedhran's forces in Ajdabiya. This included the Ali Hassan Jabber Brigade and the Martyrs of al-Jazeera Brigade, the latter of which comprised mainly members of the Zuwiya tribe, a traditional competitor to the Magharba that had objected to the port closures. With the situation threatening to escalate, tribal leaders, including al-Atyush, stepped in to diffuse tensions and both sides agreed to withdraw their forces. Although tribal diplomacy averted conflict, Jedhran made use of the situation and negotiated a deal with Tripoli, securing himself 300 million Libyan dinars in return for his ending the blockade. The ports were eventually re-opened in the summer of 2014, Jedhran having held the country's economy in a stranglehold for the best part of a year and through his exploits having turned himself into a key powerbroker. As Abduljawad Badeen described, 'Jedhran was very important… He had four ports under his control, as well as four airports, hundreds of vehicles, and fighters, including officers. More than half of his fighters were from the Magharba but he also had groups from the al-Awaqir, Zuwiya, al-Obeidat, Amarna and others… He received all their salaries.'[40] In Badeen's view, by the time he struck his deal with the government, Jedhran had become a serious competitor to al-Atyush.[41] Al-Atyush was to complain later on, 'The PFG was entrusted with protecting the ports and oilfields so its presence there was natural. But things started changing. They started making it as if the ports were their own… Jedhran started making money out his control of these places. He received millions from the state and the government.'[42]

Yet while the port blockade was ongoing, Haftar had emerged on the scene. Initially welcomed by Jedhran, who saw in Haftar an ally who could help deflect the Misratan threat, the pair fought side by side in December 2014 when Misratan forces deployed under the banner of Operation Sunrise and attacked the Ras Lanuf and Sidra

TRIBES AND THE STATE IN LIBYA AND IRAQ

ports. This attack quickly took on the hue of a clash between regions of Libya and was expressed in shrill rhetoric. Misratan cleric Salim Jabber outraged the east when he called in a sermon for Misratans to fight the 'ignorant Bedouin people of Cyrenaica', dismissing easterners as shepherds who were only fit to herd sheep and cows.[43] He also proclaimed Misratans to be the 'masters of Libya' and the 'kings of jihad'.[44] Jedhran's brother, Salim Jedhran, who was mayor of Ajdabiya, retaliated by asserting, 'We break the nose of the man who advances on us... He must smell the dirt and he must contend with us. History doesn't remember you [Misrata], because you were busy with commerce and trading, busy collecting money, busy with your bad habits. As for us, we have high morals, we are Bedouins, and we are proud of that... Even if we have become civilised and sophisticated, this Bedouin characteristic stays with us'.[45] This fight was depicted therefore as a battle of honour between the more tribal forces of the east against the more mercantile Misrata.

Jedhran's forces and the LNA fought alongside each other to successfully rebuff this attack. However, relations between Jedhran and Haftar soon soured. Haftar did not want any competitor in the east and expected Jedhran, who was not a military professional, to bring his forces under the LNA's command. Jedhran refused to countenance such a move, publicly refuting comments made by the head of the LNA's air force, Suqour al-Juroushi, at the end of December 2014 that the PFG belonged to the LNA.[46] This battle of wills worsened the following year when Haftar launched an LNA operation to root out what he described as terrorists in Ajdabiya. Haftar's attempt to intervene in what was the hometown of both men and in what Jedhran considered to be his area of control aggravated the situation, prompting Jedhran to accuse Haftar of seeking to 'destroy Ajdabiya, as he destroyed Benghazi'.[47] Relations deteriorated further when Jedhran threw in his lot with the internationally recognised GNA, a body that Haftar had rejected and did not recognise. For Jedhran, aligning himself with the GNA was a means of bolstering his position, especially vis-à-vis Haftar, and he announced not only that he was aligning his forces with these authorities in Tripoli, but that he was willing to hand over the oil ports to them. Jedhran's move infuriated Haftar, who took decisive action. In September 2016, Haftar launched a sur-

122

prise attack on the oil ports, taking them over and prompting Jedhran to flee. Yet what looked on the surface to have been a lightning military operation on the LNA's part was in fact the culmination of a carefully crafted plan that had been worked out between Haftar and the leadership of the Magharba tribe, who had decided that Jedhran had become too much of a liability.

Jedhran's behaviour had continued to embarrass the tribe and the Magharba had decided that its ultimate interests lay with Haftar rather than with its own son. Magharba sheikhs set about working on Jedhran's young supporters in the PFG to persuade them to move away from him. Playing heavily on kinship sensibilities, the sheikhs held a series of meetings with the families of Jedhran's supporters to impress upon them the need to convince their sons 'to return to the bosom of their tribe and not to confront the Libyan National Army'.[48] In one such meeting al-Atyush declared, 'Our army is the national army that is under the leadership of Khalifa Belqassim Haftar. Let everyone know that Haftar is from Ajdabiya. We have no problems with Khalifa Haftar. Haftar knows the Magharba tribe, knows its history and knows what it gave in terms of jihad and what it gives now. We support him and we support the army. Therefore, I ask all my cousins in front of me, I ask you, my cousins, to demand that you pull your sons out of these armed groups and bring them back to legitimacy'.[49] Al-Atyush also declared that 'any son of the tribe who deviates from the tribe's decision and violates legitimacy will bear the responsibility'.[50]

Given this tribal pressure, when the LNA advanced on the ports, most PFG who had supported Jedhran dropped their weapons and did not stand in its way. Al-Atyush described, 'Members of the PFG militia put down their weapons because they implemented the instructions of their fathers and the sheikhs of the Magharba tribe and didn't confront the army.'[51] Although some youth opted initially to ignore the call of their fathers, fleeing to Nawfalia, when the LNA started to advance on the town, many returned to the arms of the tribe, the pull of kinship proving greater than their loyalty to Jedhran. As Badeen observed, 'Hundreds of PFG returned [to the tribe] after al-Atyush gave them guarantees. These people cannot live without the tribe.'[52] The Magharba also made good on its threat

TRIBES AND THE STATE IN LIBYA AND IRAQ

to disown Jedhran after he had tried to stage a counter-offensive to retake the port, with al-Atyush declaring, 'The tribe will take away social cover from Jedhran. The armed forces [LNA] are free to do whatever they want with him.'[53]

Ultimately, therefore, the Magharba opted to stand on the side of stability, having concluded that, in Sheikh al-Atyush's words, 'the interests of Libya lie in the army taking control of the oil. There was no interest in confronting the army or waging a war inside our area and inside the oil ports.'[54] While tribes are often characterised as going after the spoils, the Magharba proved here that it was willing to relinquish its control of a key economic asset for the sake of stability and in the interests of upholding its relations with Haftar and with other tribes. This reflects the fact that tribes do not exist in a vacuum and have to balance their relations with other tribes and powerbrokers accordingly.

Through the Magharba therefore Haftar succeeded in eliminating his most potent competitor in the east, while simultaneously expanding his control into the Oil Crescent. However, his control over the Oil Crescent did not extend as far as Sirte at this juncture. Qadhafi's hometown had become embroiled in a conflict of its own. In May 2015, Sirte fell into the hands of ISIS. There were many complex reasons why ISIS was able to seed itself in Sirte, something it failed to do elsewhere in the country where the plethora of competing Islamist forces served as a bulwark to the group. In Derna for example ISIS was hounded out by other Islamist brigades and forces. In Sirte, the post-Qadhafi landscape evolved somewhat differently. Given Sirte's close association with the regime, in 2011 it held out until the bitter end. When it finally fell, the town was taken over by revolutionaries from outside, mainly from Misrata, who, as noted in Chapter 3, ransacked the place, prompting thousands of terrified residents to flee. Once the dust settled, the victors left Sirte in the hands of the newly created Sirte Revolutionaries Brigade, which comprised hard-line Islamists, many of them veterans of the Afghanistan and Iraq jihads. Although some members of this force came from Sirte, the brigade was strongly linked to Misrata, many of its cadres having been trained by the al-Farouq Brigade, a Misratan force known for its militant Islamist outlook.

The Sirte Revolutionaries Brigade went on, in via various reincarnations including the Sirte Supreme Security Council (SSC), to form

TRIBES AND THE POST-2014 ORDER

the basis of the Sirte branch of Ansar al-Sharia that was established in 2013 and that comprised jihadists from across Libya and beyond. With Sirte devastated, its social fabric shattered and many of the town's prominent sheikhs, including those of the Qadhadhfah, having fled, the way was clear for Ansar al-Sharia to take over. Indeed, there was no competing Islamist-revolutionary force from the town that could oppose the takeover. Although there were some armed elements that tried to fight back, such as the Zawiya Martyrs' Brigade, led by former army officer Saleh Bu Haliqa, from Benghazi, these were unable to prevent Ansar al-Sharia from dominating. Thus when ISIS appeared on the scene, the town was ripe for the group, and many Ansar Al-Sharia members swore allegiance to ISIS in what was effectively a change of brand rather than a takeover of one group by the other.

Notably, ISIS in Libya did not act as a magnet for former regime personnel. Despite reports in some media outlets that tribes or notables from tribes linked to the Qadhafi regime gave their allegiance to ISIS,[55] there is little concrete evidence to suggest this is the case. While certain tribesmen may well have joined as individuals, neither the Qadhadhfah nor other tribes from Sirte swore loyalty to the group. Most of these tribes refused to engage with ISIS, just as they had refused to engage with the authorities in Tripoli, preferring to remain outside of the entire post-Qadahafi landscape. As such, ISIS proved unable to use tribal bonds as a mobilising force in their favour.[56] While Sirte's tribes were opposed to ISIS's dominance of the town, especially as the group became increasingly entrenched and increasingly indulged in its own brutal practices, they proved too weak and divided to be able to resist. Although tribal elders in Sirte came together to try to forge an agreement over how to form a common front against the group, they could not agree on how to go about it, the more powerful Qadhadhfah refusing the Ferjan's insistence that they should rely upon assistance from revolutionary currents in Misrata.[57] Thus ISIS was able to retain control of Sirte until it was finally dislodged in December 2016 by a coalition of brigades mainly from Misrata supported by US air power. Misrata retook control of Sirte and the town remained in its hands until Haftar took it over in 2020. Sirte was never comfortable with being under the yoke of

125

TRIBES AND THE STATE IN LIBYA AND IRAQ

Misrata and when Haftar's LNA forces made their move, components from the town facilitated his way. In particular, Brigade 604, whose members were mainly from Haftar's own Ferjan tribe, many of them Salafist in orientation, switched allegieance when the opportunity presented itself, allowing LNA forces to take over. They were helped by other tribal components in Sirte who may have been wary of Haftar's ambitions, but who viewed his as a lesser curse than Misrata.

Managing the Tribes

Although Haftar had succeeded in using the tribes to extend his control, managing tribal relationships brought its own difficulties. Tribal loyalty is neither guaranteed nor unconditional, and while tribes may be flexible and pragmatic, there are always limits to how far they will bend to accommodate. Like Qadhafi before him, Haftar found himself forced to manage a succession of challenges that arose in his relations with the eastern tribes. This included with the Dersa tribe, a tribe that had stood solidly behind Haftar and that included several senior LNA commanders. This relationship was put under serious strain in January 2016, when LNA spokesperson Mohamed al-Hijazi, a member of the Dersa tribe, broke away from Haftar. Al-Hijazi issued a statement in which he lambasted Haftar, accusing him of corruption and of unleashing destruction and bloodshed on Benghazi. The LNA responded immediately, ordering al-Hijazi's arrest.

The situation threw the Dersa tribe into disarray; while it did not want to upset its relations with Haftar, it could not depart from its traditional role of protector of its members and thus could not simply hand over its son to the LNA. The tribe opted to steer a middle path therefore. In a statement dated 24 January 2016, it declared that it would not allow anyone to harm al-Hijazi, 'in word or deed', until the issue had been properly investigated.[58] At the same time, it was explicit in its continued support for Haftar, stressing that it would not be apprioriate for the tribe to break away from the LNA on account of the actions of one of its sons. Given that the tribe was not going to break free of its own traditions, Haftar and the tribe came to an agreement, namely that al-Hijazi would not actually be arrested on the understanding that he refrain from any further attacks against Haftar

126

TRIBES AND THE POST-2014 ORDER

and the LNA. In this way, they averted 'fitna' and were able to maintain a mutually beneficial relationship.

Haftar was to face a similar dilemma with the al-Awaqir tribe, but this time on a larger scale. The al-Awaqir were one of the LNA's most important supporters, serving as a critical pool of support from the time of the launch of Operation Dignity in 2014. This relationship came up against a serious challenge in April 2016, when the Presidency Council in Tripoli nominated the commander of the 204 Tank Brigade, Mehdi al-Bargathi, to serves as its defence minister in the Government of National Accord (GNA). Al-Bargathi, who is from the Baragatha House of the al-Awaqir, was proposed by Presidency Council member Fathi Majberi in conjunction with Jedhran. Al-Bargathi commented, 'I was chosen because I was from the east and I was strong. The PFG [Central Branch] chose me because I am related to them through my uncles on my mother's side.'[59] He also explained, 'There was a block comprising some al-Obeidat and al-Awaqir and some members of the House and the PFG who agreed to select me through Fathi Majberi.'[60]

Al-Bargathi's nomination for the post infuriated Haftar, who, given his rejection of the Presidency Council and the GNA, viewed it as a direct challenge to his authority. He saw it as a deliberate attempt by the new powers in the capital to undermine him and fracture his power base. LNA air force chief Saqr al-Jaroushi described, 'Nominating al-Bargathi for the defence minister post is aimed at cracking the firmly united army in Benghazi.'[61] Haftar was also not going to stomach the slight of somone who was less senior than him in military rank taking up the defence minister's post. Pro-Haftar elements in the east mobilised therefore to block the appointment; the House of Representatives refused to approve it, while senior LNA officials warned that al-Bargathi would not be able to even set foot in Benghazi were he to be appointed. In April 2016, the LNA went further and attempted to detain al-Bargathi at a checkpoint near Haftar's headquarters in Benghazi, while al-Juroushi described him as 'a traitor'.[62]

Yet Haftar didn't only have to consider al-Bargathi, he also had to contend and deal with al-Bargathi's tribe. The al-Awaqir welcomed al-Bargathi's nomination, viewing it as a well-deserved honour, and

127

one that was long overdue. As Sheikh Breiq al-Lwatti of the al-Awaqir asserted at the time, 'The Magharba got the oil portfolio, the al-Obeidat took the parliament [Aqeela Saleh is from the al-Obeidat], the Barassa got the interim government, and now it is our turn to have the defence ministry.'[63] Although the tribe was aware of the need to maintain its relations with Haftar and he held meetings with the LNA to try to smooth things over, it wasn't prepared to give up the status that would accompany one of its members holding a key portfolio in an internationally recognised government. On 14 May 2016, the al-Awaqir sheikhs met in Sidi Khalifa and announced, 'We appreciate Haftar and the General Command, and we appreciate wholeheartedly what they are doing but we don't want the defence ministry taken away from us.'[64] The tribe stood firm, therefore, making it clear that there were limits to the compromises it was prepared to make for the sake of the LNA. The tribe refused to disown al-Bargathi, despite Haftar's pressurising it to do so. As al-Bargathi described, 'Haftar tried to get the tribe to lift social cover from me, but he never managed.'[65] Tellingly, al-Lwatti commented, 'The al-Awaqir are united around al-Bargathi. General Khalifa Haftar must adhere to Libya's social fabric.'[66]

To Haftar's fury, the tribe stood by its son and al-Bargathi was duly appointed as GNA defence minister, a post he was to hold until July 2018. Yet while relations between al-Bargathi and Haftar were to deteriorate further, Haftar's relations with the al-Awaqir were upheld. Haftar knew that he could not afford to alienate such an important tribe, while both he and the al-Awaqir understood the importance of the mutually beneficial relationship they had forged. However, further strains emerged between the two in September 2017, when Faraj al-Qaim, a member of the al-Abdeli clan of the al-Awaqir, was appointed as deputy interior minister in the GNA. Like al-Bargathi, al-Qaim had been a senior commander in Operation Dignity, serving as head of its Special Counter Terrorism Task Force in Benghazi. Al-Qaim had already fallen out with Haftar, having launched a very public attack on him and his forces at the time of al-Bargathi's appointment, in which he accused the LNA of involvement in abduction, torture and killing. Haftar viewed the appointment as another bid by the GNA to chip away at his tribal support base and ordered all LNA forces to ignore any orders issued by al-Qaim.

TRIBES AND THE POST-2014 ORDER

Once again, the al-Awaqir were faced with a dilemma and had to weigh up its desire for status and recognition with the need to uphold its relations with Haftar. In this instance, the appointment created a division inside the al-Awaqir. Some members of the tribe, including Sheikh Hussein Attiya, welcomed the appointment publicly, while others more wedded to Haftar rejected it. On 3 September 2017, a group of al-Awaqir members issued a statement criticising Serraj and dismissing the GNA as an 'illegitimate body' that was implementing a foreign agenda.[67] Forty-eight hours later, a group of youth from the tribe held a separate meeting in which they gave their blessing to al-Qaim's appointment and declared that they were ready to support the GNA.[68] In the face of these divisions, the tribe did its utmost to balance its interests by steering a middle path. It issued a statement welcoming al-Qaim's appointment, but made clear that it would only give the appointment its blessing if it was 'accepted in Cyrenaica'.[69] This rather ambiguous stance was the tribe's way of trying to stand by al-Qaim while simultaneously upholding its relations with Haftar.

Nevertheless, al-Qaim forged ahead and took up the appointment. He also inflamed tensions further by appearing on television and accusing Haftar and the LNA of committing various crimes. He demanded too that Haftar hand over the head of the LNA's Saiqa Special Forces, Wanis Bukhamada, for prosecution. This public attack was too much for Haftar, who couldn't afford to let it go unpunished. Calculating correctly that the tribe would stand by him, Haftar issued orders for al-Qaim's arrest and took over his headquarters in the Bersis area, ejecting his supporters. In the face of the LNA's might, al-Qaim was left with no option but to hand himself in. Although some al-Awaqir youth staged demonstrations calling for his release, the rest of the tribe was more reticient. For many senior figures in the tribe, al-Qaim had gone too far, and was stirring up too much trouble, putting the tribe's relations with Haftar in jeopardy. In December 2017, sheikhs from the al-Awaqir apologised publicly for al-Qaim's televised accusations. The tribe also stood back when al-Qaim's supporters were being routed from their bases. Some of this reticence to defend al-Qaim may have been down to fears that it might generate a heavy-handed response on the LNA's part. It may also have been related to the fact that the GNA had struggled to impose itself in the capital since its arrival there in March 2016, and was looking increasingly like a lame duck that was representing the interests of western Libya only. Ultimately, the tribe opted not to sacrifice its relationship with Haftar for the sake of an individual. Rather, it tried to patch things up and build bridges. As al-Bargathi described, 'Al-Qaim sorted out his problem tribally through tribal rapprochement and personal rapprochement. The tribe intervened and told Haftar it didn't want fitna and that they should reconcile with each other.'[70] Haftar responded positively to these overtures, and al-Qaim was released and eventually readmitted to the LNA's fold. Indeed, Haftar did not have free rein, and was forced to show a degree of flexibilty in order to accommodate the eastern tribes that made up an important component of his core constituency and which he could not afford to alienate.

Following his victory in Benghazi, Haftar made further gestures towards the tribes including allowing prominent tribal figures who had held senior positions in the former regime to return to the country. Many sheikhs and tribal leaders had fled at the time of the revolution, fearing they would become the victims of revenge attacks. Haftar permitted many of them to return to the bosom of their tribes. This included the likes of former senior Qadhafi-era official Saad al-Asfar, who returned to Benghazi in April 2017 to a rapturous welcome from the al-Awaqir. Another prominent al-Awaqir member, Mohamed Bureiz al-Kezza, also went back, as did Mustafa Zayidi and Tayib Safi, the latter of whom is from the al-Menfa tribe and who was received by Haftar in his al-Marj headquarters upon his return. For the tribes, this flexibility on Haftar's part was welcomed. However, it was accompanied by serious efforts on Haftar's part to consolidate his control, and as the LNA military machine became ever stronger, Haftar began to look beyond the east and set his sights on the capital.

Haftar had never made any secret of the fact that his ambitions extended beyond Cyrenaica and that he sought to take control of the whole of Libya. Following his victory in Benghazi, he not only set about strengthening his position in eastern Libya, but also looked to expand his area of control. In January 2019, he carried out a major operation to seize the south. His success in this operation was partly down to the fact that in 2018, he had struck an alliance with the

TRIBES AND THE POST-2014 ORDER

powerful Awlad Suleiman tribe, something that enabled him to take Sebha with relative ease. Indeed, Haftar's courting of the large Arab tribes in the south, including the Awlad Suleiman and the Zuwiya, may have lost him the backing of Tebu forces, with whom he had been in alliance, but it enabled him to claim the south as his own. Early 2019 also saw Haftar take control of Derna, a town that had long been in the hands of various hard-line Islamist forces. By April 2019, therefore, just as the UN was preparing to hold a long-awaited National Conference in Ghadames aimed at bringing all the country's factions together to reset the political track, the general commander was ready to set his sights on the main prize of Tripoli, in a move that was to end up placing his relationship to the eastern tribes under the greatest strain.

Given the success he had had in drawing on the Cyrenaican tribes to eject his opponents in the east, Haftar looked to some of the western tribes to facilitate his entry into the capital. Prior to the launch of his attack, he had invested significant energy into trying to strike deals with tribes in the areas around the capital. He met with some degree of success, incluing in parts of Gharyan in the western mountains. On 4 April 2019, therefore, LNA forces took control of Gharyan before moving on towards Tripoli, prompting Haftar to proclaim, 'The bell has rung and the time has come and our appointment with al-Fatah al-Mubeen [a manifest victory] has arrived'.[71] Haftar also found some support among tribes in other western areas including Warshefana, Surman and Sabratha, who were disillusioned with the GNA and were willing to countenance some sort of LNA takover. Haftar also went on to bring Tarhouna on side, although this occurred at a later stage. Tarhouna, a stronghold of the former regime comprising some sixty tribes that come under the umbrella of the 'Tarhouna tribes', had initially rejected allying itself with Operation Dignity, considering Haftar to have 'violated their sanctity' through his participation in the 2011 revolution.[72] After Qadhafi's downfall, the town had fallen into the hands of revolutionary forces in the form of the notorious al-Kaniat militia, also known as the 7th Brigade, which was famed for its brutality. While these forces initially allied with the GNA in Tripoli, this alliance became strained and the force staged a number of incursions into the capital,

TRIBES AND THE STATE IN LIBYA AND IRAQ

including in 2018 and in January 2019. Frustrated with the situation, tribal representatives in Tarhouna began urging the al-Kaniat to throw in their lot with Haftar, and during a large tribal gathering in the town, it was agreed to open Tarhouna to the LNA.[73] A tribal delegation was duly dispatched to Benghazi to meet with Haftar, where it was agreed that the al-Kaniat would be merged with the LNA's 20th Brigade under the command of Abdulwahab al-Magri. Indeed, Haftar was wary of aligning himself with the al-Kaniat, given that he considered them to be a militia. Thus the al-Kaniat was absorbed by the LNA and put nominally at least under the control of an LNA commander in order to provide a veneer of professionalism and respectability through which both it and the LNA could attack the capital. This relationship proved pivotal in the early months of Haftar's campaign, as Tarhouna facilitated the LNA's penetration of the area south-east of the capital; with residents of the nearby areas of Ain Zara, Wadi Rabea and Qasr Bin Ghashir representing tribal extensions of Tarhouna, the LNA was able to advance further.

Yet, Haftar had failed to predict the strength of resistance his assault would engender and his hopes that elements inside the capital would also make common cause with him and rise up did not materialise. Instead, various forces and factions in western Libya pulled together and made common cause to defend the capital against the onslaught. Furthermore, while some western tribes may have been open to Haftar, they did not join him wholeheartedly. This includes those tribes and areas associated with the former regime that remained suspicious of Haftar and his motives given that he had joined the 2011 revolution. Zintan was also unwilling to support the attack. The LNA became bogged down in a bloody and protracted war therefore that was made worse by the intervention of foreign powers and forces on both sides, including Turkish troops and mercenaries bolstering the GNA's position and Russian Wagner Group mercenaries backing the LNA.

The extended nature of this conflict proved a serious drain on the eastern tribes who formed a large contingent of the LNA's rank and file. The tribes' Facebook pages were full of posts at this time lamenting their young members who had been 'martyred' in the cause of the Tripoli battle. More importantly perhaps, some of the eastern sheikhs

TRIBES AND THE POST-2014 ORDER

and tribes were deeply uncomfortable about going to war with Tripoli, especially for a battle that clearly couldn't be won. Rallying around Haftar to defend what they considered to be their own territory was one thing, but engaging in an offensive operation away from home against their fellow countrymen was something else. While the tribes were willing to support Haftar in the fight to achieve their dream of controlling their own areas, they were not so ready to supply their sons to achieve his. As one eastern tribesman observed, 'Haftar made a strategic mistake and the tribes were reluctant to join him in that war.'[74] Sheikh al-Senussi Buheleq expressed similar sentiments, describing, 'The tribes were unhappy about attacking the capital. The Zuwiya was one of those tribes, as we wanted reason, wisdom and negotiation. We didn't want the war and we were unhappy that a Libyan would kill another Libyan because of political differences. The decision to attack was unstudied.'[75] Even some senior commanders who were part of Operation Dignity and members of the al-Awaqir tribe were opposed to the attack.[76]

However, despite the LNA's humiliating failure in Tripoli, the eastern tribes did not abandon Haftar, as predicted by many commentators at the time. While these tribes may have resented the bloodshed and the many tribesmen who were sacrificed in the name of what turned out to be a fruitless war, in the main, they remained steadfast and continued to view Haftar as their best option. This was evidenced by the willingness of these tribes to blockade the country's oil fields and ports, especially those located in the Oil Crescent, as occurred in January 2021 and again in April 2022. This blockade was orchestrated by the LNA as a means to undermine and pressurise the government in Tripoli to distribute the country's oil wealth more equitably. Thus while the protests were a genuine reflection of the very real grievances felt by many tribes and tribesmen regarding the lack of jobs, services and development in their areas, the tribes were willing to make common cause with Haftar in order to achieve their objectives. In spite of the tensions therefore, the interests of Haftar and those of the eastern tribes remained still largely in alignment, with the tribes continuing to view Haftar both as a strongman and as the best protector of their interests.

Indeed, Haftar has, for the most part, dealt with the tribes shrewdly, providing them with space and also appeasing them where necessary.

TRIBES AND THE STATE IN LIBYA AND IRAQ

However, there are still strains in these relationships, not least because of the increasingly repressive way in which Haftar has extended his control over the eastern area. The iron grip he now wields as a result of the way in which he has been able to build up his military machine has left the eastern tribes looking increasingly as though they are being forced back into a vertical relationship with a single pole. This means that once again, they feel they are at risk of being used as clients rather than partners. Furthermore, Haftar is increasingly empowering his own children at the expense of tribal leaders and social components in the east. This, along with his general way of managing the tribes, has promped some commentators to liken Haftar to Qadhafi. Yet such comparisons are overwrought, not least because Haftar has never had the same innate proclivity towards tribalism as Qadhafi. While Haftar may have appealed to the eastern tribes at a certain moment in history and for particular reasons, and while he may have offered a kind of continuity with the past, he cannot match Qadhafi's ability to manipulate and subjugate the tribes. Some Libyans have been less generous in their assessment, with one member of the Qadhadhfah tribe describing Haftar as 'a bad copy of Muammar'.[77]

Nevertheless, tribes have clearly served as one of the foundations of Haftar's power and their willingness to mobilise on his behalf has had a major impact on Libya's political and security trajectory. One of the weaknesses of successive internationally backed governments installed in the capital has been their failure to reach out to the tribes in any meaningful fashion. Although the GNA tried to chip away at Haftar's tribal support base, it failed to harness the tribes or pay them sufficient attention, prompting one sheikh of the Awlad Busaif to quip that the GNA needed someone like Khalifa H'neish to help bring the tribes on board.[78] Indeed, while some urban Libyans may downplay the importance of the tribe, large parts of Libyan society are still strongly tribal in character, and as the events of post-2011 have shown, tribes' ability to mobilise, mediate and either support or push back against key stakeholders can have far-reaching consequences.

134

SECTION II

IRAQ

5

TRIBES AND THE IRAQI REPUBLIC

The relationship between the sheikh and the sons of the tribe was both historical and human.

Sheikh Sami al-Majoun[1]

More than a decade before Qadhafi staged his coup in Libya, a group of upstart military officers in Iraq were plotting a coup of their own. Inspired by the Arab nationalist and anti-imperialist ideas that were sweeping the region, this group of Free Officers, led by Brigadier Abdulkarim Qassim, moved against the monarchy and on 14 July 1958 established the first Iraqi Republic. These young officers were drawn mainly from the urban lower middle classes and with the exception of Qassim himself, who was of mixed Sunni-Shi'ite parentage, were mainly Arab Sunnis. They vowed to turn a page on the past and build a modern state that would see Iraq cut its ties with its British overlords. They also sought to put an end to the 'reactionary and outdated' practices of the monarchy, under which Iraqis had suffered rising inequality, growing repression and the continued dominance of foreign powers over the kingdom's polity and economy. Yet while Qassim and his fellow revolutionaries set about implementing a raft of policies to dismantle the old system, their rule was to prove short-lived and in 1963, they were toppled by another military coup. The events of 1958 ushered in a decade of

137

TRIBES AND THE STATE IN LIBYA AND IRAQ

extreme turbulence, characterised by chaos and by coups and counter-coups, as successive military cliques overturned the ruling entity to impose their authority over the country.

Although these ruling military regimes were of varying ideological hues—from Nasserite to Nationalist to Ba'athist—they all shared a broadly nationalist outlook and espoused a discourse that rebuked the reactionary forces of the *ancien régime*. Foremost among these forces were the tribes, or more accurately, the powerful tribal sheikhs who had served as one of the main pillars of the monarchy. The monarchy had incorporated these tribal sheikhs into the ruling elite at the time of state formation, and some had been able to amass vast fortunes and landholdings. To the new breed of revolutionary youth who were inspired by the nationalist ideas that had gripped the region, these sheikhs had become powerful symbols of what was wrong with the system and were viewed by successive revolutionary regimes as feudalistic tribal overlords, doing the bidding of colonial powers. These regimes adopted a discourse that equated tribalism with feudalism and denounced the tribal sheikhs, vowing to put an end to their outdated practices. They also took more practical steps to undermine the sheikhs' power in a bid to curb their wealth and influence. The coup of 1958 was a watershed moment for the tribes therefore, and it shook the foundations of the tribal system that had been in place for centuries.

These developments and the coming to power of what purported to be modern nationalist regimes prompted a general supposition that 1958 marked the beginning of the decline of the tribes. Some scholars shared these assumptions, arguing that the tribe was greatly weakened during this time.[2] Jabar went as far as to assert that tribes had 'disappeared', with tribalism existing only as a 'social and cultural space'.[3] He also described Iraq as the 'graveyard of the tribes'.[4] Yet 1958 did not mark the death knell of the tribes—far from it. This is not to suggest that the overturning of the old order and the policies of successive regimes didn't weaken the tribal sheikhs, or at least those sheikhs who had benefitted under the monarchy. Those sheikhs who had been part of the monarchy lost their political power, as well as some of their land, undermining their status and their influence over their tribesmen. At the same time, rural-to-urban migration flows

138

TRIBES AND THE IRAQI REPUBLIC

were gathering momentum, as the cities expanded and attracted increasing numbers of peasants who sought to escape the harshness and misery of the countryside. Such changes also served to erode old patterns of social organisation, transforming relations between the sheikh and his tribesmen. However, the coming of the Republic did not herald the end of tribalism, and the picture is far more complex than the generalised assertions of tribal decline would suggest.

Not only did these regimes adopt a half-hearted approach to actually dismantling the old elites, meaning that many of the old social patterns were unbroken, tribes themselves remained intact as units of social organisation. It wasn't only social and cultural tribalism that survived. In many tribes the leading houses and sheikhs stayed the same and tribal patterns of organisation persisted. Kinship ties and traditions that have been ingrained over generations cannot be undone that easily. Moreover, not all tribal sheikhs had benefitted under the monarchy, let alone been bound into its political system. There were plenty of sheikhs whose fortunes had not soared after Iraq gained independence, and lumping them together as if they formed a single class or unit, as the literature tends to do, is misrepresentative.[5] Not all sheikhs owned large tracts of land, with some forming part of the rural-to-urban migration flows of the time and settling into neighbourhoods of Baghdad and other cities from where they continued their sheikhly duties. Thus while social organisation patterns may have changed, they were far from decimated. The caricature of the greedy overlord exploiting his tribesmen who fled to the cities to escape servitude in what has been described as a 'vote of no confidence' by the tribesmen in their sheikh[6] is to ignore the nuances of kinship relations. This doesn't mean that landlord sheikhs didn't exploit and abuse the peasants who worked for them. However, the relationship between a sheikh and his tribe is not purely transactional. As Iraqi intellectual Majed Safa'ah observes, 'It's not just about economic relationships. Cultural bonds are rooted deep in history.'[7] Thus, the sheikh may have been weakened, but his influence and status did not disintegrate altogether.

In addition, the very regimes that vowed to eliminate tribalism soon understood that they could not step over the tribes, or do without them. Just like Qadhafi in Libya, these military elites extolled the

139

TRIBES AND THE STATE IN LIBYA AND IRAQ

greater Arab nation, yet were unable to bypass the kinship alliances that were woven deep into the fabric of their own society. Tribes still formed the bedrock of social organisation and were still deeply rooted. While the regimes may have been unwilling to acknowledge it publicly, they continued to rely on kinship relations and on the tribal sheikhs that they castigated as feudalists and had vowed to destroy. They wove tribal webs around their regimes, creating protective layers to shield them from challenges and buttress their power in a pattern that was to continue until 2003. That they should have done so was unsurprising; these young military officers—most of whom came from tribes concentrated in the north and north-west of Iraq—may have sought to embrace the new ideas of the time, but they were steeped in tribalism and tribal traditions. As such, some of the jostling for power that took place during this decade took on the mantle of a competition for control between towns and areas. While there were attempts to diminish the role of tribes during this fraught decade, kinship relations continued to represent an important element both in society and in the political arena.

Tribes and Monarchy

When Abdulkarim Qassim and his group of Free Officers seized power in 1958, one of their first targets were the powerful tribal sheikhs who had not only benefitted from the monarchical system, but had been bound tightly into its ruling elite. Although the fortunes of Iraq's tribes had fluctuated under successive regimes and rulers, it was under King Faisal I, who came to the throne in 1921, that their situation was enhanced considerably. Not that tribes had fared badly under the British mandate, which was established in 1914 and lasted until independence in 1932; after Ottoman rulers had tried to break up and diminish the power of the large tribal confederations, British colonial powers looked to the tribes to stabilise and control the countryside, mandating local authority to the sheikhs, who oversaw administration in their own areas. As Batatu has described in his 1978 study of Iraq's social classes, 'The Sheikh was the readiest medium to hand through which they [the British] could carry on the administration of the countryside—better than the distrusted officials of the

140

TRIBES AND THE IRAQI REPUBLIC

former Turkish government and the semi-educated young townsmen.'[8] In return for economic privileges, therefore, the British entrusted the sheikhs with collecting taxes, maintaining order and keeping their own tribesmen in check.

Tribal influence grew under the monarchy and after being installed by the British, King Faisal I turned immediately to the tribes for support. That he should have done so was inevitable. Iraq's population was still overwhelmingly rural at this time, much of it Bedouin and illiterate, with tribes forming the bedrock of society. Faisal was faced with the challenge of building the state from above and trying to find a way to bring a sense of nationhood and unity to the three Ottoman wilayas of Baghdad, Basra and Mosul that had been brought together to create modern-day Iraq. As Faisal noted in 1920, 'There are no Iraqi people in Iraq yet. There are imaginary human blocks, devoid of any nationalistic idea.'[9] Furthermore, the tribes were armed and powerful. As Faisal famously remarked in a memo to his confidants, 'In this Kingdom, there are more than 100,000 rifles [in the hands of the tribes], but the government has only 15,000.'[10] Thus, the king needed to build a social base and bind the tribes into the new state.

The monarchy relied upon the sheikhs, therefore, along with a small Sunni urban elite comprised mainly of military officers known as the Sharefan—those officers whose roots lay in the class of Sunnis who sent their sons to Istanbul to study during Ottoman rule, and deployed largesse as a means of binding them to it. In return for their loyalty, tribal sheikhs were showered with privileges and perks, including subsidies and cash presents. However, it was through land that these sheikhs were able to gain real power and prestige. After Iraq gained independence in 1932, the monarchy introduced a new land law enabling tribal sheikhs to own land, effectively institutionalising and regulating a process that had started under the Ottomans, and been strengthened by the British. In 1858, the Ottomans had introduced a new kind of land tenure called *tapu*, under which the state owned the land, but granted usufructuary possession to individuals, who were mainly tribal sheikhs.[11] The sheikhs' control over land was extended further by the British with the introduction in 1918 of the Tribal Criminal and Civil Disputes Regulation, which granted tribes the right to settle land disputes

141

TRIBES AND THE STATE IN LIBYA AND IRAQ

and other legal matters through their own customary laws and tribal norms. The monarchy's 1932 law took things further by permitting land to be registered in the name of individual owners.[12] Although senior civil servants and influential merchants all rushed to register land in their names, it was the tribal sheikhs who proved the main beneficiaries of this new legislation.

This is not to suggest that all sheikhs benefitted from this change in the law. Rather, those powerful sheikhs, especially those who had provided a 'sheikhly anchor for British policy'[13] during the mandate, were able to capitalise on the situation and register whole swathes of land in their names, becoming wealthy landowners. In 1958, 3 per cent of large and very large landowners controlled almost 70 per cent of land.[14] The large Shammar tribes, which stretch across the Iraqi-Syrian border, were a case in point. By the end of the 1950s, fifty-two members of the al-Jarba family from the Shammar tribe owned over 500,000 acres, with Sheikh Mish'an Ibn Faysal controlling over 100,000 acres singlehandedly.[15] These sheikhs brought in others to work their land or they rented it out to wealthy individuals from Mosul, as the sheikhs were 'used to the nomadic Bedouin life' rather than the world of settled agriculture.[16] In the large Amarah governorate (now called Meesan), known for its agricultural richness and the fertility of its land, seventeen sheikhs from the Bu Mohamed, al-Izeirij, Bani Lam, Bu Daraj and Bani Said tribes controlled almost 2.5 million ha of land.[17] Possessing so much territory, these landowning sheikhs turned away from their traditional tribal role and took on the mantle of feudal overlords, their tribesmen now forced into servitude as peasants and sharecroppers. Thus the patriarchal unity that had once characterised kinship relations was broken, and these landowning sheikhs were somehow dislocated from their tribesmen.

The position of these powerful sheikhs was further enhanced by their integration into the political system through the parliament. Those sheikhs who were willing to provide political and popular support for the monarchy were rewarded with seats in the legislature, and the number of them who became MPs increased steadily during the monarchy's rule. In 1925, 17 out of the 88 MPs were sheikhs or aghas (Kurdish tribal leaders), representing 19.3 per cent of members, while by 1958, this number had jumped to 52 out of 145, rep-

TRIBES AND THE IRAQI REPUBLIC

resenting 35.9 per cent.[18] Although on the one hand, this connection weakened the sheikhs in so far as they were now reliant on the state for their power, on the other, it enabled some to extend their influence and reoriented their focus. Under the monarchy therefore certain large landowning sheikhs developed new political and socio-economic interests, which connected them to Baghdad, and they became part of the elite and the centralised authority. This served to further alienate them from their tribesmen, not least because they were now absent for large parts of the year, leaving their estates in the hands of sirkal (agents) who managed the land on their behalf. American anthropologist Robert Fernea, who lived among the Shabana tribe in southern Iraq in the mid-1950s, describes how the largest estate owners in the area were 'men without interest in their tribal affiliations, who spent as much time in Baghdad or Beirut as they could afford, and those who had little contact with the tenants on their estates'.[19]

Yet one should be careful of generalising from this depiction of the absentee landlord, more preoccupied with the pursuit of power and pleasure in the urban centres than with his tribesmen tenants. While many rich sheikhs certainly spent time in Baghdad, not all large landowning sheikhs disconnected with their land or their tribesmen. Sheikhs Ajil al-Yawar and Ahmed al-Yawar of the Shammar tribes were major landowners yet chose to spend a substantial portion of each year encamped with their tribesmen in the desert.[20] Sheikh Mohamed al-Minshed of the al-Ghazi wa Fudoul tribe, who was a large landowner in Nasseriyah and an MP, was closely involved in his tribe and its affairs.[21] This was not uncommon. These sheikhs may have been powerful landlords, but they were careful to preserve their tribal traditions and ties.

Meanwhile, those sheikhs who owned small or middle-size estates generally retained a close relationship to their land and their tribesmen. Fernea also describes, 'It might, somewhat cynically, be argued that these less well-propertied landlords could neither afford to spend so much money in urban surroundings nor to hire truly competent agents to run their estates. On the other hand, men like Sheikh Mujid of the El-Shabana apparently have conservative tastes which do not run to the fleshpots of city life. For whatever reasons, such men were

143

TRIBES AND THE STATE IN LIBYA AND IRAQ

deeply involved in tribal affairs, regularly sitting in their mudheefs, arbitrating disputes, holding traditional feasts, and representing the tribe vis-à-vis the local government officials. They were a power in local affairs and it could be both advantageous to remain in good standing with such men and somewhat risky to provoke them.'[22]

It is evident then that those large landowning sheikhs who were bound into the monarchy were limited in number and did not amount to a new class. As Sheikh Sami al-Majoun, of the leading house of the al-Ghanem tribe, describes, those sheikhs who formed part of the ruling elite weren't representative.[23] This was particularly true in relation to those sheikhs who had become MPs. Al-Majoun explains, 'They were individuals and not a class. Each tribe was made up of 50,000 or 100,000 members but had only a handful who knew how to read and write so the MPs weren't representative of the tribal landscape'.[24] Of the large numbers of tribal sheikhs who were scattered across Iraq, only some succeeded in taking advantage of the opportunities that opened up under monarchical rule, and these sheikhs were more of a wealthy clique than an expression of tribal power. Harling's assertion that the emergence of a state, 'further alienated the sheikhs from their social base by incorporating them into a centralised apparatus of power and urbanised elite',[25] is only partially true and ignores the large number of sheikhs who were not part of the monarchy's elite structures.

However, the fortunes of the narrow elite whose interests were staked firmly in the monarchy were to be transformed by the coup of 1958, which shook the tribes that were already undergoing changes due to shifting patterns of social organisation. The miserable situation in the countryside combined with the new opportunities that were opening up in the cities, especially in light of the development of the oil sector, prompted many rural dwellers to migrate to the large urban centres. As had occurred in Libya during this decade, rural migrants from the same areas moved to certain neighbourhoods of the capital and other large cities existing in what were effectively shanty towns peopled with residents from the same clans and tribes. Urban centres, where communities from the same area still lived together in neighbourhoods, became extensions of the tribe. As Iraqi sociologist Dr Saleem Ali al-Wardi has observed, the distribution of the

144

TRIBES AND THE IRAQI REPUBLIC

population living in urban centres including Baghdad was based on mahalla (neighbourhoods), which represented ethnic, sectarian, tribal and sometimes professional extensions and which limited the social integration that characterises modern civil society.[26] Most of these new migrants, large numbers who came from the southern predominantly Shi'ite governorates, lived crammed into single-room mud or reed huts in neighbourhoods like Shakariya and Khalf al-Seda in Baghdad. In 1956, there were 16,413 such huts housing 92,000 inhabitants in the capital, while it was estimated that there were nearly 120,000 rural migrants in the city as a whole, 25 per cent of whom came from the southern area of Amarah.[27] Although these migrants did not cut the connection with their home areas or shed their tribal identity and traditions, the shift had started to dislocate traditional settlement patterns. Meanwhile, as society modernised, a new urban middle class was starting to emerge and the monarchy, with its dual concentration on the same old tribal landowning elite and Sharefan officers, was looking increasingly anachronistic. There was gaping economic inequality, an increasingly heavy reliance on repression, which included the banning of political parties, and, most importantly, an ongoing dependence on Britain at a time when Arab nationalism was sweeping the region. By the late 1950s, resentment was rising and the country was ripe for change.

Turbulent Decade: Tribes and the Republic

This 1958 Free Officers' coup, led by Abdulkarim Qassim and Abdulsalam Aref, was warmly received by large swathes of the population, who believed that their new leaders would tear down the vestiges of the old order and bring about an improvement in their livelihoods. These young military officers looked as though they represented the new; Arab nationalism was in its heyday and nationalist fervour was sweeping the region. They looked to be at the vanguard of a new era that could deliver a brighter future. The majority of these Free Officers came from middle- or lower-middle-class families and were part of the newly emergent modern urban class whose sons had entered the military, thereby achieving social mobility. Yet, the fourteen-member Free Officers' Central Committee that took over

TRIBES AND THE STATE IN LIBYA AND IRAQ

once the monarchy was toppled was hardly representative and marked the beginning of decades of control by Sunni military cliques. Twelve members of the committee were Arab Sunnis; there were only two Shi'ites, and no Kurds or other ethnic groupings. This imbalance was a reflection of the fact that under the monarchy, the officer class was dominated by Sunnis, particularly those Sunni officers who had studied in Istanbul and who came from the wilayas (provinces) of Mosul and Baghdad. The Shi'ites by contrast made up the majority of the rank and file.

These young officers sought from the outset to overturn the injustices of a system that rewarded a small elite and left most to struggle in dire poverty. They turned their attentions almost immediately therefore to the powerful tribal sheikhs and landowners who had become such a potent symbol of inequality and corruption. Yet they did not engage in a particularly aggressive purge. Although some sheikhs were arrested and imprisoned, such as Sheikh Mohamed al-Ar'aibi of the Bu Mohamed tribe in Amarah, who was an MP and a large landowner, there wasn't any blanket arrest or revenge policy. Rather, those sheikhs who held positions in the state were forced out of their posts or forcibly retired. Nevertheless, the regime did not hold back in its rhetoric. It launched a propaganda campaign against the sheikhs, depicting them in the state media as greedy 'feudalists' who were exploiting the peasants and amassing vast fortunes through land seizure. Anti-feudalism slogans were commonplace. The front page of the *Al-Hurriya* newspaper on 28 July 1958 for example proclaimed, 'No to feudalism after today!'[28] Articles and books also started appearing denigrating the 'unjust feudalists' and accusing them of having been active in supporting the reactionary system that had ruled Iraq between 1920 and 1958 and in implementing colonialist schemes to dominate Iraq and loot its resources.[29] The word 'landowner' became synonymous with feudalism and greediness, the target clearly being the 'reactionary' sheikhs who had propped up the old system.

Particularly debilitating for the sheikhs was the regime's cancellation of the Tribal Criminal and Civil Disputes Regulation, which severely curtailed the sheikhs' influence, stripping them of their right to arbitrate and serve as mediators between the state and the people.

146

TRIBES AND THE IRAQI REPUBLIC

The annulling of this act reduced the sheikhs' political power and clout at the local level. No less shattering—initially at least—was the regime's land reform initiative. Less than three months from taking power, the new government introduced the 1958 Agrarian Reform Law, which was modelled on similar legislation in Egypt. This law limited the maximum amount of land an individual owner could retain to 1,000 dunums (100 ha) of irrigated land or 2,000 dunums (200 ha) of rain-fed land. Any holdings above the maximum amount were to be expropriated by the government. Although presented as an exercise in redistribution and fairness, this land reform package was driven more by political than economic considerations, and was aimed at undermining the power of the large landowners and sheikhs who represented a potential challenge to the new order. When Qassim proclaimed the law's introduction on Baghdad Radio on 30 September 1958, he declared that its purpose was 'to destroy the political influence which the feudal lords enjoy as a result of their ownership of vast areas of land… influence which [has been] used to place obstacles in the way of governmental administration'.[30]

Yet while this agrarian reform law certainly injured the large landowning tribal sheikhs, especially in the south, where most agriculturally viable land was located, its effects were limited. There were many reasons for this. Firstly, the inexperience of the country's new leaders meant that the redistribution process was slow and chaotic, resulting in a torrent of disputes over land and water rights, with local government offices suddenly inundated with complaints and demands by landlords, which choked off the process. This chaos enabled some landowners to evade the new measures. Secondly, the peasants and sharecroppers, who were the main beneficiaries of the law, were not equipped to farm the land they now owned. Without the managerial services and resources of the landlord or his representative, they could not cultivate their land efficiently. With the landlord and his manager gone, there was no one at hand to supply the seed, repair the pump, organise the canal work, settle disputes between cultivators or run the irrigation system.[31] The new regime had been in such a rush to target the landowners that it had failed to consider how to properly assist the peasants. The situation was worsened by the actions of some landlords who deliberately obstructed the process,

TRIBES AND THE STATE IN LIBYA AND IRAQ

with some going as far as to damage and set fire to land earmarked for redistribution and others diverting water flows away from land taken over by peasants. Some even intimidated and attacked the peasants, with dozens killed in the process.[32] Alternatively, some landlords tried to take charge by taking over the peasant co-operatives and unions that were permitted under law 139 that was passed in September 1959. As a result of the chaos, agricultural production dropped by 40 per cent at the time, while peasants deserted their holdings and streamed into the cities in ever greater numbers. Despite Qassim's attempts to prevent such flows, including by distributing thousands of loans to the new cultivators (that were never repaid), the disaster in the countryside meant that families continued to move to the big urban centres in search of better opportunities. They were further attracted by the fact that, giddy with power, the new regime was making wild promises to provide all its citizens with 'palaces and cars'.[33] Baghdad and Basra became even more overcrowded therefore, as family upon family joined those who had already hitched their fortunes to the urban environment.

Agrarian reform was further hampered by a lack of political conviction on the part of Qassim and some of his fellow Free Officers, as well as those officials implementing the policy. The land reform committee that oversaw the process was headed by Hadeeb al-Haj Hmoud, who was the sheikh of the Hmeidat tribe and who was himself a large landowner.[34] In fact, three members of this six-member committee owned large tracts of land. Thus while there were certainly Communist elements in the new regime who were pushing hard to implement the land reform law in full, Qassim was focused more on the propaganda opportunities than actually stripping the large landowners of their wealth. Salam Ibrahim Kubba, the son of Ibrahim Kubba, economic minister and acting agrarian reform minster at the time, describes, 'Qassim wasn't serious about implementing the agricultural land reform. Ibrahim Kubba realised that Qassim had no intention to apply the land reform in accordance with legislation introduced by the revolution. He put a set of obstacles in place to prevent the agrarian reforms being implemented by the ministry.'[35] Kubba also describes how Qassim allowed large landowners to contact him directly and to lobby him for a postponement in the

148

TRIBES AND THE IRAQI REPUBLIC

takeover of their land.[36] Despite the regime's promises to tear down and destroy the feudal class, therefore, many landowners succeeded in preserving or regaining their land and businesses, enabling them to retain local leadership in the rural areas and to continue to dominate social and economic relations. In Karbala for example, by 1962, only 1,635 donums had been confiscated and had been re-distributed between eighty-five beneficiaries.[37]

Thus, while there was clearly some disruption to patterns of social organisation and while some sheikhs lost land and influence, the changes were not as far-reaching as the regime had promised, and certainly did not result in the dissolution of tribal ties and loyalties. As Kubba also observed, the agrarian reform law didn't bring an end to 'tribal traditions and values'.[38] The link between the sheikh and his tribesmen remained strong. Kinship ties were about more than just land ownership, and 'longstanding ties of obligation and responsibility existed between the sheikh and certain of the tribesmen'.[39] The regime's attempt to change the feudalist system by introducing a law from above did not annul the patriarchal tribal relationship. This relationship had a long history and ingrained traditions and customs including that the peasant or tribesman should remain docile and submissive and work in the interests of the clan and the tribe.[40] While there was undoubtedly resentment on the part of tribesmen towards their sheikhly overlords, they still identified as tribesmen and the sheikh still retained status and commanded respect. Sheikh al-Majoun observed, 'The sheikh's status was not destabilised much at that time because the relationship between the sheikh and the sons of the tribe was both historical and human... Even though their influence may have declined, there was still respect for the heads of tribes.'[41] Furthermore, it was mainly the large landowning sheikhs who were hit by the agrarian reform. Sheikh Jawad al-Assad of the Abada tribe in Nasseriyah explained, 'The land reform law touched the large feudal landowners. The majority of sheikhs had smaller amounts of land and were loved by their tribesmen and respected by their own tribe. No one touched their land. They were well-respected.'[42]

Thus the resentment towards the landlord sheikh was by no means universal. In some instances, the attack against the feudal class had the

149

TRIBES AND THE STATE IN LIBYA AND IRAQ

opposite effect of what was intended and fortified bonds of tribal *asabiya* as it was interpreted by the peasants as an attack against the sheikhs and the tribes. Sheikh al-Majoun explains how the influence of the sheikhs may have dipped when their land was taken away but how, 'the psychological feeling and the tribal association between the head of the tribe and the sons of the tribe became stronger because the government was against the tribes and the sons of the tribes were not keen on governments, which were alien to them… When the sons of the tribe learned that the sheikhs were being targeted by the government, they moved closer around us.'[43] There were ingrained human relationships therefore that transcended ideological posturing about land redistribution and about the relationship between landowner and peasant and that prevented the new regime from succeeding in shattering the social bonds that served as the glue of Iraqi society.

However, the change of regime still created anxiety among the tribal sheikhs. While the republic's bark may have been worse than its bite, and while many sheikhs had proved able to use the bureaucracy to their advantage to retain their land, the winds of change were blowing and many sheikhs feared that they may end up being swept away like the monarchy. It looked at this time as though the future lay with the progressive ideas of the regime rather than the 'reactionary' rule of the sheikh. Particularly worrying for these sheikhs was the advance of the Iraqi Communist Party, whose ranks were swelling fast, especially among the young Shi'ite poor in the southern governorates. The sheikhs feared as though the country and the mood was travelling in the opposite direction to their interests and fearing for the future, some decided to act. In March 1959, Sheikh Ahmed Ajil al-Yawar, one of Iraq's largest landowners and the sheikh of the Shammar tribe, conspired with Colonel Abdulwahab Shawaf, a member of the Free Officers and the commander of the Mosul garrison, to try to topple Qassim. Shawaf was becoming increasingly disillusioned with Qassim's lack of commitment to the pan-Arab cause and his growing closeness to the Communists and decided to stage a revolt in Mosul. Sheikh al-Yawar saw Shawaf as the best vehicle for putting a stop to Qassim and his agrarian reform policies, and threw his weight behind him. The sheikh smuggled weapons across the Syrian border into Iraq and dispatched his tribesmen into Mosul to

150

TRIBES AND THE IRAQI REPUBLIC

join the uprising. However, the attempt failed and Shawaf was killed, triggering a bout of serious violence in Mosul in which some 400 Shammar tribesmen were killed by Kurdish tribes who overran the area.[44] Sheikh al-Yawar was tried in absentia before a people's court in Baghdad and sentenced to death. Yet, less than a month after the attempted coup, Qassim granted a general pardon to the Shammar tribesmen who had taken part in the uprising and managed to flee the country, prompting hundreds to return.

Yet another, larger revolt was brewing. In September 1959, a group of fifty-one sheikhs from tribes drawn from across the country and from different sects and ethnicities established a tribal bloc as a reaction to the land reform law. Sheikh Sami al-Majoun, who became the bloc's general secretary, described, 'We felt at the time that the collapse of the monarchy was the end of Iraq. We met and decided to work underground to bring the monarchy back. We comprised sheikhs and the sons of sheikhs who had taken part in the 1920 revolt.'[45] This tribal bloc received support from the *Marja'iya*, Iraq's Supreme Shi'ite religious authority.[46] The interests of the Shi'ite tribes and the *Marja'iya* had long been intertwined, with the sheikhs looking to the *Marja'iya* as their religious reference. Both had been deeply unsettled by Qassim's coup. The *Marja'iya* feared the more secular orientation of the new regime, as well as the space being afforded to the Communists given their atheistic ideology, which was fast spreading among the Shi'ite poor. It also feared the new regime's land policies. The *Marja'iya* was supportive of this tribal bloc therefore and as Sheikh al-Majoun remarked, 'The tribal bloc had a direct relationship to Sayid Mehsen al-Hakim [the *marja'*]. We used to take guidance from him. He was willing to help us and he was against the republican system.'[47]

While these sheikhs sought to overturn the new order, they could not do so alone. These sheikhs did not represent an organised force and needed to tap into military structures in order to effect regime change. They reached out therefore to a group of disaffected Free Officers who were also unhappy at the turn Qassim's rule was taking, believing him to be giving insufficient attention to the pan-Arab cause. Despite the fact that the objectives of the tribal bloc and this group of republican officers, who included the President, Najib al-Rubai, were

151

TRIBES AND THE STATE IN LIBYA AND IRAQ

wildly divergent, with the Free Officers having no interest in restoring the monarchy, both proved willing to collaborate to bring Qassim down. As with the Mosul uprising, therefore, the sheikhs proved pragmatic and willing to put their hand in those of the republican officers to try to bring a halt to Qassim's project.

However, the plan collapsed after the tribal bloc made a misstep. Having agreed with al-Rubai that they would approach a Shi'ite military officer whom the sheikhs believed would be a suitable leader for the armed rebellion, things started to go wrong. Al-Majoun, who was working as a legal advisor in the defence ministry and who was chosen as the bloc's main point of contact with this group of officers, recalled, 'That Shi'ite officer came in November 1959 and I spoke with him. He considered me as his son and I told him that he had been nominated to stage a coup. The reason why we nominated him was because we had studied his personality and we chose him on that basis. My room in the defence ministry was eight metres away from Qassim's room. When I opened the subject with the officer, he became hysterical. He grabbed me by the shoulders and said, "This leader [Qassim] saved Iraq." His voice started getting louder and I was terrified.'[48] Al-Majoun went on to describe how, fearful of the consequences of being overheard, he pretended that he had suddenly come to his senses, 'I told him, "Master, I was asleep and you woke me up. I was mad and you brought me to my senses." I started kissing him and thanking him for waking me up. He left me after five minutes and I saw that my shoes were wet with the sweat that had fallen from my forehead.'[49] When al-Majoun recounted the news of this unfortunate exchange to al-Rubai, the president told him that the sheikhs had chosen the wrong officer and that they were responsible for the error. The plot was aborted, therefore, leaving the sheikhs too terrified to even meet for fear of being discovered. In al-Majoun's words, from then on, 'Everything was confined to the nationalists and the Ba'athists.'[50] As this episode demonstrated, despite their weight and numerical strength, the tribes could not match the country's new rulers, who were to spend the next nine years locked in a conflict that plunged Iraq into further turbulence as it underwent a succession of coups and counter-coups.

152

TRIBES AND THE IRAQI REPUBLIC

The Shield of Kinship

All of the post-1958 regimes that were to rule Iraq until the Ba'athists consolidated their grip in 1968 adopted ideologies that were grounded in nationalism and socialism. They also all denounced tribalism as the antithesis of unity and progress, associating it with the monarchy and with colonialism. Indeed, they all adopted big narratives and slogans with transnational dimensions and ambitions, seeking to move beyond the confines of local identities and parochial interests. Yet, all also adopted this discourse while simultaneously engaging with tribes as a means of garnering support. Not that they did so publicly or openly; they were all keen to conceal any reliance on traditional modes of social organisation, this being at odds with the image they wished to portray. Yet with tribes still comprising the basis of social organisation and interaction, these regimes could not do otherwise but engage with the sheikhs. As in Libya, the regime may have espoused a progressive, outward-looking discourse, but it could not vault over society. Moreover, the successive regimes, who had themselves emerged out of traditional and tribal backgrounds, also looked to kinship as a means of buttressing their rule. Wrapping themselves in the cloak of tribalism was the most obvious way for them to shield themselves from challenges and shore up power. As Jabar has observed, the power struggle that developed between different sections of the military elite gave the impression to the outside world of being modern, but 'its spirit was traditional and tribal'.[51]

This reliance on the tribe was particularly pronounced during the first period of Ba'athist rule. In February 1963, Abdulsalam Aref (a Sunni and Qassim's former deputy) and Ahmed Hassan al-Bakr (a Sunni and Free Officer) seized power in a coup. From the outset the regime belied its fiercely anti-tribal rhetoric by turning to particular Sunni tribes to swell the ranks of its military forces. Abdulkarim Farhan, who took part in the 1963 coup and who was responsible for military affairs in Mosul, recounted how he received a phone call from Prime Minister al-Bakr instructing him to meet with Sheikh Ahmed Ajil al-Yawar in Mosul to discuss how to bring Shammar tribesmen into the army.[52] He described, 'Sheikh al-Yawar came to me and I welcomed him and praised him for his bold decision and told

153

TRIBES AND THE STATE IN LIBYA AND IRAQ

him I considered it to be a big transformation in the life of the tribe. These soldiers would leave their harsh Bedouin life for a better life... He was pleased with what I said and he promised me that no less than 1,500 men from his tribe would volunteer.'[53] The new regime was willing to employ the old practices of going through the sheikh to recruit tribesmen to its military apparatus. This development wasn't without its difficulties. Farhan went on to describe how during training, these tribesmen had refused to lie flat on their stomachs when they were being shot at because they preferred the nobler, more courageous Bedouin response of standing tall in the face of attack.[54]

This leaning on the tribe was to continue. While the civilian leadership of the Ba'ath party at this time was genuinely nationalist in ideological orientation, and while Aref's regime comprised different components including Shi'ites, the military leadership displayed a proclivity to rely on kinship relations, looking to Tikrit in particular. The top military posts all went to individuals from Tikrit including the Chief of Staff of the army, Tahar Yahiya al-Tikriti, the general military ruler, Rashid Muslah, and the commander of the air force, Hardan al-Tikriti. The prime minister, who was also from Tikrit, pulled more and more of his relatives into his regime, wrapping himself in kinship layers. According to Farhan, 'al-Bakr was the first to appoint his relatives. He appointed more than twenty people from Tikrit in the general security directorate as informants and agents... Others followed suit and exaggerated the number of relatives and friends they appointed despite the fact there were no vacancies and they lacked qualifications and there was no work, resulting in government bodies becoming overcrowded'.[55] This had the effect of the offices of state being flooded with 'villagers'. Thus while the regime's ideology proclaimed adherence to a loyalty that went beyond national borders and that encompassed the concept of one Arab nation, through al-Bakr, it predicated itself on the loyalty of locality and kinship. Sunni kinship alliances were prioritised over alliances of representative political forces, and the power of the village established itself in the name of the greater nationalist state.

However, the Ba'athists' attempts to coup-proof themselves through tribal layering proved unsuccessful and their first stint in power was short-lived. In November 1963, Aref and his fellow pro-

154

TRIBES AND THE IRAQI REPUBLIC

Nasserists in the regime, who wanted closer union with Egypt, staged another coup and pushed the Ba'athists out. After taking power, they banned the Ba'ath party and all other political parties and declared the Arab Socialist Union of Iraq to be the only legal party in the republic. Aref also upheld the regime's anti-tribal posture, publicly denigrating feudalism and tribalism. Yet he also could not do without the tribes, and although his regime included military officers, Nasserites and others, he bound tribalism and kinship alliances into the core of his regime. This included through a heavy reliance on his own tribe, the Jumailat, a poor tribe from Ramadi, which formed part of the Dulaim tribes. After seizing power, Aref doled out jobs and posts to members of the Jumailat, particularly those from Ramadi and the nearby town of Anah. Just like the previous two republican regimes before it, the core of this new ruling elite was drawn almost exclusively from conservative tribal desert areas in the Sunni heartland. As Jabar has noted, during this period, when ideology was weak or insufficient to stabilise the state, the regimes relied increasingly on tribal *asabiya* to create loyalty and cohesion among the ruling elite, but this occurred at unprecedented levels during Aref's rule.[56]

Aref also looked to tribes outside of his own for support, opening up space for some of the prominent tribal sheikhs whose room for manoeuvre had been curtailed after 1958. This included Sheikh Mohamed al-Minshed, who like other wealthy landowners had come under pressure when the new republican regime had confiscated some of his land and had tried, albeit unsuccessfully, to force him to leave his area of Sayah in Nasseriyah. During Aref's rule, the pressure on the sheikh decreased, and he succeeded in bargaining with the regime to regain some of the land that had been taken away.[57] However, Aref's rule was also to be cut short as he died in a plane crash in April 1966, after which he was replaced by his brother. By this time, however, the Ba'athists had regrouped and, under al-Bakr's command, moved in again, seizing power in July 1968 and dismissing Aref's regime as having been made up of 'opportunists, thieves, illiterate, ignorant people, Zionists, agents and spies'.[58]

While 1958 was to mark a distinct and radical rupture with the past, ushering in a chaotic decade in which the old certainties and established power relations were shaken, it did not bring about the

155

TRIBES AND THE STATE IN LIBYA AND IRAQ

wholesale decline of the tribe or the tribal sheikh. Social organisation patterns were affected by the policies of successive regimes, but were not broken. The same was true of kinship bonds, which extend beyond mere transactional relationships. Thus while this decade may have undermined the power and political influence of the large land-owning sheikhs, Iraq did not witness a retraction of tribalism at this time. Rather, tribalism was pushed to the background, as new ideas and ways of ruling took centre stage. The more serious business of undercutting the tribe was to come after 1968, when the second period of Ba'athist rule took the country down a far more radical and uncompromising path.

6

TRIBES AND THE BA'ATHIST STATE

The sheikh seemed to be alone in his mudheef, as if he lost everything—first power and then the people. People were preoccupied with slogans while the sheikh stood still in his mudheef.

Sheikh Takleef al-Minshed[1]

In the monarchy, sheikhs were partners. Now they became followers.

Sheikh Jawad al-Assad[2]

The Ba'athists' return to power in 1968 under the leadership of Ahmed Hassan al-Bakr took Iraq in a dramatic new direction. Although the group of military officers who seized control were of the same nationalist mould as the previous post-monarchy regimes, they were far more radical in their approach. They vowed to put the country on a new footing and to build a modern Socialist-style state with a secular, progressive society that would be in tune with the Arab nationalist ideals they espoused. Extolling the principles of 'Unity, Freedom and Socialism', they adopted a raft of leftist and anti-imperialist policies, nationalising the oil sector and making use of the surge in global oil prices after 1973 to build a health and welfare system and engage in largescale industrialisation. This was to be a brave new Iraq in which the Ba'ath would remake society and 'create a [new] Arab man'.[3]

157

TRIBES AND THE STATE IN LIBYA AND IRAQ

These new leaders also sought a more decisive cut with the past, and were bent on dismantling the vestiges of the old monarchical system, which had been disrupted but not fully undone by ten years of nationalist rule. Thus they turned their attentions to the tribes. Like the Qadhafi regime that was to come to power in Libya just one year later, the Ba'athists viewed tribalism as the antithesis of Arab nationalism and equated tribal sheikhs with reactionary forces of the past. This anti-tribal outlook echoed the anti-tribal platform upon which the Ba'ath party had been founded, its 1954 founding constitution asserting, 'National identity is the only identity in the Arab state that guarantees harmony among citizens and their fusion into one crucible and that combats all sectarian, tribal, ethnic and regional solidarities.'[4] From the outset, the Ba'ath were, 'vigorously anti-tribal',[5] and adopted a rhetoric that denigrated tribalism and posited tribes as standing against the modern, progressive state. In its first communiqué of 1968, the regime proclaimed, 'We condemn sectarianism, racism, and tribalism', and the 'remnants of colonialism'.[6]

The Ba'athist regime did its utmost to bury the tribe therefore, and there was a general assumption that both it and society—with Iraq's still expanding cities and growing urban population—had moved on. Yet, like their predecessors, the new Ba'athist leaders soon discovered they could not ignore their own reality. While Iraq may have been changing and while the regime may have aspired to mould the masses around their modern Ba'athist ideals, ignoring the tribe was not a choice if the regime was to survive, especially given its limited legitimacy and the narrow appeal of its ideology. While it may have espoused an anti-tribal rhetoric, the new regime based the foundations of its rule on kinship relations in order to protect itself and guard against rebellion. Furthermore, while the regime may have tried to destroy the old tribal elites that were associated with the monarchy and that it viewed as a potential threat, it could not move wholeheartedly against the tribes or the tribal system. Instead it found itself forced to engage with the very tribal elite it was bent on destroying. From the outset, the regime employed a two-pronged approach, repressing the tribal sheikhs on one hand, while simultaneously courting them and accommodating them on the other. While such engagement remained largely hidden on account of the taboos surrounding

TRIBES AND THE BA'ATHIST STATE

tribalism, this relationship served both ruler and ruled, enabling the regime to tap into the tribal networks that had formed the bedrock of society over generations and enabling the tribes to carve out space for themselves under Ba'athist rule. The tribe was not merely a passive actor in this relationship, but engaged in bargaining and pushback against the regime.

This didn't mean that the tribes weren't weakened during the Ba'athist period; they lost significant power and influence under the shadow of a state that sought to dominate and control every aspect of life. Furthermore, the relationship between tribe and state was unequal. The regime forced the tribe, or at least certain tribes, to be subservient to and dependent upon it. Nevertheless, while the sheikh may have become secondary to the man of the party, the regime was unable to break the tribe or to replace tribal *asabiya* with loyalty to the state. As Sheikh Adel al-Assad from Nasseriyah commented, 'The regime tried to create party loyalty and political loyalty as an alternative to the tribal system. This failed. You cannot create artificial loyalty.'[7]

Arguments in the literature suggesting that Saddam Hussein brought the tribe back to the fore, or revived tribal politics, or that he somehow re-tribalised society in the 1990s at a time when the state was weak, need re-examination. It is true that Saddam turned to the tribes in a more overt fashion during this period, incorporating them into the regime's political iconography and openly celebrating tribal rituals and customs in what was arguably more a pastiche of tribal values and traditions. Yet this did not represent a re-tribalisation of society. Saddam certainly didn't turn the tribal sheikhs into legitimate partners for power sharing, as some have argued. Rather, this open courting of the tribes was more a rendering visible of a relationship that had been in place since 1968. Turning tribalism on or off was never within the purview of any regime, and successive leaders had to deal with the society that they inherited. While statistics might show that the country became increasingly urbanised during this period, and while this may have given the impression that tribalism was disappearing, this wasn't the case. Regardless of whether or not they dismissed tribes or were opposed ideologically to tribalism as a concept, these most modern of ideologues had no choice but to deal

159

TRIBES AND THE STATE IN LIBYA AND IRAQ

with the tribes and their sheikhs. These were a concrete reality that they could neither get around nor break.

Forging Tribal Networks

While the 1968 coup was staged by a group of military officers, including both Ba'athist and non-Ba'athist elements, it became apparent early on that the strongest components in the new regime were al-Bakr, who became president, and Saddam Hussein, who became his deputy and who, despite not being a military officer, quickly took control of the regime's security apparatus. Although a Revolutionary Command Council (RCC) was established to run the country, these two figures moved quickly to establish their dominance, ruthlessly eliminating everything and everyone that got in their way. Desperate to avoid the factionalism that had brought the Ba'athists' first stint in office to an abrupt end, the two leaders engaged in a series of purges aimed at safeguarding the regime from factionalism and internal challenges. Al-Bakr and Saddam rooted out first the non-Ba'athists, then those Ba'athists and military officers they deemed to be a threat, including some who had taken part in the coup. As Saleh Omar al-Ali, a former RCC member, observed, al-Bakr was fearful of repeating the same mistakes that had occurred in 1963, and thus started co-ordinating with Saddam in order to divide up power between the two of them.[8] Al-Ali noted how, at this time, he and the other military officers who formed part of the new regime became little more than 'members of staff working for Saddam Hussein and Ahmed al-Bakr'.[9]

Yet purging the regime of potential opponents was insufficient. Both al-Bakr and Saddam knew they needed to strengthen their regime further to shield it from potential revolt, both from within the ranks of the military and from outside it. The challenges facing them were immense. Externally, the regime had a hostile and powerful neighbour in Iran, which at that time was supported by the US, while it was facing an armed revolt in the Kurdish area that was gathering momentum under the leadership of Mustafa Barzani. It was also up against the Iraqi Communist Party, whose membership far outweighed that of the Ba'ath Party, which had undergone a major transformation in the four-year interregnum, having suffered the imprison-

TRIBES AND THE BA'ATHIST STATE

ment of its leaders and a bitter fight with its sister branch in Syria.[10] In the process, the party's civilian leadership had been all but decimated and the party had come under the control of a small military wing, which was predominantly Sunni and came from the north-west of Iraq. Where it had once comprised a genuine partnership between Sunni and Shi'ite pan-Arab youth, by 1968, the role and position of the Sunni component had increased significantly, while that of the Shi'ites had declined, prompting Batatu to observe that its leadership had become 'more homogenous but less representative'.[11] It was struggling to compete therefore with the appeal of the Communists that was still popular among the urban Shi'ite poor. In addition, these young officers, with their limited experience, had to deal with the complexity of a multi-faith, multi-sect and multi-ethnic society that had undergone decades of instability, and where the sense of national identity was still in its infancy. On top of that, many Iraqis remembered the Ba'athists' first stint in power despairingly, as they had drowned the country in blood, killing, arresting and torturing. There was limited appetite for its return and the new regime, which had come through another putsch and was thus imposed from above, had no solid constituency upon which to build a base and an ideology that could not travel far.

In such a context, the new officers had little choice but to turn to their tribal roots in order to create a loyal body upon which they could depend. Al-Bakr and Saddam, who were blood relations, looked to kinship to build a strong machine that would enable them to survive, bringing in loyal elements drawn largely from their home area of Tikrit and connected to them by lineage. Thus while espousing the virtues of the greater Arab nation, the regime rooted itself in the village, ultimately unable to make the ideological leap it had demanded of society. This resulted in Tikritis being disproportionately represented in the new regime's leadership and military structures. The RCC was certainly Tikrit-heavy, while Tikriti military men swelled the ranks of the Republican Guard and other military and security institutions. This didn't mean that all Tikritis were accepted into the fold; those deemed to be of questionable loyalty or who represented a potential threat were duly disposed of. This included Hardan al-Tikriti, one of the plotters of the 1968 coup, who was appointed as defence minister immediately afterwards, but who was forced out in 1970 after he clashed with Saddam. He was assassinated in Kuwait one year later. These individuals aside, the new regime emerged as a tightknit core of individuals from certain families and tribes in Tikrit.

That al-Bakr and Saddam should have wrapped themselves in kinship was not only a function of necessity, it was also a reflection of where they came from. Tikrit, which includes the town of Tikrit itself, along with a handful of smaller villages and settlements, was a small and impoverished town, with 'nothing to distinguish it'.[12] The landscape is arid with most of its farmland concentrated in small plots that are dispersed along the Tigris River. This topography meant that Tikrit's tribal landscape developed differently to that of other parts of Iraq, such as the south or the centre. Tikrit did not experience the same feudalistic system that other areas of Iraq were subjected to during the monarchy, with only two clans—the Shyasha and the Buhaji Shahab—possessing land or farms.[13] It did not have the kinds of large landowning sheikhs or large tribal groupings that were present in other areas but comprised mainly small tribes or clans that did not have extensions beyond their own local areas. Their leaders were more akin to the heads of extended families rather than powerful tribal sheikhs. These tribes were also more Bedouin in character, meaning that they tended to be more close-knit. Furthermore, unlike in other parts of the country where tribal *asabiya* is forged not only out of shared ancestry but also through alliances forged between different groupings and clans, in Tikrit solidarity tends to be based more upon blood lineage. There was a strong internal cohesion and solidarity among the clans in Tikrit, and Bedouin traditions were still very much upheld.

It was in this strongly tribal environment that both al-Bakr and Saddam were raised. Both were members of the Albu Nassir tribe, which is concentrated in the village of al-Awja, south of Tikrit town. Al-Awja was even more impoverished than Tikrit, its residents mainly made up of farmers or servants of the Tikriti rich. In his largely autobiographical novel, *Men and the City*, Saddam describes what is presumed to be his home area as 'miserable countryside', where people were so poor there wasn't even a slice of onion to give to an ailing

TRIBES AND THE BA'ATHIST STATE

patient (onions were believed to have curative properties). Saddam wrote, 'Whoever was ill would cross the river in the hope that one of his relatives would give him an onion. The patient who had a chicken cooked for him when he was ill was considered very lucky.'[14]

Despite being part of Tikrit, al-Awja sat somehow apart from the town, its inhabitants looked down upon. Although there are many different accounts and stories about the origins of the Albu Nassir tribe, it was always considered to be lower down the pecking order than other Tikriti tribes, including the original Tikritis or Tarkarta tribes, who claim to be the descendants of the pre-Islamic Tikrit, and the Hadithiya tribes, who originated in nearby Haditha but who settled in Tikrit on account of their commercial activities.[15] The Albu Nassir settled in Tikrit at a later stage and thus were deemed to be outsiders, meaning that they were largely excluded from intermarriage practices between Tikriti clans. Iraqi writer Fayez Khafaji describes, 'Because of the social structures of Tikrit, everyone became a relative of everyone else as families married each other in a very expansive and unique way. No one was a stranger to anyone else from Tikrit as there was a blood connection. However, there was one exception: the Albu Nassir that lived in al-Awja. They didn't mix with other tribes in Tikrit, they were a minority that kept itself to itself and you couldn't find anyone who would give them wives or marry into them.'[16] Although one should be wary of caricaturing these tribes and areas, the Albu Nassir were certainly less well-regarded in Tikrit and less well integrated than other tribes in the area.

Yet al-Bakr and Saddam didn't only belong to the same tribe, they also came from the same clan—the Beijat, which is the strongest of the Albu Nassir clans. Al-Bakr was also part of the Nada family, the leading family in the Beijat. The Beijat's sheikh, Sheikh Nada Hussein, was al-Bakr's maternal uncle as well as his father-in-law—al-Bakr having married his cousin, who was the sheikh's daughter. Sheikh Nada Hussein, meanwhile, was related to al-Bakr through his maternal uncle, Khairallah Tulfah, who brought him up on account of his father being absent and his mother having abandoned him as a small child. Tulfah was also al-Bakr's uncle, making Saddam and al-Bakr cousins, while Tulfah also became Saddam's father-in-law after Saddam married his eldest daughter, Sajida Khairallah Tulfah.

TRIBES AND THE STATE IN LIBYA AND IRAQ

Khairallah Tulfah, who became governor of Baghdad in 1968, was a powerful force in the clan as both al-Bakr and Saddam were growing up. A military man who had a reputation for being deeply religious, the youth of the tribe used to pray behind him in the mosque in Tikrit.

Like other clans in the Tikrit area, the Beijat were, and still are, socially conservative and cling to their Bedouin traditions and values. In 2012, Sheikh Ali al-Nada, who inherited the Beijat sheikhdom from his father, explained how his father had been a tent-dwelling camel herder, adding, 'I was born on the back of a camel.'[17] He also explained how the clan still didn't like its women to be seen by outsiders, noting that it still refuses to give its women in marriage to anyone other than their relatives.[18] Not that this is unique; it is a common practice among tribes in more rural areas. Nevertheless, it is reflective of the kind of mentality in which Saddam and al-Bakr grew up. Notably, the personal secretary of Saddam's son Uday recounted how Uday used to describe his father as 'a simple village man'.[19] This does not mean that these figures were one dimensional; al-Bakr and Saddam were also part of the generation of young men from Tikrit who expanded their horizons by attending military college and spending time outside of their own area.[20] Furthermore, these new leaders had clearly been attracted by the progressive ideology of the Ba'athists. Yet this does not belie the fact that, like many Iraqis, they had been brought up and immersed in a thoroughly conservative and tribal area where families were still living a semi-Bedouin existence. It was entirely natural for al-Bakr and Saddam to use their kinship connections to create a Tikriti core to underpin the regime. As former Ba'athist and Iraqi writer Hassan Allawi describes of al-Bakr, 'Despite the radical discourse al-Bakr used when required, he was a conservative, who came from a rural tribal background. In spite of his Arabism, he was acutely aware of the differences that differentiate tribes, clans and sub-clans.'[21] Saddam was no different in this respect. As Sheikh Sami al-Majoun described, 'When the Ba'athists came to power in 1968, Saddam al-Tikriti—as he was known then—took the tribes' file in his hand. He was of tribal origin and understood tribal society. He showed the sheikhs his respect for them. He brought the heads of tribes in; he assisted some of them and strengthened others while also strengthening his own influence within his tribe.'[22]

164

TRIBES AND THE BA'ATHIST STATE

Although al-Bakr and Saddam brought their relatives into the top tiers of the regime, including into the RCC, the Tikritisation was especially acute in its military and security apparatus. Saddam is alleged to have established a tribal committee at the start of 1970, which he used as a channel for recruitment and mobilisation from his own area into the Republican Guard and other forces. He also set up a special protection unit comprised primarily of young recruits from Tikrit who would be selected when they were 15 or 16 years old, from when they would be bound into the regime, which took over the minutiae of their daily existence. Not only were they housed in special complexes around the presidential palace, where they were rarely exposed to engagement with the outside world, the regime also paid for their weddings, their furniture and their daily needs.[23] The ruling elite recruited the semi-educated from their own peripheral towns to build its repressive apparatus, this protection unit representing the place where 'tribal values came together with modernist tools'.[24] It was clear from the start that this regime was to be based upon a family alliance between two cousins who were to consolidate their control by bringing in their kinsfolk. This was not only a regime that was anchored in Tikrit, but one that prioritised particular Tikriti families and clans. Despite all the aspirations to a transnational ideology, the new leaders staked themselves on the smallest, most local unit of social organisation as a means of survival.

The new leaders were well aware of the contradiction in their discourse and behaviour, and did their utmost to conceal this reliance on kinship and area. While Saddam came to power referring to himself as Saddam al-Tikriti, he soon dropped the al-Tikriti name and started referring to himself as Saddam Hussein. Around the same time, tribal surnames were banned. Official Ba'ath Party publications and magazines were replete with condemnations of tribalism, and slogans such as 'No to tribalism in Iraq after today!' started to appear at every turn, while studies on tribes were banned. Eric Davis recounts a conversation with a Baghdad University faculty member who was imprisoned for three months in the 1970s after he had returned from his studies in the UK, where he had given a talk to Arab students in which he had mentioned that tribal factors still influenced recruitment to posts in the foreign ministry.[25] Upon

165

TRIBES AND THE STATE IN LIBYA AND IRAQ

release, the individual was warned that if he ever repeated the remark, he would return to prison and never come out. Ba'athist rule was full of contradictions, not least being the fact that the individual who signed off the order banning the use of tribal surnames did so using his tribal surname, an incident that became a well-known joke during this period![26]

Tribes and the Early Years: 1968 to 1979

Despite its reliance on kinship, the regime was aware of the threat that the tribes could pose. This was particularly the case with the large Shi'ite tribes of the centre and the south. These tribes' historical relationship to the monarchy and its colonial backers, as well as their close ties to the *Marja'iya*, was a serious cause for concern. The *Marja'iya* was less than enamoured with the coming to power of yet another secular-oriented regime, and for the Ba'athists, this link between it and the tribes—two powerful forces that were deeply rooted in the majority Shi'ite population—posed a concerning prospect. The new leadership was also wary of the tribes' mobilising power and its potential to destabilise the fledgling regime. The new leaders immediately set about trying to weaken the sheikhs of these prominent Shi'ite tribes. As one Shi'ite sheikh put it, while the regime 'piled money on the heads of the Sunni tribes in order to get their support', it didn't do the same for the heads of the Shi'ite tribes because 'terrorising them was sufficient'.[27]

Targeting the sheikhs would serve the dual purpose of intimidating the tribal elite while simultaneously demonstrating that the regime was prepared to strike against the 'feudalists' who its predecessors had failed to eliminate. Going after the sheikhs would also weaken the tribal structures and modes of social organisation that stood in the way of the Ba'athists' aspiration to achieve mass political participation. The Ba'athists had dreamed of creating a new society in which the masses would sign up to its ideology and march towards progress and 'emancipation' from imperialism and injustice. As such, they honed in on the tribal sheikhs as a means of weakening their hold over their tribesmen and breaking the power of the tribe, or as one sheikh from Nasseriyah commented, 'Undermining the standing of the

166

TRIBES AND THE BA'ATHIST STATE

sheikh was done in order to undermine the tribe.'[28] One of its early moves in this respect was to arrest and banish a large number of sheikhs to the Sunni town of Ramadi. Although not an official RCC decision, the leadership entrusted its interior ministry to arrest and exile any sheikh it deemed to 'pose a security threat.'[29] Many sheikhs found themselves suddenly uprooted and forced to relocate, including the likes of Sheikh Hameed Ferhoud of the Bani Khikan tribe; Sheikh Mehsen al-Khayoun of the Bani Assad; Sheikh Fahad Shirshab of the Libdour; and Sheikh Thamar Hamouda of the al-Hassan tribe, among many others. Also included was Sheikh Mohamed al-Minshed, the sheikh of the Ghazi wa Fadoul tribe in Nasseriyah. His son, Sheikh Takleef al-Minshed, recounted, 'When the regime took over, it targeted the tribal system directly. Three or four months after the coup, my father, Sheikh Mohamed, was arrested and exiled to Ramadi for no reason. My father had no connection or affiliation to any political party. They wanted to guarantee that they would remain in power so they used to detain and exile anyone they believed had the potential to pose a danger. The purpose was to put an end to the tribe.'[30]

Like Sheikh Mohamed, the majority of the others arrested at this time were leading sheikhs who were the overall heads of their tribes rather than those smaller sheikhs who led only their clans.[31] The regime wasted no time in targeting those influential tribal figures who had come through the previous decade with their influence and power intact. As Sheikh Adnan al-Danbous, whose father was also among those exiled, observed, 'al-Bakr's philosophy was to hit the sheikh at the top so the smaller one would be frightened', with those arrested being told they had been displaced for 'disciplinary reasons'.[32] The regime had made a show of uprooting these Shi'ite sheikhs and banishing them to the Sunni heartlands. However, the Ba'athists employed a somewhat chaotic and contradictory approach towards this tribal elite, mixing punishment and inducement. This was not unique to its way of dealing with the tribes; it dealt with other components in a similar fashion, reaching out with one hand to the Communists or the Kurds for example, while simultaneously repressing them with the other. All the while it was arresting and trying to intimidate these tribal sheikhs, it was also reaching out and trying to reach some sort of accommodation with them. Most sheikhs were exiled for a matter

TRIBES AND THE STATE IN LIBYA AND IRAQ

of months only, and conditions in Ramadi were not exactly gruelling. The sheikhs were hosted by Sunni tribal sheikhs in Ramadi, who, in the words of Sheikh Takleef al-Minshed, 'looked after them'.[33] More importantly, following their release, these sheikhs were offered inducements by the regime. Sheikh Adel al-Assad described, 'al-Bakr "honoured" seven to ten sheikhs from Nasseriyah alone by offering them money and cars'.[34] Thus, as Majed Safa'ah observes, 'The state gave back to the sheikhs whatever it took'.[35] The regime was cutting the tribe down to size with one hand, while courting it and trying to bind it to the state with the other.

Thus, the regime had an almost schizophrenic attitude towards these sheikhs. This contradictory approach is encapsulated in an incident that occurred not long after the coup when al-Bakr and Saddam invited a group of prominent sheikhs to meet them in Baghdad, where they were put up in hotels. When he met them, al-Bakr asked them immediately what they wanted. Sheikh Mohamed al-Minshed, who was representing the sheikhs of Nasseriyah, replied by reminding al-Bakr that it was he who had called the sheikhs to meet with him. In the words of the Sheikh's son, al-Bakr responded by telling them, 'We want you to understand that the slogans you see in the streets against the tribe are empty. We don't want you to feel threatened. Don't pay attention to them. We are against these kinds of slogans. All we need is for you to uphold your honour and respect.'[36] Sheikh Mohamed told al-Bakr that ever since the coup they had been threatened and disrespected, to which al-Bakr replied that no one would touch them, assuring them that they would be well respected. Following this exchange, Saddam asked Sheikh Mohamed to stay behind. The sheikh reprimanded Saddam, telling him, 'The way you behave is wrong. Your ways are wrong. Your behaviour towards the notables is wrong. These sheikhs have their own status, they need respect. Why are you insulting the sheikhs?'[37] Saddam became agitated and told the sheikh, 'Why are you talking with me in this way? You talk to me as if I am a foreigner, as if I am Iranian or Turkish and have no idea about Iraq. I know who you are and I know your history and I know the status you have. I know the details of your history.'[38]

These new leaders sought to both accommodate and intimidate these sheikhs to try to make them subservient, often dealing with

168

TRIBES AND THE BA'ATHIST STATE

them in such a way that reflected their own tribal backgrounds and understanding of tribal norms and behaviours. The way in which the new regime dealt with Sheikh Sami al-Majoun is another case in point. Sheikh al-Majoun was imprisoned on 4 January 1969 upon his return from a visit to London, and was interrogated about what he had been doing in the UK and his relationship with the sheikhs of other tribes. He recalled how despite the fact that prison guards had mocked him for being a feudalist after he was sent some silk pyjamas, he overheard these same guards talking about him in positive terms, describing him as a 'good man' and the 'son of a tribe'.[39] Al-Majoun's arrest prompted some southern tribes to push back against the regime, with more than 100 sheikhs from Muthanna, Diwaniyah and Nasseriyah coming together to plot a rebellion in protest against his detention.[40] However, the intelligence services got wind of what was being planned and put a stop to it by 'terrorising certain sheikhs'.[41] Despite this, al-Majoun's own tribe continued to protest at his treatment, prompting the regime to kill two of al-Majoun's cousins and set fire to his mudheef in Muthanna governoate. Yet while the regime was heavy-handed in its efforts to repress this tribal rebellion, it clearly concluded that it wasn't prudent to continue to aggravate the tribes in this way. Khairallah Tulfah contacted a number of tribal sheikhs and instructed them to go to al-Bakr to ask him to forgive Sheikh al-Majoun. They duly went to al-Bakr, after which al-Majoun was released from prison and acquitted by the court. Sheikh al-Majoun recalled, 'I left the prison and went to my house in the Yarmouk neighbourhood of Baghdad. I found all the sheikhs sitting in my house. Fifty or sixty sheikhs were there and they told me, "Khairallah Tulfah freed you and you must go and thank him"'.[42] Al-Majoun went to Tulfah, who had been a friend of his father's, to thank him. In what he described as 'pure theatre', Tulfah apologised and told al-Majoun that his arrest had been a 'mistake'.

The Ba'athists also employed land reform policies that served to undermine the sheikhs, specifically those landed sheikhs of the Shi'ite tribes in the south and centre. The Qassim regime's half-hearted attempts at agrarian reform had left many of the most powerful land-owners still in possession of large holdings. The Ba'athists adopted a more radical approach therefore, passing Agrarian Reform Law

TRIBES AND THE STATE IN LIBYA AND IRAQ

No. 117 of 1970, which imposed considerably more stringent conditions upon the amount of land that could be owned by an individual. While there was a sliding scale of maximum holdings dependent on where the land was located and how it was irrigated, the upper limit for irrigated land was brought down to 600 donums (400 donums less than the 1958 legislation), with lower ceilings for other types of land. The law also stipulated that any holdings over the maximum were to be appropriated by the state, while the only compensation payable was for the value of 'trees and installations, pumps and agricultural machinery'.[43] In contrast to the 1958 law, the landowner did not have the right to decide which plots of land he could retain and which the state should confiscate.

As in 1958, this law left the sheikhs of the predominantly Sunni governorates of the north-west largely unscathed, as once again their holdings were not large enough to be affected. The legislation did not affect the Kurdish Aghas (sheikhs) either, as the regime opted not to extend the regulations to the Kurdish areas, which were still embroiled in a struggle for greater autonomy, making it all the more imperative for the Ba'athists that they keep the Aghas and large land-owning sheikhs on its side. The regime reversed this leniency after the Kurdish revolt collapsed in 1975, introducing Law 90, which set an even lower landowning ceiling than the 1970 law. The main victims of the 1970 law were, once again the large landowning Shi'ite sheikhs of the centre and the south. This time, the Ba'athists were more efficient in their implementation of the law and many sheikhs found the very resource from which a significant amount of their power derived confiscated by the state. Some of these sheikhs pleaded with the regime to get their confiscated land back. Sheikh Mohamed al-Minshed, for example, asked a senior Ba'athist official (Naim Haddad) to lobby al-Bakr on his behalf. The message came back that the sheikh could not regain possession of his land, but that the regime was ready to make him the official agent of the African Company for Electricity in order to compensate for the loss.[44] The sheikh refused, making it clear that what mattered to him was not the money, but the land itself. As Sheikh Takleef al-Minshed described, 'Economically, the sheikh is not a sheikh without land. It is his resource and his power. That law of 1970 was passed to end the sheikh as a power.'[45]

170

TRIBES AND THE BA'ATHIST STATE

Not that the land redistribution process was any less chaotic than it had been in 1958. The state expropriated holdings but was slow and arbitrary in its reallocation policies. As a result the government ended up retaining large areas of arable land, which was left fallow. Agricultural production suffered, and with the urban centres becoming ever more attractive poles of work and prosperity, rural-to-urban flight continued to the point where Egyptian farmers had to be invited into the country in their masses to plug labour shortages.[46] By the end of the 1970s, the towns were home to 69 per cent of the population, while the countryside was plunged into negative growth.[47]

However, this mass appropriation of land enabled the regime to bolster its support base. It started giving away plots of what was often prime agricultural land to those who showed loyalty, deepening the patronage system upon which it was becoming increasingly reliant. The ranks of the Ba'ath party began to swell as people cottoned on to the fact that membership was the route to jobs, money, status and other perks. In this way, the Ba'ath succeeded in using its economic power to expand and create a social base, increasing its patriarchal influence.[48] The party built on this further, especially in the rural areas, where it sought to dislodge the power of the sheikh and the tribal elite. The Ba'athists were determined to extend their control into the countryside and to uproot the old rural leadership and replace it with their own cadres. To this end, they established peasant co-operatives and associations, which peasants were forced to join in order to access fertilisers, water and other necessities. These associations became alternative centres of power in the rural landscape, and the authority afforded to the heads of the peasant co-operatives became equal to, if not more important than, that of the sheikhs.[49] The Ba'ath also opened party offices in every village, seeking to pull everyone into the orbit of the state, and demanding that any party official who was stationed in the village must, 'in the first place, himself be liberated from tribalism'.[50]

Thus local Ba'athist officials started to eclipse the sheikhs as they began to wield more power in their local areas. Ba'athists were told at this time that a sheikh must never be ahead of a Ba'athist and that the Ba'athist must always go in front of the sheikh.[51] They were also warned that any Ba'athist who permitted the sheikh to have priority

TRIBES AND THE STATE IN LIBYA AND IRAQ

would be punished.[52] Sheikh Takleef al-Minshed recounted how his father was warned by the head of security in his local area that it would be better for him if he left Iraq and settled in another Arab country. When the sheikh protested and offered to hand himself in to be arrested, the security official told him, 'I am just giving you advice. I don't want you to be humiliated. This regime doesn't want people like you and you could be arrested at any time.'[53] Thus, a new dynamic was created in which local power shifted increasingly from the sheikh to the state and where the local official became the link between the state and the people. As Sheikh Jawad al-Assad described, 'In the monarchy, sheikhs were partners. Now they were followers.'[54]

This shift had a devastating effect on the sheikhs. This wasn't only in the countryside; in all state institutions, the sheikh found he could no longer open the doors he once could, and the respect he once commanded within the state apparatus was gone. Sheikh al-Minshed described, 'A sheikh who was well-respected before 1968 would no longer be given special treatment by government employees afterwards. This had a psychological impact and affected the standing of the sheikh.'[55] The sheikh also found himself unable to lobby on behalf of his tribesmen, a role that formed one of his key sheikhly duties. In 1976, the regime issued a decision banning sheikhs from attending public offices and institutions on business other than that which was personal to them.[56] Traditionally, the sheikh's job had been to go from office to office, and official to official, resolving matters for his tribesmen over tea. By preventing the sheikh from being able to do so the state started to break the tribe's reliance on its sheikh, who was no longer the main conduit to the authorities.

The regime succeeded in chipping away at the sheikh's power and the party came to dwarf the sheikh. As Sheikh Takleef al-Minshed also observed, 'When the Ba'athists came to power, the image of the sheikh was shaken. He lost his centrality.'[57] Sheikh Takleef describes, 'The tribe's sense of duty to the sheikh started weakening. His presence was no longer required. Respect was no longer what it used to be and attending his mudheef was no longer a duty. Communication between the sheikh and his tribe was weakened hugely. For example, tribesmen used to come to greet the sheikh at Eid and his mudheef would be overcrowded with tribesmen. Later, this number became

172

TRIBES AND THE BA'ATHIST STATE

less and less and only dozens would come and they would only stay for half an hour and leave. Before that, they would stay in the mudheef for a day or two days.'[58] The sheikhs could feel their power and influence ebbing away. Sheikh Takleef also observed, 'The sheikh seemed to be alone in his mudheef, as if he lost everything—first power and then the people. People were preoccupied with slogans while the sheikh stood still in his mudheef.'[59]

This shifting environment prompted many tribesmen, including the sons of some of these sheikhs, to conclude that their best option was to join the Ba'ath Party. Not that they all joined themselves—doing so deemed to be beneath them. Instead, some sheikhs pushed their sons to the fore and they lined up with the thousands of others who filled the party's ranks. As Sheikh Jawad al-Assad remarked, 'Prior to 1968, the Ba'ath Party concentrated on trying to attract the sheikhs and their sons, and many of the sons of sheikhs were Ba'athists and military officers. After 1968, this equation was turned on its head. After 1968, the sons of sheikhs started tripping over themselves to join the Ba'ath Party.'[60] For their part, the sheikhs and their sons had no ideological barrier to joining the party in order to further their personal ambitions and the interests of their tribes. Both the Ba'athists and the sheikhs found a way to accommodate each other.

Notably, the sons of the sheikhs often went on to hold prominent positions in the party and its organisations. Some became the heads of the peasant co-operatives. Mehsen Shalaan, for example, who was the son of a sheikh from Khufaja, a Shi'ite tribe from Hillah in central Iraq, was appointed as the head of the peasants' association in his local area. In this way, the younger generation of the tribal elite of certain tribes were absorbed into the system, simultaneously enhancing their own positions within their tribes. As Sheikh Jawad al-Assad described, 'The closer the sheikh was to the authority, the more he would be able to solve the tribe's problems... The Ba'athist sheikh was more able than the non-affiliated sheikh to secure a job for one of his tribesmen, to get one of his tribesmen transferred from an office in one governorate to another, to secure loans, to mediate among families and to get access to the authorities. The sheikh after the 1960s realised that the shortest way to the authorities was by joining the party. The non-Ba'athist sheikhs couldn't solve their own problems or the prob-

173

TRIBES AND THE STATE IN LIBYA AND IRAQ

lems of their tribes, and quite often these non-Ba'athist sheikhs went to the Ba'athist sheikhs to mediate on their behalf.'[61] Similarly, Sheikh Adnan al-Danbous remarked, 'In my district in Amarah, the sons of the sheikhs joined the Ba'ath in order to protect their own interests. As a result they started having double the power. They were respected because they were the sons of the sheikh and also because they were members of the Ba'ath Party.'[62]

Yet, while the sheikhs were undoubtedly bent to the will of the state, the Ba'athists were unable to shatter tribal structures and tribal modes of organisation. They failed too in their attempts to replace tribal *asabiya* with loyalty to the state. While tribesmen may have come to rely on the state, and while they may have afforded their sheikhs less attention and respect than before, such structures did not simply disappear. Rather, they became less visible for a while. As the regime acknowledged itself in 1971, it may have eliminated the manifestation of feudal rule, but it had 'not achieved anything in regard to tribal structures'.[63] Tribes continued to operate as units of social organisation, to resolve disputes and to lobby the state on behalf of their members.[64]

Furthermore, the regime could not simply cancel out the role or standing of the sheikh within his own community. Sheikh Jawad al-Assad recounted an exchange over a land dispute that took place in 1971 between his grandfather, the sheikh of the Ibada tribe, and the governor of Dhi Qar.[65] The governor started threatening the sheikh telling him, 'We will exile you to Diyala', to which the sheikh responded that he could do so. The governor then warned, 'We will hang you from the ceiling', to which the sheikh also responded that he could do that. The governor came back by threatening, 'I will imprison you', to which the sheikh again told him he could do so. Finally, the governor threatened, 'We will take the sheikhdom away from you', to which the sheikh responded, 'neither you, nor your father nor whoever sent you to me can do that; the sheikhdom is inherited from father to son'.[66] Various stories of a similar ilk were recounted by a number of sheikhs indicating that this version of events was somehow constructed and woven into the tribe's history. However, it was aimed at demonstrating the unique status afforded to the sheikh of the tribe. For all that the regime under al-Bakr curbed

174

TRIBES AND THE BA'ATHIST STATE

and curtailed the sheikh and the tribe, both continued to represent a solid and deep-rooted reality that may have been in the shadows, but that was still very much present.

The Saddam Hussein Years

In July 1979, Saddam Hussein, whose grip on power had been growing progressively stronger, forced the by-now ailing al-Bakr to resign and formally assumed the presidency. By this point, Saddam was already the de facto leader of Iraq, but he used the opportunity to further consolidate this power, including by engaging in a major purge of the Ba'ath Party. Famously, he convened an assembly of party leaders on 22 July 1979 and announced the discovery of a plot by sixty-eight alleged co-conspirators. The accused were removed from the room one by one and subsequently tried and convicted for treason, with twenty-two of them sentenced to death. Further executions followed and by the end of July, hundreds of high-ranking Ba'ath Party members had been killed, cementing Saddam's dominance over the party and the country. Indeed, Saddam had been working since the mid-1970s to crush all opposition, repressing the Communists, the Kurds and Shi'ite Islamist parties and movements alike. In this way, he succeeded in bending the state to his will and, as Tripp has observed, sought to impose a political unity on Iraq that found expression chiefly in his person, with obedience to him to serve as the common cause of Iraq's heterogeneous inhabitants.[67]

This consolidation of power around the persona of Saddam was tightened further through kinship. Certainly, the new president's coming to power did not herald any sudden change of tribal policy; Saddam maintained a discourse that was dismissive of tribes and tribalism while simultaneously relying on kinship networks to shore up his regime. He brought more of his relatives into the regime's elite security apparatus, as well as members of key tribes from the Sunni triangle. Members of the loyal Jubour and Dulaim tribes for example were recruited to the Republican Guard, the security service and Saddam's inner circle. In this way, Saddam hoped to ring-fence his power base, counting on kinship as the best means of pre-empting any potential coup or challenge to his regime.

175

TRIBES AND THE STATE IN LIBYA AND IRAQ

This reliance on the tribes of the Sunni heartland did not preclude his looking to tribes and sheikhs from other parts of Iraq to help reinforce his rule. He tried to lure the sheikhs of the centre and the south, understanding that tribal identity did not conflict with national identity or constitute an Iraqi's sole conception of self.[68] In some instances, he called on the sheikhs to serve the regime by becoming its 'eyes' and serving as local informants. Sheikh Kadhem al-Anaizan of the Bin Sweilem tribe in Basra explained how in 1979 he was summoned by a leading Ba'athist who tried, unsuccessfully to recruit him as a 'semi-agent'.[69] Others were more obliging; three sheikhs wrote to Saddam in 1988 offering to deal with some of their own tribesmen who had committed an offence, pledging 'to be faithful to the revolution and its great leader', and declaring, 'If it is proved that those mentioned are the ones who committed the event, we will soon execute them ourselves'.[70] As Sheikh Jawad al-Assad remarked, 'As soon as Saddam came to power in 1979, he supported the sheikhs of the tribes. He and the tribes served each other politically'.[71] This did not mean that there weren't tribes who remained opposed to the regime and who had an antagonistic relationship to it. This included the Juwaiber, the Jamamla and the Nawashi.[72] Saddam famously detested and dispised the marsh tribes of the south. Sheikh Kadhem al-Anaizan describes, 'He hated the heads of the marsh tribes. He loathed them. He hated the Sweilem, the Siamar, the Bani Assad—all the Ma'dan tribes [marsh tribes]. He used to describe them as Indians, or Pakistanis who came to live in Iraq with their cattle in the Abassid time'.[73]

Despite this, most sheikhs were willing to work with the regime and had a good relationship with it.[74] This was not out of any particular love for Saddam or the Ba'athists, but was a pragmatic response to living under a repressive ruling power that was increasingly bent on the complete Ba'athification of both state and society. As Iraqi sociologist Karim Hamza notes, the sheikhs realised that as they were unable to rebel against 'the hand that was repressing them, they had no choice but to kiss it'.[75] Hamza also observed how, 'This pragmatic approach enabled them to gain more privileges, especially after they displayed certain loyalties, such as joining the ruling party or taking part in the "political game" by joining the opposition'.[76] As had occurred before, rather than oppose it, most sheikhs were willing to work within the

176

TRIBES AND THE BA'ATHIST STATE

confines of the state. However, this dual accommodation remained concealed, and open discussion of tribes and tribalism continued to be taboo, with Saddam playing down public consciousness and discussion of tribalism in Iraqi politics and society.[77]

Nevertheless, the regime started to shed some of these taboos during the Iran–Iraq War that erupted in September 1980. Riding high on his own sense of power and ambition, and believing that the recently installed Islamic Republic in Tehran was weak and fragmented, Saddam instigated a war, abrogating the 1975 Algiers Agreement that delineated the countries' maritime boundary and proclaiming Iraqi sovereignty over the whole of the Shatt al-Arab waterway. Saddam had expected Iran to capitulate quickly, anticipating that it would be forced into negotiating an end to hostilities on terms favourable to Baghdad. These expectations turned out to be a gross miscalculation; Iraq was dragged into an eight-year war of attrition that resulted in the deaths of an estimated 1 million Iranians and between 250,000 to 500,000 Iraqis.

Waging war against a Shi'ite power posed particular dilemmas for the regime given that there were elements among Iraq's own Shi'ite population who were sympathetic to the Islamic Republic. The regime feared that communal Shi'ite unity might prove stronger than Iraqi nationalism, especially among disenfranchised Shi'ite youth, who were being conscripted to join the frontlines in their droves. To counter such concerns, the regime deployed propaganda depicting the war as a battle between Arabs and Persians rather than as a confessional conflict between a Sunni-dominated secular regime and a Shi'ite theocracy. In so doing, it invoked the seventh-century Battle of al-Qadisiyyah in which the Arab Rashidun army defeated the Persian Sasanian Empire and incorporated territory that comprises modern-day Iraq into the Caliphate. The war against Iran was dubbed as 'Saddam's al-Qadisiyyah' or the 'second al-Qadisiyyah' and references to this historic battle began to permeate public life. Not only were military battalions, public buildings, roads and squares named after the conflict, images of heroic Arab horsemen appeared on murals, stamps and banknotes.[78] This huge propaganda campaign was clearly aimed at depicting the fight against Iran in nationalist terms.

Yet while the regime was anxious about how Iraqi Shi'ites would respond to the conflict, one should not overplay these concerns.

TRIBES AND THE STATE IN LIBYA AND IRAQ

Although the Iranian revolution had galvanised certain politicised Shi'ite elements and movements in Iraq, these did not command mass support among Iraq's Shi'ite population. Shi'ite revivalism had limited appeal at this juncture and the bulk of Iraq's Shi'ites were unconnected to these political organisations and 'endured the hardships of the war in much the same spirit as other Iraqis'.[79] Moreover, by the time the war intensified in 1982, the regime had already all but decimated political articulations of Shi'ite Islamism in Iraq. It had made membership of Shi'ite Islamist parties a capital offence and had carried out severe crackdowns against the Dawa Party and other Shi'ite currents. In April 1980, it executed Shi'ite cleric Mohamed Baqir al-Sadr and his sister, Bint al-Huda, after the former had publicly expressed support for Khomeini's regime. This strategy of repression was accompanied by attempts to woo and placate the official Shi'ite religious establishment, with the regime investing heavily in the Holy cities and their shrines and mosques, and succeeding in gaining the *Marja'iya*'s official backing for the war. While the regime was certainly alert to the potential ramifications of engaging in a conflict with a Shi'ite state, it encountered little solid opposition among the Shi'ite population and whole areas of the south became militarised, their sons called up to fight.

Nevertheless, aware of the status they still possessed, the regime was keen to garner the support of the southern sheikhs and to rally them behind its cause. Suggestions in the literature that certain Shi'ite tribes mobilised spontaneously against Iran and were supplied with weapons by the regime[80] are questionable. It is true that the regime was mobilising and providing weapons to some Kurdish tribes as part of its struggle against Kurdish nationalist insurgents. It also supplied weaponry to Sunni tribes whose loyalty could be guaranteed along the border with Syria, keeping meticulous records of what weapons were handed out to which tribesmen through their sheikhs.[81] Yet there is little concrete evidence to support the assertion that loyal Shi'ite tribes were also armed, or that they were given space to form their own tribal militias. Not only was the regime not in need of additional forces at this time given the large number of military forces and personnel at its disposal, it remained acutely wary of arming the Shi'ite tribes, fearing that weapons could be used against it or would fall into

178

TRIBES AND THE BA'ATHIST STATE

the hands of Shi'ite deserters and opponents, some of whom were hiding out in the marshes.[82] It would have been almost unthinkable for the regime to take such a radical approach.

The regime's main interest in the Shi'ite sheikhs at this time was in using them to demonstrate that it had the full support of every component of Iraqi society. To this end, the Ba'ath Party actively sought statements of support from the sheikhs of the tribes. These statements and telegrams began to appear in state newspapers and on state television with tribes pledging their loyalty to Saddam and their support for the war against Iran. Other sheikhs complied and not only sent telegrams but also contributed materially to the war effort, collecting significant sums of money and gold.[83] Not that all sheikhs obliged. The father of Sheikh Yousef al-Baidani, who was general sheikh at the time, refused to send any letter of support for the war. Sheikh Takleef al-Minshed recounts how the general secretary of the Nasseriyah branch of the Ba'ath Party stopped his father—the general sheikh of his tribe—demanding to know why he wasn't supporting the war and informing him that he would send him a telegram to sign that evening.[84] Sheikh Takleef described how after a long discussion with his relatives and tribesmen, his father opted not to sign the telegram, apologising to the general secretary. Despite the sheikh fearing that such a move would result in execution, in the event, there was no comeback for his actions. This lack of retribution was a reflection of the fact that while the sheikhs represented an important constituency, they were not the regime's top priority at this time. It could afford to turn a blind eye to individual sheikhs who did not respond to overtures by Ba'ath Party officials to collect statements of loyalty, presumably in an attempt to extract money and favour from the regime.

The willingness of the regime to publish these telegrams and statements in the media marked a new opening towards the tribes. Yet this shift in approach should not be overplayed. Assertions that this period represented a 're-tribalisation' by the authorities of the social and cultural landscape[85] are exaggerated. Firstly, these telegrams usually appeared in the back pages of the newspapers and were afforded little space compared to those received by other types of organisations. Secondly, Iraq's social and cultural landscape was already strongly

179

TRIBES AND THE STATE IN LIBYA AND IRAQ

delineated along tribal lines and it was not within the purview of the authorities to 're-tribalise' something that may have been pushed to the back but that was still very much present. Thirdly, while the regime may have invoked 'tribal' values of honour, heroism and bravery in its effort to stir up nationalist feeling in the conflict with Iran, including through promoting images depicting Arab horsemen of old, these values were part and parcel of Arab cultural iconography. Appealing to such motifs did not signify any serious attempt to 're-tribalise' the cultural arena, nor did it sit at odds with the Arab nationalist narrative promoted by the Ba'athists. As Haddad argues, the re-entering of the tribe into the political discourse in the 1980s should not be overstated.[86] Rather, Saddam opened some limited space for expressions of tribal support as part of his efforts to Ba'athify every aspect of society and to show to the outside world that Saddam had support from every quarter. As a result, during the 1980s, tribalism 'floated to the surface and became more visible'.[87]

This visibility included within the regime itself. Saddam's anchoring his regime in the tribes of north-western Iraq had facilitated the ascendance of certain groups from powerful Sunni tribes, some military elements of which became overly ambitious and sought to challenge the regime. In 1989, a plot by a group of military officers from the Jubour tribe was uncovered. The officers, who were from the Special Guard and who were led by Sattam Ghanem al-Jubouri, had been planning to assassinate Saddam on Iraqi Army Day on 6 January 1990. After the plot was uncovered, Saddam met with notables and sheikhs of the tribe. After telling the sheikhs that he had been mistaken to have recruited the officers, noting that in future he would only bring in individuals from trusted families, he instructed the sheikhs to gather all the plotters and tell them that they had 'blackened not only the image of the tribe, the village, a family or two houses, but the surface of all rivers'.[88] He continued, 'They [the perpetrators] have to see a punishment coming from you'.[89] Saddam also chastised the tribe himself through collective punishment, expelling a large number of members of the Jubour from their posts in the state administration. With the Jubour disgraced, Saddam turned to the Dulaim to plug the gaps. Yet, betrayal was to emerge from within this tribe too. In October 1994, a plot involving a group of disaffected

TRIBES AND THE BA'ATHIST STATE

officers led by Air Force general Mohamed Mazlum al-Dulaimi was uncovered, prompting the regime to execute the plotters and purge other Dulaim tribesmen from senior positions in the military. Dulaimi's execution and the return of his body, which bore signs of torture, to his family prompted rare protests in Ramadi. Saddam had vowed he wouldn't execute the ringleaders and his doing so ignited uproar. The uprisings were swiftly put down, prompting the regime to question hundreds of relatives of Dulaimi military personnel and to arrest thousands.[90] Despite this challenge, Saddam was able to contain the crisis. He rooted out those involved in the attempted plot and was able to maintain his relations with the tribe.

The following year, Saddam was to face a challenge even closer to home. His two son-in-laws, Saddam Kamel al-Majid, who was head of Iraq's secret weapons progamme, and Saddam Kamel Hassan al-Majid, defected to Jordan following differences that had evolved between them and Saddam's sons, Uday and Qussay. In Jordan, the pair declared their intention to overthrow the regime. In 1996, both returned to Iraq, having been given assurances for their safety. However, Saddam was to dispose of them. After their return, their wives were forced to divorce them and they were then attacked and killed by more than thirty of their clan members headed by senior official Ali Hassan al-Majid, who was Hussein Kamel's uncle, and also the uncle of Saddam Hussein. After their deaths, Saddam is reported to have told a group of sheikhs that the clan had 'cleansed their bodies of the shame by severing the rotten finger'.[91] Saddam dealt with the crisis in the most tribally minded way possible.

The regime also came up against challenges from outside Saddam's tribal base. In March 1991, an uprising gripped both the north and the south of the country simultaneously. It began with largely spontaneous revolts that erupted in Basra, Amarah, Nasseriyah, Najaf and Karbala, and was followed by an uprising in the Kurdish region. The southern revolts were in large part a spontaneous response to the ongoing repression and to the declining economic situation and growing poverty. They were also fuelled by an overwhelming sense of anger and frustration at the regime's having dragged the country into a pointless conflict with Iran and at its disastrous invasion of Kuwait in 1990, a move that left the Iraqi army devastated. Furthermore,

181

there was a widespred belief at this time that the regime had been so weakened by its failed military adventurism that it was on the verge of collapse.

When the powder keg exploded and the revolts erupted, some elements from the southern tribes joined in. A number of scholars have downplayed the tribal element in this rebellion, stressing its urban character and denying that tribal loyalties played any role in mobilising people to rebel in the south.[92] Yet in fact the Shi'ite tribes formed an important component of the uprising. Several well-known sheikhs took part in the rebellion, including Sheikh Hussein Ali al-Sha'alan, who had been elected to the parliament in 1984 and who led the uprising in Diwaniyah.[93] A number of sheikhs from Souq al-Shayouk in Nasseriyah also took part, including Sheikh Kadhem Risaan al-Kassid of the Hacham tribe, as well as sheikhs of the Juwaibar.[94] Sheikh Takleef al-Minshed of the Ghazi wa fudoul tribe, who also participated, described, 'No one was dreaming of revolt or of taking up arms prior to 1991. I told my brothers that I would move against the regime in Nasseriyah. I agreed with my brothers and with the sheikhs of the clan and the sub-clan that we would attack the governorate building.'[95] Naji Sultan meanwhile recounted, 'The tribes took part and fought. Those who fought in Nasseriyah were the tribes. Nasseriyah was divided into two sections, one that was under the control of the government and the other that was under the control of the tribes.'[96] He described how in Souq al-Shayouk, 'The post office was taken over by the Nawashi, the bank by the Hacham, while the al-Hassan took over a different utility and al-Asaqar took over another. They turned them into headquarters and from there, went out to fight.'[97]

Furthermore, while the uprisings may have been primarily urban, the areas that rose up against the regime were often those neighbourhoods that were populated by tribesmen who had migrated to the towns and where tribal values were particularly strong. This includes the al-Hayania neighbourhood of Basra, which is where the first uprisings began, as well as neighbourhoods along the eastern banks of the Shatt al-Arab, which were populated mainly by members of the Halaf al-Suwaijit, al-Bahla, al-Mansour and al-Sawakin.[98] In Dhi Qar, youth who revolted only did so after obtaining the blessing of their elders and sheikhs.[99] Meanwhile in some areas, the sheikhs may not have

182

TRIBES AND THE BA'ATHIST STATE

joined in the fighting, but they provided logistical support by allowing the rebels to sleep in their mudheefs and by providing them with food, clothing and bedding.[100]

Ba'athist records from this period also indicate that the southern tribes played a significant role in the revolt. A report by the head of the al-Qadisiyyah branch of the General Union of Iraqi Women dated 13 March 1991 described the violence and looting, as well as the killing, that took place in the Hamza district of Diwaniyah, noting how the 'saboteurs' were working in conjunction with the tribes there.[101] The report mentions Sheikh Hussein Ali Sha'alan and his brother, as well as Sheikh Hussein al-Ribat of the Bani Arid tribe as being involved. Records also report a meeting in Shanafiya in Muthanna organised just prior to the uprising by soldiers who had returned from Kuwait and who called on the sheikhs to support the revolt, explaining that they wanted them to provide the uprising with a 'reasonable and known face'.[102] The sheikhs agreed to take part, but only on the condition that Ba'athists who came from Shanafiya and who were their tribesmen would be permitted to flee or to be spared by those staging the uprising. This, the sheikhs argued, was the way to uphold social cohesion in Shanafiya and to ensure that revenge killings did not ensue.

The fact that the uprisings were primarily urban does not mean that they didn't include or involve the tribes. This is not to suggest that these tribes joined in en masse or that all clans of these tribes took part. One clan in the al-Nawashi tribe remained loyal to the regime throughout, its sheikh sending a message to Saddam apologising for the actions of what it described as illiterate elements in the tribe.[103] Sheikh Takleef al-Minshed estimated that less than 10 per cent of his tribe took part, explaining, 'The majority turned us down. People don't like politics.'[104] Moreover, some sheikhs opted to stand by the regime, with some assisting in its brutal suppression of the uprising. A letter written by the secretariat of the Ba'ath Party in Diwaniyah dated 23 March 1991 described how a member of the al-Ashour clan of the al-Hayal tribe in the Hamza district of the town had provided information about tribes in the governorate who had taken part in the rioting, including the Jubour tribe, the al-Khaza'el tribe and the Bani Arid tribe.[105] The clan member had offered to help the party, noting

183

TRIBES AND THE STATE IN LIBYA AND IRAQ

that it had between 170 and 200 people who could help fight the rioters.[106] Yet, the southern tribes, or at least parts of these tribes, played a major role in the uprisings, along with other components that took part in the revolt. Assertions that the 1991 uprisings and the mobilising dynamics they unleased proved that 'tribalism is not effective in forging loyalties in Iraq'[107] are perplexing.

The 'Sheikhs of the Nineties'

The rebellion shocked the regime to its core. With fourteen out of eighteen of Iraq's governorates out of its control, it retaliated hard and moved rapidly to quash both the Kurdish rebellion in the north and the Shi'ite uprising in the south. Within a couple of weeks, Republican Guard divisions had recaptured all towns held by rebels and inflicted massive destruction and loss of life on the southern areas. Tens of thousands were killed, while others fled across the borders into Saudi Arabia, Kuwait and Iran, or hid out in the marshes. Although the regime succeeded in retaking control, the rebellion forced it to take stock. Ideology mixed with repression was evidently insufficient to ensure conformity, and could not prevent societal components from mobilising to challenge the state. The regime woke up to the power of society and to the power of the tribes. While tribes may have been weakened, and while the sheikh was no longer the Bedouin sheikh of old, able to order his tribesmen into battle, the power of the tribe could still be turned against the state, including in the urban setting. As one Nasseriyah resident described, 'Through this uprising, Saddam discovered the capabilities and the real size of the tribes.'[108] He also awoke to the fact that for some Ba'athists, the pull of tribal loyalty could prove stronger than that of the party.

The regime responded to this realisation by shifting its approach towards the tribe, turning to the sheikhs in a more public and visible fashion and making space for them along with other currents and articulations of social organisation. This was part of a wider ploy aimed at giving the impression that the regime was open and pluralistic, and it opened—superficially at least—to Salafist currents at this time too. The regime also allocated a number of seats in the parliament for tribal sheikhs, bringing them formally into the political system that served as a front to rubber stamp the regime's decisions.

TRIBES AND THE BA'ATHIST STATE

This didn't mean that there was any departure from Ba'athification, or that, as some scholars have suggested, the regime's tribal policy suddenly morphed into what has been described as 're-tribalisation', or 'neo-tribalism', or as a 'resurrection' of tribalism.[109] This wasn't about re-tribalising society or reinventing tribalism. Rather, it was the regime's way of trying to harness and subjugate those components of society that it had failed to quash. The tribe's sudden visibility after 1991 represented a more overt expansion of previous efforts by the regime to bring the tribes, particularly those in the south, under central government control.[110] A General Security Directorate report from this time, drawn up in response to the 'Page of Treason and Treachery', as the regime named the uprising, details recommendations for harnessing the tribes in order to better control them. These included instilling nationalist sentiment and moral obligation among tribesmen; improving relations between tribal leaders and Ba'ath Party officials; incorporating the sons of tribal leaders into government positions; and empowering tribes to combat crime and protect national borders.[111] Rather than a grand effort to 're-tribalise' society or to empower tribes or tribalism, this was a targeted effort to bring the Shi'ite tribes under more direct control. As Saddam's press secretary, Abduljabbar Mohsen, recounted, Saddam looked to the tribes after 1991 to repair what had happened in the uprising, noting how the president believed that tribal mobilisation would help him fight opposition activists in the south as well as any other international attack. Mohsen explained how the regime's thinking towards the tribes was: 'Let us start anew. We were not against you; we want to rely on you'.[112] Thus, the focus on the tribes during the 1990s should be viewed within the context of Saddam's efforts to Ba'athify all components of the state and society in order to defend the regime against future threats.

The beginnings of this engagement emerged immediately after the failed uprisings, when state media began to print telegrams of support from tribal sheikhs. *Al-Thawra* and other state newspapers regularly carried pledges of loyalty by tribal sheikhs, including from the south, to their 'heroic leader'.[113] However, this tribal engagement was still low-key at this point; these pledges were still relegated to the back pages and sat among other such pronouncements from different com-

185

TRIBES AND THE STATE IN LIBYA AND IRAQ

ponents of society. The regime was clearly still flirting with the idea and hadn't yet committed itself fully. Tribal engagement became more obvious in the years that followed. The regime tried to lure back sheikhs who had fled after the uprisings, offering them clemency if they returned. Many sheikhs came back at this time, including Sheikh Ali al-Minshed and Sheikh Kenan Tamimi, the latter of whom was killed in 1994 after he was found to have links to the opposition. Saddam also began inviting Shi'ite tribal sheikhs to meet with him. Sheikh Kadhem al-Anaizan described how, following the imposition by Western powers of the southern no-fly zone in August 1992, Saddam invited a small delegation of Shi'ite sheikhs including himself, Sheikh Sabri Sadoun, Sheikh Abduljabbar al-Hdhal (from the Anza tribe) and Sheikh Kadhem al-Ribat (from the Qatarna tribe) and others to meet with him.[114] Sheikh al-Anaizan claims that this meeting— the first of its kind—was organised at the suggestion of Sheikh Aziz Saleh Noman, a leading Shi'ite Ba'athist and a sheikh of the Khufaja tribe, who had advised Saddam to give the Shi'ites more of a role.[115] Sheikh al-Anaizan recounted how during the meeting, Saddam had reproached the sheikhs for the 1991 events, asking them, 'How did those people who are Iranian bring Basra down? What is your role? You are the tribes.'[116]

Most noticeable was the flood of visits by tribal sheikhs and notables to the presidential palace that began in 1993. These were often highly theatrical displays at which the sheikhs would swear oaths of allegiance to Saddam and recite tribal poetry composed for the occasion. State newspapers from this time were replete with reports of sheikhs and heads of clans going in their hundreds to Baghdad to pledge their devotion to the 'heroic leader'. On 2 April 1993, *al-Thawra* reported how 328 sheikhs, notables, clan heads and religious scholars from Dhi Qar had sworn an oath of loyalty in front of the president.[117] The sheikhs acknowledged the leadership of the Ba'ath Party and of Saddam and promised that no 'terrorist or agent' would be permitted to enter their clans. They also swore that their clans would 'be one man and one weapon against vandals and greedy people', and that their leadership would be 'the first to sacrifice in deed and not in word alone'.[118] Three days later, *al-Thawra* reported on 266 sheikhs and notables from al-Qadisiyyah who had gathered in

186

TRIBES AND THE BA'ATHIST STATE

front of Saddam to pledge a similar oath of allegiance in what was clearly a set-piece text.[119] This exercise was evidently about ensuring that the tribes were rallying behind the regime and about demonstrating that Saddam had support from the tribes in those areas that had rebelled. Sheikh Jawad al-Assad considers that the purpose of these televised tribal visits was to prove to the Arab world, as well as to the region, that the tribes were standing behind the Ba'ath Party and supporting it.[120] With Iraq under international sanctions and having been humiliated in its war with Kuwait, Saddam wanted to put on a show of strength and to demonstrate that he had Iraqi society behind him. As Sheikh al-Anaizan described, 'The sheikh that didn't go to visit Saddam was considered hostile. He wanted loyalty from us— loyalty to him and to the party, but ultimately to him'.[121]

Saddam did not leave things there. In the mid-1990s, the regime issued a decision aimed at categorising the sheikhs and the tribal lineage of all citizens. As part of this process, the regime set up a bureau for tribal affairs in every governorate at which all sheikhs were required to register. The sheikhs were categorised according to their importance, with general sheikhs labelled as 'Sheikh A', heads of clans as 'Sheikh B', lesser sheikhs as 'Sheikh C', and so on. To this end, the head of the tribal affairs section of the president's office, Rukan Abdulghafour, who was also Saddam's cousin, met with sheikh after sheikh to determine their status. These meetings were often televised, with the sheikhs—who had no written record or documentation proving their status—forced to explain and prove their lineage.

This categorisation system was used as a way to manipulate the tribal system, with the regime moving sheikhs up and down the sheikhly status ladder. Those general sheikhs whose loyalty was deemed insufficient would find themselves undercut as the regime turned to other lesser sheikhs or individuals in their tribe, making them Sheikh A and foisting benefits and status upon them, thereby creating new loyal centres of power inside the tribes. Sheikh Kadhem al-Anaizan described how he was initially registered as Sheikh A, but was subsequently demoted to Sheikh B, explaining, 'The party was the one that decided. The reason why [I was demoted] was because one of my cousins was very rich and he slaughtered sheep and made feasts for Ali Hassan al-Majid [a leading Ba'athist and cousin of Saddam, known

TRIBES AND THE STATE IN LIBYA AND IRAQ

as 'Chemical Ali'] and al-Baki Sadoun [a leading Ba'athist who was in charge of all Ba'athist organisations in the south who was also a leading sheikh of the Sadoun tribe] and sent them dates and fish. He begged the authorities until they made him Sheikh A.'[122] Sheikh al-Anaizan also recounted asking his cousin one day why he had spent so many millions of dinars in this way, to which he responded, 'All I need is to be called sheikh. That is the thing I lack.'[123] Another sheikh recounted how when the general sheikh of his tribe died, his uncle was courted by Saddam because Saddam wanted this uncle to be Sheikh A rather than the son of the dead sheikh.[124]

In this way, the regime was able to bind the tribes to it, creating loyal sheikhs who would do its bidding and serve as a chorus to cheer on Saddam in return for 'honours'. As Sheikh Jawad al-Assad remarked, 'Every tribal sheikh was registered in the tribal affairs bureau. The sub-sheikhs were also registered. If a sheikh was to be honoured, the honour would come through that bureau'.[125] This was also a way for the regime to use these officially recognised sheikhs as a form of social control. One Nasseriyah resident remarked, 'The regime wanted the sheikhs to serve as its eyes. He wanted them to become members of the Ba'ath Party so he would buy them by giving them "allocations"... Being an eye for the regime is not the role of a general sheikh. General sheikhs would not want to inform on their tribesmen, so the regime sought to create alternatives in parallel to the real sheikhs'.[126]

The regime's policy ended up creating a scramble inside the tribes, with many lesser sheikhs rushing to be recognised as general sheikhs, and with some breaking away from their tribes in order to create their own clans. Their doing so was partly an attempt to access funds. Sheikh Adel al-Assad recounted how during the 1990s, many sheikhs were so poor they couldn't afford to provide coffee for guests in their mudheef, forcing them to compete with each other for the regime's attention and largesse.[127] Yet being recognised officially as sheikh wasn't solely about money; it was also about status. Wealthy individuals would often seek to enshrine and strengthen their prestige by being recognised officially as a sheikh because, 'Becoming a sheikh was the shortest route to consolidate status'.[128] These newly made sheikhs became known disparagingly as the 'Sheikhs of the Nineties',

188

TRIBES AND THE BA'ATHIST STATE

or the 'Made in Taiwan Sheikhs'. One Nasseriyah resident described, 'In our area, there was a taxi driver who had no connection to any sheikhly house. Suddenly he had a mudheef and a special car and he was surrounded by people who followed him everywhere while he issued tribal orders. These are the Nineties Sheikhs'.[129] There was a sudden proliferation of sheikhs competing to demonstrate loyalty to the state, and encouraged by Ba'ath Party officials, who would try to bring in tribesmen and categorise them as sheikhs in order to receive honorary payments from Saddam.[130] Sheikh Jabbar al-Assad estimated that in Basra there used to be around thirty sheikhs but during the 1990s, their numbers increased to between 300 and 400.[131] These sheikhs would host dinners, commission poetry and stage televised war dances in support of the regime and hand dissidents over to the authorities in return for receiving medals, epaulettes, certificates, money, rank and guns.[132]

Yet, while these new sheikhs may well have served as conduits to money and power, they could not replace the 'authentic' general sheikhs who were well known to their tribesmen and among their own communities. Sheikh Jabbar al-Assad explained, 'Every tribe in Iraq knows its sheikh. Some of the Nineties Sheikhs were known as social faces but not as sheikhs.'[133] Sheikh Jawad al-Assad meanwhile described the Nineties Sheikhs as 'bubbles' who emerged, became sheikhs for a certain period but later disappeared because the general sheikh of the tribe would not accept them, noting, 'The dwarf sheikh appeared for a while and then disappeared, but the general sheikh remained.'[134] While not necessarily recognised by the regime, the general sheikhs maintained status and could still elicit loyalty from their tribesmen. Harling is incorrect to assert that during this period, the sheikh's clout was conditioned only on absolute loyalty to the regime's core interests rather than the traditional sources of their authority or more recent power bases.[135] The picture was far more complex and nuanced, with competing sheikhs taking recognition and status from different sources.

Through this policy of subjugation Saddam succeeded nevertheless in weakening the tribe. Sheikh Mansour al-Tamimi commented, 'Saddam destroyed the tribes in the 1990s because he brought ordinary people and made them sheikhs who were loyal to him. He

TRIBES AND THE STATE IN LIBYA AND IRAQ

ignored the tribal codes and created conflicts inside the tribe.'[136] Thus while it looked on the surface as though Saddam was deliberately reviving tribalism and its structures, in reality, he was forcing the tribe and the sheikhs to submit to him and his regime. This wasn't neo-tribalism; it was another means of coercion and control that the Ba'athist regime foisted upon existing social structures.

7

TRIBES, OCCUPATION AND SHI'ITE IRAQ

After 2003, there was a clear vacuum in the state and the state became weak. That placed the largest responsibility ever on the shoulders of the sheikh. It was a responsibility that went beyond their [tribal] domain.

Sheikh Jabbar al-Assad[1]

The Islamists don't like the tribes. They respect the tribes and show them all the courtesy, but it is without content.

Sheikh Sami al-Majoun[2]

When coalition forces invaded Iraq in March 2003, Iraqi tribes were thrown into turmoil. While it is impossible to talk about tribes as single units capable of taking collective decisions or unified stances, in general, the tribes in the north-west of Iraq couldn't stomach regime change. Those Sunni tribes that had formed the core of the Ba'athist regime took up arms and went on to become the core of the resistance. Others took the opposite route, with some sheikhs, especially those who lived abroad, taking the side of the Americans and entering Iraq with coalition forces. Most tribes, however, were more circumspect, with many divided between clans and houses. The al-Khaza'el tribe is an illustrative example. One of the largest Shi'ite tribes in Diwaniyah, the clans responded differently to the new reality; those who had suffered heavily under the former regime tended to support the change, while those who had held important posts and

191

TRIBES AND THE STATE IN LIBYA AND IRAQ

who had now lost both their jobs and their status opposed it. Other clans 'sat in the middle' and remained neutral.[3] This is not to assert that these neutral tribes and their sheikhs didn't want change. The sheikhs may have been bound into the Ba'athist regime, but like the rest of Iraqi society, had been ground down by years of repression and dysfunctional governance. They had also been degraded by the international sanctions that had been in place since the early 1990s. As Sheikh Adnan al-Danbous remarked, 'At the time of the invasion, many sheikhs had nothing. The vast majority of them were living in real poverty.'[4] With the state and society in such decay, many sheikhs, along with their tribesmen and the population at large, felt suffocated and wanted a way out.

Yet for all that the tribes may have wanted regime change, they were reticent about the way events were unfolding. Not only do tribes prefer stability and continuity, their natural instincts are to oppose any invading power. Over the decades, Iraqi tribes had curated a narrative, which held that they were the founders of the Iraqi state, their 1920 revolt against British rule having been a pivotal moment in Iraq's road to independence. As Sheikh Mansour al-Tamimi described, 'The state was established on the 20th revolution... The body of the state is tribal. The tribes formed the Iraqi state... Iraq was born thanks to the tribes and not the other way around. We revolted against the English. Whenever the Iraqi state deviates, it returns to its origins, the tribe.'[5] The tribes saw themselves as the natural guardians of the state and as such were predisposed to resist invasion by foreign forces, regardless of these forces' objective. In addition, for all that the tribes may not have liked the Saddam regime, they were fearful of what might replace it. Having been so deeply intertwined with the Ba'athist state, the sheikhs and their tribesmen feared that the regime's departure would unleash a cycle of vengeance, and that they would be vulnerable to retribution and retaliation. Some sheikhs were so afraid of what was to come that they abandoned their sheikhdoms and handed them over to their sons or relatives.

Despite the bloodletting and chaos that enveloped the country after 2003, the aftermath of the regime's toppling saw the tribes propelled to the fore. In the disorder that accompanied the regime's

192

TRIBES, OCCUPATION AND SHI'ITE IRAQ

downfall, the tribes moved to centre stage and began exercising tribal agency in ways previously unseen. The collapse of the state did not leave the sheikhs 'helpless',[6] but instead provided them with space to try to assert their authority in new ways. The tribes not only began running and securing their local areas, providing protection for utilities and strategic installations, and in some areas establishing councils to keep the peace, they also saw an opportunity to recover a political role. Ever since the overturning of the monarchy in 1958, the sheikhs had lost political power, their connection to the polity having been transformed into the role of client. With the power vacuum that now opened up, the sheikhs moved to assert themselves politically both at the local and national levels. To this end, they began organising tribal conferences, issuing political statements and writing bylaws, all very 'strange measures' for what were social units of organisation to take, the tribe suddenly taking on the aspect of a political party.[7]

For the first time in decades, it looked as though the tribe was going to be a major player in the new Iraq. It may be tempting to argue, as some scholars have done, that the emergence of the tribe at this time can be accounted for by the weakness of the state.[8] Yet such a well-worn paradigm is overly simplistic. This binary view of the weak state-strong tribe relationship doesn't account for the fact that the Iraqi state was weak during the 1990s, yet the tribes were weak too. Saddam may have encouraged certain aspects of tribal pageantry and may have created new sheikhs in order to compensate for state weakness, but this did not translate into a strengthening of the tribe. Rather, the opposite occurred, and tribes were arguably weaker by the time 2003 came around than they were when the Ba'athists took power. After 2003, the tribes filled the vacuum that was left when the regime disappeared not because they were suddenly 'strong', but because, with the army, security forces and administration dissolved, they were the only organised social force able to step in. The tribes wanted to recover from the clientelistic relationship that had characterised republican rule and to become participants in the new Iraq. They also considered themselves to be the only force that was capable of uniting the country politically. Ethno-sectarian divisions were already coming to fore, as the various political factions—especially those opposition groups who were returning from abroad—adopted

193

TRIBES AND THE STATE IN LIBYA AND IRAQ

communal narratives as a means of positioning themselves in the new Iraq. Moreover, the Americans appeared to view the country through a neat, but erroneous prism of a Kurdish north, Shi'ite south, and Sunni centre, and were also making it clear that the majority Shi'ite population would be the dominant power in the new political configuration. The de-Ba'athification exercise that began within weeks of the regime's downfall was made to fit partisan ambitions and sectarian narratives rather than the requirements of state-formation and transitional justice.[9] With the direction of political travel clear, the tribes, which cut across sect and aspired to national unity, believed it was their role to prevent the country from falling apart.

More importantly perhaps, for the tribes this was an opportunity to assert themselves without the patronage of a larger power. Some scholars have argued that the tribes immediately sought a sponsor to replace the old regime, asserting that they wanted recognition from the Coalition Provisional Authority (CPA), this serving as 'compensation for their former sponsor who revived them and then disappeared'.[10] The idea of their 'floating around in a political vacuum' looking for a pole to which they could attach themselves in order to access the spoils is misplaced and risks caricaturing the tribes as if they hadn't moved on and were still stuck in some sort of archetypal Bedouin existence. Rather than seeking a new patron, some tribes wanted to assert themselves independently of any larger force, including the US and British occupiers. This is not to deny that like any other component of society, they were out for what they could get. Many individual sheikhs and heads of clans certainly made the most of the opportunity to reap what they could sow from the sudden opening up and the inflows of money and contracts that accompanied it. However, the tribes' primary interest at this point was to become a power in their own right.

The tribes' attempt at asserting themselves as a political force proved short lived, and the tribes soon found that not only was it impossible for them to unite and become a coherent force, but that there were other, stronger powers able to outmanoeuvre them. As Iraq's troubled transition unfolded, the tribes were overtaken by a host of components and competing forces, including the Americans, the political Islamist parties, militias and extremist groups. Some of

TRIBES, OCCUPATION AND SHI'ITE IRAQ

these elements, especially the Shi'ite political parties that took control of the state, tried to force the tribes back into the role of client. In the atomised landscape that characterised post-Saddam Iraq, there were now many masters, all competing with each other to try to simultaneously subdue and win over the tribes. Indeed, new relationships emerged and a new bargain was struck between ruler and ruled in which the latter was to play a more visible and more active role.

After the Fall

The collapse of the Iraqi state in 2003 created a gaping power vacuum, triggered in no small part by the expansive nature of the CPA's efforts to dismantle the Ba'athist regime. As well as rushing to disband the army and the security forces, the CPA introduced its notorious de-Ba'athification orders, the first of which entered into force on 16 May 2003. These ruled that all members of the Ba'ath Party, from senior leadership to those at the rank of Udw (member), should be 'removed from their positions and banned from future employment in the public sector'.[11] State institutions began to implode as their employees were discharged and the state was stripped bare as the remnants of a party that had touched the lives of almost every family in Iraq were targeted for removal or investigation.

With these poles of regime power eliminated, the country quickly slid into chaos. Looting began on a large scale, offices and public buildings were set on fire, while militias such as the Mehdi Army and Fadhila began to spring up. These militias, which had ransacked military camps for weapons, went on the rampage, hunting down those linked to the former regime in a bid to exact revenge. The chaos prompted many tribal sheikhs to feel as though they had a responsibility to provide security for their own areas and to protect their tribesmen, including those who were part of the former regime, this being within the traditional purview of the tribe. The tribes served as a place of refuge for their members who had been Ba'athists and who now found themselves hunted down and chased by the armed groups and militias. In some areas, there was a deliberate push to go after particular tribal sheikhs who were closely entwined with the regime. In Ramadi for example, graffiti was daubed on the houses of some

TRIBES AND THE STATE IN LIBYA AND IRAQ

sheikhs, the words, *Shayukh Al-'asha'ir 'umala'* (the tribal sheikhs are collaborators) being one such example.[12] The tribes stepped in therefore to protect their own.

Tribes also took on the role of security providers for their own areas. As Iraqi academic Dr Falah al-Zuhairi has described, 'Based on their feeling of responsibility, the Iraqi tribes started moving to fill the security vacuum that had opened up with the collapse of the state. The first act they did was to protect state properties from thieves and vandals. They protected many schools, health centres and other institutions especially in districts and sub-districts.'[13] Many sheikhs expressed this sense of duty. Sheikh al-Danbous explained, '[CPA head] Paul Bremer pushed Iraq into a dark ravine when he decided to dissolve the army, the police, state institutions. The state collapsed. When that happened, the tribes and their tribesmen rushed to protect the state as much as they could.'[14] He continued, 'After 2003 the tribe and clans played a major role in maintaining the security of Iraq. They kept the towns and state buildings running as best they could. In Sadr City in Baghdad, the sheikhs and their tribes protected schools, hospitals, electricity cables. This was also true in Kut, Amarah, Basra, Diwaniyah and everywhere else.'[15] Likewise, Adel Shirshab, former antiquities minister, whose father was sheikh of the Bidour tribe, commented, 'After 9 April 2003, the tribes moved and started protecting their areas.'[16] In a similar vein, Sheikh Ahmed Salal Abdulaziz al-Badri, the head of the al-Badri tribe and an MP, recalled, 'The tribes played a major role in maintaining society [after 2003]. As a result of the invasion and the collapse of the security situation, the tribe took the initiative and played a major role in stopping the bloodshed and resolved so many problems.'[17] The same was true of the Sunni areas. Sheikh Hamid Showka of the Budiab tribe, one of the most important of the Dulaim tribes, described, 'It was the Anbar tribes that protected the state and the people after 2003.'[18] While some of these comments may well represent a self-reflexive view of events, the sheikhs certainly felt as though they had a duty to protect their local areas and communities and to serve as a moderating force, even when that meant engaging in duties that would normally be beyond their responsibility. Sheikh Jabbar al-Assad from Basra observed, 'After 2003, there was a clear vacuum in the state and the state became weak. That placed the largest responsibility ever on the shoulders of the sheikh. It was a responsibility that went beyond their [tribal] domain.'[19]

Tribes in some areas, however, took it upon themselves to resist the occupying forces. Many Sunni tribes that had formed the core of the regime began organising to try to counter the invading forces and to prevent them from entering their territory. Sheikh Mazhar Kharbit, a prominent sheikh in Anbar, was proactive in this respect. He described how US forces had called on two officers from the Iraqi army to sign control of Anbar over to them, promising that this would be the way to avoid US forces entering the governorate.[20] The sheikh recalled, 'We, as sheikhs of Anbar, convinced these two military officers to sign that document but after it was signed, six American Hammerhead tanks entered Ramadi. When they entered, the young put these tanks under siege and fighting ensued.'[21] US military personnel met with the sheikhs but now insisted that they needed to enter Anbar. This prompted all but two sheikhs in Anbar to agree to the announcing of a resistance front on 18 April 2003. Some of the tribes in these Sunni areas engaged directly in the fighting. The Zobah tribe for example set up the 20th Revolution Brigade, while others such as the Bu Nimmer in Anbar or the Jubour in Salehedinne, provided logistical support.[22]

Many sheikhs saw 2003 as an opportunity to re-establish some sort of political role and to regain their status. They wanted to retrieve a role that would enable them to be partners rather than servants or clients of the state. In June 2003, Sheikh Ra'ad Ouda al-Hamdani proclaimed, 'History did not die; the tribes and notables who emerged in 1920 and created our modern state in 1921 are here to stay with all the others who came into being thereafter.'[23] The most natural arena for the tribes to engage was at the local level. A number of sheikhs took up local governance posts almost immediately, often appointed in conjunction with the Americans, who had earmarked particular individuals for certain jobs. These individuals were largely sheikhs known for their opposition to the Ba'athist regime, many of them having resided outside the country for years. Sheikh Sami al-Majoun recounted how, returning to Iraq to attend a CPA-organised conference in Nasseriyah on 15 April 2003, a US

TRIBES AND THE STATE IN LIBYA AND IRAQ

commander came to his mudheef and told him that the Americans wanted him to be made governor of Muthanna.[24] Sheikh al-Majoun initially refused the Americans' request, but was subsequently persuaded to take on the role of civil ruler of the governorate. Sheikh Ali al-Minshed was made governor of Dhi Qar, a move that was not supported by a large section of his tribe,[25] while Sheikh Wael Abdullatif of the Shirsha tribes became governor of Basra. Sheikh Hussein Ali al-Sha'alan, the general sheikh of the al-Khaza'el tribes, who had played a leading role in the 1991 uprising, became head of the governorate council in Diwaniyah in September 2003, while his cousin, Hazem al-Sha'alan, was appointed by the CPA as governor of Diwaniyah, something other clans reportedly opposed on the grounds that he wasn't the general sheikh of the tribe.[26] The appointment of tribal sheikhs to local governance structures was replete with pitfalls, as the sheikhs and clans squabbled over who should get what. CPA Deputy Governorate Co-ordinator in Meesan Rory Stewart describes vivdly the difficulties of deciding which sheikhs should be appointed to the seven places that had been allocated for the tribes on the Meesan Provincial Council, with different sheikhs and heads of clans demanding that they rather than their cousins be appointed, recounting, 'I had four people in a day deisgareeing about the paramount sheikhs and there was no reason for one tribe to vote for another tribe, and no formula for weighing the big tribes against the small tribes.'[27]

Yet, the sheikhs did not want to be confined to the realm of the local. They envisaged a national role both for themselves and for their tribes and to this end, they set about trying to bring the tribes together under a single umbrella. Their efforts reflected the belief of some activist sheikhs that the tribes could serve as a force to unite the country at a time of sharpening sectarian and ethnic divisions. The emergent political discourse was already being shaped along communal lines, reflecting the fact that the political parties that had spent the previous decades in exile and that were now returning to Iraq were mainly delineated along sectarian lines. These parties were mainly Islamist, most of them Shi'ite and with close ties to Iran, while the Kurdish parties that had been pushing for liberation for decades saw 2003 as an opportunity to push their nationalist demands. Some tribal

TRIBES, OCCUPATION AND SHI'ITE IRAQ

sheikhs deemed these parties to be poisoning the political scene. Sheikh Mansour al-Tamimi, who berated the parties, asserted, 'The opposition—whether Sunni, Shi'ite or Kurd—played a malicious role. The Kurds raised the temperature of nationalist feeling, while the Sunnis and the Shi'ites brought sectarianism alive. These were their goods and they promoted them in order to take hold of power.'[28] Thus there was a feeling that the county was at risk of travelling down a path of sectarian and ethnic fragmentation and conflict.

Certain sheikhs were equally aghast at the overly simplistic sectarian and ethnic prism through which the Americans were approaching rebuilding the political system. Some Sunni sheikhs were certainly fearful that they would lose out through the installation of a system based on allocation. Sheikh Mazhar Kharbit recounted how he and other sheikhs were summoned by the CPA's then Director of Governance, Ryan Crocker, who went on to become US Ambassador to Iraq.[29] According to Kharbit, Crocker told the sheikhs that the Americans had decided to give the majority of posts to the Shi'ites. When Kharbit retorted, 'If you have already decided upon that, why did you summon us?' Crocker allegedly told him, 'Don't worry! We reserved some posts for you Sunnis.' The sheikh described, 'I became really tense and left when Crocker said he would give us ministerial jobs.'[30] As this comment reflects, the sheikhs were coming to feel as though they were not being treated with sufficient respect in their own land.

In this divisive atmosphere, some sheikhs believed they could serve as a social glue to hold the country together. Sheikh Kharbit was a key proponent of this line of thinking and reached across the sectarian and ethnic divide to bring the tribes together with the aim of setting a timetable for the withdrawal of foreign forces and uniting the country. He described, 'I called the Iraqi tribes to gather and to form a council to unite the Iraqi tribes. The reason why I wanted this council for Iraqi tribes was because after the fall of the Ba'ath Party, we wanted something to unite all Iraqis, and the tribes were most important in this respect because there are historical connections that bring them together. So I brought all Iraqi tribes together.'[31] Kharbit, a Sunni, reached out to Shi'ite and Kurdish tribes and began to plan for a large tribal conference. This isn't to suggest that the tribes had

TRIBES AND THE STATE IN LIBYA AND IRAQ

ambitions of a nobler order than other actors that had moved in to try to fill the power vaccum, or that the sheikhs were any less bent on muscling in to secure their interests. The sheikhs wanted to pursue this grand coming together in order to regain power and status, as well as the benefits, including financial, that this would entail. However, unlike the political parties that were more narrowly focused and divided along communal and ideological lines, the sheikhs genuinely believed they were best placed to hold the country together at a time when it appeared to be at risk of falling apart.

Although the sheikhs that took the lead on this conference had sought to pursue the event without external assistance, once the Americans got wind of what was being planned, they asked to be involved and attended a preparatory meeting in the capacity of observers. At this meeting, which was attended by thirty tribal sheikhs, one of the most contentious issues was the date on which the conference was being planned. The sheikhs were intending for it to go ahead on 30 June 2003, this being the anniversary of the start of the 1920 tribal revolt against the British. Given the importance Iraqi tribes ascribe to this revolt and its place in forging the Iraqi state, this was a deeply symbolic date for the tribes and one of which they are particularly proud. Despite this, the Americans intervened. Sheikh Kharbit described how Crocker and Yael Lempert, a CPA Governance Officer, told them to change the date. The sheikh's anger was palpable, as he describes: 'They came to me in my office. I was sitting with the sheikh of the Zubaid tribe and with Sheikh Hussein Sha'alan and other sheikhs and Lempert said, "If you don't change the date, Bremer won't attend the conference." I told her, "If Bremer doesn't attend, we will call on Saddam Hussein to do so." The other sheikhs told me to soften my tone. I said to her, "Why do you need us to change the date?" She said that the date would irritate the British.'[32]

This kind of insensitive treatment was part of a far wider problem related to how tribes, and Iraqis more widely, perceived the way in which they were treated at the hands of CPA officials. Certain sheikhs did not take kindly to the fact that there was a US push to 'teach' the tribes democracy, including through an initiative to establish four centres for the tribes in Diwaniyah, Najaf, Karbala and al-Hillah that would run courses for sheikhs and religious scholars.[33] A number of

200

TRIBES, OCCUPATION AND SHI'ITE IRAQ

sheikhs responded to this initiative by issuing a statement demanding that people's status be respected.[34] One sheikh who had been appointed to run one of the southern governorates complained that the Americans 'believe everything they hear and are short-sighted and they came to Iraq without knowing the country'.[35] He recounted how the CPA had sent him a thirty-year-old economy graduate who had worked previously in Kenya and who wanted to draw up a constitution for the governorate. The sheikh responded positively to his suggestion but was surprised when the same individual returned soon afterwards with a written constitution already in his hand. When the sheikh asked him how he had managed to write a constitution so quickly, the young official told him it was the constitution of the state of Florida. The sheikh mocked, 'Just imagine, a representative of Bremer wants to apply the state of Florida constitution in a governorate of Iraq!'[36] Meanwhile, Ahmed Hashim has described in some detail the 'missteps' and 'boorish behaviour' displayed by American military personnel, especially in their trampling over tribal traditions and honour, and in their treatment of detainees, served to agitate tribal communities, fuelling support for the resistance.[37]

Yet, as far as the tribal conference was concerned, the sheikhs complied with Crocker and Lempert's demand and the gathering was moved to July. A host of prominent sheikhs from most of Iraq's tribes attended the event and agreed upon a broad set of goals, including that the tribe should be responsible for maintaining security and for setting a timetable to end the occupation, and that the army and security forces sould be rebuilt under tribal supervision. Some scholars have sought to belittle or dismiss these kinds of tribal gatherings, asserting that the tribal organisations and unions formed at this time were run by leaders who inflated the number of their followers and who 'typically lacked legitimacy and were challenged by their own kin'.[38] While this is true to a certain extent given the large number of gatherings that took place at this time, in this instance at least, participants included many prominent tribal sheikhs who formed the core traditional leadership of many of the country's tribes from across the sectarian divide and who could claim respect and status from their tribesmen.

Yet despite these ambitious objectives, the tribes were struggling to make their mark in an overcrowded political arena and found

TRIBES AND THE STATE IN LIBYA AND IRAQ

themselves outmanoeuvred and overtaken by other forces. There were several reasons for this. Firstly, the tribes may have adopted a discourse of national unity, but by their very nature they were not a coherent or cohesive body, having no ideological platform that could serve as a unifying dynamic. Secondly, there was still considerable distrust of the tribes and their sheikhs. Having been demonised by the discourse of successive regimes since 1958, the sheikhs were still associated in people's minds with the past, both with the period of the monarchy and with colonial rule. In the mind of the urban elite, the sheikhs were perceived as illiterate, embarrassing, criminal, powerless anachronisms who should be given no recognition.[39] They were also widely viewed as being preoccupied with going after the spoils, an image fuelled by the fact that some sheikhs and heads of clans started tripping over each other in the rush to secure contracts, including from the CPA. Although tribes still formed the bedrock of Iraqi society and while their influence extended into urban areas, they did not fit with the view of the Iraqi elite—both Islamist and secular—which considered Iraq to have moved on.

Most importantly, the tribes were no match for the political parties that had clear ideological poles around which people could gather. The Shi'ite space was filled immediately with a host of competing factions, many of which had returned from abroad. The Islamic Supreme Council of Iraq led by the prominent al-Hakim family returned from exile in Iran, as did the Islamic Dawa Party and the Fadhila Party. The Sadrists, under the leadership of cleric Moqtada al-Sadr, were more of a local product, but also succeeded in moving into the foreground, the combination of al-Sadr's firebrand anti-Americanism and the party's focus on Shi'ite identity attracting young recruits, especially among the urban Shi'ite poor. These forces were ideologically aligned with states and political forces in the regional space, giving them additional clout. This was in stark contrast to the tribal sheikhs, many of whom had been living in the closed environment of Saddam's Iraq. Some of the political parties, meanwhile, had their own militias, strengthening them further. The Islamic Supreme Council of Iraq (ISCI) had its al-Badr Brigade, while the Sadrists had the Mehdi Army and the Fadhila had its own armed force. While the sheikhs could still muster the respect of their tribesmen, they could

202

TRIBES, OCCUPATION AND SHI'ITE IRAQ

not mobilise in the same way as these ideologically driven political parties, which appeared on the scene looking ready to rule.

Furthermore, the Americans were unwilling to give the sheikhs the space they craved in the national political arena, preferring to curb their role to the local level. As Iraqi academic, Isra Alla Aldeen Nouri observed, 'The Americans didn't focus on the tribes as much as they focused on doctrinal affiliation, religious and sectarian. There was some attempt to revive the tribal factor, as it was suitable for the Iraqi situation being less divisive and with tribes spread across the country and comprising different sects, but this didn't develop.'[40] The tribes certainly felt as though the Americans were using them rather than engaging with them as partners. In fact, US officials and their coalition partners were perplexed about the extent to which they should be working with the tribes and the sheikhs. Mark Etherington, who was the CPA's administrator in Wasit governorate, described how the CPA struggled to calculate how much it should lean on the tribes, grappling with key questions: How much power did the tribes really have? How was this power to be measured? And how might it be used?[41] However, some senior US officials clearly had an ideological resistance to the idea of embracing what they perceived to be backwards forces. A US army officer who served as a strategist in Iraq explained how he had been in a meeting at which (Deputy Secretary of Defense Paul) Wolfowitz responded to the suggestion that the tribes were a powerful part of the social structure by asserting, 'This disturbs me greatly. Iraq is a cosmopolitan society.'[42] Similar views were clearly held in the CPA. A former US army intelligence officer described how their plan to strike a deal with nineteen sub-clans of the Dulaim in Anbar had been rebuffed by the CPA, noting, 'All it would have required from the CPA was formal recognition that the tribes existed... but we couldn't get the CPA to move... The standard answer we got from Bremer's people was that tribes are a vestige of the past, that they have no place in the new democratic Iraq... Eventually they paid some lip service and set up a tribal office, but it was grudging.'[43]

The US focused mainly on engaging the tribes at a low level, using them mainly for security provision. This opened the door for competition between different sheikhs and clans as they rushed to secure contracts. This doling out of contracts by the CPA and foreign com-

203

TRIBES AND THE STATE IN LIBYA AND IRAQ

panies enabled certain families and clans to either build on their existing wealth or to create new wealth. Families such as the al-Bunnia, al-Janabi, al-Kubaseen and al-Hateen for example were able almost immediately to engage in lucrative contracts with the CPA and international companies in return for providing security in the energy sector.[44] In the electricity field, KEC International, which had a US$150 million contract for transmission work in the northern and southern regions of Iraq, contracted with local tribes to provide security and prevent sabotage.[45] Thus the CPA tied them back into the role of client. In this way, the CPA ended up creating what some have described as the 'Sheikhs of the Millennium', or the '4x4 Sheikhs', namely those individuals or would-be sheikhs who went to the CPA cap in hand to secure what they could for themselves and their relatives. This policy did not sit well with some of the traditional sheikhs and tribal leaders, who saw in it a deliberate attempt by the US to play the tribes. Sheikh Hamid Showka, the sheikh of the Budiab tribe, one of the largest of the Dulaim tribes and also head of the Anbar sheikhs' council, observed, 'When the Americans came, they tried to create replacement sheikhs. They started coming to these weak souls. They came and said they wanted to build a school and they would sign with a contractor for 750,000 dollars. They would give the individual 250,000 and put the rest in their own pockets. That individual takes the money and goes and paints a building, then he sets up a mudheef and calls himself sheikh'.[46] In an apparent replication of what had occurred during the 1990s, many individuals who had managed to make some money out of regime change set themselves up as sheikhs, this being their way to status and influence.

The US also used the sheikhs as monitors in their counter-insurgency efforts. The CPA's Special Assistant for Tribal Affairs, Lieutenant Colonel Alan King, explained in December 2003, 'The idea is not to build controlling little warlords, but to use the information that the sheikhs have to benefit the country.'[47] In this role, King was tasked with identifying prominent sheikhs who could assist US troops in peacekeeping but also in hunting down insurgents and former high-ranking Ba'athists. The *Christian Science Monitor* reported, 'King has asked them [tribal sheikhs] for help in finding insurgents and former Ba'athist bigwigs. So far, tips from sheikhs have helped King capture

204

TRIBES, OCCUPATION AND SHI'ITE IRAQ

numbers 23, 62, 85, 91, 97, and 99 on the US military's Most Wanted list, as well as other miscellaneous evildoers.'[48] Once again, the tribes were relegated to a local role and asked to act as 'eyes.'

This is not to deny that certain tribal sheikhs were given posts in the first government that was appointed after sovereignty was partly handed over to Iraq in June 2004. This government included Sheikh Adnan Janabi of the Janabi tribe, as a minister of state; Sheikh Malek al-Hassan from the Jubour tribe as justice minister; and Laila Abdulateef from the Bani Tamim as labour minister. However, these individuals were not chosen because of their positions in their tribes, but rather because of their professional capabilities.[49] They were not in post as representatives of their tribes either. A more overtly tribal appointment was that of Sheikh Ghazi al-Yawar, who became president of Iraq in June 2004. A sheikh of the powerful Shammar tribe—although not the tribe's general sheikh—al-Yawar was born in Nineveh but had spent most of his life abroad including in Saudi Arabia, where he ran a successful communications company. Although he had the support of the Americans and while his appointment may have been in part to appease the Shammar,[50] al-Yawar was little known to most Iraqis and could not be described as a tribal heavyweight. This handful of so-called tribal appointments certainly didn't amount to any sense for the tribes that they had any real agency or ability to shape Iraq's future.

This sense of being outside the main action was further confirmed in the January 2005 elections to the National Assembly, a body that was meant was to supervise the constitution-writing process and serve as an interim legislative body until the new constitution came into effect. Despite several tribal blocs contesting these polls, they fared badly. The Democratic Assembly of Iraqi Tribes failed to take any seats, as did the Islamic Conference for the Tribes of Iraq, the Council of the United Tribes of Mosul, the National League of Iraqi Sheikhs–National Tribes Organisation, and the Assembly of Grandsons of the Ashreen Revolution. These tribal blocs could not even begin to compete wtih the Shi'ite Islamist parties or with the Kurds, the Sunnis having boycotted the polls. This did not mean that there was no tribal presence in the National Assembly, as some sheikhs had thrown in their lot with these parties and had won seats

205

TRIBES AND THE STATE IN LIBYA AND IRAQ

as candidates of these coalitions, but the results were further evidence to the tribes of their irrelevance in the emerging political scene. However, if there was one episode that revealed to the tribes their place in the political pecking order, it was the constitution-writing process. The constitution was drawn up by a drafting committee comprising fifty-five members of the National Assembly. Reflecting the composition of the Assembly, this committee was heavily dominated by members of the Shi'ite religious parties and the Kurds.[51] Some of the sheikhs who had been elected to the National Assembly through the coalitions saw the constitution-writing process as an opportunity to reassert the political role and enshrine the statues of the tribes in law. Among them was Sheikh Sami al-Majoun, who had been elected to the National Assembly as part of the United Iraqi Alliance and who described, 'I was a member of the constitution committee and I told the sheikhs, "I want to revive the status of the tribes through the constitution. I will write a text that will give you back your rights and will consolidate your importance inside your tribes."'[52] The sheikhs were supportive of this ambition and once the draft text had been drawn up, Sheikh al-Majoun showed it to them. He explained, 'There were three articles, including one to compensate the sheikhs for the land that was taken away from them under agricultural reform laws. I told them that this would give power back to the leading tribal houses and that they would regain their psychological status. They agreed with me and we swore on the Qu'ran that we would push for these articles to be included in the constitution and if they were not accepted, we would boycott the political process. These forty-five sheikhs signed and took the oath and went on television and announced to the media that we had agreed on these articles and would do our best to implement them.'[53] Sheikh al-Majoun then went to Grand Ayatollah Ali al-Sistani to canvas his support on the issue.

Yet, these articles were never to see the light of day. A huge debate erupted within the constitution committee about a series of contested issues, including the role of the tribe. The Islamist parties, being ideologically disposed to tribes, did not want to give the tribes any more space. Thus, in the final part of the drafting process in which a six-member committee comprising senior political figures that supervised the process settled on the final text, most of what Sheikh al-Majoun had drawn up was ditched. As he commented, 'They emptied the content out of what we had written and they returned it to us to sign. They changed everything, not just about the tribes. The word "tribe" is there but it has no meat to it. They told us, this is the *Marja'iya*'s constitution. I disputed that but the Islamists insisted that the *Marja'iya* had agreed to it and we had to sign it.'[54] The final wording relating to the tribes was lukewarm at best; the second clause of article 45 states, 'The State shall seek the advancement of the Iraqi clans and tribes, shall attend to their affairs in a manner that is consistent with religion and the law, and shall uphold their noble human values in a way that contributes to the development of society. The State shall prohibit the tribal traditions that are in contradiction with human rights.'

This was not a victory for the tribes therefore, and the sheikhs came to the realisation that they were not going to be able to exercise agency at the national level in the way they had desired. They had neither the cohesion nor the political muscle to be able to impose themselves, and Islamism in its various permutations took over. The tribes and sheikhs were dwarfed, and were left with little option but to work within this new reality and to find a way to coexist with and alongside these Islamist parties that had filled the political arena and that, thanks to the support of their armed militias, were entrenching themselves at every level.

Tribes under Maliki

The adoption of the constitution following its approval in a national referendum on 15 October 2005 opened the way for Iraq to go to the polls. Although the Sunnis did not boycott the parliamentary elections that took place on 15 December, the vote threw up another overwhelming victory for the Shi'ite parties. The United Iraqi Alliance—the main Shi'ite bloc—won 128 out of 275 seats and over 41 per cent of the vote. The Democratic Patriotic Alliance of Kurdistan came second, taking 53 seats, while the Iraqi Accord Front, a Sunni coalition created by the Iraqi Islamic Party (the Iraqi branch of the Muslim Brotherhood), came third with 44 seats. Once again, the tribes were notable by their absence. This didn't mean that sheikhs or tribal figures weren't elected to the parliament; many had stood on party lists, this being the surest way to win a seat given the adoption of a list-based electoral system.

Following its victory, the United Iraqi Alliance set about choosing a prime minister. This proved challenging as the two main components in the alliance—the Sadrists and the Islamic Supreme Council of Iraq (ISCI)—refused to yield control of the executive to the other. A compromise candidate was finally agreed and Nouri Maliki, the head of the Islamic Dawa party, which had only won 12 of the alliance's 148 seats, was appointed. The Dawa Party was an elitist party whose membership comprised a small section of the urban elite, most of whom returned to Iraq from Iran after 2003. Maliki started his tenure as a weak figure, caught between competing and powerful components within his own bloc. His job was made even harder by the enormity of the challenges facing the country when he took power. If the immediate aftermath of the toppling of the Ba'athist regime was filled with chaos, by the mid-2000s, the situation had become significantly worse. The sectarianism that had surfaced partly as a result of the way in which regime change had been managed, was now fully unbridled, and the country was sliding into full-scale sectarian conflict. Militias and Islamist groups, many linked to the ruling parties, were running amok in the main urban centres and had started to engage in what amounted to ethnic cleansing campaigns, with whole neighbourhoods of Baghdad now delineated along Sunni or Shi'ite lines as terrified residents were hounded out of their neighbourhoods. In May 2006, the month when Maliki took power, the Iraqi government was reporting some 3,000 violent attacks a month.[55] The militias began to have the upper hand and the country was engulfed in violence.

Maliki's most pressing challenge when he took power was to get a grip on security, and just one day after naming his cabinet, he held meetings with US government and military heavyweights vowing to use 'maximum force against terrorists and criminals'.[56] One of the most pressing concerns in this respect was the insurgency that had taken hold in the Sunni areas. It was here that al-Qaeda, along with other Sunni militant groups, was gaining ground. Al-Qaeda had implanted itself in Iraq as early as 2003, but under the leadership of

TRIBES, OCCUPATION AND SHI'ITE IRAQ

Jordanian-Palestinian Abu Musab al-Zarqawi, had expanded its presence, particularly in Anbar. Part of the group's appeal lay in its ability to tap into the grievances felt by some Sunni elements, including some Sunni tribes. These tribes had not recovered from the CPA's insistence on dismantling the former regime's army and security apparatus, which they had populated. The complete undoing of these forces had undercut these tribes' economic power, as well as their status. Their sudden disenfranchisement in 2003 rendered them impotent and left them feeling incriminated for the former regime's reliance on Sunni kinship networks. These Sunni tribes also viewed the sudden ascendance to power of Shi'ite Islamist parties with alarm. They viewed these parties as little more than extensions of Iran, and believed the US was deliberately facilitating their dominance in order to emasculate the Sunnis.

With disaffection running high, some of these Sunni tribal elements proved a willing pool of recruits for al-Qaeda that swelled its ranks with young tribesmen from these areas. As one of al-Zarqawi's lieutenants, Abu Jafar al-Ansari, noted, 'Everyone should know that the tribesmen of Anbar are the backbone of the jihad.'[57] This doesn't mean that al-Qaeda found it easy to implant itself in these traditional tribal areas. Tribes thrive on flexibility and accommodation, and some could not abide al-Qaeda's strict puritanical outlook or its brutality, let alone the fact that it was a 'foreign' entity with a foreign ideology. Indeed, tribes reflect the interests of local society and local culture, whether economic, social or political, and their cultural values run contrary to the ideological purism of the '*Takfiri* man'.[58] The adoption and implementation by al-Qaeda of such a literal interpretation of Islamic sharia was far removed from their own way of thinking and being. Aware of these challenges, al-Qaeda deliberately targeted disenfranchised young local elements, impressing upon them the un-Islamic nature of the tribal system.[59] Sheikh Ali al-Hatem of the Dulaim tribes referred to those who joined the group in particularly disparaging terms, describing them as 'riffraff' and 'low-lifes', condemning how al-Qaeda 'bought them and raised them up to the rank of Emir… A homeless man, wandering the streets, and now he has become an Emir!!'[60] This is not to deny the fact that some sheikhs either supported the insurgency or were will-

TRIBES AND THE STATE IN LIBYA AND IRAQ

ing to send their sons to join it. However, many of al-Qaeda's foot-soldiers were from the lower echelons.

Some scholars have framed the willingness of these recruits to join al-Qaeda as evidence of an internal 'class war' within the tribes. Harking back to the old trope of the greedy sheikhly landlord exploiting his peasant tribesmen, some commentators have suggested that disenfranchised tribesmen joined al-Qaeda because they saw an opportunity for social mobility and for retribution against senior tribal elements who mistreated them in the past.[61] Characterising the struggle for local control that unfolded in Anbar in this way is somewhat contrived. Al-Qaeda may well have recruited from the lower rungs of society, but these tribesmen did not join in order to exact revenge upon their sheikhs or to turn tribal hierarchy on its head. Joining al-Qaeda was more of an opportunistic move by young marginalised elements who had been won over by ideological conviction and who desperately needed money and status. As Sheikh al-Hatem also observed, the sons of the tribes joined al-Qaeda for 'a simple reason… unemployment'.[62] He continued, 'There was no work. Neither the Americans nor the government were providing us with jobs.'[63] Thus while it is possible that some individual elements may have used al-Qaeda as a vehicle to take revenge against certain elements in the local hierarchy, for most this was a desperate solution to a desperate situation.

Yet while al-Qaeda was able to attract recruits, there were limits to what it could achieve, and many tribal sheikhs became increasingly hostile towards the group, resenting its attempts to impose itself and its ideology on the local population. These sheikhs also resented al-Qaeda's willingness to kill those who stood in its way, including tribal sheikhs. While tribes have their own codes of behaviour and often brutal vengeance traditions, one of their main functions is to mediate and to settle disputes in order to avert further bloodshed. Al-Qaeda's insistence on punishing or killing for minor infractions was anathema to the tribes, while its killing of sheikhs unleashed bloody cycles of revenge. The sheikhs did not like being told how to practise their religion either. Sheikh Hamid al-Heiss remarked, 'We are Muslims. We know our religion and we have a solid moral structure that was formed according to authentic Iraqi traditions. We don't need politi-

210

TRIBES, OCCUPATION AND SHI'ITE IRAQ

cal clerics to control all aspects of life… The intervention of religion in political matters corrupts both.'[64] The tribes also recoiled at the way in which al-Qaeda trampled on tribal traditions and values. This included its insistence on forcing families in the area to provide brides for its fighters. Tribes generally prefer their women to marry within their own tribe, and the Sunni tribes of Anbar were particularly conservative in this respect. Being forced to hand over their women to these so-called 'guests' was particularly troubling and violated local traditions. While some sheikhs in Anbar had been willing to give space to al-Qaeda initially in order to fight against the occupying forces, they resented its efforts to dominate. Sheikh Ali al-Hatem described, 'The jihadists ignored the enemy and instead held us in a stranglehold. They started slaughtering our sons. They cut Anbar off from Iraq and instead of raising the flag of Iraq they raised a flag of what they called the Islamic State. We Iraqi tribes rejected that.'[65] Sheikh al-Hatem also summed up the desperation of the tribes at the time, describing, 'We have land and dignity and we needed to protect that… We despaired that no one would come to protect us. No tank came to protect us. Things went to the abyss so the tribe had to do something. There was nothing protecting us. We had men and we had weapons and we waited for someone to come and free our necks from this tragedy. And no one came.'[66]

Some tribes started to fight back and their doing so caught the attention of the US administration, where attitudes towards tribal engagement were shifting. There was a growing realisation among US policymakers that their initial sidelining of the Sunni sheikhs had been misguided and that these tribes could be instrumentalised in the fight against al-Qaeda.[67] The US began to focus its attention on trying to engage the Sunni tribes in the fight to drive out al-Qaeda. Some of the tribes were receptive and proved willing to work with US forces. In early 2005, several sheikhs from the Albu Mahal tribe around Qaim, a small town next to the Syrian border, co-operated with US troops to drive al-Qaeda out of its territory.[68] This co-ordination increased with the arrival in Iraq of General David Petraeus, who took command of US troops in 2006. Petraeus recognised the importance of the tribal context and brought in anthropologists, who were integrated on the ground and imbedded into combat units. This proved

211

TRIBES AND THE STATE IN LIBYA AND IRAQ

highly controversial and generated major debate in academia about the morals of using academic staff to support military missions.[69] Nevertheless, the US formalised its tribal engagement through Sahwat, or Awakening Councils, providing these councils with financial resources, weapons and support. Much has been written about these Sahwat and their relationship to the US and it is not the intention of this book to go over the same ground. However, the tribes clearly saw this relationship with the US as an opportunity to put an end to what Jabar describes as 'the insult of the guest having become the master'.[70]

The tribes' willingness to work with the US in this way elicited commentary denigrating the tribes for being 'mere opportunists', whose loyalty could be bought by the highest bidder.[71] There is undoubtedly some truth in these allegations; tribes are no less opportunistic or focused on securing their interests than other components, while tribes also have a habit of attaching themselves to the strongest pole. Yet, such characterisations oversimplify the issue and diminish the extremity of the situation in which the tribes found themselves. It is problematic to characterise the Sahwat as if their primary purpose was to benefit from being 'bought'. Their decision to work with the US was driven by the real and pressing need to regain control of their own territory and to eject a force that had become an intolerable burden. As Sheikh Ali al-Hatem described, 'Local resistance [against al-Qaeda] emerged in order to ensure a stable and secure life. The Awakening Councils... took it upon themselves to confront al-Qaeda, which had taken control of and darkened every aspect of life in Anbar.'[72] Sheikh Ali al-Hatem also remarked, 'We didn't want chaos in the name of jihad... one could no longer distinguish between honest resistance and jihad. So we took up our role as tribes.'[73] The tribes' only hope at this time was to look to the Americans, especially as they knew they were not going to get help from the Shi'ite-dominated government. Mistrust between the Shi'ite parties and the Sunni tribal sheikhs was running high, and it was evident that the Maliki-led government had neither the ability nor the desire to arm or fund them. Thus partnering with the Americans was the surest way to achieve their objectives, and although militant Sunni groups were to flourish in these areas again, the success of the Sahwat in defeating

TRIBES, OCCUPATION AND SHI'ITE IRAQ

al-Qaeda was striking, and by mid-2007 insurgent hotbeds such as Ramadi and Fallujah had been 'cleansed and relatively pacified, to the surprise of the most sceptical'.[74]

Engaging the Tribes in the South

The success of the Sahwat in Anbar served as a major boost to Maliki and encouraged him to look to the Shi'ite tribes as a means of securing the southern governorates. This included in Basra, where the security situation had become critical. In 2007, British troops, who had long been coming under attack by insurgents, had transferred control of Basra province to the Iraqi authorities, and began to withdraw from the centre of the city. If security was poor before their departure, it deteriorated further once these forces had pulled out. Militia forces including the Mehdi Army and the al-Badr Brigades, which had been able to infiltrate the political establishment through their ties to senior political figures, were running riot. Assassinations, kidnappings and clashes had become a daily occurrence, while rival militias and criminal gangs vied for control of Basra's infrastructure and resources. Sheikh Mansour al-Tamimi from Basra described how the official security apparatus in Basra was 'broken', commenting, 'Two armed militia men could go to a police station of 200 police officers and terrorise them and take over the police station'.[75] The Mehdi Army and the al-Badr Brigades were also using their control of the public space to enforce their strict interpretation of sharia on the local population, while the economic situation for ordinary citizens was worsening. Basra residents may have welcomed the downfall of the Ba'athist regime, but they were becoming increasingly frustrated at the hand they had been dealt since its toppling. As one Basra resident bemoaned, 'Electricity is absent for most of the day and gasoline is very expensive. Ordinary people can never get a job at the state security forces because it is entirely controlled by the militias. People think those who used to live abroad came and controlled everything while the common citizens still cannot get basic life needs'.[76]

Maliki, who had criticised the British army's handling of security in the city since 2003, realised he needed to get a handle on the situation and impose his authority over both Basra and Iraq. The need was

TRIBES AND THE STATE IN LIBYA AND IRAQ

all the more pressing because some Shi'ite powers were calling for Basra to become a region in its own right. The head of the ISCI, Abdulaziz al-Hakim, and his son Ammar al-Hakim, who took over the party in 2009, as well as the head of the al-Badr Organisation, Hadi al-Ameri, had all mooted the idea of creating an autonomous region in the south and the federal solution was gaining some traction among these currents. Maliki needed to do something impactful that would pull the southern governorates under his control. On the morning of 25 March 2008, the prime minister launched Operation Saulat al-Fursan (Charge of the Knights) in a bid to clear Basra of all militia and criminal forces. Maliki dispatched Iraqi security forces to Basra, where they were to carry out a grand purge of the city, forcing out all militia elements but particularly those linked to the Mehdi Army, which had become especially powerful.

These mostly inexperienced forces met with heavy resistance and fighting spread quickly from neighbourhood to neighbourhood. It was becoming increasingly evident that these units were not capable of turning the tide against the militias. The operation was hampered further by mass desertion, with around 1,000 members of the army and police fleeing or refusing to fight, some of them having been instructed to do so by militia elements that had infiltrated the security apparatus.[77] With the situation becoming increasingly desperate, Maliki sent in reinforcements, dispatching more Iraqi security forces to the city. Critically, he also turned to the southern tribes for help.

The tribes were not natural bedfellows for Maliki. Like other political Islamist parties, the Dawa Party had been formed as a response to modernisation and secularisation, and it saw Islam as the ultimate unifying force. Its ideological outlook was dismissive of tribes and tribalism as divisive and antithetical to the aspiration to the Ummah (one Islamist nation). Sheikh Mohamed Zeidawi from the Bu Zeid tribe in Basra noted how these political parties look at the tribes as 'backwards entities'.[78] Maliki clearly embodied this way of thinking. Sheikh al-Majoun recalled sitting next to Maliki during an Iraqi opposition conference in Beirut in 1991, 'He was an effendi [an educated man]. He was wearing a jacket and glasses and was very young. I didn't know him. We talked about tribes and their history. He said, "There are no tribes in Iraq", and he started attacking the tribes in a big way. I learned later that his name was Nouri Maliki and he was a representative of the Dawa Party.'[79] Sheikh al-Majoun explained that in 2006, he reminded Maliki of what he had said in Beirut and asked him whether his view of the tribe had changed, to which Maliki replied that it had. However, al-Majoun commented, 'The Islamists don't like the tribes. They respect the tribes and show them all the courtesy, but it is without content.'[80]

Whatever his view of the tribe, Maliki could see that the southern tribes could serve as one of the keys to bringing Basra under his control and he was pragmatic enough to use them. Sheikh Adnan al-Danbous of the Kenana tribe was correct to note, 'Political Islamists don't like tribes. They are against them in their discourse but ironically, they are keen on using them.'[81] Maliki engaged with tribal sheikhs in the south and centre therefore and agreed for tribal forces to be established and armed, calling on tribal leaders to form armed auxiliaries to the Iraqi Security Forces.[82] These tribal forces were organised through a tribal committee that was responsible for nominating and approving tribal recruits and pressurising tribal members linked to the Mehdi Army to lay down their weapons. The committee was effectively led by Sheikh Muazhem al-Tamimi, the sheikh of the large and influential Bani Tamim tribe, but also comprised other prominent sheikhs from the most important Basra tribes.[83]

In general, the tribes of Basra responded positively to these overtures, viewing this initiative as an opportunity. Many tribes and sheikhs had found themselves increasingly sidelined by the militias and the Shi'ite political parties that these militias were linked to. The tribes had found themselves dwarfed by these forces who had weaponry and Iranian backing. Sheikh Wael Abdullatif, a judge, who was appointed as the first post-2003 governor of Basra, expressed this sense of being eclipsed, 'Basra was the first province in Iraq to organise local elections. The British worked well, they met with local sheikhs and attended their tribal councils. When I asked their military for a bridge, they built it in one month… They, the Iranians, worked against us from day one, directly or through their Islamic parties that dominated the city council. Every time I wanted to start a major project or bring investment to the city, the council members would hamper all my efforts and block any new project.'[84] Other tribal lead-

TRIBES AND THE STATE IN LIBYA AND IRAQ

ers felt sidelined by the militias but equally ignored by the British, who they accused of considering them to be irrelevant.[85]

These sheikhs grasped at the *Saulat al-Fursan* as a way of downsizing the militias and restoring a sense of stability and order to Basra. They were not indifferent either to the promise of financial support. More importantly, the sheikhs saw this operation as a way for their tribes to become formalised components of the state security apparatus. Many hoped and expected that the tribal battalions they established for this fight, such as the al-Qurnah Battalion that comprised mainly Bani Malik tribesmen and the Shatt al-Arab Battalion, which was mainly from the Bani Tamim, would be incorporated into the official security forces, providing the sheikhs with status as well as jobs and wages for their tribesmen. The tribes proved willing recruits therefore. In April 2008, Acting Justice Minister Safa al-Safi, who supervised the tribal engagement process, told the Iraqi media that hundreds of tribesmen, including 480 sheikhs, were supporting Iraqi forces in the Basra operation.[86] However, this operation went wider than just the tribes of Basra. Two coachloads of fighters were recruited and sent from Samawah in Muthanna to Basra. As Iraqi analyst Ammar al-Ameri described, 'At that time, people were reluctant to join the army or the police because of the chaos, the poor pay. So when they announced they needed volunteers, people went.'[87]

This tribal support proved decisive for Maliki and served as a key determinant in the campaign's success. This is not to overplay the tribes' role; other factors contributed to the curtailing of the militias in Basra as well, especially the fact that al-Sadr himself called for a ceasefire and demanded his Mehdi Army fighters hand in their weapons. Nevertheless, the tribes played an important part in the operation and helped turn it around. As Sheikh Mansour al-Tamimi described, 'The tribes supported *Saulat al-Fursan*. If it wasn't for the support of the tribes, Basra would have collapsed. I fought myself. We fought against criminals and murderers. We fought against the militias and because of the tribe, they were defeated. We agreed with the state. All of the tribes almost agreed with the state to take part with the security forces. We formed regiments. The security services were beyond the point of collapse. They were under the control and domination of the political parties. The soldier and the policeman

TRIBES, OCCUPATION AND SHI'ITE IRAQ

were frightened. That was the positive tribal act. The tribes changed the fate of the Iraqi state.'[88]

Yet despite this positive outcome, the tribes were to be bitterly disappointed. Sheikhs started to complain that their battalions were not receiving the salaries, weapons and equipment they had been promised.[89] In a meeting with US government officials at the end of June 2008, the leaders of the Shatt al-Arab Battalion, which comprised 760 tribesmen, mostly from the Bani Tamim tribe in the Shatt al-Arab district of Basra city, expressed their frustration that the government had only supplied them with 170 AK47s, 12 PK machine guns and 10 vehicles for which they received just 20 litres of petrol a day.[90] Such complaints became commonplace among these armed battalions. Furthermore, access to the US$ 100 million emergency reconstruction fund for Basra, which had also been promised when the tribes were engaged, was proving elusive. Worse for these sheikhs, it was becoming evident that there was no real political will to absorb them into the official security apparatus. On 22 May 2008, Sheikh Salam Maliki, the sheikh of the Bani Malik tribe and his brother, Sabah Maliki, complained to US policymakers at the State Department's Basra Regional Embassy Office that the Iraqi government had promised to incorporate their tribal battalions into the official security forces but that not only had this promise not been fulfilled, their tribesmen had not received salaries, equipment or weapons.[91] This was particularly disappointing to Sheikh Salam, who had met with Maliki during the first days of the *Saulat al-Fursan* and who had been promised significant support.[92] With Basra now secured, there was a clear reluctance in the government to empower tribal forces in the south, and as a result, these tribal battalions died a slow death through lack of support.

However, Maliki sought to capitalise on the success of his tribal engagement strategy, seeing in the tribes a way to build a base for himself. He began to institutionalise tribal support through the establishment of isnads, or Tribal Support Councils, which were populated by tribal sheikhs and meant to serve as a conduit between the state and the people. During the mid-2000s, these isnads were rolled out across the south and centre of the country. By October 2008, every southern governorate except Basra had at least ten functional

217

TRIBES AND THE STATE IN LIBYA AND IRAQ

isnads, comprising approximately twenty members per council.[93] Once again, the sheikhs were willing recruits. It wasn't only in Basra that the tribes had felt sidelined by more powerful militia forces; in other southern towns and cities, militias and political parties had become dominant and were acting with impunity and the sheikhs were desparate to alter the balance of power. Sheikh Takleef al-Minshed described an incident in Nasseriyah that demonstrated the extent to which these militia forces had taken hold. He recounted how two local tribes had started fighting each other after a member of one of the tribes had killed a member of the other, prompting local tribal leaders to decide that the best way to prevent further bloodshed was for the state to arrest the killer, enabling the two tribes to come together to start mediation. Sheikh Takleef described going to the police station and begging the police to arrest the perpetrator, recalling, 'I explained that if this individual wasn't arrested within the next hour or two, more blood would flow. The officer responded by saying, "I know the killer. I am from here and I know where he is and where he is hiding. But this killer has a political bloc behind him and I don't want to sacrifice myself or the life of my children [by going to arrest him].'"[94]

The tribes saw in the isnads a way to empower themselves and downsize the influence of the militias. It also appeared to be a way in which the sheikhs could revive their political role. Sheikh Jabbar al-Assad, who was elected as the head of the isnad council in Zubair in the Basra governorate, explained how he believed the purpose of the councils was to 'create a communication channel between the tribes and state institutions'.[95] He went on, 'It was an attempt to create a strong role for the sheikhs of the south and a way to give them responsibility for dealing with the offices of the state'.[96] To the sheikhs, it looked as though their role as intermediaries between the state and the people was being revived, enabling them to fortify their influence both locally and within their own tribes. In addition, there were financial benefits to be reaped. Upon formation, each council began receiving monthly payments within the range of 8 to 10 million Iraqi dinars per month, with each individual member receiving around 500,000 dinars (US$400).[97] Moreover, as Ammar al-Amiri observed, most sheikhs agreed to take part, even those who were not loyal to

TRIBES, OCCUPATION AND SHI'ITE IRAQ

Maliki, because they knew that if they turned down the invitation, their cousins would accept, and they would find themselves facing new sheikhs or new poles of influence within their own tribes.[98] Just as Saddam Hussein had brought up new sheikhs during the 1990s in an effort to weaken the traditional tribal leadership, there was a fear that, through this initiative, Maliki might try to do the same. Although not all sheikhs joined, many rushed to take part.

However, these isnads turned out not to be the passport to greater power and influence that the sheikhs had hoped. Firstly, the sheikhs soon found that their role through these councils was nowhere near as expansive as they had anticipated. Sheikh Jabbar al-Assad explained, 'The problem with this council was that it was confined to the elite and to the sheikhs and the idea didn't permeate the tribes themselves. I worked in the council. We divided up into committees—administrative committees, a dispute resolution committee and others. The only committee worth talking about was the dispute committee. Why? Because it was able to get close to the authorities. Other committees, such as the services committee, were unable to achieve anything because of the weakness of co-ordination with the relevant state bodies that looked at us or looked at our council as a hybrid formation.'[99] The sheikh also complained, 'Our role was confined to a consultative one. We had no teeth. Our function was merely to convey the people's demands to the authorities. As for solving tribal disputes, this was already our role as sheikh, so these isnad councils were useless.'[100] He went on to pinpoint the crux of the problem, 'The state didn't deal with us as if we were part of the state. It dealt with us as if we separate to it.'[101] Once again, the tribes' hopes of being partners to the state rather than subjugated to it were dashed. Secondly, it was becoming increasingly apparent that Maliki was using these isnads to build up his own support base and to strengthen his position vis-à-vis his political rivals. As a result, the Dawa Party laid an increasingly heavy hand on the councils. In Muthanna, there were twenty-four isnad councils, but they were overseen and controlled by members of the Dawa Party, who would select who should be on the council.[102] Additionally, the Dawa Party would select one sheikh on each council who would receive the money allocated to the entire council and be responsible for distributing it among its members. This left the system open to abuse.

TRIBES AND THE STATE IN LIBYA AND IRAQ

The isnads also met with resistance from inside the Shi'ite alliance. Maliki's attempt to commandeer the sheikhs for his own benefit agitated other political players, especially those in his own Shi'ite coalition. These parties were wary that Maliki was trying to craft himself a web of tribal support and that he was deliberately doing so ahead of the governorate council elections that were due in January 2009. One individual linked to the al-Badr Organisation remarked, 'Maliki tried to attract all sorts of sheikhs, both general sheikhs and others, into the isnads. The most important thing was that they had to be loyal to the Dawa Party and to Maliki personally.'[103] The ISCI was especially opposed to these isnads, not least because it had always had a presence inside the southern tribes by virtue of its strong grassroots support base in the south. In contrast to the more elitist Dawa Party that had focused its attentions on attracting the educated middle class, the ISCI had long cast its net wide and thus counted on support from inside the tribes. The ISCI was also closely associated with the *Marja'iya* through Mehsen al-Hakim, who was the *marja'* until his death in 1970, and who was the father of the ISCI's leader. Given the intertwined nature of the relationship between the tribes and the *Marja'iya*, the ISCI considered the tribes to fall within its own domain. As Ali al-Adeeb, a leading Dawa Party member commented at the time, 'The ISCI's objection to the supporting councils is because clan mobilisation is their domain. They are objecting because they fear that this role will be taken away from them and that it will be institutionalised by the state.'[104] The ISCI, along with other parties in the Shi'ite alliance, rejected what they deemed to be Maliki's attempt to woo the sheikhs and turn the tribes into partisan entities as a means of expanding the Dawa Party's support base, something that would aid it in the elections.

Maliki's efforts were hampered by his political rivals, with governorate councils and other entities that were dominated by these rival Shi'ite parties rejecting them. The Muthanna governorate council, which was controlled by the ISCI, refused the isnads along with other ISCI-led provincial councils and sought to block them. Some MPs from rival parties also tried to use the parliament to hinder them. Sheikh Jabbar al-Assad described, 'The other political parties looked at these isnad councils as if they were part of the Dawa Party and they

TRIBES, OCCUPATION AND SHI'ITE IRAQ

thought that this would make them an additional force in elections. When we were talking in the parliamentary finance committee and discussing the isnad allocation in the budget, some Islamists objected to money being allocated to them because they viewed the isnad councils as being part of a political party or a particular political body and not in the public interest.'[105]

This suspicion of the isnads was shared by some sheikhs who supported other political currents. Sheikh Hussein al-Sha'alan, an MP from Diwaniyah, who was part of Ayad Allawi's Iraqiya Alliance, said in October 2008 that he had been disappointed that the isnads—the idea of which he had supported originally—had become dominated by the Dawa Party.[106] The Kurdish parties were also unsettled by the councils, especially when Maliki tried to form them in Kirkuk and Mosul. Iraqi President Jalal Talabani criticised the policy, as did other Kurdish leaders, who feared that Maliki was trying to use the tribes to challenge Kurdish influence in both areas. They also accused Maliki of trying to replicate a force akin to the notorious Command of the National Defence Battalions, a primarily Kurdish force whose members were commonly referred to as Jhoush (mules), who worked for the regime by monitoring the Kurdish areas to root out dissent, acting as spies and guides for the Iraqi military in these areas.

Resistance to these councils notwithstanding, Mailki's efforts with the tribes paid off. When it came to provincial elections in 2009, Maliki, who stood on a separate platform to the other Shi'ite parties, swept the board. His State of Law Alliance took control of six southern governorates and came second in Karbala. This is not to suggest that Maliki's electoral victories were entirely down to tribal support—far from it. There were many other factors that enabled the State of the Law Alliance to win such a large share of the vote. Maliki's success in bringing Basra under control, in containing the worst of the violence in Baghdad, and in presiding over the Sahwat's victory in the Sunni governorates made him in the eyes of many the man who could impose order. Furthermore, his determination to push for American troop withdrawal had made him appear like someone who could stand up to the US, while he looked to many to be more independent of Iran than some of the other Shi'ite blocs. He was also proving willing to take on the Kurdish parties and to face

221

TRIBES AND THE STATE IN LIBYA AND IRAQ

down their nationalist demands. To many Iraqis, Maliki appeared to be the man of the moment and the strong, independent figure in whom the Iraqis could trust.

Yet despite all these factors, the tribes had undeniably been part of the equation, and had helped facilitate Maliki's victory. As Sheikh Fawaz al-Jerbi, the head of the Shammar tribe, stated, 'Maliki wouldn't have been able to put an end to terrorism in Basra if it wasn't for the support of the tribes and he wouldn't have been able to succeed in the elections if it wasn't for the support of the tribes.'[107] His willingness to reach out to the tribes and engage the sheikhs, however clumsily, had brought him votes and support. Thus the tribes became part of the political arena, but in a way that they had not envisaged themselves. They had hoped that the post-Ba'athist period would enable them to return to the centre ground. Yet, they ended up caught in a new clientelistic relationship that was set in motion by Maliki and his political rivals, and that was to persist into the rest of Maliki's rule and beyond.

8

TRIBES AND MOBILISATION

POLITICS, POWER AND PROTESTS

The political parties have corrupted the tribes. They work to tear off the meat of the tribe... They pushed the tribes into a political arena that is alien to them.

Sheikh Mohamed Zeidawi[1]

Giving votes is an expression of love by the sons of the tribe for the candidate who is from the tribe not for the political party itself.

Sheikh Adel al-Assad[2]

There is no separation between the sheikh and the Marja'iya. *The sheikh of the tribe is ultimately in the service of the* Marja'iya.

Sheikh Takleef al-Minshed[3]

Although political parties had been reaching out to the sheikhs since the fall of the Ba'athist regime, the governorate elections of January 2009 had highlighted the power of the tribe. This power was still somehow intangible in character but it was evident that despite being a social force, the tribe could affect the direction of political travel. The political parties woke up to these possibilities and increased their efforts to win over tribal support. The main parties opened offices dedicated to engaging with the tribes and courted the sheikhs in a

TRIBES AND THE STATE IN LIBYA AND IRAQ

more concerted way. They focused these efforts in areas they deemed to be 'fertile', namely those areas with a strong tribal presence, where, by virtue of their more cohesive kinship structures, electoral participation tended to be highest.

While this wooing of the sheikhs occurred across the country, it was particularly pronounced in the Shi'ite areas where the main Shi'ite parties competed for votes. Not that tribes, or even clans, expressed a unified political view or stance. As Dr Ali Juwad Witwit has argued, there has been no unified political orientation inside a clan since the 1950s.[4] Tribes are not politically cohesive and do not follow one party or another, their role being primarily social. They are a reflection of wider society and with tribesmen split across different political, religious and ideological currents. This means that a single clan contains individuals belonging to a host of different orientations. As Sheikh Mansour al-Tamimi observed, 'The tribe is not a political party or an ideological force. It is a social body without the thorns of ideology. My tribe is a small society. You can find in it the Communist, the Ba'athist, the Sadrist, the Dawaist, the nationalist, the Nasserite. However, we live in one body and what we have in common is more than what divides us.'[5]

While the tribe may not articulate a single political view, it can still have political impact through its ability to mobilise, including in elections, where it can provide a critical mass of votes. This mobilising power proved particularly important in the Iraqi context given that many of the parties that appeared on the scene after 2003 were either newly established or recently returned from long years in exile, meaning that they had limited constituencies and depth. In spite of their ideological resistance to tribes and tribalism, the Islamist political parties invested heavily in trying to win over tribal support. Sheikh al-Danbous observed, 'Political parties say tribes are backwards and cannot enter politics, yet they use them when elections come along.'[6] The parties found that they could not do without the tribes and that, as previous regimes had come to realise, the tribes were a reality that could not be avoided or ignored. The relationship between the tribes and the state was to continue therefore. However, the nature of this relationship had changed immeasurably. Whereas in the past, the tribe had maintained a vertical relationship to the state through its

TRIBES AND MOBILISATION

clientelistic ties to the Ba'athist regime, the atomised nature of the political arena meant that the tribes were now free to engage with a range of different political actors and power centres that were competing for their attention.

Yet it wasn't only in the political space that tribes proved potent. The mass tribal mobilisation that occurred in 2014 in response to the fatwa issued by the *Marja'iya*, calling on all able-bodied males to volunteer to fight against ISIS, was a case in point. The tribes responded to this call in their hundreds of thousands, joining or forming their own Popular Mobilisation Units. While many tribesmen were keen to volunteer in order to defend the state, seeing it as a matter of duty and honour, the key to this mass recruitment was the involvement of the *Marja'iya*, reflecting the longstanding and interdependent relationship between the tribes and the Shi'ite religious establishment. Shi'ite tribes consider themselves to be the 'sword' or the 'army' of the *Marja'iya*, and deem its fatwas to be binding. Thus the combination of the tribe and the *Marja'iya* mobilised the masses in a way that eluded the state, with the tribes serving as a critical component of the effort to preserve the state.

The tribes were also critical actors when it came to the protests that gripped whole swathes of the country from 2018 onwards. Here, the tribes worked as a buffer between the protestors and the state, which had responded to the unrest with a repressive response aimed at crushing the demonstrations by force. Although the tribes were initially reluctant to get involved, leaving it up to their tribesmen to decide whether or not to join the mass protests, they found themselves forced to intervene in order to both protect their tribesmen and preserve stability. While some scholars have claimed that the sheikhs adopted an 'equivocal and vacillating position' towards dealing with the protests, a stance attributed to the 'youthful, civic and urbanised nature of the demonstrations',[7] this is to belie the important role played by the sheikhs. It also once again relegates the tribe to the periphery or the rural space, as if the tribes themselves are not capable of existing or acting within the urban environment. In fact, the tribes' contribution was critical to the trajectory of the protests, particularly in Nasseriyah. As post-2003 Iraq demonstrated, although the tribes' power is localised and somehow intangible, they are still a

TRIBES AND THE STATE IN LIBYA AND IRAQ

potent force that has had a significant impact on the dynamics of post-Ba'athist Iraq.

Politics, Parties and Sheikhs

While all the political parties that emerged in large numbers after 2003 rushed to make use of the tribes, as described in Chapter 7, Maliki, despite his ideological orientation, was a key proponent of this effort and became particularly visible in the tribal arena early on. After securing his 2009 local election victory, Maliki continued to reach out to the tribes, making high-profile visits to tribal gatherings and to sheikhs in their mudheefs, where he would distribute gifts and money. He also sponsored a number of large tribal conferences such as in March 2009, when more than 600 sheikhs came together in the Babylon Hotel in Baghdad under the banner of the 'General Conference of the Sheikhs of Iraqi Tribes and Clans'. Maliki entrusted Sheikh Sami al-Majoun to organise this conference. Sheikh al-Majoun recalls, 'I said to Maliki, "Abu Isra [father of Isra], working with the tribes is very difficult and we need to be credible with them, otherwise I will be lost and you will be lost." At that time, Maliki had 150 million dollars that had been given by President George Bush for reconciliation… I organised the conference made out of 600 sheikhs. Most of them were genuine sheikhs whom I knew.'[8] These sheikhs were drawn from Shi'ite, Sunni and Kurdish tribes, as well as from tribes comprising Iraq's other religious and ethnic minorities. Sheikh al-Majoun gave a speech at the conference in which he told the tribes that they should consider themselves as a political front.[9]

Maliki used the occasion to curry favour with the tribes, lauding their role in establishing security, supporting the state and defeating terrorism. He also made sure to promote himself and his vision for Iraq, speaking of the need to move beyond the allocation system in order for the country to transcend consensus politics and start working as one. Maliki used this conference as a way to present himself as guardian of the whole of Iraq rather than as just guardian of one sect. His message chimed well with the sheikhs, who still saw themselves as the best force to unify Iraq and serve as a bulwark against sectarianism and extremism. Sheikh Abdelila Farhim al-Farhoud, the head of

TRIBES AND MOBILISATION

the Bani Zerij tribes in Muthanna, sought to convey this message, telling the media at the time how he had worked with a number of sheikhs in Ramadi to force the expulsion of a terrorist from the governorate.[10] The sheikhs were keen to show that they were able to cut across sect and thus were deserving of the state's support. While the ability of tribes to actually go beyond these communal lines is highly questionable, even in mixed Sunni-Shi'ite tribes, the sheikhs continued to promote the self-reflexive narrative they had developed in response to the country's unravelling. The tribes hoped that through Maliki they could return to the fore. Sheikh Fasal al-Gaoud, who was governor of Anbar between July 2004 and January 2005, commented at the time of the tribal conference, 'This conference has restored the status of the clan to its natural position of harmony and brotherhood and everyone supports the prime minister's initiative.'[11]

Maliki didn't only try to woo the sheikhs at flashy tribal gatherings and events that brought together large cross-sections of different tribes; he also courted tribes individually, including those of lesser standing. On 29 January 2010, he sponsored a conference for the elite and professionals of the Soudan tribe, a tribe from Meesan. In a speech, he proclaimed, 'We have to tell the world that these are the Iraqi clans we talk about today. We don't want to go back to a tribal system [of old]; today's tribes have the competence, the elites and the cadres who can build our country on a scientific, cultural and civilised basis.'[12] Such language surprised some Iraqis who had never associated the urbane Dawa Party leader with tribes or tribalism. Yet like the other political players, Maliki saw the value in harnessing the tribe to his advantage, especially when it came to elections. His doing so paid off, and in the 2010 elections, he scored another success. Although Ayad Allawi's Iraqiya list came first, Maliki's State of Law Alliance came second, taking 89 of the 325 seats in the parliament. The Alliance won in Babil, Basra, Karbala, Muthanna, Najaf, Wasit and Baghdad, and fared well in other Shi'ite governorates. Particularly striking was that Maliki smashed the individual candidate vote, taking 622,961 votes, putting him well ahead of the other main political players. As in the provincial elections the previous year, Maliki's success wasn't only predicated on tribal support; the same factors that had propelled him to victory in 2009 drove many Iraqis to vote for him again. However, his ability to appeal to the tribes played a significant part in his ability to turn his fortunes around, transforming himself from a mouse caught between the two giants of his political rivals into a giant in his own right.

Although Maliki's success was to dissipate later on, especially in light of his sectarian policies that laid down the foundations for the Sunni revolt that began with the protests in December 2012, for now, the prime minister was the man of the moment. Many Iraqis looked to him as the leader who could unite and stabilise the country, and who could create the strong central state that would enable Iraq to get back on its feet. Yet, Maliki's stellar rise was deeply problematic for the other Shi'ite parties who saw him as a competitor that threatened their hegemony among the Shi'ite masses. These parties also saw the tribes as a vehicle for votes and for expanding their power base.

Thus the parties embarked upon a race to win over the tribes and threw money, gifts and promises at the sheikhs, using state resources in order to do so. While the tribes may have 'put themselves up for auction, eliciting patronage from a range of parties and lists in exchange for their pledges of "loyalty"',[13] the parties were tripping over themselves competing for the sheikhs' support. As one Iraqi analyst commented, 'Since 2003 the political parties started running after the sheikh and not the other way around.'[14] The parties fought each other therefore to win the support of the sheikhs and the tribes became 'a tool in the conflict that developed between the religious parties especially in the Shi'ite-Shi'ite context'.[15]

This competition was played out within the fragmented political arena that characterised Iraq after the toppling of the Ba'athist regime. Whereas in the past, the tribes had navigated a relationship with a single centralised force, the post-2003 environment meant that they were now facing myriad poles of influence and a panoply of parties delineated along communal lines, all of whom were seeking to win over tribal support. Sheikh Raed al-Freiji, who is part of the Council of Basra Tribes, described, 'The political parties opened special offices for tribal affairs in order to attract tribal figures to their side and to win their loyalty to the bloc or even sometimes to specific political figures… We have been contacted a few times and they put so many offers to us, but we refused. Even the heads of political parties con-

TRIBES AND MOBILISATION

tacted us. They tried to steer our loyalty their way, although not to the bloc so much as to its head. A very well-known minister who belongs to one bloc suggested that he would open offices for us and give us money but only providing that we worked in the interests of Maliki's government.'[16]

This more open environment not only gave the parties space to canvas mass support, it created greater possibilities for the sheikhs to exert tribal agency and influence by choosing which parties and individuals they were willing to engage and bargain with. As Ammar al-Ameri notes, 'Never before was there so much space open for the tribes on the political level.'[17] Although the sheikhs had been able to push back against successive republican regimes to a certain degree, they could finally start laying down some of their own conditions. Yet it wasn't only the political environment that had been transformed; the tribes had also undergone significant changes themselves and were more divided and diffuse than in the past. As noted in previous chapters, this shift had started long before 2003, but accelerated after it. Iraqi academic Hayder Mohamed described the scene in Basra in 2011 thus: 'The erection of mudheefs is on the increase. These meeting houses are built not by recognised tribal sheikhs but by men with ambitions who create a space in the front of their house or rent a patch of land where men gather for tea or Arabic coffee and a chat. If a man is savvy enough and makes contacts with government officials, senior religious leaders and political figures, and if he looks as if he has enough money and power, more people begin to visit his mudheef. Within a short period of time, the man will assert himself as a sheikh, and as long as he has enough clients who are content in the relationship, his sheikhly status will not be questioned by anyone other than those competing for prominence. This ability of anyone to claim himself to be a sheikh, if he has enough money and power, points to how malleable and open the category of "tribe" is in Iraq today and why it is so resistant to coherent definition.'[18]

Yet while the number of sheikhs continued to multiply, it didn't mean that the traditional tribal leaderships disappeared. These new sheikhs, who were not generally rooted in the leading houses of the tribes, could not replace the traditional sheikhs who had their own established connections to the authorities. As Sheikh Jabbar al-Assad

TRIBES AND THE STATE IN LIBYA AND IRAQ

described, 'Claiming sheikhdoms undoubtedly increased. Claiming to be a sheikh is quite a widespread phenomenon in Basra, perhaps more so than in any other governorate. But the real sheikhs are very well known.'[19] The parties were able to distinguish between 'authentic sheikhs' and 'pretenders,' and knew exactly who to target at election time. As one tribesman in Muthanna observed, 'Political parties try usually to go for those who are Sheikh A or Sheikh B, as these are the most influential.'[20]

However, the parties have also sought to break into the tribe and create loyal sheikhs of their own. Like the Ba'athists before them, they have foisted money and attention on certain clan heads and tribal figures in order to secure support and votes, thereby contributing to the multiplication of 'sheikhs.' These parties have 'encouraged these sheikhs to challenge the general sheikhs by giving them and their sub-clans money and support... Some of these sheikhs decided that being connected to the party is more important than their own tribes.'[21] Sheikh Subhi Bu Kelal from Najaf describes, 'These days the political parties are shattering the tribes as they are not respecting the status of the sheikh. The non-traditional sheikhs go to whoever pays money and so we have more than one sheikh in a tribe. Rather, we have more than one in a clan, a sub-clan and a house.'[22] Sheikh Mohamed Zeidawi from the Bu Zaid tribe in Basra is even more explicit about the impact these parties have had, 'The political parties have corrupted the tribes. They work to tear off the meat of the tribe... They pushed the tribes into a political arena that is alien to them.'[23] He also asserts that those sheikhs who do not comply make themselves vulnerable to assassination attempts, or malicious court cases, noting 'The tribes who have connection to the higher power are safe, but those who don't have someone high up will be subjected to marginalisation, creating conflict between tribes or inside them.'[24]

Thus both tribe and party have played each other in the pursuit of new political bargains that serve the political, economic and religious interests of both. This marriage of convenience has been most apparent during elections, when tribe and party have come together to manoeuvre mutually acceptable candidates into positions of power. Working with the tribe in this way has been essential for the parties, which need to be able to tap into the mass of votes that the tribe can

TRIBES AND MOBILISATION

provide. This is especially important outside of the main urban centres, where political parties have little real reach or constituency. With electoral participation tending to be higher in rural areas, where services are lacking and where the tribes are strongest, the parties have had no option but to woo the sheikhs in return for support. They have also done so in the popular neighbourhoods of the cities, where tribal components have a strong presence. Although there are many factors—political, religious, ideological—that drive individuals to support particular candidates at elections, in general, the parties have relied on the tribes to deliver the critical mass of support.

The tribe has been equally reliant on the party to ensure the election of its chosen candidate, who, once elected, provides the tribe with access to the state, to jobs and to services. For the tribe, the party is an important source of funds required for laying on feasts, celebrations and mass rallies during the campaign period, as well as for the gifts and financial bonuses that are distributed as inducements of support. Many tribal candidates simply do not have the means to support such a huge campaign.[25] Sheikh Raed al-Freiji describes, 'You can see the political parties moving from one mudheef to another and behind them there is a long queue of food eaters and people doing howsat. Some of the sheikhs of the tribes joined these political blocs and joined parties.'[26]

More importantly, the list-based electoral system that was used up until the 2021 elections did not favour small parties or independents, making the chances of winning on a tribal ticket particularly challenging. Tribal candidates had little option but to stand on party lists, whether as independents or as a member of the party itself. This doesn't mean that certain sheikhs haven't contested the polls as individual candidates or as part of tribal blocs that are not tied to the parties. Yet, those who have done so have not fared well, and in the main, politically active sheikhs have opted to join party lists, this being the best way to secure election, whether locally or nationally. Sheikh Jabbar al-Assad explained why he decided to contest the 2010 elections on Maliki's State of Law Alliance list: 'I joined them because the electoral system wouldn't allow any independent figure to win. I am an independent man and not a member of the Dawa Party. Other members from my tribe nominated themselves because of their rela-

231

TRIBES AND THE STATE IN LIBYA AND IRAQ

tionship to a political party, but the tribe chose me rather than them.'[27] He went on to explain how not all members of his tribe voted for him but how, as the tribe's chosen candidate, he gained the support of many tribesmen, reflecting the fact that many make little distinction between one Shi'ite party and another, opting to support the sheikh upon whom their tribe has settled.

However, the candidates are not always sheikhs. Not all tribes can boast prominent sheikhs who have the political clout or standing to be able to contest and win elections, while some sheikhs may be qualified but are not politically inclined. Furthermore, the sheikhs of smaller or lesser tribes are not always best placed to enter the political arena as they would not garner sufficient support. In such instances, it is common for the tribe and the party to agree jointly on an individual from the tribe who has the necessary credentials to stand as a candidate. Tribes have often settled upon the son of a sheikh or member of the leading family, or a businessman, senior official or well-respected figure from within the tribe to rally behind. Sheikh Adel al-Assad described the process as follows: 'If Ammar al-Hakim [the then leader of the ISCI] came to me and said, "Sheikh I want you to be with me and give me a candidate", I would choose someone who is a heavyweight. I would tell him, "This is the person." The tribesmen wouldn't vote for Ammar al-Hakim, they would vote for the person I chose. This is the impact of the general sheikh.'[28] Similarly, Sheikh Takleef al-Minshed noted, 'The party comes to the sheikh and asks him to nominate someone and they will support him and finance him. Sheikhs still have influence and are not clients. The State of Law Alliance contacted me and asked me to nominate someone for their list.' He went on to explain how the candidate is normally not bothered about which list he stands on, noting that he just 'needs to nominate himself for election. The party is meaningless to him.'[29]

Thus, many individuals who have stood on party lists have been tribesmen with the support of their tribes behind them. In Muthanna for example, a number of tribesmen stood as candidates in the 2018 parliamentary elections on party lists. Among those elected was the grandson of Sha'alan Abu Jun, a legendary figure who had been one of the leaders of the 1920 tribal revolt against the British. Abu Jun's grandson's candidacy was agreed between the al-Badr Organisation

232

TRIBES AND MOBILISATION

and the al-Zuwalem tribe in Muthanna. Through this arrangement, Abu Jun's grandson, who had resigned from his job as a policeman in order to stand for the elections, won a seat in the parliament. In a similar vein, the Sadrists struck a deal with Sheikh Yousef al-Baidani of the al-Baidan tribe (Huwais house)–in Baghdad to rally behind a particular candidate in the same elections. The candidate was a member of the Communist Party, with whom the tribe had historical links, and which was standing on a joint list with the Sadrists as part of the Sa'iroun alliance. Sheikh al-Baidani described, 'We put all our effort as a tribe behind the candidate to get as many votes as possible. We went to the heads of the clans to rally support. What we did for the candidate was more than what Sa'iroun did for him.'[30]

This is not to suggest that the sheikh, including the general sheikh, has the power to command his tribesmen to vote in a particular way. The sheikh's authority in tribal or social matters has never been matched in the political arena. Nevertheless, the sheikh can steer the general direction of the tribe, including by getting it to rally behind particular candidates, relying on tribal solidarity to mobilise his tribesmen. Sheikh Adel al-Assad also explained, he could not tell his tribesmen to vote in a certain way, but that any candidate he selected would inevitably receive votes, noting, 'Giving votes is an expression of love by the sons of the tribe for the candidate who is from the tribe not for the political party.'[31] Another sheikh described, 'The tribesmen who are elected officially represent a political party, but as a matter of fact, they are serving their tribe. The tribe doesn't follow any political party and the elected tribesman is often not a member of the party upon whose list he stood. There is co-operation between the two, but loyalty to the tribe is stronger than loyalty to the party.'[32]

This process is by no means smooth or without conflict. Rather, the electioneering has created competition between and within clans and tribes, with multiple candidates often emerging out of the same tribe. One tribesman in Muthanna commented, 'We have many different types of sheikh. This has generated major conflict because all the sheikhs of these clans try to push their own candidate.'[33] In the 2018 parliamentary elections, the al-Abs tribe, which had succeeded in having an MP in previous terms, failed to win a seat because so many candidates from the tribe joined different lists, shattering the tribe's

233

TRIBES AND THE STATE IN LIBYA AND IRAQ

vote between the State of Law and al-Hikma currents. In the 2021 parliamentary elections, every major tribe in Basra's fourth electoral district put more than one candidate forward, fragmenting the tribal vote.[34] However, the post-2003 period has seen the tribe and the party serve each other in such a way as to impact the political landscape. As Riyadh al-Baddawy, a civil servant from the Huwais house of the al-Baidan tribe put it, 'The party needs the tribe and the tribe needs the party.'[35] Rather than the sheikhs running after the spoils—a loaded image associated with the raiding Bedouin tribes of the past—this has been a mutually convenient arrangement in which both have sought to use the state for their own ends. Both the tribe and the parties have used the state as a cash cow and both have sought to use the political arena to serve their own interests above everything else.

Tribes, Marja'iya and Popular Mobilisation

While the post-2003 period saw the Shi'ite tribes enter into a new type of relationship with the parties, there was another component to this dynamic in the form of the *Marja'iya*. As noted previously, the ties between the Shi'ite religious establishment and the Shi'ite tribes date back over generations and the two entities are inextricably linked through a shared history of interdependence, 'one completing the other.'[36] As Naji Sultan observed, 'The relationship between tribes and the state is unstable, but the relationship between tribes and the *Marja'iya* is very stable.'[37] Sheikh Wael Abdullatif meanwhile described, 'The *Marja'iya* is part of belief. The *Marja'iya* explains the rulings of Islam that the Muslim is obliged to apply so its fatwas must be applied.'[38]

The bond between the tribe and the *Marja'iya* is partly transactional; the sheikh pays khums, a 20 per cent tax paid on any profits that is one of the ten obligatory acts of Shi'ite Islam. More importantly, the tribes also provide the *Marja'iya* with critical mass and support. Sheikh Takleef al-Minshed observes, 'There is no separation between the sheikh and the *Marja'iya*. The sheikh of the tribe is ultimately in the service of the *Marja'iya*.'[39] In return, the sheikh receives the *Marja'iya*'s blessing, serving as the 'spiritual platform' for the tribe. As Ali Juwad Witwit describes, 'Sheikhs are committed to pay

234

TRIBES AND MOBILISATION

khums to the *Marja'iya* while the *Marja'iya* blesses the power of the sheikhs and the way in which they run their tribes.'[40] This spiritual recognition is critical for the Shi'ite sheikhs and any sheikh who does not have such religious approval would struggle to be accepted by his tribesmen. Sheikh Abdullatif commented, 'The tribe would never give up on the *Marja'iya*; it is their source of legitimacy.'[41] Thus the two entities are deeply interlinked and interdependent, hence the sheikhs routinely referring to the tribes as the 'shield' or the 'army' of the *Marja'iya*.

This doesn't mean that the tribes have applied the rulings of the *Marja'iya* to the letter. Tribal norms and customs have sometimes overridden Islamic directives, as in the case of *degga*. *Degga* is a custom in which members of one tribe shoot at the house of a member of a tribe with whom they are in dispute, the shooting meant as a warning that the tribe has three days to come and settle the dispute through mediation or else face more serious forms of tribal revenge. Not only was the practice outlawed by the state in 2018, the *Marja'iya* has spoken out against it, classifying it as a pre-Islamic tribal norm. However, *degga* continues to be practised by some clans, including in urban centres. The same is true of other tribal traditions that the *Marja'iya* has denounced, including *nahwa* (whereby male uncles and cousins can block a woman's right to marry anyone other than them) and fasliya (whereby females from a family that committed an offence against another tribe are handed over to the wronged tribe for marriage, with multiple females sometimes handed over in a single incident). Yet in general, the tribes would not dare to go against the *Marja'iya* in an overt or explicit manner.

Not that all members of a tribe follow the same *marja'* (religious reference). While Grand Ayatollah al-Sistani, who is based in Najaf, is considered to be the most senior *marja'* in Iraq, serving as the main religious reference for the Shi'ites, other *marja'*s also command followings of their own. This includes Ayatollah Sayid Kadhem al-Ha'iri, who is deemed to be the *marja'* of the Sadrist current. Al-Ha'iri is based in Iran and follows in the tradition of the teachings of the late Ayatollah Mohamed Sadiq al-Sadr (Moqtada al-Sadr's father), whose more radical and politicised stance proved popular with some Shi'ite youth, especially among the urban poor.[42] Ayatollah Mohamed Sadiq al-Sadr's teachings still hold sway among the Sadrist current, who look to both to al-Ha'iri and increasingly to Moqtada al-Sadr himself for spiritual guidance. While most sheikhs and tribes follow al-Sistani, some tribesmen including some sheikhs have aligned with the other current. Sheikh al-Minshed explained, 'The tribe can split in two parts if there is a contradiction between al-Sadr and al-Sistani. Those who follow al-Sadr will stay with al-Sadr and those who follow al-Sistani will stay with al-Sistani.'[43]

However, most sheikhs still follow the more pragmatic al-Sistani, who advocates for the separation of fiqh (jurisprudence) and politics and who has tried to resist the politicisation of the religious sphere, considering the *Marja'iya*'s role to be to protect the spiritual and religious welfare of Iraqis and the Islamic identity of Iraq. Al-Sistani's more moderate and traditional teachings have chimed well with the majority of sheikhs, who are not naturally disposed to the radical calls for political action that have characterised the teachings of more hard-line currents including the Sadrists. Thus, while sheikhs may not always comply with the *Marja'iya*'s rulings, in general they consider them binding. As one Iraqi tribesman from Nasseriyah commented, 'No sheikh, whoever he is, would announce publicly that he is against the *Marja'iya*. In every statement issued by a sheikh, he has to include the phrase, "Based on the instructions of the *Marja'iya*", even if he isn't convinced with those particular instructions. If he doesn't do that, no one will attend the Ashura rituals in his area and no one will come to his mudheef'.[44]

Al-Sistani has considerable power and influence within the tribal context therefore. This influence has extended to the political and even the security arenas. While the *Marja'iya* is generally reluctant to engage in politics, the situation has been so extreme that al-Sistani has found himself drawn directly into the political realm in the name of protecting social order. This included at the time of the 2003 invasion. In contrast to the Sadrist current, which called for armed resistance against occupying forces, al-Sistani adopted a more judicious line. Despite proclaiming prior to 2003 that any aggression against Iraq should be resisted, when coalition forces attacked, al-Sistani stopped short of calling for jihad and did not advocate taking up arms. This did not mean that he wasn't opposed to the presence

TRIBES AND MOBILISATION

of coalition forces on Iraqi soil. For the *Marja'iya*, the occupation by foreigners, and especially non-Muslims, risked degrading Iraqi society and corrupting its Islamic character. This view sat well with the tribes' natural suspicion of invading forces and the need to defend the honour of the land and the Iraqi man. However, he was restrained when it came to calls for action. During the early days of the occupation, the *Marja'iya* was asked by a group of vendors and shopkeepers how they should react when American or British forces came to buy goods from them. Al-Sistani responded by telling them, 'You sell to them but you ask every single one of them, "When are you going to leave our country?"'[45]

While it is impossible to ascertain the extent to which al-Sistani's stance contributed to the Shi'ite tribes' decision not to take up arms against the occupiers, it is likely to have had a significant impact. Given tribes' natural resistance to foreign forces, and the fact that many Shi'ite sheikhs were invested in the Ba'athist regime, or at the least were fearful of what would happen were it to fall, one might have expected some of the Shi'ite tribes to put up some sort of armed resistance. While there were many complex reasons why most Shi'ite sheikhs did not advocate taking up arms against the occupying forces, al-Sistani's cautious stance towards the invasion will have been of fundamental importance to many. Or put another way, had the *Marja'iya* issued a fatwa urging jihad, the tribes would have felt obliged to comply. They certainly would have been reluctant to work with coalition forces or the CPA.

The *Marja'iya*'s appeals for restraint after the regime's toppling were also significant. Early on, al-Sistani cautioned against revenge killings and went on to issue a fatwa prohibiting attacks against Ba'athists, stressing that those Ba'athists who had engaged in criminal acts should be referred to the courts. He also warned against sectarian strife, in some cases instructing the tribes directly not to get engaged in such conflict. After explosions carried out by Sunni extremists that killed over 170 people in Karbala and Kadhimiya during Ashura in 2004, al-Sistani received a group of sheikhs who asked him to authorise them to respond to the attacks in kind. Al-Sistani told them, 'I don't permit anything like this. Even if they exterminate entire cities, I won't allow us to be drawn into a sectarian conflict... Even if I were

TRIBES AND THE STATE IN LIBYA AND IRAQ

to be killed by some of these entities or in such situations, I wouldn't allow anyone to be drawn into sectarian strife.'[46] While there were certainly many young Shi'ites who did not adhere to the *Marja'iya*'s calls, al-Sistani served as a restraining influence on some of the Shi'ite tribes and sheikhs at a time when the country was entering a dark tunnel of sectarian violence.

The *Marja'iya* was also instrumental in shaping the tribal response to the unfolding political context. The CPA's initial plan for the transition, which had been agreed by the caretaker interim government in November 2003, had been for indirect elections via a complex system of provisional caucuses that would elect representatives to a new assembly. Yet, al-Sistani encapsulated the feelings of many Iraqis, including many tribal sheikhs, when he objected to this plan, viewing the American hand as being too heavy in what was a critical process for Iraq's future. Al-Sistani openly opposed the proposal and called for direct elections that would enable Iraqis to take back control of their country more quickly. In January 2004, al-Sistani's office released a statement that declared, 'The Ayatollah invoked his position that the planned transitional national assembly cannot represent Iraqis in the ideal manner... In this situation, experts think it is possible to organise fair and transparent elections in the coming months.'[47] His calls triggered large demonstrations in Basra, and many tribesmen were among the tens of thousands who marched through the streets, some of them chanting 'No to America' and holding up al-Sistani's portrait.

Many sheikhs looked to al-Sistani for guidance during this period. This included a group of sheikhs from Samawah and Rumaitha who met the *Marja'iya* to ask for direction. Tapping into Iraq's tribal history, al-Sistani told them that if the Iraqis weren't going to be permitted to be the political decision makers of their country, the *Marja'iya* would be forced to announce jihad as it had done in 1920 against the British, noting that this was a call to which the tribes of Rumaitha and Samawah had responded.[48] Such was the power of the *Marja'iya* that the CPA agreed that indirect elections would be shelved and that direct elections would go ahead in 2005. These elections clearly had al-Sistani's approval, something that was instrumental in encouraging some sheikhs to support the polls. Sheikh Sami al-Majoun recounted

238

TRIBES AND MOBILISATION

how when he told US Ambassador Ryan Crocker that he wasn't certain Iraq was ready for elections, Crocker told him that the *Marja'iya* had ruled that an election should go ahead, prompting the sheikh to accept the polls because he couldn't object to what the *Marja'iya* had decided.[49] The *Marja'iya* also intervened regarding the constitution, instructing Iraqis to vote to approve the text that was put forward in the referendum of October 2005. An official from al-Sistani's office explained how, 'Anyone who contacts the grand ayatollah's office is told that he instructs Iraqis to vote "yes"... The Iraqi faithful must go to the polling stations to vote in favour of the text.'[50] There was not only a high turnout for this vote—estimated to be 69 per cent—there was overwhelming support for the constitution in the southern governorates. In all the Shi'ite majority governorates, over 94 per cent of voters voted in favour of the text and in Muthanna, the yes vote reached as high as 98.9 per cent. There will have been many different reasons why these predominantly Shi'ite governorates voted in favour of the constitution, which also received a strong endorsemen in the the Kuridsh areas. Nevertheless, the *Marja'iya*'s intervention will have contributed to the high levels of endorsement in the Shi'ite areas.

Yet it was in June 2014 that the *Marja'iya*'s mobilising power was to come together with that of the tribes to have perhaps the greatest impact on Iraq's political and security trajectory. At this time, ISIS was expanding across large swathes of Iraq, taking territory as the Iraqi army all but dissolved in the face of the advancing militant forces. The speed with which ISIS was able to take control of so many areas and towns, including major towns like Mosul, was rooted in the festering grievances that had long been brewing in Iraq's Sunni population. Despite Maliki's pretensions to be the man who could unite Iraq and go beyond sect, his continued marginalisation of the Sunnis had provoked anger and resentment. This marginalisation was evident in the political arena, where despite the Sunnis having a share of government posts through the allocation system, they had little tangible political power. It was apparent in the security field too. Not only were the *Sahwat* still feeling abandoned by the state, which despite its promises, had not absosbed the Sunni tribal fighters into the official security apparatus, while thousands of young Sunni males had been detained on terrorism-related charges having been arrested under

239

TRIBES AND THE STATE IN LIBYA AND IRAQ

draconian anti-terrorism legislation. These resentments against Maliki's overtly sectarian approach erupted in the Sunni protest movement that began in Fallujah on 21 December 2012 following a raid on the home of Sunni Finance Minister Rafi al-Issawi, and the arrest of ten of his bodyguards on terrorism-related charges. The protests spread across the Sunni governorates, with protest camps established in various locations.

In December 2013, Maliki sent security forces to shut down the main protest camp in Ramadi, killing hundreds of civilian demonstrators in the process. This attack provoked an armed Sunni revolt, with former Ba'athists, Islamists and Sunni tribal leaders coming together to fight back. Although the Sunni tribes were a key component of this attempted revolt, they soon found themselves overtaken by other forces. This included ISIS, which had seeded itself in the protest movement and was fast gaining new recruits, especially among the disaffected urban poor whose origins lay largely in the countryside.[51] Inevitably, many of the group's recruits were tribesmen drawn from across tribes in the Sunni governorates and who saw in ISIS a form of redemption and a way to challenge the marginalisation they had experienced at the hands of the Shi'ite-dominated government. As one tribal leader in Haditha observed, the Maliki government, 'isolated Sunni tribes, designated us enemies and stripped us of all benefits, like social status and posts in the government, army and police… As a result, many tribesmen joined Daesh to get revenge from the state.'[52]

This did not mean that particular tribes rallied wholesale behind ISIS. While the relationship between the Sunni tribes and ISIS has been covered in the literature, it is worth noting that while some tribal elements may have been willing to work or co-operate with the militant group, whole tribes or clans did not generally commit themselves to it. Assertions made by some commentators that certain Sunni tribes joined ISIS or were split between clans that joined it and clans that stood against it are overplayed. While individual tribesmen may have joined ISIS, the tribes did not give collective allegiance to the group. As Sheikh Nawaf Dulaimi of the Dulaim tribe asserted, 'There is no clan or tribe in its entirety that pledged allegiance to ISIS or other militant groups in Syria or in Iraq… There are some individuals within the tribes or clans who support them but they do not

240

TRIBES AND MOBILISATION

represent their whole tribe or clan.'[53] Although some sheikhs joined the group, those who did rarely came from leading sheikhly houses.[54]

Indeed, ISIS's Takfiri ideology and brutality, as well as its insistence that the tribes submit to its control, served as a barrier to most tribes regardless of their shared interests in defending Sunni interests against a repressive Shi'ite-led government. Thus while the shifting and fragmented nature of the tribe may have allowed some individuals and families to join the group, the tribes as a whole did not do so. Jabar has observed in relation to this issue that kinship groups don't live in an isolated environment but represent a group of interests that are intertwined with other components of Iraqi society, meaning that, 'The tribe or lineage group is not a cohesive unit that can take unified political action.'[55] Given the complexity and diffuse nature of kinship networks, as well as the fact that the sheikh does not direct or command his members when it comes to political issues, it is almost impossible to categorise tribes into neat sections or parts that either supported or didn't support ISIS. The picture is far more confused.

ISIS focused its attentions therefore on chipping away at the tribes and the sheikhs to try to force them to submit. Long before the group staged its mass takeover in June 2014, it subjected the sheikhs to a campaign of intimidation and violence. As early as 2012, ISIS members routinely entered villages and small towns warning local tribal leaders and notables that they had to submit and should not be co-operating with the state. In some instances, the group sent members of a tribe who it had recruited to their own tribes to warn their own sheikhs.[56] During this period, ISIS also forced sheikhs into swearing allegiance to the group and its emir, killing many who refused to comply or who continued to remain in contact with the central government. Between 2013 and 2014, ISIS killed thirteen sheikhs in Nineveh alone.[57] It also killed Sheikh Barazan al-Badrani, an influential sheikh in Mosul, who had played a prominent role in opposing the US occupation and who had also been a leading figure in the Sunni protest movement. According to the sheikh's brother, from 2012, ISIS had been secretly trying to gain the allegiance of sheikhs in and around Mosul, chasing those who refused, including Sheikh Barazan.[58] This was corroborated by one ISIS member, Abu Qatada, who described how two years before the group took control of Mosul, it had worked

TRIBES AND THE STATE IN LIBYA AND IRAQ

relentlessly to coerce the sheikhs of Mosul to commit themselves to 'supporting and building the caliphate through souls and money', explaining that if these sheikhs didn't comply, they would be deemed to have gone back on Islam, the punishment for which is death.[59] As such, the group intimidated many sheikhs who lived in the popular neighbourhoods surrounding Mosul and forced them into swearing allegiance to it upon the threat of death. Sheikh Mustafa al-Obeidi from the Obaid tribe, south of Mosul, described, 'ISIS only attacked Mosul to control it when it had gained the allegiance of the tribes surrounding the town and imposed punishment on those who rejected it. Most were forced into giving their allegiance.'[60] Thus some of those sheikhs who co-operated with ISIS did so out of intimidation and fear rather than ideological or political commitment.

ISIS certainly made the most of those sheikhs who had sworn allegiance to the group, using them to claim that it had succeeded in winning over tribal support. Illustrative of this effort was a propaganda video filmed by ISIS on 23 March 2015. This video, which was filmed in an engineering club in the east of Mosul, purported to show thirty sheikhs from Nineveh pledging allegiance to ISIS Emir, Abu Bakr al-Baghdadi. In the video, titled 'Nineveh Tribes Renew Allegiance and Will Confront', an ISIS member can be heard telling the sheikhs, 'You sheikhs are the crowns on our heads.'[61] Yet while ISIS presented this video as evidence of tribal support, many of the sheikhs in the video were what one Iraqi journalist described as 'shayouk duwasa' and 'shayouk azaim', namely 'fake sheikhs' who claimed sheikhly status in order to attend feasts and political occasions and to obtain jobs.[62] Many sheikhs in the video clip are presented as the general sheikhs of their tribes, whereas in fact they did not represent the authentic leadership of these tribes. Sheikh Mohamed Abdulsalam, for example, who was referred to as the sheikh of the Ibada tribe, was not the tribe's general sheikh, a position held by Sheikh Barak Ligoud.[63] Some of the sheikhs in the footage meanwhile had been imprisoned by ISIS but were wheeled out for the video after they had agreed to 'repent'. From the footage, it is also evident that some of these 'sheikhs' were intimidated into appearing in the video. One sheikh who participated explained later how it had been made clear to him and the others that they would be killed if they didn't co-

242

TRIBES AND MOBILISATION

operate, describing, 'We were frightened. We didn't know how to behave and we avoided talking to each other or looking directly into the faces of the group's leaders'.[64] Sheikh of the Hadideen tribe commented meanwhile, 'The tribe in Nineveh was a victim and only a few of its sheikhs took part voluntarily. The majority were forced to submit'.[65] While one cannot discount the fact that such comments were made in hindsight and may have been made in order to deny any hint of these sheikhs or tribes having collaborated with ISIS, it is evident that many sheikhs and tribesmen were intimidated into co-operating with ISIS and had little option but to comply.

By contrast, others took the decision to resist ISIS despite the violence that had been unleashed against them. The largest and most influential tribes in many areas stood against the group. This includes in Anbar, where the dominant tribe in many districts remained broadly hostile to the group. This included the Jagayfa tribe in the Haditha area, the Obeid tribe in al-Baghdadi, the Bufahad tribe in Khalidiya, the Bu Alwan tribe in Ramadi, the Bu Issa tribe in Amiriyat al-Fallujah and the Bu Mahal tribe in al-Qaim. Again, this did not mean that some members of these tribes hadn't joined ISIS, but the general tribal direction was to stand against the group despite the heavy price that many paid. While some Jubour tribesmen held senior positions in ISIS, for example, the tribe was among those who fought hardest against the militant group. Regardless of the actions of some individuals, the tribes, with their traditional and more pragmatic outlook and their desire to retain power and status in their own areas, served more as a bulwark against ISIS than an enabler of it.

While many Sunni tribes put up resistance to ISIS, with many paying the ultimate price, Iraq's Shi'ite tribes also played their part. By June 2014, the situation was looking desperate; ISIS had not only taken control of large areas in the Sunni governorates with astonishing speed, it was looking as though the capital was at risk of falling. The urgency of the situation, made worse by the near collapse of the Iraqi army and security forces, prompted the government to act. On 11 June, a ministerial committee that had been appointed by Maliki three months earlier in response to ISIS's growing power, including its gains in neighbouring Syria, announced that it had established volunteer brigades to serve as an 'alternative army'. These so-called

243

Popular Mobilisation Forces (PMF) were to be tasked with supporting the official security services through the newly formed Popular Mobilisation Directorate. Although some Iraqis responded to this call, the volunteer effort escalated significantly two days later, when the *Marja'iya* issued a fatwa calling on all able-bodied men to defend the country. In a Friday sermon, the *Marja'iya*'s representative Sheikh Abdulmehdi Karbalai announced, 'Citizens who are able to bear arms and fight terrorists, defending their country and their people and their holy places, should volunteer and join the security forces to achieve this holy purpose'.[66] He also appealed to Iraqis' readiness to sacrifice themselves for the sake of 'preserving the unity of our country, its dignity, and the defence of its holy places'.[67] Karbalai declared the mass mobilisation as a 'jihad kifaye', namely an obligation that is imposed upon the community with the proviso that if the duty is fulfilled by some members of the community, the remainder are not under obligation to comply.

Although this fatwa was meant to appeal to all Iraqis across sect and ethnicity, the fact that it emanated from the supreme Shi'ite religious establishment meant that some Sunnis interpreted it as a call to sectarian war that was backed by Tehran. The Mufti of Iraq, Rafa Rafa'i, for example condemned the fatwa, declaring, 'We won't accept Iraq being a back garden for Iran, and al-Sistani's call to fight is a sectarian one.'[68] In a similar vein, media outlets in various Sunni Arab countries attacked the call, describing it as an irresponsible move that risked enflaming sectarian violence.[69] The reaction prompted the *Marja'iya* to issue an explanatory addendum to clarify the fatwa's meaning and to try to reassure Iraqi Sunnis that this was not a sectarian call to arms, but was intended to apply to all able-bodied Iraqi males in the cause of defeating terrorism.

This fatwa inevitably galvanised many Shi'ite tribes. So much so that the government was surprised by the large numbers who volunteered. Al-Sistani's call to arms clearly resonated much more deeply with the Shi'ite population than Maliki's call for volunteer fighters ever could. To the tribes, al-Sistani's words were binding and they embarked upon a mass mobilisation effort to send their sons to the front lines. As Ammar al-Ameri described, 'When ISIS entered Iraq in June 2014 and the *Marja'iya* called for jihad, the sons of the Iraqi

TRIBES AND MOBILISATION

tribes responded to the call and rose up to defend their territory.'[70] Sheikh Wael Abdullatif described, 'When al-Sistani issued his fatwa, the tribes and young people all came out in the street in support of it.'[71] Adel Abdulmehdi, who went on to become prime minister of Iraq, observed, 'When ISIS came along and the *Marja'iya* issued the fatwa the tribes stood up and took their position. They filled the fighting fields with their men. When we said they were the army of the *Marja'iya* and the army of the people; we didn't exaggerate.'[72] Almost as soon as al-Sistani's fatwa was declared, the tribes rushed to erect tents to organise tribal mobilisation efforts, including in urban areas. Many of the tribesmen who volunteered to fight were drawn from poor urban neighbourhoods of the south and centre. In the Qarma area of Basra, which is known for being strongly tribal, some 80 per cent of youth volunteered in response to al-Sistani's call.[73]

The tribes had much pride in their response to al-Sistani's fatwa, which they deemed to be a national rather than a sectarian call to arms. They felt strongly that they were defending the country as a whole rather than just one sect. Sheikh Mohamed Zeidawi of the Bu Zaid tribe in Basra commented, 'Members of the tribes are the ones who rose up to save Iraq based on the fatwa of al-Sistani. The tribes competed to give martyrs and money and to defend their Sunni brothers. It was the tribes who defeated ISIS.'[74] These tribes were so keen to take part that it often seemed as though they were trying to outdo each other in their mobilising abilities. Sheikh Sadoun Ghulam Ali, the general sheikh of the Bani Lam tribe, for example recounted, 'As soon as the *Marja'iya* issued the decision, we were the first who gathered militarily in this mudheef and this garden. We responded to the demand and I contacted a large number of Bani Lam tribesmen in Wasit, Meesan, Sheikh Saad, al-Kut, Ali Shergi and al-Kumait. They all came armed. All of Bani Lam announced their willingness [to fight] and volunteered themselves.'[75] Similar sentiments were expressed by other sheikhs, who clearly exulted in the role played by their tribes.

While many tribesmen were spurred into action by al-Sistani's fatwa, the mass of volunteers was such that various Shi'ite militias took advantage of the situation to recruit for their own ranks. The Popular Mobilisation Forces were split between three main currents: the Hashd al-Atabat (Mobilisation of the Shrines), which comprised

245

TRIBES AND THE STATE IN LIBYA AND IRAQ

forces loyal to al-Sistani;[76] the Saraya Salam Brigades, which were loyal to Moqtada al-Sadr; and the *Hashd al-Wilayee*, which comprised more hard-line forces that had been in existence for years, such as Badr Brigades, Asaib Ahl al-Haq, Saraya al-Kharasani, Hizbollah and Al-Nujaba, and that had close ideological and operational ties to Iran, which provided training and finance. This Hashd al-Wilayee current was the most powerful by far, comprising more fighters and controlling most of the PMF.[77] Around 80 per cent of the administration and leadership structures of the Popular Mobilisation were run by this current, while those who followed al-Sistani didn't have any senior or middle-ranking posts inside its organisational structure.[78] This didn't mean that the *Marja'iya*'s current had no importance; the Hashd al-Wilayee needed to keep it on board to justify the existence of the PMF and provide them with religious cover.[79] However the Hashd al-Wilayee profited hugely from the government's inability to absorb the large number of volunteers who responded to al-Sistani's fatwa, successfully recruiting from among the many thousands who came forward. This included many tribesmen who ended up joining these more ideologically driven forces that had been established long before al-Sistani's fatwa.

While some of these young tribesmen were doubtless ideologically motivated and attracted to these more hard-line Islamist forces, others joined simply by virtue of circumstance in the rush to defeat ISIS. Sheikh Sabah Faris al-Rumaidha, the general sheikh of the Bu Saleh tribe in Dhi Qar, described, 'We formed a full fighting brigade led by Nadhem Faris al-Rumaid and within days and through self-financing, we set up the brigade and we trained them and moved to protect Karbala… This brigade joined the al-Abbas force [linked to *Marja'iya*], while some of our brothers joined under the banner of the Islamic parties like Asaib Ahl al-Haq.'[80] Some tribes became deeply embedded in some of these al-Wilayee PMF, therefore, crafting a highly complex web of interests and affiliations.

These forces went on to capitalise on their military triumphs against ISIS, translating them into political success by contesting the 2018 parliamentary elections under the banner of the al-Fatah Alliance. This alliance, which posited itself as defender both of Iraq and of the PMF, came second in the polls, having gained a large

TRIBES AND MOBILISATION

groundswell of support among the Shi'ite population in the central and southern governorates. Some PMF continued to try to court the tribes and mobilise their support, serving as yet another force that has tried to turn the tribes into clients. In 2018, the Popular Mobilisation Committee in Diwaniya held a large tribal conference entitled 'Our Iraqi Tribes are Our Strategic Depth and Support our Sacred Popular Mobilisation'. This conference was attended by a large number of tribal sheikhs who proclaimed their support for the PMF and called for the families of their martyrs to be looked after. Like the political parties, these PMF have looked to the tribe to provide critical mass and support.

However, the dominance of these Hashd al-Wilayee forces has proved troubling for the traditional sheikhs, especially given their close ties to Tehran. One sheikh from Basra complained that Iran was intervening and using the PMF to tighten its grip on Iraq.[81] Others expressed frustration about the way in which the PMF had been taken over and hijacked by the militias. Sheikh Mansour al-Tamimi remarked, 'The Popular Mobilisation Forces are our sons. They have no relationship to the militias. The militias used the Popular Mobilisation. We mobilised our sons based on al-Sistani's fatwa and we fought because we consider ourselves to be part of the state not part of militias.'[82] Some, meanwhile, are unhappy about the myriad problems these forces have brought back with them to their own areas. Notwithstanding, the tribes still have a near sentimental attachment to the PMF and remain fiercely proud of the 'noble' achievement of their sons, many of whom were martyred in the struggle. Although these Popular Mobilisations may be led by hard-line radical figures with strong ties to Iran whose ideology and connections do not sit comfortably with many sheikhs, the tribes still revere the PMF as an institution and deem their mobilisation to have been blessed by al-Sistani. For many, it represents the fulfilment of their role as the army of the *Marja'iya*.

Tribes and Protests

The tribes were to mobilise again, but in a different guise, after mass demonstrations engulfed the south from late 2019 onwards. Faced

TRIBES AND THE STATE IN LIBYA AND IRAQ

with the extremity of the situation, especially in Nasseriyah, where the governorate looked to be on the point of collapse, the tribes were catapulted to the fore and forced to go beyond the purview of their traditional role, deploying security measures in order to restore order and forestall further bloodshed. Indeed, with state legitimacy in crisis, the tribes felt duty bound to step in.

The protests, that came to be known as the Tishreen (October) Movement, were driven primarily by disenfranchised youth, frustrated at the grinding poverty, lack of services, corruption and general bad governance they had been forced to endure. The demonstrations were an articulation of the festering resentments that had been building for years especially among Iraq's Shi'ite population, where there was a feeling that the Shi'ite-led government was ignoring their plight, despite the fact that they had sacrificed so many of their sons for the war against ISIS. These resentments were well known to the sheikhs, who understood and in many cases shared the grievances that had been building over the years and that had already triggered a number of smaller-scale protests in the south. Sheikh Jawad al-Assad recounted how in 2018, he and a group of fellow sheikhs from Dhi Qar had gone as a delegation to the *Marja'iya* to impress upon the *marja'* the seriousness of the situation. The sheikhs were received by al-Sistani's representative, Sheikh Abdulmehdi Karbalai, to whom they expressed their concerns. Sheikh Jawad recalled, 'We talked about the tension in the street. We told them that the streets were boiling and that things risked getting out of control. We explained that there was a huge class division and injustice.'[83] Sheikh Jawad continued, 'I asked him, "Do you eat the rice that is distributed by the government?" He said, "no". I said, "When your wife is ill, do you take her to a government hospital?" He said, "no". I said, "Do you drink water from the tap or do you buy bottled water?" He said, "bottled water". I told him, I came from a governorate where half the people are living below the poverty line. These people cannot take their families to a private hospital but state hospitals are tumbling down. There are people in Dhi Qar wearing shirts that cost more than 1,000 dollars, but the rest cannot afford shoes'.[84] Despite the delegation's pleas for the *marja'* to intervene, and despite Karbalai promising to pass on a letter they had brought for al-Sistani, no response was forthcoming.

248

TRIBES AND MOBILISATION

The Dhi Qar sheikhs' predictions that things would get out of hand materialised, and in October 2019, large-scale protests erupted in Baghdad but also in different parts of the south, especially in Nasseriyah. Panicked by the unfolding situaiton, the authorities adopted a heavy-handed response, and by mid-October, security forces had killed 150 protestors and wounded more than 6,000 across Baghdad, Diwaniyah and Nasseriyah. This violence only spurred the protestors on, and some took to more direct action to express their frustration, including setting fire to political party offices and government buildings. On 4 November, protestors attacked the Iranian embassy in Karbala, setting it alight and pulling down the Iranian flag and demanding that Tehran stop intervening in Iraq's internal affairs. Despite the escalating situation, the authorities pursued the same course of action and deployed more force to try to contain the unrest, while pro-Iranian PMF infiltrated the crowds to kill and abduct protestors. In Basra, Diwaniyah, Karbala, Meesan, Nassiriyah and Wasit, armed men regularly showed up at prominent protesters' homes to deliver threatening notes.[85] The situation became particularly tense in Nasseriyah on 17 November, when security forces shot live ammunition into the crowds.

Worried about the potential for full-scale destabilisation, the government reached out to the tribes in the knowledge that they were the only force with the requisite social power to contain the unrest. Not that the sheikhs could have commanded their youth to stop protesting; but were they to take a clear stance against the demonstrations, the impact would have been less. Prime Minister Adel Abdulmehdi called on the sheikhs therefore to meet him to try to 'find solutions' to the unrest. A group of sheikhs responded to his call and met him in Baghdad on 20 November. Abdulmehdi told those present that they should tell the protestors to wait for the government to complete its long-term development plan, while making it clear to the sheikhs that it was their responsibility to stop the demonstrations and calm the streets.[86] He did so while lavishing praise on the tribes, declaring in a statement, 'The tribes were on the front lines at all times. They sent brave men to the battlefields to fight against the Islamic State. They are truly the army of the *Marja'iya* and the people. They stood by our forces until we achieved victory.'[87]

249

TRIBES AND THE STATE IN LIBYA AND IRAQ

However, few sheikhs responded positively to the prime minister's overtures. In fact, only some sheikhs attended the Baghdad meeting and many of those who showed up were lesser sheikhs rather than general sheikhs. Many others refused to attend altogether. There were several reasons for their refusal to engage. Firstly, many sheikhs felt that the demands of the protestors were legitimate and they backed their calls for basic rights and services. Secondly, many sheikhs were outraged at the heavy-handed way in which the authorities had responded to the demonstrations. Furthermore, given the way in which the tide was turning against the government, the sheikhs did not want to be seen to be sitting with the very prime minister whose security forces had killed and maimed unarmed protestors. It was important therefore that they were seen to be protecting rather than betraying their tribesmen. Notably, there was a strong reaction among the protestors towards those sheikhs who accepted Abdulmehdi's invitation. One protestor in Baghdad decried, 'What about the martyrs and those who have been injured? How could they forget about them and sit around the same table with the government?... We condemn all the tribes that took part in that meeting. All they have done is just mock the martyrs and what they fell for.'[88] Another declared, 'If they were real tribesmen, they would have never taken part in this scam.'[89]

Many sheikhs opted instead therefore to turn their back on the government and stand behind the protestors, supporting their demands for change. In Nasseriyah, many sheikhs went to the town's Haboubi Square—the centre of the protests—to perform tribal *housa* in order to show their solidarity with the protestors.[90] Others issued expressions of support. The sheikhs also saw it as their duty to try to protect the protestors from the government's violent onslaughts. The sheikhs of Bani Tamim, for example, held a meeting in one of their mudheefs in Basra to discuss how to shield the demonstrators from attack. After the meeting, Sheikh Mansour al-Tamimi posted a video online in which he threatened to set up armed groups to protect the town on account of the fact that the government had become 'unable to protect its people'.[91] He also explained, 'We, Bani Tamim, announced that if one of the demonstrators [in Basra] felt their life was at risk, we would protect him. We also announced that the state

250

TRIBES AND MOBILISATION

has to protect us. I myself was subjected to assassination attempts. So if the state is unable to protect us, let it tell us so, and we will form brigades to defend ourselves. What the tribe did in these demonstrations is to remind the state that it needs to act and to remind it of its responsibilities towards its citizens'.[92]

In Nasseriyah, the sheikhs of the Bidour and Abouda tribes engaged with the local police forces and succeeded in separating the protestors from the authorities. However, things continued to deteriorate. On 28 November, a security force came from outside the Dhi Qar governorate and attacked protestors in Nasseriyah, killing 32 and wounding 225 more. This violence prompted the sheikhs to demand that Marshal Jameel Shimmeri, an army commander whose forces had killed protestors in the town, be brought to justice. On 4 December, the Dhi Qar tribes issued a joint statement demanding that the government resign and that a new government be appointed. Sheikh Karim Mahawar, a notable from the Bidour tribe, meanwhile, threatened at the time, 'If the judiciary doesn't punish those who were involved in killing our sons, we will take our rights by our own hands.'[93]

Despite these efforts, the situation continued to escalate, including in Nasseriyah, where in mid-January 2020, hundreds of protestors not only surged into the squares but also cut off roads and bridges to prevent security forces from trying to enter. The situation looked to be running out of control fast, especially after 26 January, when more than eighty protestors were injured by the police. Alarmed at the potential for the governorate to collapse and for bloodshed to ensue, the sheikhs realised that they needed to intervene more forcefully. Sheikh Hussein Ali Khayoun, the sheikh of the Abouda tribe, telephoned Sheikh Adel al-Assad, who was at a meeting with the sheikhs of the Bidour tribe in the Mudheef of Sheikh Abar Fahad Shirshab in Battha'a, north of Nasseriyah.[94] Sheikh Khayoun pleaded with Sheikh Adel to return to the city with immediate effect, explaining that protestors were rounding on the police directorate and were about to attack it, and that he needed help to pull the demonstrators back in order to prevent the situation from spiralling completely out of control.[95]

The prospect of the police directorate being taken over was particularly alarming to the sheikhs, not least because it may have opened

251

TRIBES AND THE STATE IN LIBYA AND IRAQ

the way for the storming of the Al-Hoot prison in Nasseriyah, which was housing large numbers of ISIS detainees. In addition, the sheikhs not only felt obliged to protect their tribesmen who were protesting, they also had a duty towards those members of the police who were from their tribes. As Safa'ah explains, 'The police directorate contains weapons and ammunition and policemen, and these policemen are the sons of tribes. There is no policeman who comes from outside the governorate. Even the police commander was from the governorate itself.'[96] Thus the sheikhs felt they had a responsibility to protect both the protestors and the police. Additionally, the sheikhs feared that if things got any more out of control, the killing that would inevitably ensue would embroil their tribes in cycles of tribal vengeance and bloodshed. They realised therefore that in the face of the state's impotence, they needed to do something to calm the situation and restore order. Sheikh Adel and the other sheikhs rushed back to the scene, going straight to the police directorate where, after immense effort, they managed to convince the protestors to withdraw from the area around the police directorate.[97] Indeed, the tribes viewed themselves as a bridge between the protestors and the local police force, and engaged with both sides to try to avert disaster.

Their triumph was short lived. The same night, which the sheikhs spent with the protestors in the square, unknown forces in government pick-up vehicles attacked again, entering the square, where they set fire to protest tents and opened fire on protestors, killing one demonstrator. Fearing that more security forces would be sent from outside, or that protestors from other governorates would flood into Nasseriyah to join the demonstrations, destabilising the situation futher, the sheikhs agreed to take drastic action and to adopt a security role. They called on their tribesmen to take up their weapons and close all the roads leading to the governorate. The tribesmen duly complied; the al-Juwaibar tribe closed the road linking Dhi Qar to Basra, the Najam and Hawashi tribes closed all the roads leading to Souq al-Shayouk, while the Bu Saleh and Nassrala tribes closed the road that links Dhi Qar to Meesan.[98] The Bani Assad tribe prevented anyone from entering the Jabayish district, while the Shwaylat, Bani Rukab, A'rgail and other tribes blocked the roads between Dhi Qar and Meesan, Diwaniyah, Baghdad and Kut.[99] The al-Ghazi and Bidour

252

TRIBES AND MOBILISATION

tribes took control of the highway west of Nasseriyah. Upon the sheikhs' call, the tribes mobilised in their own local areas to force an effective shutdown of the governorate. Some sources claimed that they did so on the orders of the *Marja'iya*, asserting that this was the reason why the tribes were able to move collectively in what was clearly a co-ordinated act.[100] However, there is no concrete evidence to support this assertion. Although one cannot discount the possibility of such intervention, for the tribes, this action was first and foremost a way to contain the crisis and to stabilise Nasseriyah at a time when things looked to be spiralling out of control.

This doesn't mean that all Dhi Qar tribes followed the same path. The interests of some tribes or clans were staked so heavily in the state and the political parties that their sheikhs opposed the demonstrations. The same was true of those tribal elements that had close links to the Iranian-backed militias, or those who believed the protestors were implementing the demands of foreign agents and forces, including the US, in order to put an end to Shi'ite domination.[101] Some tribes and clans were split, meanwhile, with one group supporting the state and another backing the protestors. In the main the sheikhs' priority was to protect their sons and avert collapse. To this end, they found themselves dragged further into the political and security scene than they would normally countenance. While they tried to resolve the situation through their characteristic role as mediators between the people and the state, when this failed, they had no alternative but to up the stakes and take concrete action in order to avert further crisis. Thus, while tribes are often portrayed as instigators and fomenters of instability, in this instance, they proved the opposite. This is not to suggest that tribes don't engage in conflict and destabilising behaviour, the intra-tribal fighting that has persisted in Basra being a case in point. Yet, when it looked as though the governorate was on the verge of collapse, and as though blood was going to be spilt, the tribes took the side of stability, even if doing so meant extending beyond their traditional role.

Despite arguments in the literature suggesting that tribes are no longer real or concrete structures, post-2003 Iraq has shown that tribes are still solid social organisations and units capable of action. Although Iraqi tribes have undoubdetly undergone far-reaching

TRIBES AND THE STATE IN LIBYA AND IRAQ

changes, including in structure and form, they have not disappeared altogether, nor can they be reduced to mere 'cultural' or 'social tribalism'. Today's tribes may be more divided and diffuse than Iraqi tribes of old, and their power may not always be evident or fully tangible, but they are still concrete organisational structures that have solid meaning in the lives of large swathes of the population. Through their ability to mosbilise and provide critical mass, as well as through their relationships to key powerbrokers, the tribes have continued to be important players in both the political and security landscapes.

CONCLUSION

Notwithstanding the decades of modernisation and urbanisation, as well as the earth-shattering changes that have gripped the Arab world in the contemporary period, tribes remain a concrete reality in both Libya and Iraq, and still represent important modalities of identity and action. Many Libyans and Iraqis still identify closely with their tribe, and while they may adopt multiple identities simultaneously, kinship continues to play a significant part in their lives. The fact that tribes have come to the fore since regime change in both states does not mean that they were absent or irrelevant before. One should not confuse increased visibility with what has been described in some of the commentary as a 're-tribalisation' of society or a 'resurgence' of tribal identity. Tribes have always been a key part of society and social interaction, and tribal identity has long co-existed with other identities and loyalties. There is no contradiction for many Libyans and Iraqis between tribal loyalty and national loyalty. This is not to suggest that all citizens of these states view tribes as relevant or meaningful; there are plenty of Libyans and Iraqis who remain dismissive of tribes and tribalism, and plenty more for whom the tribe is only relevant in times of need or when the state is absent or unable to respond. Furthermore, tribes are just one component among many that have shaped the modern histories of these states, and their role should not be inflated. However, the tribe remains the key unit of social organisation and the foundation of society in both countries.

TRIBES AND THE STATE IN LIBYA AND IRAQ

This does not mean that tribes have remained static. As the experiences of Libya and Iraq demonstrate, tribes have undergone transformative changes over the decades, adapting to the modernisation process and to the shifting nature of the state. Long gone are the days when the tribe was part of an untamed rebellious periphery and when the sheikh could command or direct his tribesmen. Today's tribes span both the rural and urban environments, and sheikhs are just as likely to be part of the professional urban classes than not. These urbanised elements may reside in the towns and cities but are not bounded by 'cultural tribalism' only, as has been suggested in some of the literature, which seems bent on denying the continued existence of tribes as concrete realities that inform and shape people's lived experiences. Rather, these elements are very much still part of organised tribal structures with their own codes and customs that are not alien to the urban setting, whether in Benghazi, Baghdad or Basra. Tribes can no longer be dismissed as part of the hinterland or framed as being in opposition to a more 'civilised' urban centre. As Sheikh Mansour al-Tamimi of the Tamim tribe in Iraq articulates, 'The tribes are a powerful resource for the country. We are part of the state. We are educated. We are doctors, engineers, etc. Our girls are educated. The image of the tribe as if it is living in the wilderness and as if it is an armed body is an old one. We, like everyone else, want a civil state. Al-Tamimi is my genealogy and I am proud of it. The tribe is genealogy and blood and it is not identity.'[1]

As well as expanding to incorporate the urban space, tribes have also changed in structure. Tribes are less cohesive than they once were, with sheikhs and clans breaking away at a faster pace than in the past. Although this phenomenon is occurring in both states, it is particularly acute in Iraq, which has witnessed a striking multiplication of sheikhs and clans, all jostling for power and influence. Where there was once a general sheikh, there are now many centres of power inside a single tribe or clan, with multiple heads of houses and families who are in competition with one another as much as they are working towards a common political goal. As Sheikh Abdulhameed al-Kezza, a leading sheikh from the al-Awaqir tribe in Libya, describes, 'We used to have one sheikh with a history behind him. Now we don't have that. We have many people claiming they are from the leading house.'[2]

256

CONCLUSION

This structural transformation is partly the result of a natural process whereby tribes expand over time, prompting elements to break off and create new clans, but it is also due to the policies of the nationalist regimes. As this book has shown, the Qadhafi regime in Libya and the Ba'athist regime in Iraq worked to create and activate alternative centres of power within the tribes. Both brought up loyal elements and provided them the financial means with which to create new poles of influence inside the tribe that could bypass and challenge the traditional tribal leadership. This dividing of the tribe accelerated following regime change as the new political landscapes that opened up in Libya and Iraq offered new opportunities for engagement. The tribe was no longer locked into a vertical clientelistic relationship with a repressive centralised power but was suddenly facing a dizzying array of powerbrokers, some of whom sought to court and use the tribes. The fragmentation of the political and security landscape created new patron–client relationships and new forms of bargaining both at the local and the national level. While on one level tribes were weakened by the fracturing that occurred, on the other they were empowered too, finding themselves with greater space to negotiate the parameters between ruler and ruled. Although tribes are still a long way from being partners of the state, they are playing a more active and independent role than in previous decades.

Furthermore, while the tribe may be more diffuse and while it may routinely find itself outmanoeuvred by more powerful armed groups and militias, it has not lost its ability to project political power, albeit not always in ways that are fully perceptible or quantifiable. Indeed, the tribe's political power lies in its ability to mobilise. Whether by providing critical mass during elections, supplying recruits for military operations, offering support and legitimacy to powerbrokers, shutting down energy infrastructure or shielding protestors from state or parastatal agencies, the tribes are informal political actors that have a tangible role in steering the course of events. The sheikh of today may not be as powerful as the sheikh of old, but he can still command influence among his tribe, clan or house, and his words still carry weight beyond the social realm. Hence the sheikhs, or sometimes the dominant elite in the tribe, are able to work from behind, rallying their tribesmen and mustering sufficient critical mass to influence the

TRIBES AND THE STATE IN LIBYA AND IRAQ

course of events. Without tribal support, Haftar would not have succeeded in defeating his Islamist opponents in Benghazi, taking over the ports of the Oil Crescent in 2016, or pressurising the authorities in Tripoli by orchestrating the shutdown of the oil infrastructure in 2020. The tribes provided Haftar with weight and depth he would not otherwise have had to achieve his objectives. In Iraq, without the tribes, the state would not have been able to defeat either al-Qaeda or ISIS, and the political parties would not have been able to reach beyond the narrow constituencies of the urban elite in any meaningful way. Furthermore, had the tribes not intervened in the protests in the south of Iraq, putting themselves in between the authorities and the protestors, even more blood would have been spilled. For all that sheikhs routinely assert that tribes are social entities, in reality they have a bigger impact and role than is often apparent.

Tribes have also been critical proponents of conflict resolution, proving to be some of the strongest advocates of national reconciliation while working hard on the ground to build bridges and contain conflict. This type of action fits with tribes' views of themselves and their natural role. Tribes put great store by the fact that by their very essence, they transcend some of the divisions that have fractured society over generations but that have come to the fore in both states since regime change. In Iraq, tribes are proud that they extend across sect, while in Libya extol the fact that they are spread across regions. Tribes also pride themselves on their ability to absorb all political orientations and creeds, their porous nature and their pragmatism, allowing them to encompass a wide range of views and ideological stances. Tribes are not prescriptive and as this book has shown, do not generally take unified political stances. Instead, they view themselves as the most natural and most authentic expression of society in all its components and believe that they are the only force capable of serving as an effective social glue that can hold things together. In contrast to some of the other sub-state components that have come to the fore in the new order and that are mobilised on sect or ideology, tribes and tribesmen are presenting themselves as exponents of the state and of national unity.

Such sentiment should not belie the fact that tribes and tribesmen in both states have been agents of violence too. Tribes have been

258

CONCLUSION

embroiled in bloody campaigns of vengeance against their fellow countrymen and have invoked history to unleash violence on their opponents. They have also engaged in inter-tribal conflict, which in some areas has been particularly acute. Yet, tribes in both states have also sought to uphold stability and promote national unity. As Ouanes observes, 'The tribe can serve as a strong "machine" to produce hatred and rekindle animosity... but it is also... a house of experience and wisdom that can diffuse tensions... spread the culture of stability and consolidate the spirit of solidarity and acceptance of others.'[3]

This is not to promote any idealised or romanticised view of the tribe. Tribes are still ultimately interested in securing their own interests and are replete with problems, including questionable tribal norms and outdated behaviours, especially in relation to gender. They are also constrained by their own locality and scope. Yet in the Libyan and Iraqi contexts, they have arguably served more as agents of stability than of conflict. This is because tribes prefer to operate within the confines of a stable and strong state. Contrary to the caricature of the tribe as working in opposition to the state and being preoccupied solely with looting its spoils, tribes in Libya and Iraq have demonstrated that they are more comfortable working within the confines of state structures rather than against them. Although tribes have been routinely framed in the literature as being opponents of the state or have been pigeonholed in the flawed binary 'strong state-weak tribe' paradigm, tribes not only seek to work within the state, they consider themselves to be part and parcel of it. The tribes still uphold and cherish the narrative that they are the defenders of the state against hostile invading powers, whether through their role fighting jihad against the Italians in Libya or against the British in Iraq. The tribes also consider themselves to be the founders of the modern state in both countries, as well as the protectors of society. For the tribes, history, however constructed, is alive and ever-present. They also rightly consider their own history as being fully intertwined with that of the state rather than as something peripheral or separate to it. Thus, the tribes—which are conservative by nature—yearn for stability and seek to be part of the nation. As Cherstich has observed, Libya is not failing to become a nation because of tribalism.[4] The same is true of Iraq.

TRIBES AND THE STATE IN LIBYA AND IRAQ

There are of course more practical reasons why tribes prefer a stable and secure state. The tribes' ultimate goal is to have autonomy over their own areas and communities, and to be left alone to administer tribal justice. This does not mean that they oppose the state or want to operate outside of its confines. Rather, they want a hybrid system whereby they can manage their own affairs while still being part of the wider framework of the state, through which they reap its rewards, namely, by accessing jobs, benefits and resources for their tribesmen. As Sheikh Adnan al-Danbous observes, 'The street is tribal because the individual cannot break the wall of the state. The tribe is his access.'[5]

However, the tribe is still opaque, including to policymakers grappling with these countries as they undergo fraught transitions. Outside of the counter-terrorism context, there has been a tendency by policymakers to ignore the tribes, not least because of the difficulty and complexity of understanding or engaging with them. Their fluid and multi-centred nature, as well as the fact that they are primarily units of social not political organisation, have served as additional barriers to engagement, as have the serious and valid questions surrounding tribes' value systems and their ability to work within democratic norms. However, within the Libyan and Iraqi contexts, tribes have proved to be no better or no worse than the other components that have filled the political vacuum since regime change. Although the old trope of tribes being unreliable partners who only serve their own interests and switch allegiance to the highest bidder may have elements of truth in it, these other components have behaved no differently, and in some cases have behaved worse. From the political parties, including those of an Islamist bent, to the militias in both states, to the LNA in Libya, they all have raided the state, viewing it as a golden goose to be exploited and controlled. As the devastating experiences in both Libya and Iraq have shown, political parties and elections do not equate to democracy and have brought neither stability nor prosperity.

Tribes are a reflection of their own societies therefore, and their norms and behaviours are a reflection of the experience of modernisation and the nature of the state in the Middle East. Tribes are neither a positive nor a negative phenomenon but are a reality of life in Libya,

CONCLUSION

Iraq and beyond. Despite the ideological onslaught they have withstood over generations in the name of modernity, nationalism and progress, tribes are organic components of their own societies and should not be ignored or dismissed as outdated bodies that are separate or different to other components. They are multifaceted, flexible and comprise urbanised, semi-urbanised and rural elements that are able to adapt and work with the prevailing political power. More importantly, they are a cornerstone of identity for large swathes of the population in both Libya and Iraq and will remain so for the foreseeable future.

pp. [2–4]

NOTES

INTRODUCTION

1. Jabar, F A, and Dawod, H (eds), 2002, *Tribes and Power: Nationalism and Ethnicity in the Middle East*, London, Saqi Books.
2. Stolzoff, S, 2009, *The Iraqi Tribal System: A Reference for Social Scientists, Analysts, and Tribal Engagement*, Two Harbours.
3. Husken, T, 2018, *Tribal Politics in the Borderland Between Libya and Egypt*, Palgrave Macmillan.
4. Fatahaly, O, and Palmer M, 1980, *Political Development and Social Change in Libya*, D C Heath & Co., Lexington, USA, Lexington Books; Mattes, H, 2011, *Formal and Informal Authority in Libya in Libya Since 1969*, in 'Libya Since 1969: Qadhafi's Revolution Revisited', Dirk Vandewalle (ed.), Palgrave Macmillan, Anderson, L, 1986, *The State Avoided in Libya: From Rentier Monarchy to Distributive Jamahiriyyah in The State and Social Transformation in Tunisia and Libya, 1830–1980*, Princeton University Press.
5. Anaya, J, 2012, *La 'Seconde Jamahiriyya' libyenne: l'échec d'une stratégie de survie*, L'Année du Maghreb, VIII, 2012, pp. 207–18; Hweio, H, 2012, 'Tribes in Libya: From Social Organization to Political Power', *African Conflict and Peacebuilding Review*, Vol. 2, No. 1 (Spring 2012), pp. 111–21.
6. Lacher, W, 2020, *Libya's Fragmentation*. London, I B Taurus, p. 72.
7. Obeidi, A, 2015, *Political Culture in Libya*, London, Routledge.
8. Davis, J, 1987, *Libyan Politics: Tribe and Revolution*, London, I B Tauris.
9. Qadhafi held that political representation was false and in his discourse espoused a society in which the people ruled themselves. This was despite the fact that he established a highly centralised authoritarian state.
10. Anderson, L, 1986, *The State Avoided in Libya: From Rentier Monarchy to Distributive Jamahiriyyah in the State and Social Transformation in Tunisia and Libya, 1830–1980*, Princeton University Press.
11. Ahmida, A A, 2014, '*The Libya We Do Not Know*', Tripoli, The Libyan Ministry of Culture.

263

pp. [4–16]   NOTES

12. Tripp, C, 2000, *A History of Iraq*, Cambridge, Cambridge University Press.
13. Baram, A, 1997, 'Neo-Tribalism in Iraq: Saddam Hussein's Tribal Policies 1991–96', *International Journal of Middle East Studies*, Vol. 29(1); Rohde, A, 2010, *State-Society Relations in Ba'athist Iraq*, London, Routledge.
14. Author interview, Abduljawad Badeen, July 2021.
15. Khoury, P, and Kostiner, J (eds), 1990, *Tribes and State Formation in the Middle East*, University of California Press, p. 5.
16. Walsh, D, 2016, *Us Against the World: Tribalism in Contemporary Iraq*, Master's thesis, Sciences-Po.
17. Cavatorta, F, 2017, 'The Weakness of State Structures in the Arab World: Socio-Economic Challenges from Below' in *The Frailty of Authority Borders, Non-State Actors and Power Vacuums in a Changing Middle East*, Lorenzo Kamel (ed.), Rome, Edizioni Nuova Cultura.
18. Husken, T, 2018, *Tribal Politics in the Borderland Between Libya and Egypt*, Palgrave Macmillan, p. 38.
19. Lacher, W, 2013, 'The Rise of Tribal Politics' in *The 2011 Libyan Uprisings and the Struggle for the Post-Qadhafi Future*, Pack, J (ed.), Palgrave Macmillan.
20. Pack, J, 2013, 'Introduction: The Centre and the Periphery' in *The 2011 Libyan Uprisings and the Struggle for the Post-Qadhafi Future*, Pack, J (ed.), Palgrave Macmillan.
21. Lacher, W, 2011, 'Families, Tribes and Cities in the Libyan Revolution', *Middle East Policy*, Vol. 18, Issue 4, Winter 2011, pp. 140–54.
22. Cherstich, I, 2014, 'When Tribesmen do not act Tribal: Libyan Tribalism as Ideology (not as Schizophrenia)', *Middle East Critique*, Vol. 23, Issue 4.
23. Zeidal, R, June 2016, *Tribes in Iraq: A Negligible Factor in State Formation in Tribes and States in a Changing Middle East*, Uzi Rabi (ed.), London, Hurst.
24. Jabar, F, and Dawod, H, op. cit.
25. Zeidal, R, op. cit.; Harling, P, 2012, 'Beyond Political Ruptures: Towards a Historiography of Social Continuity in Iraq' in *Writing the Modern History of Iraq: Historiographical and Political Challenges*, Riccardo Bocco, et al., World Scientific Publishing Company.
26. Wardi, A (1969–1978); Jabar, F A (2017); Jabar, F A and Dawood, H (eds) (2002); Hweio, H (2012); Hamza, K (2017).
27. Genat, M, 15 September 2021, 'Tribal Justice and State Law in Iraq', *International Journal of Middle East Studies*, Cambridge, Cambridge University Press, pp. 507–11

1. FROM PALACE TO REVOLUTION: TRIBES AND THE COMING TO POWER OF THE NATIONALIST STATE

1. *Alsijil Alqawmi*, Vol. 1, Speech 2 January 1970, p. 191–2.
2. Author interview, Abdulsalam Jalloud, Paris, February 2022.
3. Dawisha, A, Winter 2003, 'Requiem for Arab Nationalism', *Middle East Quarterly*, Vol. 10, No. 1, Philadelphia, pp. 25–41.
4. The Senussi religious order, a Sunni revivalist movement that had implanted itself

NOTES

pp. [16–20]

mainly in eastern Libya during the nineteenth century, where it became intertwined with local tribes, which sought to attract and protect its lodges in return for giving up some arable land and wells. The order was the source of Idris's religious legitimacy.

5. Proclamation of the Republic, 1 September 1969.
6. First, R, 1975, *Libya: The Elusive Revolution*, New York, Penguin Books, p. 78.
7. Bulugma, M R, 1964, *The urban geography of Benghazi*, thesis, Durham University, pp. 265–66. Available at http://etheses.dur.ac.uk/9559
8. *Alsijil Alqawmi*, Vol. 1, Speech, 2 January 1970, pp. 191–2.
9. Wehrey, F, November 2018, Review of *Tribe, Islam and State in Libya: Analytical Study of the Roots of Libyan Tribal Society and Evolution Up to the Qaramanli Reign (1711–1835)* by Faraj Najem, *Libyan Studies*, London.
10. Notable exceptions are Davis, J, *Tribe and Revolution*, Husken, T, *Tribal Politics in the Borderland Between Libya and Egypt*.
11. Al-Shadeedi, A, and Ezzedine, N, 18 February 2019, 'Libyan tribes in the Shadows of War and Peace', CRU Policy Brief, Clingaendal. Available at https://www.clingendael.org/publication/libyan-tribes-shadow-war-and-peace; Joffe, G, 2013, 'Civil Activism and the Roots of the 2011 Uprisings' in *The 2011 Libyan Uprisings and the Struggle for the Post-Qadhafi Future*, Jason Pack (ed.), Palgrave Macmillan.
12. Jalloud, A, 2021, *Memoirs of Abdulsalam Ahmed Jalloud: The Epic*, Doha, Arab Centre for Research and Studies.
13. Najem, F, 2004, *Tribe, Islam and state in Libya: analytical study of the roots of the Libyan tribal society and interaction up to the Qaramanli rule (1711–1835)*, PhD thesis, University of Westminster School of Social Sciences, Humanities and Languages, p. 147. Available at https://westminsterresearch.westminster.ac.uk/download/926d7d076329ed28eba6c6893c17630fb1ec633a9e37b4a2ac4ea32394f484ed/19198678/Najem.pdf
14. Keddie, O, January 2015, 'The Ink of Exile', *Al-Moustaqil Magazine*, p. 107 and Shouker, A F, *Al'iihya' Baed Al'iinsa'*, part 1, Dar Alkilma, p. 91.
15. Interview with Qadhafi by *Kulushay Magazine*, Lebanon, 1 September 1972. (In Arabic) Reproduced in *Alsijil Alqawmi*, Vol. 3, pp. 31–2.
16. Ahmida, A A, 2020, *An Introductory Study on the Status, Challenges and Prospects of the Libyan Society. Part II of a Baseline Study for the Libya Socioeconomic Dialogue Project*. E/ESCWA/CL6.GCP/2020/TP.2.
17. Shalgam, A, *2012, Figures Around Qadhafi*, Tripoli, Dar al-Madariq and Ferjani, p. 266.
18. Heitman, G, July 1969, 'Libya: An Analysis of the Oil Economy', *The Journal of Modern African Studies*, Vol. 7 Issue 2, Cambridge, Cambridge University Press, pp. 249–63.
19. Wright, J, 1981, *Libya: A Modern History*, London, Routledge, p. 100.
20. Ibid.
21. Elbendak, O, June 2008, *Urban Transformation and Social Change in a Libyan City: An Anthropological Study of Tripoli*, PhD thesis, National University of Ireland Maynooth,

NOTES

Maynooth, p. 139. Available at https://mural.maynoothuniversity.ie/1332/1/Ph.D._Thesis.pdf and see Fig. 11.2, map of tribal distribution from Hajjaji, S A, 1969, *The land use patterns and rural settlement in the Benghazi plain*, thesis, Durham University, p. 47. Available at: http://etheses.dur.ac.uk/9644

22. Ahram, A, 2019, *Break All the Borders: Separatism and the Reshaping of the Middle East*, Oxford, Oxford University Press.
23. Bulugma, op. cit., p. 99.
24. Ibid.
25. Wright, op. cit. p. 100.
26. First, op. cit. p. 115; Mansfield, P, 1976, *The Arabs*, New York, Allen Lane; Vandewalle, D, 2006, *A History of Modern Libya*, Cambridge, Cambridge University Press.
27. First, op. cit. p. 115.
28. Ashraf Waddan refers to the Murabitoun tribes of the Waddan oasis—those tribes that claim special holy status.
29. Ouanes, M, 2018, *The Libya that I Saw, the Libya that I See: The Calamity of a Country*, Tunis, Mediterranean Publisher, p. 81.
30. *Alarabiya Net*, 'The Political Memory: Abdulsalam Jalloud Interview', part 1, 24 August 2012. Available at https://rb.gy/eegz1
31. 'Qadhafi's Five-Part Account of the Libyan Revolution', published in the Libyan press, 1969. Available at https://rb.gy/zap0ty
32. Author interview, Abdullah Othman, Tunis, October 2019.
33. Conversations with Libyans in Tripoli and Benghazi during the 2000s.
34. Husken, op. cit. p. 88.
35. Ibid.
36. Al-Houni, A, 2015, *Saif Qadhafi: The Cunning Art of Politics and the Irony of Fate*, Tripoli, Dar Madariq, p. 11.
37. Ibid.
38. Al-Deeb, F, 1986, *Abdulnasser and Libya's Revolution*, Cairo, Dar al-Mostaqbel Alarabi, p. 31.
39. Nabil, M, 1969, *Libya and the Revolution*, Kitab Almusawir, Cairo, Dar al-Hilal. Available at https://rb.gy/vgrwt4
40. Author interview, Abdulsalam Jalloud, Paris, February 2022.
41. Husken, op. cit. p. 88.
42. Joffe, G, op. cit.
43. *Alsijil Alqawmi*, Vol. 1, Speech 2 January 1970, pp. 191–2.
44. *Alsijil Alqawmi*, Vol. 3, 1972, p. 51.
45. Author interview, Sharif al-Abbar, November 2019.
46. Fatahaly, O, and Palmer, M, 1980, *Political Development and Social Change in Libya*, D C Heath & Co., Lexington, USA, Lexington Books, p. 56.
47. Author interview, Sheikh Mohamed Aujail Hasnawi, August 2021.
48. The counsellor was responsible for informing his tribe of all government decisions and for relaying his tribe's demands, concerns and complaints to the authorities.

NOTES pp. [27–31]

Food and Agriculture Organisation of the United Nations, Report to the Government of Libya. Development of Tribal Lands and Settlements Project, Vol. II. 1969. No government official or minister would take action affecting the sectional interest of a tribe without consulting its counsellor and the counsellor had the right to go over the government's head directly to the king. Morone, A, 2017, 'Idrīs' Libya and the Role of Islam: International Confrontation and Social Transformation', *Oriente Moderno*, Anno 97, No. 1, C A Nallino, Istituto per l'Oriente, pp. 111–32.

49. Ibrahim, S and Otto, J M, 201, *Resolving real property disputes in post-Gaddafi Libya, in the context of transitional justice*, the Centre for Law and Society Studies, Benghazi University and Van Vollenhoven Institute for Law, Governance and Society, Leiden University, Van Vollenhoven Institute. Available on https://rb.gy/dlwtu5

50. Law No. (142) of 1970 on Tribal Lands and Wells. Available at https://security-legislation.ly/en/law/101411

51. Ibrahim, and Otto, op. cit. and El-Kikhia, M O, 1997, *Libya's Qadhafi*, *The Politics of Contradiction*, Florida, University Press of Florida.

52. Food and Agriculture Organisation of the United Nations, Report to the Government of Libya. Development of Tribal Lands and Settlements Project, Vol. II, 1969.

53. Hajjaji, op. cit., p. 265.

54. Author interview, Abdulsalam Jalloud, Paris, February 2022.

55. Law 123 of 1970.

56. Ibrahim and Otto, op. cit.

57. Author interview, Abdulsalam Jalloud, Paris, February 2022.

58. Author interview, Musa Rumaila, January 2022.

59. Fathalay and Palmer, op. cit. p. 58; Alexander, N, April 1981, 'The Continuous Revolution', *Middle Eastern Studies*, Vol. 17, No. 2, pp. 210–27; Mattes, H, 2011, 'Formal and Informal Authority in Libya in Libya Since 1969', in *Libya Since 1969: Qadhafi's Revolution Revisited*, Dirk Vandewalle (ed.), Palgrave Macmillan; Vandewalle, D, *Libya Since Independence*, London, I B Taurus, p. 67.

60. Author interview, Abdulsalam Jalloud, Paris, February 2022.

61. Author interview, Sheikh Mohamed Aujail Hasnawi, August 2021.

62. Husken, op. cit. p. 88.

63. Fatahaly and Palmer, op. cit. p. 35.

64. Dumasy, François and Di Pasquale, 2012/1, Francesca, 'Être historien dans la Libye de Kadhafi. Stratégies professionnelles et pratiques mémorielles autour du Libyan Studies Center', *Politique africaine* (No. 125), pp. 127–46.

65. Author interview, Abdulsalam Jalloud, Paris, February 2022.

66. Al-Deeb, op. cit. p. 74.

67. *Alsijil Alqawmi*—Vol. 1, 1969–1970, pp. 266–7.

68. Ibid.

69. Author interview, Absuldalam Jalloud, Paris, February 2022.

pp. [32–40] NOTES

70. El-Kikhia, op. cit. p. 45.
71. Author interview, Sheikh Mohamed Aujail Hasnawi, August 2021.
72. Author interview, Sharif al-Abbar, July 2021.
73. El-Khoja, M, 14 January 2006, *The Terrorism Triangle, Episode 2*, Libya Watanona. Available at https://rb.gy/sgfkca
74. El-Kikhia, op. cit. p. 90.
75. Ibid.
76. Shalgam, op. cit. p. 39
77. Ibid.
78. Author interview, Abdullah Othman, Tunis, October 2019.
79. Ibid.
80. Author interview, Sharif al-Abbar, July 2021.
81. Ibid.
82. Author interview, Kamila Othman, Tunis, October 2019.
83. Bleuchot, H, *Chroniques et documents libyens, 1969–1980*, Editions CNRS, Paris, p. 92.
84. For a discussion of *The Green Book*, see Pargeter, A, 2012, *Libya: The Rise and Fall of Gaddafi*, Yale University Press.
85. Qadhafi, M, 1982, *The Green Book*.
86. Ibid.
87. *Alsijil Alqawmi*, Vol. 10, 4 January 1979, pp. 358–9.
88. Bleuchot, op. cit. p. 88.
89. *Libya TV Channel*, 'An Interview with Nasser al-Hassouni,' 6 May 2011. Available at https://rb.gy/8iijq; https://rb.gy/u76b2; https://rb.gy/0iib4
90. Author interview, Abdulsalam Jalloud, Paris, February 2022.
91. Ibid.
92. Author interview, Saleh Ibrahim, Tunis, October 2019.
93. Author interview, Moncef Ouanes, Tunis, October 2019.
94. Author interview, Saleh Ibrahim, Tunis, October 2019.
95. Author interview, Abdullah Othman, Tunis, October 2019.
96. Jalloud, A, 2021, *Memoirs of Abdulsalam Ahmed Jalloud: The Epic*, Doha, Arab Centre for Research and Studies, p. 34–6.
97. Author interview, Abdulsalam Jalloud, Paris, February 2022.
98. Ibid.
99. Charbel, G, January 2012, *Inside Qadhafi's Tent: The Colonel's Companions Reveal the Secrets of His Regime*, Beirut, Riad al-Rayyes Books, p. 85
100. St John, R, 2015, *Libya, Continuity and Change*, London, Routledge, p. 177.
101. Other brigades included the Fadil Bu Omar Brigade in Benghazi; the Hamza Brigade in Misrata; the Sahbane Brigade in Gharyan; and Battalion 32 in Tripoli, which went on to be headed by Qadhafi's son Khamis.
102. Keddie, O, 23 February 2014, *The Army of Muammar and the Army of Bubaker*, Al-Wasat. Available at https://rb.gy/flvedj.
103. Kane, S, 2015, 'Barqa Reborn?: Eastern Regionalism and Libya's Political

NOTES

pp. [40–49]

Transition' in *The Libyan Revolution and Its Aftermath*, Peter Cole and Brian McQuinn (eds), Oxford, Oxford University Press.

104. Author interview, Sheikh al-Senussi Buheleq, October 2021.

2. TRIBES AND QADHAFI'S REVOLUTIONARY TOOLBOX: FROM KHOUT AL-JED TO SOCIAL CONTROL

1. Author interview, Sheikh Mohamed Omar Benjdiriya, Tunis, October 2019. Benjdiriya also noted that there was some differentiation; while budgets in the west were usually passed quickly, Qadhafi used to monitor and often reduce budgets that had been proposed by congresses in the east as part of his efforts to maintain control.
2. *Alsijil Alqawmi*, Vol 7, p. 135.
3. Author interview, Sheikh Mohamed Omar Benjdiriya, Tunis, October 2019.
4. Jalloud, A, 2021, *Memoirs of Abdulsalam Ahmed Jalloud: The Epic*, Doha, Arab Centre for Research and Studies.
5. *Alarabiya Net*, 'The Political Memory: Abdulsalam Jalloud Interview,' part 1, 24 August 2012. Available at: https://rb.gy/eegz1
6. Shalgam, A, 2012, *Figures Around Qadhafi*, Tripoli, Dar al-Madariq and Ferjani, p. 301.
7. Ibid.
8. Ibid.
9. Author interview, Mousa Rumaila, January 2022.
10. Author interview, Kamila Othman, Tunis October 2019.
11. Shalgam, op. cit. p. 37.
12. Ibid. p. 38.
13. Keddie, O, January 2015, 'The Ink of Exile', *Al-Moustaqil Magazine*, Cairo, p. 109.
14. Ibid.
15. Author interview, Abdulrahman Shalgam, August 2021.
16. Aqeel, A H, 2012, *Secrets and Facts from Qadhafi's Time*, Al-Majmua Al-Dawliya li Nashr wa Tawzia, p. 122.
17. Ibid.
18. Shalgam, op. cit. p. 37.
19. Author interview, Saleh Al-Ghazal Zwai, August 2020.
20. Author interview, Sheikh Mohamed Aujail Hasnawi, August 2021.
21. Author interview, Abdulsalam Jalloud, Paris, February 2022.
22. Author interview, Sharif al-Abbar, July 2021.
23. El-Khoja, M, 14 January 2006, *The Terrorism Triangle, Episode 2*, Libya Watanona. Available at https://rb.gy/sgfkca
24. Shoukri, S, 1 June 2009, *The Time of the Monarchy: Men Around the King*, Part 7, Libya Al-Mostakbal. Available at: https://rb.gy/kgmzqr
25. Author interview, al-Senussi Buheleq, October 2021.
26. Ibid.

269

pp. [49–55]   NOTES

27. Najm, F, 2004, *Tribe, Islam and state in Libya: analytical study of the roots of the Libyan tribal society and interaction up to the Qaramanli rule (1711–1835)*, PhD thesis, University of Westminster School of Social Sciences, Humanities and Languages, p. 187. Available at https://westminsterresearch.westminster.ac.uk/download/926d7d076329ed28eba6c6893c17630fb1ec633a9e37b4a2ac4ea32394f484ed/19198678/Najem.pdf

28. Cited in Najm, op. cit. p. 189.

29. Author interview, Sheikh al-Senussi Buheleq, October 2021.

30. Author interview, Mehdi al-Barghathi, July 2021.

31. Lacher, W, and Labnouj, A, 2015, 'Factionalism Resurgent: The War in the Jabal Nafusa' in *The Libyan Revolution and Its Aftermath*, Peter Cole and Brian McQuinn (eds), Oxford, Oxford University Press, p. 261.

32. Author interview, Abdulsalam Jalloud, Paris, February 2022.

33. Ibid.

34. Ibid.

35. Ibid.

36. El-Khoja, op. cit.

37. Keddie, O, 15 December 2014, *Where Did Libya's Leaders Come From and Where Will They Come From?* Correspondents. Available at https://rb.gy/bynpap

38. Charbel, G, January 2012, *Inside Qadhafi's Tent: The Colonel's Companions Reveal the Secrets of his Regime*, Beirut, Riad al-Rayyes Books, p. 56.

39. Ibid. pp. 55–6.

40. Shalgam, op. cit. p. 572–3.

41. Author interview, Abdulsalam Jalloud, Paris, February 2022.

42. Ibid.

43. See Cole, P, 2015, *Bani Walid: Loyalism in a Time of Revolution* in *The Libyan Revolution and Its Aftermath*, Peter Cole and Brian McQuinn (eds), Oxford, Oxford University Press.

44. Author interview, Sheikh Mohamed Omar Benjdiriya, Tunis, October 2019.

45. Ibid.

46. Author interview, Abdulsalam Jalloud, Paris, February 2022.

47. Author interview, Saleh Ibrahim, Tunis, October 2019.

48. Author interview, Sheikh Mohamed Omar Benjdiriya, Tunis, October 2019.

49. Author interview, Sheikh Dr Mabrouk Buamid, Tunis, October 2019.

50. Author interview, Sheikh Mohamed Omar Benjdiriya, Tunis, October 2019.

51. Ibid.

52. Ibid.

53. Ibid.

54. Ibid.

55. Cole, op. cit. p. 290.

56. Muammar Gaddafi's reception of a delegation from Bani Walid in al-Sadadah area, published on 14 June 2020. Available at https://www.youtube.com/watch?v=vFmrKm2U74g

NOTES pp. [55–61]

57. International Crisis Group. 'Divided We Stand: Libya's Enduring Conflicts', Report No. 130, 14 September 2012. Available at https://rb.gy/ynuunb
58. Author interview, Sheikh Mohamed Omar Benjdiriya, Tunis, October 2029.
59. Mogherbi, M Z, 1995, *Civil Society, Economic Liberalisation and Democratisation in Libya*, Cairo, Ibn Khaldoun Centre for Development and Studies.
60. Butaleb, M N, October 2011, *The Political Dimensions of the Tribalism Phenomenon in Arab Societies: A Sociological Approach to the Tunisian and Libyan Revolutions*, Doha, the Arab Center for Research and Policy Studies. Available at https://rb.gy/uy2yoj
61. Anaya, J, 2012, *La 'Seconde Jamahiriyya' libyenne: l'échec d'une stratégie de survie, L'Annee du Maghreb, VIII.* Available at https://journals.openedition.org/anneemaghreb/1470?lang=ar
62. Faraj, A A, 30 January 2022, *Qadhafi visits Baghdad, apologises to Iraqis, describes Hafez Assad in harsh words*, Kitabat website. Available at https://kitabat.com
63. Attir, M, 2016, *Conflict Between the Tent and the Palace: A Critique of the Libyan Pattern of Modernity*. CreateSpace Independent Publishing Platform.
64. Author interview, Abdullah Othman, Tunis, October 2019.
65. Al-Awqali, S, 2 August 2015, *The Gaming Table of the Country and the Dice of the Tribe*, Al-Wasat. Available at https://rb.gy/wqcof2
66. CSDS Centre, *The Role of the Tribe in Libya*, 18 February 2019. Available at https://rb.gy/7o5mz.
67. Attir, op. cit.
68. Saqar, S S, 2002, *Gharyan and its Relationship with Surrounding Countryside*. Master's thesis. Available at https://drive.google.com/file/d/1AIc8CK4JYU_8SCoUotUcXHyN3I5raUj/view
69. Keddie, op. cit. p. 107 and Mzoughi, S B, 2008, *Genealogy of the Qadhadhfah tribe*. Libyajil site. Available at https://aboezra.yoo7.com/t13724-topic#24971
70. Ibid.
71. Mogherbi, op. cit.
72. Attir, op. cit. pp. 115–16.
73. Ibid.
74. Ibid.
75. Author interview, Sheikh Mohamed Omar Benjdiriya, Tunis, October 2019.
76. Ibid.
77. Obeidi, A, 2015, *Political Culture in Libya*, London, Routledge, p. 119.
78. Ibid.
79. Ibid.
80. Mrgin, H S, 2018, *The Protest and Social Movements in Libya: Between the Crisis of the State and Societal Fracturing*, Majalat Buhuth, London, Markaz Lundan Lildirasat Walbuhuth Waliastisharat. Available at https://rb.gy/nugjvk
81. Al-Shadeedi, Al-Hamzeh and Ezzedine, Nancy, 18 February 2019, *Libyan tribes in the Shadows of War and Peace. CRU Policy Brief, Clingaendal.* Aailable at: https://rb.gy/yi5g8g, and Riis, L (ed.), *January 2013, How the Local Matters: Democratization in Libya, Pakistan, Yemen and Palestine*, Danish Institute For International Studies. Available at https://rb.gy/hvja3d and Husken op. cit. p. 102 and Anderson.

pp. [61–64]　　　　NOTES

82. Lacher, W, 4 September 2019, 'Libya's local elites and the politics of alliance building' (2), *Libya Tribune*. Available at https://rb.gy/f8jaty; St John, R, *Libya, 2015, Continuity and Change*. London, Routledge, p. 71; and Myers, C, 2013, 'Tribalism and Democratic Transition in Libya: Lessons from Iraq', *Global Tides: Vol. 7*, Article 5. Available at https://rb.gy/b1hmor
83. Author interview, Sheikh Mohamed Aujail Hasnawi, August 2021.
84. Attir, op. cit. pp. 115–16, p. 110.
85. Cole, P, 2015, 'Bani Walid: Loyalism in a Time of Revolution', in *Libyan Revolution and its Aftermath*, McQuinn, B and Cole, P (eds), Oxford University Press, p. 293.
86. Author interview, Abdulrahman Shalgam, August 2021.
87. Al-Magariaf, M Y, March 2009, *Libya from Constitutional Legitimacy to Revolutionary Legitimacy*, Libya almostakbal. Available at https://rb.gy/h5nip
88. Author interview, Sheikh Abdulrahim Alburki, November 2019.
89. Mrgin, op. cit. *The Protest and Social Movements in Libya*.
90. Author interview, Sheikh Mohamed Aujail Hasnawi, August 2021.
91. Ibid.
92. Author interview, Abdullah Othman, Tunis, October 2019.
93. Author interview, Sheikh Mohamed Aujail Hasnawi, August 2021.
94. Mrgin, op. cit.
95. *Libya News and Views Website*, 10 March 1997. Available at https://rb.gy/g7zro
96. Libyan TV, Tripoli, 1951 gmt 9 September 1995, excerpts from recorded speech by Libyan leader Col Qadhafi to the masses of Bani Walid and Warfallah; broadcast by Libyan TV on 9 September; BBC Monitoring.
97. Qadhafi addresses Zintan tribes: traitors must be eliminated. BBC Summary of World Broadcasts. 6 August 1994, Section: Part 4 Middle East; THE MIDDLE EAST; Libya; ME/2067/MED. The speech includes the following telling example regarding a 'traitor' named Ja'akah: 'Libyans began to look for Ja'akahs. They found a family with the surname Ja'akah in Souq al-Jum'ah. They were about to burn their house and tear them into pieces in front of me but I managed to save them at the last moment. Had people not shown me respect they would have slaughtered them in front of me. However, his father came in; he made a public statement at Souq al-Jum' ah. He said that his son was a culprit and a traitor. He said that he was washing his hands of him and that he would cut his throat himself if he were to catch him. He said, furthermore, that the Libyans should not spare his blood; they should cut his throat as soon as they caught him. Thus, he washed his hands of treachery; treachery was disclaimed by the closet members of the family: Even the father washed his hands of his traitor son. And this is what is required: It is imperative that treachery must be contained and checked… Now the family of Ja'akah, actually, has been acquitted because the family itself; the father, the brother and the mother have disowned this traitor who is called Ja'akah. That is it. They said his blood was proscribed and said: If we catch him we will murder him. And we allow the Libyans to do the same. This family is no longer to be harmed by anybody because it disowned him. The traitor bears the responsibility himself. If the family

NOTES pp. [64–73]

did not disown this individual, the family itself would become a traitor family because it approved and did not reject treason. This must be clear.'

98. Author interview, Sheikh Mohamed Aujail Hasnawi, August 2021.
99. Ibid.
100. Ibid.
101. *Libya TV Channel*, 'An Interview with Nasser al-Hassouni', 6 May 2011. Available at https://rb.gy/8iijq; https://rb.gy/u76b2; https://rb.gy/0iib4
102. Ibid.
103. Ibid.
104. Qadhafi, M, 1999, *Escape to Hell and Other Stories*, London, Blake Publishing.

3. TRIBES, REVOLUTION AND REVENGE

1. Author interview, Sheikh Mabrouk Buamid, Tunis, October 2019.
2. *Aljazeera*, 'Supporting the Libyan Revolution, Today's Interview Programme with Juma al-Ma'arafi', 25 September 2011. Available at https://rb.gy/otnhvj
3. Al-Shadeedi, A, and Ezzedine, N, 18 February 2019, *Libyan Tribes in the Shadows of War and Peace. CRU Policy Brief, Clingaendal*. Available at https://rb.gy/yi5g8g
4. Mogherbi, Z, 2011, 'Social change, regime performance and the radicalisation of politics: The case of Libya', in *Islamist Radicalisation in North Africa, Politics and Process*, George Joffe (ed.), London, Routledge.
5. Pargeter, A, 2012, *Libya: The Rise and Fall of Gaddafi*, Yale University Press.
6. Shalgam, A, 2012, *Figures Around Qadhafi*, Tripoli, Dar al-Madariq and Ferjani, p. 58.
7. Ibid.
8. Al-Houni, A, 2015, *Saif Qadhafi: The Cunning Art of Politics and the Irony of Fate*, Tripoi, Dar al-Madariq, p. 30.
9. The families had rejected the regime's offer of compensation and wanted death certificates to be issued stating the cause of death, and for the perpetrators to be brought to justice. The SPLs became a kind of buffer for the regime, enabling it to look as though it was reckoning with the past without yielding to the families' demands.
10. Author interview, Sharif al-Abbar, November 2019.
11. Menas Associates, Libya Focus, December 2005.
12. 'Al-Qadhafi's son sympathetic to Lebanese model of power sharing', BBC Monitoring Middle East, London, 28 April 2005: 1.
13. Al-Houni, op. cit. p. 22.
14. Ibid.
15. Information imparted to author as part of an asylum claim in 2010.
16. Ibid.
17. Al-Houni, op. cit.
18. Author interview, Abduljawad Badeen, July 2021
19. *Libya TV Channel*, 'An Interview with Nasser al-Hassouni', 6 May 2011. Available at https://rb.gy/8iijq; https://rb.gy/u76b2; https://rb.gy/0iib4

pp. [73–78] NOTES

20. Author interview, Sharif al-Abbar, November 2019.
21. Author interview, al-Senussi Buheleq, September 2021.
22. 'An Interview with Nasser al-Hassouni,' op. cit.
23. Author interview, Moncef Ouanes, Tunis, October 2019.
24. Menas Associates, Libya Focus, March 2011.
25. Ibid.
26. Kane, S, 2015, 'Barqa Reborn?: Eastern Regionalism and Libya's Political Transition' in *The Libyan Revolution and Its Aftermath*, Cole, P and McQuinn, B (eds), Oxford, Oxford University Press; Lacher, W, 2011, 'Families, Tribes and Cities in the Libyan Revolution', *Middle East Policy*, Vol. 18, Issue 4, Winter 2011, pp. 140–54; Al-Shadeedi, A, and Ezzedine, N, op. cit.
27. Al-Houni, op. cit. p. 9.
28. Author interview, Abduljawad Badeen, July 2021.
29. 'An Interview with Nasser al-Hassouni,' op. cit.
30. Author interview, Mehdi al-Barghathi, July 2021.
31. Author interview, Abduljawad Badeen, July 2021.
32. *Africa Gate News*, 'Discover 11 Facts about al-Senussi al-Waziri, the Last Security Minister during the Qadhafi Era', 23 December 2018. Available at https://rb.gy/wkwn1
33. Author interview, senior al-Awaqir member who preferred to remain anonymous, 2021.
34. 'Gaddafi spent millions for tribal support', Al-Jazeera, 21 May 2012, https://www.aljazeera.com/news/2012/5/21/gaddafi-spent-millions-for-tribal-support
35. Ibid.
36. Author interview, Salah Gazal Senussi, August 2021.
37. Notably some commentators cited Sheikh Faraj Zuwiy, who on 20 February 2011 threatened to shut down oil production unless the regime stopped the bloodshed, as evidence that the Zwiya tribe had joined the revolution. Zuwiy is referred to repeatedly in the literature as the sheikh or head of the Zuwiya tribe. In reality, Sheikh Faraj was nothing of the sort and his intervention was what one leading sheikh in the Zwiya described as a 'media bubble that had no basis in reality'. A former Abu Slim prisoner, Shaiekh Faraj, later acknowledged that he had issued the declaration himself because he hoped it would result in European intervention to bring down the regime (https://www.youtube.com/watch?v=GsGejA9tdYM).
38. Bamyeh, M, 25 March 2011, 'Is the 2011 Libyan Revolution an Exception?', Jadaliyya. Available at https://www.jadaliyya.com/Details/23828
39. Lacher, W, 2020, *Libya's Fragmentation*, London, I B Taurus, p. 97.
40. Author interview, Abduljawad Badeen, July 2021.
41. Lacher, *Libya's Fragmentation*, op. cit. p. 75.
42. *Libya al-Ahrar*, 'An interview with Sheikh Taher al-Judai', 2011. Available at https://rb.gy/e7ep1
43. Author interview, Sheikh Mohamed Aujail Hasnawi, August 2021.
44. Author interview, Sheikh Omar Benjdiriya, Tunis, October 2019.

NOTES

pp. [78–84]

45. Aqeel, A H, 2012, *Secrets and Facts from Qadhafi's Time*, Al-Majmua Al-Dawliya li Nashr wa Tawzia, pp. 136–7.
46. Author interview, Sheikh Mabrouk Buamid, Tunis, October 2019.
47. Author interview, Sheikh Abdul Raheem al-Burki, November 2019.
48. Ibid.
49. *Al-Jazeera*, 'Interview with Giuma al-Ma'arafi', 25 September 2011. Available at https://rb.gy/snit9
50. Author interview, Sheikh Mohamed Aujail Hasnawi, August 2021.
51. Author interview, Abdullah Othman, Tunis. October 2019.
52. Author interview, Sheikh Mohamed Omar Benjdiriya, Tunis, October 2019.
53. Ibid.
54. 'Toutes les tribus de Libye n'en font qu'une', *La Regle du Jeu*, 27 April 2011. Available at https://laregledujeu.org/2011/04/27/5465/toutes-les-tribus-de-libye-nen-font-quune/
55. Bernard-Henri Lévy, 'L'Appel de Benghazi', *La Regle du Jeu*, 27 April 2011. Available at https://laregledujeu.org/2011/04/27/5468/lappel-de-benghazi/
56. Those of Turkish origin, mainly the descendants of Janissaries, Ottoman elite soldiers who were the dominant force in Ottoman Libya.
57. Lacher, *Libya's Fragmentation*, op. cit. p. 87.
58. Author interview, Nureddin Abumanhar, Tunis, October 2019.
59. Keddie, O, 2015, 'The Ink of Exile', *Al-Moustaqil* magazine, p. 87
60. Whilst deliberating over candidates, al-Keib was threatened by Zintani commander, Abdullah Naker, the leader of the Tripoli Revolutionary Council, which comprised mainly Zintani residents of the capital, who warned, 'We'll see whether he is working for the interests of the revolutionaries. If not, he will fall as Qadhafi fell. We won't stand for any of the names that we think are unqualified to be in the new government and we will decline and announce our approval or disapproval… The rebels should be recognised… we demand to have a role in the new government especially in the transitional period.' (Menas Associates, Libya Focus, November 2011).
61. Al-Houni, op. cit. p. 1.
62. Rania El Gamal, 'In Gaddafi's hometown, residents accuse NTC fighters of revenge', Reuters, 16 October 2011. Available at https://www.reuters.com/article/libya-sirte-looting-idUKL5E7LG0CV20111016
63. 'Libya fighters take revenge on Qaddafi's tribe', the Associated Press, 5 October 2011. Available at https://www.cbsnews.com/news/libya-fighters-take-revenge-on-qaddafis-tribe/
64. Despite Tawerghan elders trying to make their peace with Misrata, even declaring at a conference in Benghazi in February 2012, 'We, the Tawergha tribes of Libya, apologise to our brothers in Misrata for any action committed by any resident of Tawergha. We affirm that their honour is our honour, their blood is our blood and their fortune is our fortune' ('Ash, Nigel, Tawergha elders say "Sorry" to Misrata', *Libya Herald*, 25 February 2012. Available at https://www.libyaherald.

275

pp. [85–91] NOTES

com/2012/02/tawergha-elders-say-sorry-to-misrata/). Misrata refused to soften its stance, and continued to prevent the Tawergha from returning.

65. This incident was triggered by the killing of Omran Sha'aban, the young Misratan who had delivered the final blow to Qadhafi, who died from injuries sustained during his capture and detention in Bani Walid. When Bani Walid refused to hand Sha'aban's killers over to Misrata, Misratan put the town under siege.

66. Menas Associates, Libya Focus, October 2012.

67. Author interview, a commander from the al-Rubaya tribe, Tunis, October 2019.

68. Ouanes, M, 2018, *The Libya that I Saw, the Libya that I See: The Calamity of a Country*, Tunis, Mediterranean Publisher, p. 80.

69. Menas Associates, Libya Focus, December 2011.

70. Author interview, Sheikh Mabrouk Buamid, Tunis, October 2019.

71. The south has its own complexities and dynamics, which are outside the scope of this book. See https://www.crisisgroup.org/middle-east-north-africa/north-africa/libya/179-how-libyas-fezzan-became-europes-new-border

72. Hatita, A S, *Libyan War Diaries (Episode 5) Map of Tribes' Loyalties in the Conflict with Extremists*, Al-sharq Awast, 21 November 2014. Available at https://rb.gy/skpetp.

73. Author interview, Abduljawad Badeen, August 2021.

74. Shalawi, H, 'Libyan Tribes and their Relationship to the Revolution', 12 May 2015, *Noon Post*. Available at https://rb.gy/lf0ug6

75. Al-Houni, op. cit. p. 12.

76. Menas Associates, Libya Focus, March 2011.

77. Author interview, Sharif al-Abbar, November 2019.

78. 'Solving the Libyan Crisis Requires Achieving Reconciliation Based on a Political Project that Builds the State and the Constitution', a symposium by the Al-Jazeera Center for Studies, Ankara, 29 August 2019. Available at https://studies.aljazeera.net/en/node/2275

79. *Libya International TV Channel*, 'Interview with Major General Suleiman Mahmoud al-Obeidi', 2019. Available at https://rb.gy/17y3s

80. Amer, A N, 'A conspiracy in every sense', Correspondents.org, 26 September 2012. Available at https://correspondents.org/en/2012/09/26/a-conspiracy-in-every-sense/

81. Author interview, Mehdi al-Bargathi, July 2021.

82. Author interview, Sharif al-Abbar, November 2019.

83. Author interview, Abduljawad Badeen, August 2021.

84. Hatita, A S, 2015, *The Wars of the Militias, Libya Post-Qadhafi*, Cairo, Dar Kenous, p. 79.

85. The event drew participants from a wide assortment of military brigades from across the country. They included the Abu Slim Martyrs Brigade and the Ansar al-Sharia Brigade, both from Derna and Benghazi, the Benghazi Martyrs Brigade and the Omar Ibn Khattab Brigade from Benghazi, the Faruq Brigade from Misarata, the Sirte Revolutionary Brigade and the Libya Shield Brigade, among others.

86. Menas Associates, Libya Focus, June 2012.

NOTES

pp. [92–101]

87. Ibid.
88. Author interview, Mehdi al-Bargathi, July 2021.
89. Ryan, Yasmine, 'US consulate "easy target" for extremists', Al-Jazeera, 16 September 2012. Available at https://www.aljazeera.com/features/2012/9/16/us-consulate-easy-target-for-extremists
90. Author interview, al-Senussi Buheleq, September 2021.
91. Interviews with tribal figures in Tunis, October 2019.
92. Cited in Libya Focus, December 2011.
93. Author interview, Tripoli resident, December 2011.
94. Low, C, and Murphy, F, 'Libyan tribes protest at new government line-up', Reuters, 23 November 2011. Available at https://www.reuters.com/article/us-libya-idUSTRE7AL0JM20111123
95. Djzeri, M, 22 February 2021, 'Tribal Power, the State, and Political Transition in Libya', Milano, OASIS Center. Available at https://www.oasiscenter.eu/en/tribal-power-the-state-and-political-transition-in-libya
96. Author interview, Faraj Najm, April 2022.
97. Author interview, Abduljawad Badeen, July 2021.
98. Author interview, Abduljawad Badeen, August 2021.
99. Ibid.
100. Author interview, senior member of al-Awaqir, September 2021
101. Author interview, Abduljawad Badeen, August 2021.
102. Cited in Abdulsattar Hatita, *The War of the Militias: Libya Post-Qadhafi*, op. cit. p. 60.
103. Zargoun, T, and Holmes, O, 15 January 2012, 'Libyan parties reject draft election law', Reuters. Available at https://www.reuters.com/article/uk-libya-law-election/libyan-parties-reject-draft-election-law-idUKTRE80E0FW20120115
104. Doherty, M, December 2012, '"Give Us Change We Can See": Citizen Views of Libya's Political Process', Washington DC, National Democratic Institute for International Affairs (NDI). Available at https://www.ndi.org/sites/default/files/Libya-FG-121012.pdf
105. General National Congress (GNC) website, https://www.temehu.com/gnc.htm
106. Bskeri, S, 23 July 2012, 'Libyan National Congress Elections and Options for the Winning Blocs', Doha, Al-Jazeera Center for Studies. Available at https://studies.aljazeera.net/en/node/3432
107. Author conversations with members of the Libyan Muslim Brotherhood, 2012.
108. Husken, T, op. cit. p. 7.
109. Menas Associates, Libya Focus, March 2013.
110. Ibid.
111. Al-Fessi, S, 30 June 2014, 'The Political Role of Tribes in Libya… Between presence and absence', *Fessaniya*, Issue 117.
112. Ouanes, op. cit. p. 170.
113. Author interview, Sheikh Abdulrahim Alburki, November 2019.

277

pp. [101–115]   NOTES

114. Video footage of the conference titled 'Achieving the 17th February Revolution and Building the State and the Constitution'. YouTube, 'https://www.youtube.com/watch?v=fAgWTkmpKFY. Accessed 2021.

115. Author interview, Sharif al-Abbar, November 2019.

4. TRIBES AND THE POST-2014 ORDER

1. 'Haftar defiant despite divisions within Libyan army', Libya Channel. 25 January 2016. Available at https://www.marsad.ly/en/2016/01/25/haftar-defiant-despite-divisions-within-libyan-army/

2. Fitzgerald, M, March 2015, 'Mapping Libya's Factions', European Council on Foreign Relations, Middle East and North Africa Programme. Available at https://ecfr.eu/archive/page/-/Libya_maps_combined.pdf

3. Author interview, Sheikh of Warshefana, Tunis October 2019.

4. Lacher, W, 2020, *Libya's Fragmentation*, London, I B Taurus, p. 179.

5. Cousins, Michel, 'General Haftar announces coup; politicians react with scorn, order his arrest', *Libya Herald*, 14 February 2014. Available at https://www.libyaherald.com/2014/02/general-hafter-announces-coup-politicians-react-with-scorn-order-his-arrest/

6. Menas Associates, Libya Focus, June 2014.

7. Ibid.

8. Statement from the Tribes of Libya Conference, Jamahiriya News Agency, 25 May 2014.

9. Video of the Official Spokesperson of the 'Libyan Cities and Tribes Conference', Khalid Buamid, posted on Facebook on 31 May 2018. Available at https://rb.gy/ldfqk

10. Author interview, Sheikh Mabrouk Buamid, Tunis, October 2019.

11. Ibid.

12. Ibid.

13. Among those released was Omar Tantoush al-Warshefani, a former high-ranking officer in the military under Qadhafi, who went on to form what was dubbed the Tribal Army, a force comprising mainly fighters from Warshefana.

14. Almahir, K, 'Libyan Tribes Pledge Allegiance to Haftar, and Misrata Rejects Him', *Al-Jazeera*, 11 March 2014. Available at https://rb.gy/ff4z9

15. Ibid.

16. Author interview, Sheikh al-Senussi Buheleq, September 2021.

17. Ibid.

18. Juma, A, 'Sheikh of the Libyan Magharaba tribe: The tribes supported the national army led by Field Marshal Haftar', *Youm 7*, 19 September 2016. Available at https://rb.gy/tm5mi

19. Author interview, Mehdi al-Barghathi, March 2022.

20. Ibid.

21. Menas Associates, Libya Focus, June 2013.

NOTES

pp. [115–123]

22. Ibid.
23. Ibid.
24. *Channel 218*, 'Interview with Sheikh Tayib Sharif', 29 August 2017. Available at https://rb.gy/uig2m
25. Author interview, Sheikh al-Senussi Buheleq, September 2021.
26. Author interview, Saad Yasser Obeidi, August 2022.
27. Ibid.
28. Ibid.
29. Al-Qzeeri, T, 'The Phenomenon of Field Marshal Haftar… a Different Approach, part 1', *Libya Al-Mostakbal*, 9 February 2017. Available at https://rb.gy/ntfje
30. Author interview, Saad Yasser Obeidi, August 2022.
31. Author interview, member of al-Awaqir tribe, October 2020.
32. Author Interview, Mehdi al-Bargathi, July 2021.
33. Author interview, Sharef Al-Abbar. November 2019.
34. Author interview, former Benghazi resident, May 2020.
35. Menas Associates, Libya Focus, September 2013.
36. *Libya Al-Mostakbal*, 'Al-Atyush: The West Seeks to Impose the "Oil-for-Food Scenario" on Libya', 13 November 2016. Available at https://rb.gy/x317d
37. VanLaningham, P, and Gupte, E, *Libyan tribe says oil terminal blockade to be lifted Sunday*, 10 December 2013. Available at https://www.spglobal.com/commodityinsights/en/market-insights/latest-news/oil/121013-libyan-tribe-says-oil-terminal-blockade-to-be-lifted-sunday and Libya Politics and Security, Menas Associates. 16 December 2013.
38. *Libya Al-Mostakbal*, 'Al-Atyush:…', op. cit.
39. Ibid.
40. Author interview, Abduljawad Badeen, August 2021.
41. Ibid.
42. Menas Associates, Libya Focus, November 2016.
43. 'Sheikh Salim Jabber's speech to people in Misrata who were mourning their martyrs for Allah and the country', undated. Available at https://s.shabakngy.com/to/to.php?q=GJJN7Z1U7NU
44. Ibid.
45. *Cyrenaica Television*, 'The Criminal Salim Jedhran', undated video. Available at https://rb.gy/vubun
46. Menas Associates, Libya Focus, January 2016.
47. Ibid.
48. *Libya Al-Mostakbal*, 'Al-Atyush:…', op. cit.
49. *Libya TV 24*, 'Speech of Saleh al-Atyush, Sheikh of the Magharba tribe, at a meeting of the tribe today in the Jlidayeh area,' 21 August 2016. Available at https://ar-ar.facebook.com/704791526314687/videos/958086924318478/
50. Ibid.
51. *Libya Al-Mostakbal*, 'Al-Atyush:…', op. cit.
52. Author interview, Abduljawad Badeen, August 2021.

NOTES

53. Menas Associates, Libya Focus, October 2016
54. *Libya Al-Mostakbal*, 'Al-Atyush:...', op. cit.
55. *Al-Quds Al-Arabi*, 'The "Islamic State" in Libya Receives Support from Tribes that were Loyal to Qadhafi', 20 February 2015. Available at https://rb.gy/8i8f9
56. Collombier, Virginie, 2017, 'Sirte's Tribes Under the Islamic State' in *Tribes and Global Jihadism*, Virginie Collombier and Olivier Roy (eds), London, Hurst & Company, p. 173.
57. Ibid., p. 174.
58. 'Al-Darsa tribe: We will not allow anyone to harm al-Hijazi until the results of the investigation are out', Al-Wasat, 26 January 2016. Available at https://alwasat.ly/news/libya/87924
59. Author interview, Mehdi al-Barghathi, July 2021.
60. Ibid.
61. *Libya Observer*, 'Al-Jroushi: Sirraj would be branded terrorist if he refuses Haftar, threatens to arrest Al-Barghathi', Libya Observer, 17 April 2016. Archived page available at https://rb.gy/cnc8g
62. Menas Associates, Libya Focus, April 2016.
63. Ramdan, S, 'The fact of the dispute in Cyrenaica', Libya Al-Mostakbal, 17 June 2016. Available at https://archive2.libya-al-mostakbal.org/news/clicked/98744
64. Menas Associates, Libya Focus, June 2016.
65. Author interview, Mehdi al-Bargathi, July 2021.
66. *Akhbar Libya 24*, 'A Meeting to Heal the Social Rift between Magharba and al-Awaqir', 17 April 2016. Available at https://rb.gy/m797q
67. Menas Associates, Libya Focus, September 2017.
68. Menas Associates, Libya Focus, November 2017.
69. Ibid.
70. Author interview, Mehdi al-Bargathi, July 2021.
71. Quoted in Menas Associats, Libya Focus, April 2019.
72. Mrgin, H S, 'Tarhouna Adopts a New Vision for the Role of Armed Groups in Tripoli', Ahewar, 6 September 2018. Available at http://www.ahewar.org/debat/show.art.asp?aid=610706&r=0
73. Interviews by author with sources from Tarhouna, 2019.
74. Author interview, eastern tribesman who wanted to remain anonymous.
75. Author interview, Sheikh al-Senussi Buheleq, October 2021.
76. Author interview, Mehdi al-Bargathi, July 2021.
77. Author interview, member of Qadhadhfah tribe and former senior member of the Qadhafi regime, Tunis, October 2019.
78. Mrgin, H S, 'The Sheikh and the Tribe in the 2019 Tripoli War', Ahewar, 11 June 2019. Available at https://www.ahewar.org/debat/show.art.asp?aid=639974

5. TRIBES AND THE IRAQI REPUBLIC

1. Author interview, Sheikh Sami al-Majoun, November 2020.

NOTES

pp. [138–145]

2. Batatu, H, 1978, *The Old Social Classes and the Revolutionary Movements of Iraq: A Study of Iraq's Old Landed and Commercial Classes and of its Communists, Ba'athists, and Free Officers*, Princeton University Press.

3. Jabar, F A, October 2017, *The Caliphate State: Advancing Towards the Past—ISIL and the Local Community in Iraq*, Beirut, Arab Center for Research and Policy Studies, p. 238.

4. Ibid, p. 235.

5. Zeidal, R, June 2016, 'Tribes in Iraq: A Negligible Factor in State Formation' in *Tribes and States in a Changing Middle East*, Uzi Rabi (ed.), London, Hurst, p. 179.

6. Ibid. p. 179.

7. Author interview, Majed Safa'ah, February 2021.

8. Batatu, op. cit. p. 88.

9. Al-Hosni, A, 2008, *Iraq's Modern Political History, Part 1*, 7th edition, Beirut, Dar al-Rafidain, p. 12.

10. Batatu, op. cit. p. 90.

11. This practice served the Ottomans' efforts to break up the large tribal confederations, creating large numbers of smaller landowning sheikhs who were no longer reliant on the heads of the large confederations.

12. See Batatu op. cit. p. 109—three types of tenure—tapu, miri or lazmah. The latter two were indistinguishable from private ownership.

13. Batatu, op. cit. p. 108.

14. Marr, P, 2012, *The Modern History of Iraq*, third edition, Boulder, CO, Westview Press, p. 69.

15. Williamson, J F, 1975, *A Political History of the Shammar Jarba Tribe of Al-Jazirah: 1800–1958*, Indiana University Dissertations Publishing.

16. Sbahi, Aziz, 2020 *Decades of the History of the Iraqi Communist Party*, Vol. 2, 2nd edition, p. 67.

17. Sbahi, Aziz, 2020, *Decades of the History of the Iraqi Communist Party*, Vol. 1, 2nd edition, p. 290.

18. Batatu, op. cit. p. 103.

19. Fernea, R A, 1970, *Shaykh and Effendi, Changing Patterns of Authority among the El Shabana of Southern Iraq*, Cambridge, Massachusetts, Harvard University Press, p. 52.

20. Williamson, op. cit. p. 193.

21. Author interview, Sheikh Takleef al-Minshed, November 2020.

22. Williamson, op. cit. p. 193.

23. Author interview, Sheikh Sami al-Majoun, November 2020.

24. Ibid.

25. Harling, P, 2012, 'Beyond Political Ruptures: Towards a Historiography of Social Continuity in Iraq' in *Writing the Modern History of Iraq: Historiographical and Political Challenges*, Riccardo Bocco, et al. World Scientific Publishing Company, p. 68.

26. Dr Al-Wardi, S A, *Approaches to the Iraqi Political Project, 1921–2003*. Available at http://iraker.dk/v/4.htm

pp. [145–154] NOTES

27. Al-Nasiri, K S, 1978, *Landlords, Lineages and Land Reform in an Iraqi Village*, PhD thesis, Durham University, p. 18.
28. *Al-Hurriya* newspaper, Issue 1,238, 28 July 1958.
29. Al-Atiyyah, H, 2004, *Tribe, Religion, Superstition and Politics in the South of Iraq*, Dar Zahar, p. 28.
30. Baali, F, January 1969, 'Agrarian Reform in Iraq: Some Socioeconomic Aspects', *The American Journal of Economics and Sociology*, Vol. 28, No. 1, pp. 61–76.
31. Al-Nasiri, op. cit. p. 76.
32. Kubba, S I A, 29 September 2014, 'A whole decade since the departure of a distinguished economist—6', Ahewar. Available at https://www.ahewar.org/debat/s.asp?t=4&aid=434991
33. Ibid.
34. Sbahi, op. cit. Vol. 2, p. 260.
35. Kubba, op. cit.
36. Ibid.
37. Cited in Kadhem, F J, 2016, *The Sacred and the Secular: The 'ulama of Najaf in Iraqi politics between 1950 and 1980*, Doctoral thesis, University of Exeter, p. 165. Available at https://ore.exeter.ac.uk/repository/bitstream/handle/10871/13621/KadhemF.pdf?sequence=1
38. Kubba, op. cit.
39. Fernea, op. cit. p. 53.
40. Dr Habib, Kadhem, 2013, *Aspects of Iraq in the Twentieth Century*, Vol 6, p. 441, Dar Arras for Printing and Publication, Erbil.
41. Author interview, Sheikh Sami al-Majoun November 2020.
42. Author interview, Sheikh Jawad al-Assad, November 2020.
43. Ibid.
44. Williamson, op. cit. p. 193.
45. Author interview, Sheikh Sami al-Majoun, November 2020.
46. The *marja'iya* was founded in the 1830s, when Mohamed Hassan Najafi became the first transnational Shi'ite religious authority (*marja'*) in Najaf. The word *marja'* means 'reference', denoting the *marja*'s role as a source of religious jurisprudence to follow.
47. Author interview, Sheikh Sami al-Majoun, November 2020.
48. Ibid.
49. Ibid.
50. Ibid.
51. Jabar, F A, October 2017, *The Caliphate State: Advancing Towards the Past—ISIL and the Local Community in Iraq*, Beirut, Arab Center for Research and Policy Studies.
52. Farhan, A, 1996, *Harvest of the Revolution*, Second edition, London, Dar Albarq, pp. 87–8.
53. Ibid.
54. Ibid.
55. Farhan, op. cit. p. 108.

NOTES pp. [155–164]

56. Jabar, F A (ed.), 2002, *Ayatollahs, Sufis and Ideologues: State, Religion and Social Movements*, Saqi Books.
57. Author interview, Sheikh Takleef al-Minshed, November 2020.
58. Hirst, D, 'Ba'athists now put Iraq first', *The Guardian*, 18 July 1968. Available at https://www.theguardian.com/world/1968/jul/18/iraq.davidhirst

6. TRIBES AND THE BA'ATHIST STATE

1. Author interview, Sheikh Takleef al-Minshed, November 2020.
2. Author interview, Sheikh Jawad al-Assad, November 2020.
3. Cited in Baram, A, 1997, 'Neo-Tribalism in Iraq: Saddam Hussein's Tribal Policies 1991–96', *International Journal of Middle East Studies*, Vol. 29 (1).
4. Constitution of the Arab Socialist Ba'ath Party. Available at https://online.fliphtml5.com/huvs/syup/#p=5
5. Dawisha, A, 1999, 'Identity and Political Survival in Saddam's Iraq', *Middle East Journal*, Vol. 53, No. 4, Autumn 1999, pp. 553–67.
6. Cited in Baram, A, op. cit.; and Khafaji, F, 11 July 2019, *17 July Statement*. Available at https://www.facebook.com/936525943185887/photos/pcb.1253431974828614/1253430198162125/?type=3&theater
7. Author interview, Sheikh Adel al-Assad, February 2021.
8. *Al-Jazeera*, 'Interview with Saleh Omar al-Ali–part 5', 15 June 2003. Available at https://rb.gy/wrpyn
9. Ibid.
10. Marr, P, 2012, *The Modern History of Iraq*, third edition, Boulder, CO, Westview Press, p. 134.
11. Batatu, H, 1978, *The Old Social Classes and the Revolutionary Movements of Iraq: a Study of Iraq's Old Landed and Commercial Classes and of its Communists, Ba'athists, and Free Officers*, Princeton University Press, p. 1120.
12. Cited in Khafaji, F, 2016, *Khairallah Tulfah, Saddam Hussein's Man of the Shadows*, Baghdad, Darstoor, p. 19.
13. Khafaji, F, op. cit. p. 22.
14. Hussien, S, 2002, *Men and the City*, Baghdad, p. 86. Cited in Khafaji, F, op. cit. p. 26.
15. Zeidel, R, November 2005, 'Tikriti Regional Identity as Reflected in Two Regional Myths and a Folkloric Tale', *Middle Eastern Studies*, Vol. 41, No. 6, pp. 899–910.
16. Al-Zubaidi, I, 2003, *The Radio's State: Iraqi Biography and Observations*, London, Dar al-Hakima, pp. 26–7. Also see: Al-Zubaidi, Ibrahim, 5 March 2003, *Saddam Hussein as remembered by a childhood friend and classmatesee*. Available at صدام حسين كما يتذكره أحد أصدقاء الطفولة وزملاء الدراسة (aawsat.com)
17. *Riyad Newspaper*, an interview with Ali al-Nada sheikh of Saddam's clan, 26 January 2016, *Saddam Bet on Street War… and Betrayal was Greater Than Sacrifices*, Defense Arab website. Available at https://defense-arab.com/vb/threads/51027/
18. Ibid.

pp. [164–171]   NOTES

19. Interview with Dhaffar Mohamed Jabber. Personal secretary and friend of Uday—Dustoor net, 15 September 2003. Available at https://rb.gy/vtvitt
20. Tikrit had a history of sending its youth to the military to train as officers thanks to Mawlud Mukhlas, an MP during the monarchy who originated from Tikrit and who was a graduate of the military college in Istanbul. Mukhlas, who married a woman from Tikrit, co-operated with a senior military officer to send the sons of the tribes of Tikrit and its surrounding areas to military college. It was these very sons who went on to stage the 1968 coup. Allawi, H, 1991, *Iraq: The State of Secret Organisation*, Saudi Research and Marketing Company.
21. Allawi, op. cit.
22. Author interview, Sheikh Sami al-Majoun, November 2020.
23. Allawi, op. cit.
24. Ibid.
25. Davis, E, 2005, *Memoirs of State: Politics, History and Collective Identity in Modern Iraq*, London, University of California Press, p. 333.
26. Author interview, Sheikh Jawad al-Assad, November 2020.
27. Author interview, Sheikh Sami al-Majoun, November 2020.
28. Author interview, Sheikh Takleef al-Minshed, November 2020.
29. Author interview, Sheikh Adnan al-Danbous, July 2021.
30. Author interview, Sheikh Takleef al-Minshed, November 2020.
31. Ibid.
32. Author interview, Sheikh Adnan al-Danbous, July 2021.
33. Ibid.
34. Author interview, Sheikh Adel al-Assad, February 2021.
35. Author interview, Majed Safa'ah, February 2021.
36. Author interview, Sheikh Takleef al-Minshed, November 2020.
37. Ibid.
38. Ibid.
39. Author interview, Sheikh Sami al-Majoun, November 2020.
40. Ibid.
41. Ibid.
42. Ibid.
43. Baumann, H (ed.), 2019, *Reclaiming Home: The struggle for socially just housing, land and property rights in Syria, Iraq and Libya*, Friedrich-Ebert-Stiftung. Law available at http://extwprlegs1.fao.org/docs/pdf/irq38269.pdf
44. Author interview, Sheikh Takleef al-Minshed, November 2020.
45. Ibid.
46. Metz, H C (ed.), 1988, *Iraq: A Country Study*. Washington: GPO for the Library of Congress. Land Tenure and Agrarian Reform. Available at http://countrystudies.us/iraq/59.htm
47. Saghieh, H, 2003, *The Iraqi Ba'ath: Saddam's Power from Resurrection to Ruin*, London, al-Saqi, p. 178.
48. Saghieh, op. cit. p. 176.

NOTES   pp. [171–178]

49. Author interview, Sheikh Adnan al-Danbous, July 2021.
50. Baram, A, op. cit.
51. Author interview, Sheikh Takleef al-Minshed, November 2020.
52. Ibid.
53. Ibid.
54. Author interview, Sheikh Jawad al-Assad, November 2020.
55. Author interview, Sheikh Takleef al-Minshed, November 2020.
56. Author interview, Sheikh Adnan al-Danbous, July 2021.
57. Author interview, Sheikh Takleef al-Minshed, November 2020.
58. Ibid.
59. Ibid.
60. Author interview, Sheikh Jawad al-Assad, November 2020.
61. Ibid.
62. Author interview, Sheikh Adnan al-Danbous, July 2021.
63. Baram, op. cit.
64. Author interview, Sheikh Yousef al-Baidani, January 2020.
65. Author interview, Sheikh Jawad al-Assad, November 2020.
66. Ibid.
67. Tripp, C, 2000, *A History of Iraq*, Cambridge, Cambridge University Press, p. 225.
68. Aaron, F, 2015, *The Ba'thification of Iraq: Saddam Hussein's Totalitarianism*, University of Texas Press, pp. 141–2.
69. *Samarra Satellite TV*, Interview with Sheikh Kadhem al-Anaizan, head of the Southern Tribes Council, 14 March 2015. Available at https://www.youtube.com/watch?v=klACeQkOocg
70. Cited in Aaron, F, op. cit. p. 144.
71. Author interview, Sheikh Jawad al-Assad, November 2020.
72. Author interview, Naji Sultan, Feburay 2021.
73. *Samarra Satellite TV*, Interview with Sheikh Kadhem al-Anaizan op. cit.
74. Author interview, Naji Sultan, March 2021.
75. Hamza, K, Winter 2017, 'A History of the Political Usage of Local Tribal Identity in Iraq: State and Sheikhs Serving Each Other', *Omran for Social Sciences and Humanities*, Issue 19, pp. 89–118, Doha, the Arab Center for Research and Policy Studies.
76. Ibid.
77. Davis, E, op. cit. p. 173.
78. Lewental, D G, November 2014, 'Saddam's Qadisiyyah': Religion and History in the Service of State Ideology in Baʿthi Iraq', *Middle Eastern Studies*, Vol. 50, No. 6, Taylor & Francis Ltd, pp. 891–910.
79. Tripp, C, op. cit. p. 247.
80. Jabar, F A, 2000, 'Shaykhs and Ideologues: Detribalization and Retribalization in Iraq, 1968–1998', *Middle East Report* (*MERIP*), No. 215, Summer 2000, pp. 28–31 and 48, and Rohde, A, 2010, *State-Society Relations* in *Ba'athist Iraq*, London, Routledge.

NOTES

81. Faust, A, 2015, *The Ba'thification of Iraq: Saddam Hussein's Totalitarianism*, University of Texas Press, p. 143.

82. The Popular Army, a paramilitary organisation established to serve as a counterpoint to the army and composed of civilian volunteers tasked with protecting the regime, ran a number of campaigns to seek out and arrest the large numbers who had deserted or absconded from military service. However, some of these Popular Army elements put tribal loyalty before that to the regime and would regularly warn their own communities ahead of arrest campaigns in order to allow their fellow tribesmen who were wanted to escape. Dr Al-Atiyyah, H, 2004, *Tribe, Religion, Superstition and Politics in the South of Iraq*, Dar Zahar, p. 46.

83. Author interview, Majed Safa'ah, Feburary 2021,

84. Author interview, Sheikh Takleef al-Minshed, March 2021

85. Dawod, H, 2017, 'Iraqi Tribes in the Land of Jihad' in *Tribes and Global Jihadism*, Virinie Collombier and Olivier Roy (eds), London, Hurst.

86. Haddad, F, 2011, *Sectarianism in Iraq: Antagonistic Visions of Unity*, Oxford, Oxford University Press, p. 95.

87. Author interview, Majed Safa'ah, Feburary 2021.

88. 'Saddam Hussein threatens the Jubour clan with genocide', video, undated. Available at https://s.shabakngy.com/go/g.php?q=YJ_D7XPw1n4

89. Ibid.

90. *New York Times*, 'Iraq Reportedly Cracks Down on Clan that Tried a Coup', 20 June 1995. Available at https://www.nytimes.com/1995/06/20/world/iraq-reportedly-cracks-down-on-clan-that-tried-a-coup.html

91. *New York Times*, 'Iraqi Offers Regrets in Killing of Defecting Sons-in-Law', 10 May 1995. Available at https://www.nytimes.com/1996/05/10/world/iraqi-offers-regrets-in-killing-of-defecting-sons-in-law.html

92. See for example, Khafaji, I, 2003, 'A Few Days After: State and Society in a Post-Saddam Iraq', in *Iraq at the Crossroads: State and Society in the Shadow of Regime Change*; Toby Dodge and Steven Simon (eds), Adelphi Paper 354, IISS, Oxford University Press, pp. 80–1.

93. Witwit, A, 2015, 'The Sociology of the Political Participation of the Iraqi Clan: a field study of social and political structure of the al-Khaza'el clans', *Al-Qadisiya Magazine, Journal of Al-Qadisiya in Arts and Educational Sciences*, Vol. 15, Issue 3, pp. 323–76.

94. Others included Sheikh Zaher al-Ajeel, Sheikh Sajit al-Doukhi, Sheikh of Nawashi.

95. Author interview, Sheikh Takleef al-Minshed, November 2020.

96. Ibid.

97. Author interview, Naji Sultan, November 2020

98. Cited in *Saddam's Cruelty Blog*, 'The Sha'aban Intifada… March 1991/ The Page of Treachery and Betrayal', part 1, 10 November 2018. Available at https://rb.gy/w2ezf

99. Ibid.

100. Author interview, Naji Sultan, December 2020.

NOTES

pp. [183–189]

101. *The Shaaban Intifada—March 1991/ The page of treachery and betrayal... 4*, June 2020. Available at http://saddamscruelty.blogspot.com/2020/06/blog-post_10.html
102. Ibid.
103. Author interview, southern tribesman, June 2021.
104. Author interview, Sheikh Takelef al-Minshed, Feburary 2021.
105. *The Shaaban Intifada... Part 4*, op. cit.
106. Ibid.
107. Khafaji, I, op. cit. pp. 80–1.
108. Author interview, Naji Sultan, December 2020.
109. Baram, A, op. cit.; Davis, E, 2005, op. cit.; Yaphe, J, 2000, 'Tribalism in Iraq, the Old and the New', *Middle East Policy*, Vol. 7, Issue 3, June 2000.
110. Aaron, op. cit. p. 142.
111. CRRC Doc. No. SH-IDGS-D-000–370, November 1991–August 1992, cited in Blaydes, L, 'Rebuilding the Ba'thist State', *Comparative Politics*, October 2020, Vol. 53, No. 1 (October 2020), pp. 93–115.
112. Pages of the Iran–Iraq War narrated by Abdul Jabbar Mohsen, Part 2, YouTube. Available at https://www.youtube.com/watch?v=-535VZAuuzg.
113. See for example, Al-Thawra, 29 March 1991, 2 April 1991 and 10 April 1991.
114. An interview with Kadhem al-Anaizan in *Testimonials for History*, presented by Dr Hamid Abdullah. Available at https://www.youtube.com/watch?v=KlO136ZPylE
115. Ibid.
116. Ibid.
117. *Saddam's Cruelty Blog*, 'The Bond of Kinship', 6 February 2009. Available at https://rb.gy/4j53e
118. Ibid.
119. Ibid
120. Author interview, Sheikh Jawad al-Assad, November 2020.
121. An interview with Kadhem al-Anaizan in *Testimonials for History*, presented by Dr Hamid Abdullah. Available at https://www.youtube.com/watch?v=KlO136ZPylE.
122. An interview with Kadhem al-Anaizan. Available at https://www.youtube.com/watch?v=KlO136ZPylE
123. *Special Testimony with Dr Hameed Abdullah*, 'What did the rich and tribal sheikhs give to gain Saddam Hussein's approval?' 3 September 2022. Available at https://www.youtube.com/watch?v=Jwmwnuwwcts
124. Author interview, Sheikh Takleef al-Minshed, November 2020.
125. Author interview, Sheikh Jawad al-Assad, November 2020.
126. Author interview, Naji Sultan, December 2020.
127. Author interview, Sheikh Adel al-Assad, March 2021.
128. Author interview, Sheikh Jawad al-Assad, November 2020.
129. Interview with resident of Nasseriyah who wished to remain anonymous.

pp. [189–196] NOTES

130. Author interview, Sheikh Mansour al-Tamimi, August 2021.
131. Author interview, Sheikh Jabbar al-Assad, February 2021.
132. Stewart, R, 2006, *Occupational Hazards*, Picador, p. 232.
133. Author interview, Sheikh Jabbar al-Assad, February 2021.
134. Author interview, Sheikh Jawad al-Assad, November 2020.
135. Harling, P, 2012, 'Beyond Political Ruptures: Towards a Historiography of Social Continuity In Iraq' in *Writing the Modern History of Iraq: Historiographical and Political Challenges*, Riccardo Bocco, Hamit Bozarslan, Peter Sluglett, Jordi Tejel (eds), World Scientific Publishing Company. Available at https://peterharling. com/2012/11/01/452/
136. Author interview, Sheikh Mansour al-Tamimi, August 202.

7. TRIBES, OCCUPATION AND SHI'ITE IRAQ

1. Author interview, Sheikh Jabbar al-Assad, February 2021.
2. Author interview, Sheikh Sami al-Majoun, December 2020.
3. Witwit, A J, 2015, 'The Sociology of the Political Participation of the Iraqi Clan: a field study of social and political structure of the al-Khaza'el clans', *Journal of Al-Qadisiya in Arts and Educational Sciences*, Vol. 15, Issue 3, pp. 323–76.
4. Author interview, Sheikh Adnan al-Danbous, July 2021.
5. Author interview, Sheikh Mansour al-Tamimi, August 2021.
6. Harling, P, 2012, 'Beyond Political Ruptures: Towards a Historiography of Social Continuity In Iraq' in *Writing the Modern History of Iraq: Historiographical and Political Challenges*, Riccardo Bocco, et al., World Scientific Publishing Company. Available at https://peterharling.com/2012/11/01/452/
7. Jabar, F A, October 2017, *The Caliphate State: Advancing Towards the Past—ISIL and the Local Community in Iraq*, Beirut, Arab Center for Research and Policy Studies, p. 242.
8. Cigar, N, 2011, 'Al-Qaida, the Tribes and the Government: Lessons and Prospects for Iraq's Unstable Triangle', *Middle East Studies Occasional Papers*, No. 2, Marine Corps University Press, Quantico.
9. Harling, op. cit.
10. Jabar, *The Caliphate State: Advancing Towards the Past*, op. cit. p. 242.
11. Coalition Provisional Authority Order 1.
12. International Crisis Group, 'Iraq After The Surge: The New Sunni Landscape', *Middle East Report* No. 74, 30 April 2008. Available at https://icg-prod.s3.amazonaws.com/74-iraq-after-the-surge-i-the-new-sunni-landscape.pdf
13. Al-Zuhairi, F K K, 2021, 'The Tribe and the Strategy of Constructing the Modern State in Iraq Post-2003', *Political Issues*, No. 64, Al-Nahrain University, pp. 218–38. Available at https://www.iasj.net/iasj/download/895b9d1a3b30724d
14. Author interview, Sheikh Adnan al-Danbous, July 2021.
15. Ibid.
16. Interview with Adel Shirshab, Sheikh of al-Bidour Tribe. Available at http://trib-arab.com/videos/777-2019-02-05-11-37-19. Accessed 2019.

NOTES

pp. [196–204]

17. *Arab Tribes*, 'Interview with Sheikh Ahmed Salal Abdulaziz al-Badri of Bu Bader Tribe'. Available at http://www.tribarab.com/videos/924-2019-02-15-21-24-06
18. Biladi Television, Interview with Sheikh Hamid Shawka, Head of the Budiab Tribe and Head of the Al-Anbar Tribal Sheikhs' Council, 5 July 2021. Available at https://www.youtube.com/watch?v=9eOmT1pBEBs
19. Author interview, Sheikh Jabbar al-Assad, February 2021.
20. Al-Arabiya, 'Political Memory: Sheikh Mazhar Kharbit', September 2022. Available at https://www.youtube.com/watch?v=zfQn9lZ7JSs
21. Ibid.
22. Jabar, *The Caliphate State…*, op. cit. p. 243.
23. International Crisis Group, Governing Iraq, 25 August 2003. Available at https://icg-prod.s3.amazonaws.com/17-governing-iraq.pdf
24. Author interview, Sheikh Sami al-Majoun, November 2020.
25. Author interview, Sheikh Takleef al-Minshed, December 2020.
26. Witwit, A, op. cit.
27. Stewart, R, 2006, *Occupational Hazards*, London, Picador, p. 234.
28. Author interview, Sheikh Mansour al-Tamimi, August 2021.
29. Al-Arabiya, Political Memory: Sheikh Mazhar Kharbit, September 2022. Available at https://www.youtube.com/watch?v=zfQn9lZ7JSs
30. Ibid.
31. Ibid.
32. Ibid.
33. *Al-Sabah* newspaper, 10 January 2004.
34. Ibid.
35. Author interview, southern sheikh, June 2021.
36. Ibid.
37. Hashim, A S, 2006, *Insurgency and Counter-insurgency in Iraq*, Cornell University Press, pp. 107–8.
38. International Crisis Group, 'Iraq After the Surge: The New Sunni Landscape', op. cit.
39. Stewart, R, op. cit. p. 231.
40. Nouri, I, 2018, 'Tribalism and Women in Iraq after 2003', *Al-Faraheedi Literature Magazine*, Issue 35, September 2018. Available at https://www.iasj.net/iasj/download/ba0ae90c6e0a1a81
41. Etherington, M, June 2005, *Revolt on the Tigris*: *The Al Sadr Uprising and the Governing of Iraq*, London, Hurst, p. 104.
42. Ricks, T, 2009, *The Gamble: General Petraeus and the Untold Story of the American Surge in Iraq, 2006–2008*, Penguin UK.
43. *Time*, 'Saddam's Revenge', 18 September 2005. Available at https://content.time.com/time/subscriber/article/0,33009,1106307,00.html
44. Menas Associates, Iraq Focus, September 2003.
45. Menas Associates, Iraq Focus, February 2004.
46. *Biladi Television*, 'Interview with Sheikh Hamid Shawka', op. cit.

pp. [204–211] NOTES

47. *Christian Science Monitor*, 'A Scholarly Soldier Steps Inside the World of Iraq's Potent Tribes…', 30 December 2003.

48. Ibid.

49. Dawod, H, 2017, 'Iraqi Tribes in the Land of Jihad' in *Tribes and Global Jihadism*, Virginie Collombier and Olivier Roy (eds), London, Hurst.

50. In his memoirs, Bremer recalls his first encounter with al-Yawar on 24 June 2003 with a dozen Sunni sheikhs from the Shammar tribe: 'The members came to the session in their flowing and perfumed white robes. Most were over sixty, but among them was a younger member, Sheikh Ghazi al-Yawar, whom we were considering as a candidate for the Governing Council. About forty years old, American educated, Ghazi was a successful businessman based in Saudi Arabia. His uncle was the prominent chief of the tribe and lived just outside Mosul.' Although al-Yawar did not speak in this meeting in deference to his elders, Bremer describes too how the leading sheikh assured him of the tribe's constant and everlasting loyalty to him and the governments that 'freed' Iraq, before going on to pledge that if the tribe should ever decide to betray him, it would give him give him one month's notice.' Bremer, P, 2006, *My Year in Iraq: The Struggle to Build a Future of Hope*, Threshold Editions, p. 91.

51. Membership of this committee broke down as follows: United Iraqi Alliance—28; Democratic Patriotic Alliance of Kurdistan—15; The Iraqis—8; Communist Party of Iraq—1; Iraqi Turkmen Front—1; National Rafidain List—1; Sunni Arab nominee—1 (later expanded to 15).

52. Author interview, Sheikh Sami al-Majoun, December 2020.

53. Ibid.

54. Ibid.

55. Menas Associates, Iraq & Kurdistan Focus, May 2006.

56. Ibid.

57. Cigar, N, op. cit. p. 6.

58. Jabar, *The Caliphate State: Advancing Towards the Past*, op. cit. p. 247 (Takfiri refers to someone who pronounces another Muslim as an infidel or non-believer).

59. Ibid.

60. Cited in Cigar, N, op. cit. p. 11.

61. Ibid.

62. Al-Jazeera, 'A symposium on the security and political role of clans', 6 April 2008. Available at https://www.youtube.com/watch?v=ZfcyYFUYaY4

63. Ibid.

64. Alrai Media, 'Al-Suleiman: There is no longer such a thing as 'al-Qaeda' in al-Anbar Governate', 2 April 2008. Available at https://rb.gy/bo38s2

65. Al-Jazeera, 'A Symposium on the Security and Political Role of Clans', 6 April 2008. Available at https://www.youtube.com/watch?v=ZfcyYFUYaY4

66. Ibid.

67. Pollack, K M, 12 January 2004, 'After Saddam: Assessing the Reconstruction of Iraq', *Foreign Affairs*.

NOTES pp. [211–216]

68. 'Insurgents Assert Control Over Town Near Syrian Border', *The Washington Post*, 6 September 2005.
69. See for example Dawod, H, *Iraqi Tribes in the Land of Jihad*, op. cit. p. 25.
70. Jabar, A, *The Caliphate State: Advancing Towards the Past*, op. cit. p. 248.
71. Benraad, M, 2011, 'Iraq's Tribal "Sahwa": Its Rise and Fall', Middle East Policy Council.
72. Alrai Media, 'Al-Suleiman: There is no longer such a thing as "al-Qaeda" in Anbar Governate', 2 April 2008. Available at https://rb.gy/bo38s2
73. Al-Jazeera, 'A symposium on the security and political role of clans', 6 April 2008. Available at https://www.youtube.com/watch?v=ZfcyYFUYaY4
74. Ibid.
75. Author interview, Sheikh Mansour al-Tamimi, August 2021.
76. *The Guardian*, 'British tactics reviewed as Basra erupts', 8 May 2006. Available at https://www.theguardian.com/world/2006/may/08/iraq.military
77. Cochrane, M, June 2008, 'Operation Knight's Charge (Saulat al-Fursan), "The Battle for Basra"', *Iraq Report* 9, Institute for the Study of War. Available at https://www.understandingwar.org/operation/operation-knights-charge-saulat-al-fursan
78. Author interview, Sheikh Mohamed Zeidawi, January 2022.
79. Author interview, Sheikh Sami al-Majoun, December 2020.
80. Ibid.
81. Author interview, Sheikh Adnan al-Danbous, August 2021.
82. CLASSIFIED BY: Howell H. Howard, Director, US Regional Embassy Office, Basrah, Department of State. 11 April 2008, 18:44 (Friday). Available at https://wikileaks.org/plusd/cables/08BASRAH28_a.html
83. The tribal committee included: Muzahim al-Tamimi (Bani Tamim), Mansur al-Kana'an al-Tamimi (Bani Tamim), Abd al-Amir al-'Atbi (al-'Atab), Abd al-Amir al-Aydani (al-Aydan), Amr al-Faiz (Bani Amr), Mohammed Ali al-Maturi (al-Mitur), Sabri al-Baydani (al-Baydan), Salam Maliki (Bani Malik), Ya'rib al-Imarah (al-Imarah), Hasan al-Kheyum (Bani Asad), Adnan al-Ghanim (al-Ghanim), Nazar al-Jabri (Sada al-Jawaaber), Najeh Shinawa (Rabiah), Sabah Hatem Ridah (Shaghanbeh), Jabar al-Ubadi (al-Ubadi), Dakhil Abd al-Zahra (Selmi). Source: CLASSIFIED BY: Howell H. Howard, Director, U.S. Regional Embassy Office, Basrah, Department of State. 11 April 2008, 18:44 (Friday). Available at https://wikileaks.org/plusd/cables/08BASRAH28_a.html
84. *The Guardian*, 'Basra after the British: division and despair in Iraq's oil boomtown', 4 July 2016. Available at https://www.theguardian.com/cities/2016/jul/04/basra-british-iraq-oil-boomtown-legacy-chilcot-saddam
85. CLASSIFIED BY: Howell H. Howard, Director, U.S. Regional Embassy Office, Basrah, Department of State, 11 April 2008, 18:44 (Friday). Available at https://wikileaks.org/plusd/cables/08BASRAH28_a.html
86. 'Iraqi Minister: Hundreds of tribesmen support Iraqi forces in Basra', Kuwait News Agency, 20 April 2008. Available at https://www.kuna.net.kw/ArticleDetails.aspx?id=1900842&language=ar

pp. [216–225]

NOTES

87. Author interview, Ammar Alameri, November 2020.
88. Author interview, Sheikh Mansour al-Tamimi, August 2021.
89. BASRAH 00000063 001.2 OF 002. CLASSIFIED BY: Won Lee, A/Director, US Regional Embassy Office, Basrah, Department of State. Available at https://wikileaks.org/plusd/cables/08BASRAH63_a.html, 2 July 2008.
90. Ibid.
91. Bani Malik Sheiks, Growing Iranian Influence in Southern Iraq. 30 May 2008, Basrah, Dept. of State. Wikileaks.
92. Ibid.
93. CLASSIFIED BY: Howell H. Howard, Director, U.S. Regional Embassy Office, Basrah, Department of State, 11 April 2008, 18:44. Available at https://wikileaks.org/plusd/cables/08BASRAH28_a.html
94. Author interview, Sheikh Takleef al-Minshed, December 2020.
95. Author interview, Sheikh Jabbar al-Assad, February 2021.
96. Ibid.
97. CLASSIFIED BY: Howell H. Howard, Director, U.S. Regional Embassy Office, Basrah, Department of State, 11 April 2008, 18:44. Available at https://wikileaks.org/plusd/cables/08BASRAH28_a.html
98. Author interview, Ammar al-Ameri, October, 2020.
99. Author interview, Sheikh Jabbar al-Assad, February 2021.
100. Ibid.
101. Ibid.
102. Author interview, Ammar al-Ameri, October 2020.
103. Author interview, advisor to the al-Badr Organisation, December 2020.
104. Al-Jazeera, 'A Project to Form Support Councils in the Southern Governorates', *Iraq Scene*, 9 October 2008. Available at https://rb.gy/s13hdq
105. Author interview, Sheikh Jabbar al-Assad, February 2021.
106. Wikileaks, Classified by Pol Min Couns Robert Ford for reasons 1.4 (b) and (d).
107. Albayan, 'Fawaz al-Jerba: Maliki and al-Hakim support the "Emirate of Shammar" in Iraq', 29 November 2009. Available at https://www.albayan.ae/one-world/2009–11–29–1.496947

8. TRIBES AND MOBILISATION: POLITICS, POWER AND PROTESTS

1. Author interview, Sheikh Mohamed Zeidawi, January 2022.
2. Author interview, Sheikh Adel al-Assad, February 2021.
3. Author interview, Sheikh Takleef al-Minshed, February 2021.
4. Witwit, A, 2015, 'The Sociology of the Political Participation of the Iraqi Clan: a field study of social and political structure of the al-Khaza'el clans', *Al-Qadisiya Magazine. Journal of Al-Qadisiya in Arts and Educational Sciences*, Vol. 15, Issue 3.
5. Author interview, Sheikh Mansour al-Tamimi, February 2021.
6. Author interview, Sheikh Adnan al-Danbous, August 2021.
7. Alhammood, T A, 2020, 'Iraqi Protests 2019: A sociological view of what happened

NOTES

pp. [226–234]

and possible outcomes' in *The Tishreen Protests in Iraq: The Death of the Old and the Difficulty of the New*, Fares Kemal Nazami and Hareth Hassan (eds), Dar Almada, p. 70. Available at https://www.ahewar.org/debat/files/665969.pdf

8. Author interview, Sheikh Sami al-Majoun, December 2020.
9. Ibid.
10. *Almada* newspaper, 'Voices from the First Reconciliation Conference… Conference Participants: There is no place for terrorists among us', undated. Available at https://www.almadapaper.net/sub/08–754/p00.htm
11. Ibid.
12. Harbi, T, 30 January 2010, 'Maliki Clans!!', *Ahewar*. Available at https://www.ahewar. org/debat/show.art.asp?aid=201608
13. Harling, P, *Beyond political ruptures: Towards a historiography of social continuity in Iraq*, 2012. Available at https://peterharling.com/2012/11/01/452/
14. Author interview, Iraqi analyst, Meesan, October 2021.
15. Harbi, op. cit.
16. Author interview, Sheikh Raed al-Freiji, August 2021.
17. Author interview, Ammar Alameri, November 2020.
18. Al-Mohammad, H, 2011, '"You Have Car Insurance, We Have Tribes": Negotiating Everyday Life in Basra and the Re-emergence of Tribalism', *Anthropology of the Middle East*, Vol. 6, No. 1, Spring 2011, pp. 18–34.
19. Author interview, Sheikh Jabbar al-Assad, February 2021.
20. Author interview, tribesman from Muthanna governate who preferred to remain anonymous, October 2021.
21. Author interview, Ammar Alameri, November 2020.
22. Alarabiya, 'Iraq's Clans are Regaining Their Influence and Turning Into a 'Kingmaker' of the Elections', 7 December 2009. Available at https://www.alarabiya.net/articles/2009%2F12%2F07%2F93426
23. Author interview, Sheikh Mohamed Zeidawi, January 2022.
24. Ibid.
25. Author interview, Sheikh Takleef al-Minshed, December 2020.
26. Author interview, Sheikh Raed al-Freiji, August 2021.
27. Author interview, Sheikh Jabbar al-Assad, February 2021.
28. Author interview, Sheikh Adel al-Assad, February 2021.
29. Author interview, Sheikh Takleef al-Minshed, December 2020.
30. Author interview, Sheikh Yousef al-Baidani, January 2020.
31. Author interview, Sheikh Adel al-Assad, February 2021.
32. Author interview, Iraqi Sheikh, who wished to remain anonymous, August 2021.
33. Author interview, tribesman in Muthanna who preferred to remain anonymous.
34. Author interview, Taleb Abdulaziz, October 2020.
35. Author interview, Riyadh al-Baddawy, May 2021.
36. Author interview, Naji Sultan, November 2020.
37. Ibid.
38. Author interview, Sheikh Wael Abdullatif, August 2021.

pp. [234–244] NOTES

39. Author interview, Sheikh Takleef al-Minshed, February 2021.
40. Witwit, A, 2015, op. cit.
41. Author interview, Sheikh Wael Abdullatif, August 2021.
42. Ayatollah Mohamed Sadiq al-Sadr is known for his criticisms of particular tribal norms, which he claimed in his book *Jurisprudence for Clans* ran counter to sharia.
43. Author interview, Sheikh Takleef al-Minshed, February 2021.
44. Author interview, tribesman in Nasseriyah who wanted to remain anonymous, October 2021.
45. Al-Jazeera, 'An interview with Hassan Mousa Safar, Shiite Marja'iya between religion and politics', Alsharia Walhayat, March 2005. Available at https://rb.gy/admoob
46. Ibid.
47. Al-Jazeera, 'Sistani Chides US for Dropping Election', 12 January 2004. Available at https://www.aljazeera.com/news/2004/1/12/sistani-chides-us-for-dropping-elections
48. Author interview, Ammar Alameri, November 2020.
49. Author interview, Sheikh Sami al-Majoun, December 2020.
50. Al-Jazeera, 'Al-Sistani calls for "yes" vote', 13 October 2005. Available at https://www.aljazeera.com/news/2005/10/13/al-sistani-calls-for-yes-vote
51. Multiple authors, 2018, *The Islamic State of Iraq and the Levant (Daesh): Formation, Discourse and Practice*, Vol. 2, Arab Centre for Research and Policy Studies, Beirut.
52. *The Arab Weekly*, 'Sunni Tribes in Iraq and Syria Split Over ISIS', 9 October 2015. Available at https://thearabweekly.com/sunni-tribes-iraq-and-syria-split-over-isis
53. Ibid.
54. Nirij, *The Nineveh Clans and the 'Caliphate State'... Networks of Interests and Violence that Drew the Map of Statebuilding and Continuity*. 30 October 2015. Available at https://rb.gy/fhsd1k
55. Jabar, F A, 2017, *The Caliphate State*, op cit.
56. Ibid.
57. Ibid.
58. Nirij, op. cit.
59. Ibid.
60. Ibid.
61. Ibid.
62. Ibid.
63. Jabar, F A, op. cit. pp. 28–9.
64. Nirij, op. cit.
65. Ibid.
66. BBC News, 'Iraq Conflict: Shia Cleric Sistani Issues Call to Arms', 13 June 2014. Available at https://www.bbc.co.uk/news/world-middle-east-27834462
67. Rudolf, I, 2018, *Holy Mobilisation: The Religious Legitimation behind Iraq's Counter-ISIS Campaign*, ICSR. Available at https://icsr.info/wp-content/uploads/2018/12/Holy-Mobilisation-The-Religious-Legitimation-behind-Iraq%E2%80%99s-Counter-ISIS-Campaign.pdf.

NOTES

pp. [244–250]

68. Alarabiya Net, *Mufti of Iraq: We will not be a back garden for Iran*, 16 June 2014, https://rb.gy/gosxc6.

69. *Huffington Post*, 'What Do You Know About Sistani's Fatwa?', 10 June 2014. Available at https://www.huffpost.com/entry/what-do-you-know-about-si_b_5576244

70. Author interview, Ammar Alameri, November 2020.

71. Author interview, Sheikh Wael Abdullatif, August 2021.

72. Al-Iraqiya News Channel, 'Prime Minister Adel Abdulmehdi's Speech During his Reception of the Tribal Sheikhs of the Central and Southern Governorates', 19 November 2019. Available at https://www.youtube.com/watch?v=2INZD3VOAeg YouTube. November 2019.

73. Author interview, Taleb Abdulaziz, December 2020.

74. Author interview, Sheikh Mohamed Zeidawi, January 2022.

75. Iraqi Public Opinion Agency, 'A Special Interview With Sheikh Saadoun Ghulam Ali, The General Sheikh of the Bani Lam Tribe'. Available at https://www.youtube.com/watch?v=nYkUW_k9k1s&list=RDCMUC2Zbld6Xdrd82MAVjc2FhLQ&start_radio=1&t=753s

76. They included the Abbas Fighting Squadron, the Brigade of the Supporters of the *marjiya*, the al-Imam Ali Squadron and the Ali al-Akbar Brigade.

77. In 2018, it had an estimated 70,000 members as opposed to the 40,000 members of the other two currents combined. Husham al-Hashemi, July 2020, 'Internal Differences in the Popular Mobilisation Forces', the Center for Policymaking in International & Strategic Studies. Available at https://www.makingpolicies.org/ar/posts/internal-dispute-in-alhashd-alshaabi.php

78. Ibid.

79. Ibid.

80. Iraqi Public Opinion Agency, 'A Special Interview with Sheikh Sabah Fares Badr al-Rumaid, Chief of the Al-Bu Saleh Clans', 1 June 2016. Available at https://www.youtube.com/watch?v=wMJiS45jfl0

81. Author interview, sheikh who wanted to remain anonymous.

82. Author interview, Sheikh Mansour al-Tamimi, August 2021.

83. Author interview, Sheikh Jawad al-Assad, February 2021.

84. Ibid.

85. International Crisis Group, *Iraq's Tishreen Uprising*: *From Barricades to Ballot Box*, Report 223 / Middle East & North Africa, 26 July 2021.

86. Prime Minister Adel Abdulmehdi's speech during his reception of the tribal sheikhs of the central and southern governorates, op. cit.

87. *The Arab Weekly*, 'Iraqi prime minister turns to tribal leaders for support as pressure mounts from protests', 24 November 2019. Available at https://thearabweekly.com/iraqi-prime-minister-turns-tribal-leaders-support-pressure-mounts-protests

88. Al-Jazeera, '"Traitors": Iraqi protesters slam tribal leaders for meeting PM', 22 November 2019. Available at https://www.aljazeera.com/news/2019/11/22/traitors-iraqi-protesters-slam-tribal-leaders-for-meeting-pm

pp. [250–260]   NOTES

89. Ibid.
90. Author interview, Naji Sultan, February 2021.
91. Alestiklal Net, 20 August 2020, 'The State was absent and the militias of Iraq increased: What is Al-Kazemi's plan to tame the tribes?'. Available at https://www.alestiklal.net/ar/view/5692/dep-news-1597756936
92. Author interview, Sheikh Mansour al-Tamimi, August 2021.
93. Anadolu Agency, 'The Nasiriyah Massacre in Iraq… Who ordered the shooting of protesters?', 4 December 2019. Available at https://rb.gy/
94. Author interview, Sheikh Adel al-Assad, February 2021.
95. *Middle East Eye*, 'Dhi Qar: The Southern Province at the Heart of Iraq's Uprising', 2 February 2020. Available at https://www.middleeasteye.net/news/demonstrators-iraqs-dhi-qar-say-they-are-inspiration-iraq
96. Author interview, Majed Safa'ah, February 2021.
97. Author interview, Sheikh Adel al-Assad, February 2021.
98. Author interview, Naji Sultan, February 2021.
99. Ibid.
100. Author interview, tribesman in Nasseriyah, September 2021.
101. Author interview, sheikh who wished to remain anonymous.

CONCLUSION

1. Author interview, Sheikh Mansour al-Tamimi, August 2021.
2. Author interview, Sheikh Abdulhameed al-Kezza, May 2022.
3. Ouanes, M, 2018, *The Libya that I Saw, the Libya that I See: The Calamity of a Country*, Tunis, Mediterranean Publisher, p. 243.
4. Cherstich, I, 2014, 'When Tribesmen do not act Tribal: Libyan Tribalism as Ideology (not as schizophrenia)', *Middle East Critique*, Vol. 23, Issue 4.
5. Author interview, Sheikh Adnan al-Danbous, July 2021.

BIBLIOGRAPHY

Books and Journal Articles

Aaron, F, 2015, *The Ba'thification of Iraq: Saddam Hussein's Totalitarianism*, University of Texas Press.

Ahmida, A A, 2014, *The Libya We Do Not Know*, The Libyan Ministry of Culture (Arabic).

Ahmida, A, 2020, *An Introductory Study on the Status, Challenges and Prospects of the Libyan Society*, Part II of a Baseline Study for the Libya Socioeconomic Dialogue Project. E/ESCWA/CL6.GCP/2020/TP.2.

Ahram, A, 2019, *Break All the Borders: Separatism and the Reshaping of the Middle East*, Oxford, Oxford University Press.

Alexander, N, 1981, 'The Continuous Revolution', *Middle Eastern Studies*, Vol. 17, No. 2, April 1981, pp. 210–27.

Alhammood, T A, 2020, 'Iraqi Protests 2019: A Sociological View of What Happened And Possible Outcomes' in *The Tishreen Protests in Iraq: The Death of the Old and the Difficulty of the New*, Nazami, F and Hassan, H, (eds), Dar Almada, p. 70. Available at https://www.ahewar.org/debat/files/665969.pdf (Arabic).

Al-Atiyyah, H, 2004, *Tribe, Religion, Superstition and Politics in the South of Iraq*, Dar Zahar (Arabic).

Al-Burasim, Q, 2004, *The Spark and the Ashes*, Dar Kanous (Arabic).

Al-Deeb, F, 1986, *Abdulnasser and Libya's Revolution*, Cairo, Dar al-Mostaqbel Al-Arabi (Arabic).

Al-Hosni, A, 2008, Iraq's *Modern Political History*, Part 1, 7th edition, Beirut, Dar al-Rafidain (Arabic).

Al-Houni, A, 2015, *Saif Qadhafi: The Cunning Art of Politics and the Irony of Fate*, Tripoi, Dar al-Madariq (Arabic).

Al-Fessi, S, 2014, 'The Political Role of Tribes in Libya... Between Presence and Absence', *Fessaniya*, Issue 117, 30 June 2014 (Arabic).

BIBLIOGRAPHY

Allawi, H, 1991, *Iraq: The State of Secret Organisation*, Saudi Research and Marketing Company (Arabic).

Al-Mohammad, H, 2011, '"You Have Car Insurance, We Have Tribes": Negotiating Everyday Life in Basra and the Re-emergence of Tribalism', *Anthropology of the Middle East*, Vol. 6, No. 1, Spring 2011, pp. 18–34.

Al-Nasiri, K S, 1978, *Landlords, Lineages and Land Reform in an Iraqi Village*, PhD thesis, Durham, Durham University.

Al-Wardi, S, *Approaches to the Iraqi Political Project, 1921–2003*, undated (Arabic). Available at http://iraker.dk/v/4.htm.

Al-Zubaidi, I, 2003, *The Radio State: Iraqi Biography and Observations*, London, Dar al-Hakima (Arabic).

Al-Zuhairi, F K K, 2021, 'The Tribe and the Strategy of Constructing the Modern State in Iraq Post-2003', *Political Issues*, No. 64, Al-Nahrain University, pp. 218–38, Available at https://www.iasj.net/iasj/download/895b9d1a3b30724d (Arabic).

Anaya, J, 2012, *La 'Seconde Jamahiriyya' libyenne: l'échec d'une stratégie de survie*, L'Annee du Maghreb, VIII.

Anderson, L, 1986, *The State and Social Transformation in Tunisia and Libya, 1830–1980*, Princeton University Press.

Aqeel, A H, 2012, *Secrets and Facts from Qadhafi's Time*, Al-Majmua Al-Dawliya li Nashr wa Tawzia (Arabic).

Attir, M, 2016, *Conflict Between the Tent and the Palace: A Critique of the Libyan Pattern of Modernity*, CreateSpace Independent Publishing Platform.

Baali, Fuad, 1969, 'Agrarian Reform in Iraq: Some Socioeconomic Aspects', *The American Journal of Economics and Sociology*, Vol. 28, No. 1, January 1969.

Baram, A, 1997, 'Neo-Tribalism in Iraq: Saddam Hussein's Tribal Policies 1991–96', *International Journal of Middle East Studies*, Vol. 29 (1).

Batatu, H, 1978, *The Old Social Classes and the Revolutionary Movements of Iraq: a Study of Iraq's Old Landed and Commercial Classes and of its Communists, Ba'athists, and Free Officers*, Princeton University Press.

Benraad, M, 2011, *Iraq's Tribal 'Sahwa': Its Rise and Fall*, Middle East Policy Council.

Blaydes, L, 2020, 'Rebuilding the Ba'thist State', *Comparative Politics*, Vol. 53, No. 1, pp. 93–115.

Blaydes, L, 2018, *State of Repression*, Princeton University Press.

Bleuchot, H, *Chroniques et documents libyens, 1969–1980*, Paris, Editions CNRS.

Bremer, P, 2006, *My Year in Iraq: The Struggle to Build a Future of Hope*, Threshold Editions.

Bulugma, M R, 1964, *The Urban Geography of Benghazi*, Durham University, Durham E-Theses Online. Available at http://etheses.dur.ac.uk/9559.

BIBLIOGRAPHY

Butaleb, M N, 2011, *The Political Dimensions of the Tribalism Phenomenon in Arab Societies: A Sociological Approach to the Tunisian and Libyan Revolutions*, Doha, The Arab Center for Research and Policy Studies. Available at https://www.dohainstitute.org/en/ResearchAndStudies/Pages/The_Political_Aspects_of_the_Tribal_Phenomenon_in_Arab_Societies_A_Sociological_Approach_to_the_Tunisian_and_Libyan_Revolu.aspx.

Cavatorta, F, 2017, *The Weakness of State Structures in the Arab World: Socio-Economic Challenges from Below* in 'The Frailty of Authority Borders, Non-State Actors and Power Vacuums in a Changing Middle East', Kamel, L (ed.), Rome, Edizioni Nuova Cultura.

Charbel, G, 2012, *Inside Qadhafi's Tent: The Colonel's Companions Reveal the Secrets of his Regime*, Beirut, Riad Al-Rayyes Books (Arabic).

Cherstich, I, 2014, 'When Tribesmen do not act Tribal: Libyan Tribalism as Ideology (not as Schizophrenia)', *Middle East Critique*, Vol. 23, Issue 4.

Cigar, N, 2011, Al-Qaida, 'The Tribes and the Government: Lessons and Prospects for Iraq's Unstable Triangle', *Middle East Studies Occasional Papers*, No. 2, Quantico, Marine Corps University Press.

Cole, P, 2015, 'Bani Walid: Loyalism in a Time of Revolution' in *The Libyan Revolution and Its Aftermath*, Peter Cole and Brian McQuinn (eds), Oxford, Oxford University Press.

Collombier, V, 2017, 'Sirte's Tribes Under the Islamic State' in *Tribes and Global Jihadism*, Collombier, V and Roy, O (eds), London, Hurst.

Dawisha, A, 2003, 'Requiem for Arab Nationalism', *Middle East Quarterly*, Vol. 10, No. 1, Winter 2003, pp. 25–41.

Dawisha, A, 1999, 'Identity and Political Survival in Saddam's Iraq', *Middle East Journal*, Vol. 53, No. 4, Autumn 1999, pp. 553–67.

Dawod, H, 2017, 'Iraqi Tribes in the Land of Jihad', in *Tribes and Global Jihadism*, Collombier, V and Roy, O (eds) London, Hurst.

Davis, J, 1987, *Libyan Politics: Tribe and Revolution*, I B Tauris.

Davis, E, 2005, 'Memoirs of State: Politics, History and Collective Identity' in *Modern Iraq*, London, University of California Press.

Dumasy, F and Di Pasquale, F, 2012, 'Être historien dans la Libye de Kadhafi. Stratégies professionnelles et pratiques mémorielles autour du Libyan Studies Center', *Politique Africaine*, 2012/1 (No. 125), pp. 127–46.

Elbendak, O, 2008, *Urban Transformation and Social Change in a Libyan City: An Anthropological Study of Tripoli*, PhD Thesis, National University of Ireland Maynooth, Maynooth, Ireland. Available at https://mural.maynoothuniversity.ie/1332/1/Ph.D._Thesis.pdf.

El-Kikhia, M O, 1997, *Libya's Qaddafi: The Politics of Contradiction*, Florida, University Press of Florida.

BIBLIOGRAPHY

Etherington, M, 2005, *Revolt on the Tigris: The Al Sadr Uprising and the Governing of Iraq*, London, Hurst.

Evans-Pritchard, E, 1954, *The Sanusi of Cyrenaica*, Oxford University Press.

Farhan, A, 1996, *Harvest of the Revolution*, Second edition, London, Dar Albarq (Arabic).

Fatahaly O and Palmer, M, 1980, *Political Development and Social Change in Libya*, D C Heath & Co., Lexington, USA, Lexington Books.

Faust, A, 2015, *The Ba'thification of Iraq: Saddam Hussein's Totalitarianism*, University of Texas Press.

Fernea, R A, 1970, *Shaykh and Effendi, Changing Patterns of Authority Among the El Shabana of Southern Iraq*, Cambridge, Massachusetts, Harvard University Press.

First, R, 1975, *Libya, The Elusive Revolution*, New York, Penguin Books.

Genat, M, 2021, 'Tribal Justice and State Law in Iraq', *International Journal of Middle East Studies*, Vol. 53, Issue 3, August 2021, Cambridge University Press, pp. 507–11.

Habib, K, 2013, *Aspects of Iraq in the Twentieth Century*, Vol. 6, Erbil, Dar Arras for Printing and Publication (Arabic).

Haddad, F, 2011, *Sectarianism in Iraq: Antagonistic Visions of Unity*, Oxford, Oxford University Press.

Hajjaji, S A, 1969, *The Land Use Patterns and Rural Settlement in the Benghazi Plain*, Durham University. Available at Durham E-Theses Online http://etheses.dur.ac.uk/9644.

Hamza, K, 2017, 'A History of the Political Usage of Local Tribal Identity in Iraq: State and Sheikhs Serving Each Other', *Omran for Social Sciences and Humanities*, Issue 19, Doha, the Arab Center for Research and Policy Studies (Arabic).

Harling, P, 2012, 'Beyond Political Ruptures: Towards a Historiography of Social Continuity in Iraq' in *Writing the Modern History of Iraq: Historiographical and Political Challenges*, Bocco, R et al. (eds), World Scientific Publishing Company.

Hashim, A S, 2006, *Insurgency and Counter-insurgency in Iraq*, Cornell University Press.

Hatita, A S, 2015, *The Wars of the Militias, Libya Post-Qadhafi*, Cairo, Dar Kenous (Arabic).

Heitman, G, 1969, 'Libya: An Analysis of the Oil Economy', *The Journal of Modern African Studies*, Vol. 7, Issue 2, July 1969, Cambridge, Cambridge University Press.

Husken, T, 2018, *Tribal Politics in the Borderland Between Libya and Egypt*, Palgrave Macmillan.

Hweio, H, 2012, 'Tribes in Libya: From Social Organization to Political

BIBLIOGRAPHY

Power', *African Conflict and Peacebuilding Review*, Vol. 2, No. 1 (Spring 2012), pp. 111–21.

Jabar, F A and Dawod, H (eds), 2002, *Tribes and Power: Nationalism and Ethnicity in the Middle East*, Saqi Books.

Jabar, F A, 2017, *The Caliphate State: Advancing Towards the Past—ISIL and the Local Community in Iraq*, Beirut, Arab Center for Research and Policy Studies (Arabic).

Jalloud, A, 2021, *Memoirs of Abdulsalam Ahmed Jalloud: The Epic*, Doha, Arab Centre for Research and Studies (Arabic).

Joffé, G, 2013, *Civil Activism and the Roots of the 2011 Uprisings* in 'The 2011 Libyan Uprisings and the Struggle for the Post-Qadhafi Future', Pack, J (ed.), Palgrave Macmillan.

Kadhem, F J, 2016, *The Sacred and the Secular: The 'ulama of Najaf in Iraqi politics between 1950 and 1980*, doctoral thesis, University of Exeter. Available at https://ore.exeter.ac.uk/repository/bitstream/handle/10871/13621/KadhemF.pdf?sequence=1.

Kane, S, 2015, 'Barqa Reborn? Eastern Regionalism and Libya's Political Transition' in *The Libyan Revolution and Its Aftermath*, Cole, P and McQuinn, B (eds), Oxford, Oxford University Press.

Khafaji, I, 2003, 'A Few Days After: State and Society in a Post-Saddam Iraq' in *Iraq at the Crossroads: State and Society in the Shadow of Regime Change*, Dodge, T and Simon, S (eds), Adelphi Paper 354, IISS, Oxford University Press.

Khafaji, F, 2016, *Khairallah Tulfah, Saddam Hussein's Man of the Shadows*, Baghdad, Darstoor (Arabic).

Khoury, D, 2013, *Iraq in Wartime: Soldiering, Martydom and Remembrance*, Cambridge University Press.

Khoury, P and Kostiner, J, 1990, *Tribes and State Formation in the Middle East*, University of California Press.

Lacher, W, 2011, 'Families, Tribes and Cities in the Libyan Revolution', *Middle East Policy*, Vol. 18, Issue 4, Winter 2011, pp. 140–54.

Lacher, W, 2020, *Libya's Fragmentation*, London, I B Taurus.

Lacher, W and Labnouj, A, 2015, 'Factionalism Resurgent: The War in the Jabal Nafusa' in *The Libyan Revolution and Its Aftermath*, Cole, P and McQuinn, B (eds), Oxford, Oxford University Press.

Lewental, D G, 2014, 'Saddam's Qadisiyyah': Religion and History in the Service of State Ideology in Ba'thi Iraq', *Middle Eastern Studies*, Vol. 50, No. 6, November 2014, Taylor & Francis, pp. 891–910.

Mansfield, P, 1976, *The Arabs*, New York, Allen Lane.

Marr, P, 2012, *The Modern History of Iraq*, 3rd ed., Boulder, CO, Westview Press.

Mattes, H, 2011, 'Formal and Informal Authority in Libya in Libya Since

BIBLIOGRAPHY

1969' in *Libya Since 1969: Qadhafi's Revolution Revisited*, Vandewalle, D (ed.), Palgrave Macmillan.

Mogherbi, Z, 1995, *Civil Society, Economic Liberalisation and Democratisation in Libya*, Cairo, Ibn Khaldoun Centre for Development and Studies in Egypt.

Mogherbi, Z, 2011, 'Social Change, Regime Performance and the Radicalisation of Politics: The Case of Libya' in *Islamist Radicalisation in North Africa, Politics and Process*, Joffé, G (ed.), London, Routledge.

Morone, A, 2017, 'Idrīs' Libya and the Role of Islam: International Confrontation and Social Transformation', *Oriente Moderno*, Anno 97, No. 1, C A Nallino, Istituto per l'Oriente.

Mrgin, H S, 2018, *The Protest and Social Movements in Libya: Between the crisis of the state and societal fracturing*, Majalat Buhuth, London, Markaz Lundan Lildirasat Walbuhuth Waliastisharat (Arabic). Available at https://rb.gy/nugjvk.

Myers, C, 2013, 'Tribalism and Democratic Transition in Libya: Lessons from Iraq', *Global Tides*, Vol. 7, Article 5. Available at https://digitalcommons.pepperdine.edu/globaltides/vol7/iss1/5.

Nabil, M, 1969, *Libya and the Revolution*, Kitab Almusawir, Cairo, Dar al-Hilal (Arabic).

Najm, F, 2004, *Tribe, Islam and state in Libya: analytical study of the roots of the Libyan tribal society and interaction up to the Qaramanli rule (1711–1835)*, PhD thesis, University of Westminster School of Social Sciences, Humanities and Languages. Available at https://westminsterresearch.westminster.ac.uk/download/926d7d076329ed28eba6c6893c17630fb1ec633a9e37b4a2ac4ea32394f484ed/19198678/Najem.pdf.

Nakash, Y, 1994, *The Shi'is of Iraq*, Princeton University Press, New Jersey.

Obeidi, A, 2015, *Political Culture in Libya*, London, Routledge.

Ouanes, M, 2018, *The Libya that I Saw, the Libya that I See: The Calamity of a Country*, Tunis, Mediterranean Publisher (Arabic).

Pack, J (ed.), 2013, *The 2011 Libyan Uprisings and the Struggle for the Post-Qadhafi Future*, Palgrave Macmillan.

Pargeter, A, 2012, *Libya: The Rise and Fall of Gaddafi*, Yale University Press.

Peters, E, 1990, *The Bedouin of Cyrenaica*, Press Syndicate of the University of Cambridge.

Pollack, K, 2004, *After Saddam: Assessing the Reconstruction of Iraq*, Foreign Affairs.

Qadhafi, M, 1999, *Escape to Hell and Other Stories*, London, Blake Publishing.

Qadhafi, M, 1982, *The Green Book*.

Ricks, T, 2009, *The Gamble, General Petraeus and the Untold Story of the American Surge in Iraq, 2006–2008*, Penguin UK.

BIBLIOGRAPHY

Riis, L (ed.), 2013, *How the Local Matters: Democratization In Libya, Pakistan, Yemen And Palestine*, Danish Institute For International Studies.

Rohde, A, 2010, *State-Society Relations in Ba'athist Iraq*, London, Routledge.

St John, R, 2015, *Libya, Continuity and Change*, London, Routledge.

Saghieh, H, 2003, *The Iraqi Ba'ath: Saddam's Power from Resurrection to Ruin*, London, al-Saqi (Arabic).

Saqar, S, 2002, *Gharyan and its Relationship with the Surrounding Area*, Master's thesis (Arabic). Available at https://drive.google.com/file/d/1AIc8C K4JYU_8SCoUot-UcXHyN3I5raUj/view.

Sbahi, A, 2020, *Decades of the History of the Iraqi Communist Party*, Vol. 1 and Vol. 2, second edition.

Shalgam, A, 2012, *Figures Around Qadhafi*, Tripoli, Dar al-Madariq and Ferjani (Arabic).

Shouker, A F, *Al'iihya' Baed Al'iinsa', part 1*, Dar Alkilma (Arabic).

Stewart, R, 2006, *Occupational Hazards*, Picador.

Stolzof, S, 2009, *The Iraqi Tribal System: A Reference for Social Scientists, Analysts, and Tribal Engagement*, Minneapolis, Two Harbours Press.

Tripp, C, 2000, *A History of Iraq*, Cambridge, Cambridge University Press.

Vandewalle, D, 1998, *Libya Since Independence: Oil and State-Building*, London, I B Taurus.

Walsh, D, 2016, *Us Against the World: Tribalism in Contemporary Iraq*, Master's thesis, Sciences-Po.

Wardi, A, 1969–1978, *Social Aspects of Iraq's Modern History*, (6 volumes), various publishing houses, Baghdad.

Williamson, J F, 1975, *A Political History of the Shammar Jarba Tribe of Al-Jazirah: 1800–1958*, Indiana University Dissertation.

Witwit, A, 2015, 'The Sociology of the Political Participation of the Iraqi Clan: a field study of social and political structure of the al-Khaza'el clans', *Al-Qadisiya Magazine, Journal of Al-Qadisiya in Arts and Educational Sciences*, Vol. 15, Issue 3, pp. 323–76 (Arabic).

Wehrey, F, November 2018, Review of *Tribe, Islam and State in Libya: Analytical Study of the Roots of Libyan Tribal Society and Evolution Up to the Qaramanli Reign (1711–1835) by Faraj Najem*, London, Libyan Studies.

Wright, J, 1981, *Libya: A Modern History*, London, Routledge.

Yaphe, J, 2000, 'Tribalism in Iraq, the Old and the New', *Middle East Policy*, Vol. 7, Issue 3, June 2000.

Zeidal, R, November 2005, 'Tikriti Regional Identity as Reflected in Two Regional Myths and a Folkloric Tale', *Middle Eastern Studies*, Vol. 41, No. 6, pp. 899–910.

Zeidal, R, June 2016, 'Tribes in Iraq: A Negligible Factor in State Formation' in *Tribes and States in a Changing Middle East*, Uzi Rabi (ed.), London, Hurst.

BIBLIOGRAPHY

Reports, Documents and Media Sources

Ahewar, 'A whole decade since the departure of a distinguished economist', 29 September 2014. Available at https://www.ahewar.org/debat/s.asp?t=4&aid=434991.

Ahewar, 'Maliki clans!!', 30 January 2010. Available at https://www.ahewar.org/debat/show.art.asp?aid=201608.

Ahewar, 'The Sheikh and the Tribe in the 2019 Tripoli War', 11 June 2019. Available at https://www.ahewar.org/debat/show.art.asp?aid=639974.

Ahewar, 'Tarhouna Adopts a New Vision for the Role of Armed Groups in Tripoli', 6 September 2018, Available at http://www.ahewar.org/debat/show.art.asp?aid=610706&r=0.

Akhbar Libya 24, 'A Meeting to Heal the Social Rift between Magharba and al-Awaqir', 17 April 2016. Available at https://rb.gy/m797q

Alarabiya, 'Iraq's clans are regaining their influence and turning into a "King Maker" for the elections', 7 December 2009. Available at https://www.alarabiya.net/articles/2009%2F12%2F07%2F93426.

Alarabiya, 'Mufti of Iraq: We will not be a back garden for Iran', 16 June 2014. Available at مفتي العراق: لن نكون حديقة خلفية لإيران (alarabiya.net).

Alarabiya, 'Sheikh Mazhar Kharbit', September 2022. Available at https://www.youtube.com/watch?v=zfQn9lZ7JSs.

Al-Bayan, 'Fawaz al-Jerba: Maliki and al-Hakim support the "Emirate of Shammar" in Iraq', 29 November 2009. Available at https://www.albayan.ae/one-world/2009–11–29–1.496947.

Al-Hamzeh, A and Ezzedine, N, 'Libyan tribes in the Shadows of War and Peace', CRU Policy Brief, Clingaendal, 18 February 2019. Available at https://www.clingendael.org/sites/default/files/2019–02/PB_Tribalism.pdf.

Al-Hashemi, H, July 2020, 'Internal Differences in the Popular Mobilisation Forces', the Center of Making Policies for International & Strategic Studies. Available at https://www.makingpolicies.org/ar/posts/internal-dispute-in-alhashd-alshaabi.php.

Al-Hurriya newspaper, Issue 1,238, 28 July 1958.

Al-Iraqiya News Channel, 'Prime Minister Adel Abdulmehdi's Speech During His Reception of the Tribal Sheikhs of the Central and Southern Governorates', 19 November 2019. Available at https://www.youtube.com/watch?v=2INZD3VOAeg.

Al-Jazeera, 'US consulate "easy target" for extremists', 16 September 2012.

Al-Jazeera, 'Libyan Tribes Pledge Allegiance to Haftar and Misrata Rejects Him', 11 March 2014.

Al-Jazeera, 'A symposium on the security and political role of clans', 6 April 2008. Available at https://www.youtube.com/watch?v=ZfcyYFUYaY4.

BIBLIOGRAPHY

Al-Jazeera TV, 'Interview with Saleh Omar al-Ali–part 5'', Shahid Ala Al-Asr Programme, 15 June 2003. Available at https://rb.gy/wrpyn

Al-Jazeera, 'An interview with Hassan Mousa Safar, Shiite Marja'iya between Religion and Politics', Alsharia Walhayat, March 2005. Available at المرجعية الشيعية بين الدين والسياسة | متوقفة | الجزيرة نت (aljazeera.net).

Al-Jazeera, 'Project to Form Support Councils in the Southern Governorates', Iraq Scene, 9 October 2008. Available at مشروع تشكيل مجالس الإسناد في المحافظات الجنوبية | متوقفة | الجزيرة نت (aljazeera.net).

Al-Jazeera, '"Traitors": Iraqi protesters slam tribal leaders for meeting PM, 22 November 2019. Available at https://www.aljazeera.com/news/2019/11/22/traitors-iraqi-protesters-slam-tribal-leaders-for-meeting-pm.

Almada newspaper, 'Voices from the first reconciliation conference… Conference participants: There is no place for terrorists among us', undated. Available at https://www.almadapaper.net/sub/08-754/p00.htm.

Al-Magariaf, M Y, 'Libya from Constitutional Legitimacy to Revolutionary Legitimacy', Libya almostakal, March 2009. Available at ليبيا المستقبل .. Libya Almostakbal (libya-al-mostakbal.org).

Al-Maarafi, J, 'Supporting the Libyan revolution', Today's Interview, Al-Jazeera, 25 September 2011.

Alrai Media, 'Al-Suleiman: There is no longer such a thing as "al-Qaeda" in al-Anbar Governate', 2 April 2008. Available at https://rb.gy/bo38s2.

', Benghazi, 1999, Education Division, Leader's Comrades Forum.

Al-Thawra newspaper, 29 March 1991; 2 April 1991; 10 April 1991.

Al-Wasat, 'The Gaming Table of the Country and the Dice of the Tribe', 2 August 2015.

Al-Wasat, 'Al-Darsa Tribe: We Will Not Allow Anyone to Harm Al-Hijazi Until the Results of the Investigation Are Out', 26 January 2016. Available at https://alwasat.ly/news/libya/87924.

Anadolu Agency, 'The Nasiriyah Massacre in Iraq… Who ordered the shooting of protesters?', 4 December 2019. Available at https://rb.gy/.

Arab Centre for Research and Policy Studies, multiple authors, 'The Islamic State of Iraq and the Levant (Daesh): Formation, Discourse and Practice', Vol. 2, Beirut, 2018.

Asharq al-Awast, 'Libyan War Diaries (Episode 5) Map of Tribes' Loyalties in the Conflict with Extremists', 21 November 2014.

Bamyeh, M, 'Is the 2011 Libyan Revolution an Exception?', Jadaliyya, 25 March 2011.

Baumann, H, (ed.), 2019, 'Reclaiming Home: The struggle for socially just housing, land and property rights in Syria, Iraq and Libya', Friedrich-

BIBLIOGRAPHY

Ebert-Stiftung. Available at https://library.fes.de/pdf-files/bueros/tunesien/15664.pdf.

BBC News, 'Iraq Conflict: Shia Cleric Sistani Issues Call to Arms', 13 June 2014. Available at https://www.bbc.co.uk/news/world-middle-east-27834462.

Bskeri, S, 'Libyan National Congress Elections and Options for the Winning Blocs', Doha, Al-Jazeera Center for Studies, 23 July 2012.

Christian Science Monitor, 'A Scholarly Soldier Steps Inside the World of Iraq's Potent Tribes…', 30 December 2003. Available at https://www.csmonitor.com/2003/1230/p01s03-woiq.html.

Coalition Provisional Authority Order 1. Available at https://govinfo.library.unt.edu/cpa-iraq/regulations/20030603_CPAMEMO_1_Implementation_of_De-Ba_athification.pdf.

CRRC Doc. No. SH-IDGS-D-000–370, November 1991–August 1992.

CSDS Centre, *The Role of the Tribe in Libya*, 18 February 2019. Available at https://rb.gy/7o5mz

Cochrane, M, 'Operation Knight's Charge (Saulat al-Fursan), "The Battle for Basra"', Iraq Report 9, Institute for the Study of War, June 2008. Available at https://www.understandingwar.org/operation/operation-knights-charge-saulat-al-fursan.

Constitution of the Arab Socialist Ba'ath Party. Available at https://online.fliphtml5.com/huvs/syup/#p=5.

Correspondents, 'A Conspiracy in Every Sense', Correspondents.org, 26 September 2012.

Djzeri, M, 'Tribal Power, the State, and Political Transition in Libya', 22 February 2021, Fondazione OASIS. Available at https://www.oasis-center.eu/en/tribal-power-the-state-and-political-transition-in-libya.

Doherty, M, '"Give Us Change We Can See": Citizen Views of Libya's Political Process', Washington DC, National Democratic Institute for International Affairs (NDI).

Dustoor.net, 'Interview with Dhaffar Mohamed Jabber. Personal secretary and friend of Uday', 15 September 2003. Available at https://rb.gy/vtvitt

El-Khoja, M, 'The Terrorism Triangle, Episode 2', Libya Watanona, 14 January 2006,. Available at https://rb.gy/sgfkca.

Faraj, A, 'Qadhafi visits Baghdad, apologises to Iraqis, describes Hafez Assad in harsh words', Kitabat, 30 January 2022. Available at https://kitabat.com/%d8%a7%d9%84%d9%82%d8%b0%d8%a7%d9%81%d9%8a-%d9%8a%d8%b2%d9%88%d8%b1-%d8%a8%d8%ba%d8%af%d8%a7%d8%af-%d9%88%d9%8a%d8%b9%d8%aa%d8%b0%d8%b1-%d9%84%d9%84%d8%b9%d8%b1%d8%a7%d9%82%d9%8a%d9%8a%d9%86-%d9%88/.

BIBLIOGRAPHY

Fitzgerald, M, 2015, 'Mapping Libya's Factions. European Council on Foreign Relations', Middle East and North Africa Programme.

Food and Agriculture Organisation of the United Nations, Report to the Government of Libya, Development of Tribal Lands and Settlements Project, Vol. II, 1969.

Hirst, David, 'Ba'athists now put Iraq first', *The Guardian*, 18 July 1968. Available at https://www.theguardian.com/world/1968/jul/18/iraq. davidhirst.

Guardian, 'British Tactics Reviewed as Basra Erupts', 8 May 2006. Available at https://www.theguardian.com/world/2006/may/08/iraq.military.

Guardian, 'Basra after the British: division and despair in Iraq's oil boomtown', 4 July 2016. Available at https://www.theguardian.com/cities/2016/jul/04/basra-british-iraq-oil-boomtown-legacy-chilcot-saddam.

Huffington Post, 'What Do You Know About Sistani's Fatwa?', 10 June 2014. Availableathttps://www.huffpost.com/entry/what-do-you-know-about-si_b_5576244.

Ibrahim, S and Otto, J M, 2017, 'Resolving real property disputes in post-Gaddafi Libya, in the context.

of transitional justice', the Centre for Law and Society Studies, Benghazi University and Van Vollenhoven Institute for Law, Governance and Society, Leiden University, Van Vollenhoven Institute.

International Crisis Group, 'Governing Iraq, Report 17', Middle East & North Africa 25 August 2003.

International Crisis Group, 'Iraq's Tishreen Uprising: From Barricades to Ballot Box', Report 223, Middle East & North Africa, 26 July 2021.

International Crisis Group, 'Divided We Stand: Libya's Enduring Conflicts', Report No. 130, 14 September 2012.

International Crisis Group, 'Iraq after the Surge: The New Sunni Landscape', Middle East Report No. 74—30 April 2008.

Iraqi Public Opinion Agency, 'A special interview with Sheikh Sabah Fares Badr Al-Rumaid / Chief of Al-Bu Saleh clans', 1 June 2016. Available at https://www.youtube.com/watch?v=wMJiS45jfl0.

Jabar, F A, 'Shaykhs and Ideologues: Detribalization and Retribalization in Iraq, 1968–1998', Middle East Report (MERIP), No. 215, Summer 2000, pp. 28–31 and 48.

Keddie, O, 'The Ink of Exile', Cairo, *Al-Moustaqil Magazine*, January 2015.

Keddie, O, 'Where Did Libya's Leaders Come From and Where Will They Come From?', Correspondents.org, 15 December 2014.

Kuwait News Agency, 'Iraqi Minister: Hundreds of tribesmen support Iraqi forces in Basra', 20 April 2008. Available at https://www.kuna.net.kw/ArticleDetails.aspx?id=1900842&language=ar.

BIBLIOGRAPHY

Lacher, W, 'Libya's Local Elites and the Politics of Alliance Building', *Libya Tribune*, 4 September 2019.

Law No. (142) of 1970 on Tribal Lands and Wells. Available at https://security-legislation.ly/en/law/101411.

Libya Al-Mostakbal, 'The facts of the Dispute in Cyrenaica', 17 June 2016.

Libya Al-Mostakbal, 'The Time of the Monarchy: Men Around the King', part 7, 1 June 2009.

Libya Al-Mostakbal, 'The phenomenon of Field Marshal Haftar... a different approach', part 1, 9 February 2017.

Libya Channel, 'Libya Zintan Revolution, an interview with Sheikh Taher Al-Jadaa'.

Libya Herald, 'General Haftar Announces Coup; Politicians Rreact with Scorn, Order his Arrest', 14 February 2014.

Libya News and Views Website, March 1997. Available at https://web.archive.org/web/20210901044802/http://www.libyanet.com/3–97nwsc.htm.

Libyan TV, Tripoli, Excerpts from recorded speech by Libyan leader Col Qadhafi to the masses of Bani Walid and Warfallah; broadcast by Libyan TV on 9 September 1995; BBC Monitoring.

Menas Associates, Libya Focus, December 2005; January 2011; March 2011; November 2011; December 2011; June 2012; October 2012; March 2013; June 2013; September 2013; June 2014; January 2016; October 2016; November 2016; September 2017; November 2017.

Menas Associates, Iraq Focus, May 2006; September 2003; February 2004.

Menas Associates, Libya Politics and Security, 16 December 2013.

Metz, H (ed.), 1988, 'Iraq: A Country Study', Washington: GPO for the Library of Congress. Land Tenure and Agrarian Reform. Available at http://countrystudies.us/iraq/59.htm.

Middle East Eye, 'Dhi Qar: The Southern Province at the Heart of Iraq's Uprising', 2 February 2020. Available at https://www.middleeasteye.net/news/demonstrators-iraqs-dhi-qar-say-they-are-inspiration-iraq.

Mzoughi, S, 2008, 'Genealogy of the Qadhadhfah tribe', Libyajil site. Available at https://aboezra.yoo7.com/t13724-topic#24971.

New York Times, 'Iraq Reportedly Cracks Down on Clan that Tried a Coup', 20 June 1995. Available at https://www.nytimes.com/1995/06/20/world/iraq-reportedly-cracks-down-on-clan-that-tried-a-coup.html.

New York Times, 'Iraqi Offers Regrets in Killing of Defecting Sons-in-Law', 10 May 1995. Available at https://www.nytimes.com/1996/05/10/world/iraqi-offers-regrets-in-killing-of-defecting-sons-in-law.html.

Nirij, 'The Nineveh Clans and the "Caliphate State"... Networks of Interests and Violence that Drew the Map of Statebuilding and Continuity', 30 October 2015. Available at https://rb.gy/fhsd1k.

BIBLIOGRAPHY

Noon Post, 'Libyan Tribes and their Relationship to the Revolution', 12 May 2015.

Nouri, I A, 'Tribalism and Women in Iraq after 2003', *Al-Faraheedi Literature Magazine*, Issue 35, September 2018. Available at https://www.iasj.net/iasj/download/ba0ae90c6e0a1a81.

Proclamation of the Republic, 1 September 1969.

Qadhafi, M, 'Sijil al-Qoumi' (Statements, Speeches and Conversations), Vol. 1, 1970; Vol. 3, 1972; Vol. 10, 1979.

Qadhafi's Five-Part Account of the Libyan Revolution, published in the Libyan press, 1969.

Reuters, 'Libyan tribes protest at new government line-up', 23 November 2011.

Reuters, 'In Gaddafi's Hometown, Residents Accuse NTC Fighters of Revenge', 16 October 2011.

Reuters, 'Libyan parties reject draft election law', 15 January 2012.

Riyad Newspaper, 'An Interview with Sheikh Al-Nada of Saddam's Clan: Saddam Bet on Street War... and Betrayal was Greater than Sacrifices', Defense Arab website, 26 January 2016. Available at https://defense-arab.com/vb/threads/51027/.

Rudolf, I, 2018, 'Holy Mobilisation: The Religious Legitimation behind Iraq's Counter-ISIS Campaign', ICSR. Available at https://icsr.info/wp-content/uploads/2018/12/Holy-Mobilisation-The-Religious-Legitimation-behind-Iraq%E2%80%99s-Counter-ISIS-Campaign.pdf.

S&P Global, 'Libyan tribe says oil terminal blockade to be lifted Sunday', 10 December 2013. Available at https://www.spglobal.com/commodityinsights/en/market-insights/latest-news/oil/121013-libyan-tribe-says-oil-terminal-blockade-to-be-lifted-sunday.

Saddam Hussein's Cruelty Blog, 'The Sha'aban Intifada... March 1991: The Page of Treachery and Betrayal... 1', November 2018. Available at http://saddamscruelty.blogspot.com/2018/11/blog-post_10.html.

Saddam Hussein's Cruelty Blog, 'The Sha'aban Intifada... March 1991: The Page of Treachery and Betrayal... 4', June 2020. Available at http://saddamscruelty.blogspot.com/2020/06/blog-post_10.html.

Samarra TV, 'Interview with Sheikh Kadhem al-Anaizan, head of the Southern Tribes Council', Samarra Guest Programme, 14 March 2015. Available at https://www.youtube.com/watch?v=klACeQkOocg.

Shabakngy.com, 'Saddam Hussein Threatens the Jubour Clan With Genocide', undated. Available at https://s.shabakngy.com/go/g.php?q=YJ_D7XPw1n4.

The Arab Weekly, 'Sunni tribes in Iraq and Syria split over ISIS', 9 October 2015. Available at https://thearabweekly.com/sunni-tribes-iraq-and-syria-split-over-isis.

BIBLIOGRAPHY

The Arab Weekly, 'Iraqi prime minister turns to tribal leaders for support as pressure mounts from protests', 24 November 2019. Available at https://thearabweekly.com/iraqi-prime-minister-turns-tribal-leaders-support-pressure-mounts-protests.

Time, 'Saddam's Revenge', 18 September 2005. Available at https://content.time.com/time/subscriber/article/0,33009,1106307,00.html.

Washington Post, 'Insurgents Assert Control Over Town Near Syrian Border', 6 September 2005. Available at https://www.washingtonpost.com/archive/politics/2005/09/06/insurgents-assert-control-over-town-near-syrian-border/028645c8-d87e-4a17-a6d8-3baf4e3abcea/.

Wikileaks, Classified by Pol Min Couns Robert Ford for reasons 1.4 (b) and (d).

YouTube, 'Pages of the Iran–Iraq War Narrated by Abdul Jabbar Mohsen', Part 2, undated. Available at https://www.youtube.com/watch?v=-535VZAuuzg.

YouTube, 'An interview with Kadhem al-Anaizan in Testimonials for History, presented by Dr Hamid Abdullah', undated. Available at https://www.youtube.com/watch?v=KlO136ZPylE.

YouTube, 'Special Testimonies, What Did the Rich and Tribal Shiekhs Give to Gain Saddam Hussein's Approval?', 3 September 2022. Available at https://www.youtube.com/watch?v=Jwmwnuwwcts.

YouTube, 'The Political Memory: Abdulsalam Jalloud Interview', part 1, 24 August 2012. Available at. https://www.youtube.com/watch?v=18QcNwObfeM.

YouTube, 'Muammar Gaddafi's Reception of A Delegation From Bani Walid In Al-Sadadah Area', 14 June 2020. Available at https://www.youtube.com/watch?v=vFmrKm2U74g.

Youm7, 19 September 2016, 'Sheikh of the Libyan Magharba tribe: The tribes supported the national army led by Field Marshal Haftar', Cairo, Youm. Available at https://rb.gy/tm5mi

INDEX

:Note: Page numbers followed by "*n*" refer to notes.

7th Brigade. *See* al-Kaniat militia
(7th Brigade)
20th Revolution Brigade, 197
204 Tank Battalion, 89–90, 118,
127

al-Abbar, Abdulhameed, 26–7, 33
al-Abbar, Sharif, 32, 34, 48, 101
Abdulateef, Laila, 205
Abdulhafiz, Masoud, 65
Abduljalil, Mustafa, 93, 97
Abdullatif, Sheikh Wael, 198, 215,
234
Abdulmehdi, Adel, 249–50
Abdulnasser, Jamal, 15
Abdulsalam, Sheikh Mohamed, 242
Abouda tribe, 251
Abu Ghaylan Mountain, 18
Abu Jun, Sha'alan, 232–3
Abu Khattala, Ahmed, 92
Abu Obeida Ibn Jarrah Brigade, 89
Abu Sleem prison massacre (1996),
71
Abushagur, Mustafa, 94
al-Adeeb, Ali, 220
African Company for Electricity,
170

Aghas (Kurdish tribal leaders),
142, 170
Agrarian Reform Law (Libya,
1958), 147–50
Agrarian Reform Law No. 117
(1970), 169–71
Ahl al-Beit (family of the Prophet),
57
Ahmed, Mousa, 36
Ajdabiya tribes, 42
Ajdabiya, 77, 121, 122
Akara tribe, 59
al-Akhdar, Mukhtar, 83
al-Abraq, 113
al-Abs tribe, 233–4
al-Ameri, Ammar, 216, 218–19,
229, 244–5
al-Ameri, Hadi, 214
al-Anaizan, Sheikh Kadhem, 176,
186, 187, 188
al-Ansari, Abu Jafar, 209
al-Ar'aibi, Sheikh Mohamed, 146
al-Arabi, Mehdi, 62
al-Asfar, Saad, 76, 130
al-Ashiq, Wasila, 97
al-Ashour clan, 183
al-Assad, Sheikh Adel, 159, 168,
232, 251, 252

311

INDEX

al-Assad, Sheikh Jabbar, 218, 219, 220–1, 233
al-Assad, Sheikh Jawad, 149, 172, 173, 174, 176, 187, 188, 189, 196–7, 248
al-Atyush, Sheikh Saleh, 120, 121, 123, 124
al-Awaqir tribes, 7, 16, 22, 27, 34, 48, 88, 94
  administrative committee, 96
  Arab Spring and, 73, 75, 76
  Brigade 204 tanks, 89–90
  Haftar and, 113, 114, 116, 117, 127–30, 133
  vs. Jawazi, 49–50
al-Aziziya tribal conference (25 May 2014), 109–10
al-Badr Brigade, 202, 213
al-Badr Organisation, 220, 232–3
al-Baida, 31, 113
al-Baidan tribe, 233
al-Breiki tribe, 72
Albu Mahal tribe, 211
Albu Nassir tribe, 162, 163
Alburki, Sheikh Abdulrahim, 62, 100
al-Dbeibahs, 82
al-Fatah Alliance, 247–7
al-Fatah revolution (1969), 15, 21, 23–4
Algeria, 60
al-Ghanem tribe, 144
al-Ghazi wa Fudoul tribe, 143
Algiers Agreement (1975), 177
al-Gurda, Libya, 64
al-Harrarat tribe, 59
al-Hayal tribe, 183
al-Hayania, 182
al-Hijazi, Mohamed, 109, 126–7
al-Hillah, 200
al-Hoot prison (Nasseriyah), 252
al-Huda, Bint, 178

al-Hurriya (newspaper), 146
Ali Hassan Jabber Brigade, 121
Ali Khayoun, Sheikh Hussein, 251
al-Ali, Saleh Omar, 160
al-Issawi, Rafi, 239
al-Izeirij tribe, 142
al-Jarba family, 142
al-Jazeera, 76
al-Jubour tribe, 180, 183, 197, 243
al-Juwaibar tribe, 252
al-Kaniat militia (7th Brigade), 82, 131–2
al-Khaza'el tribe, 183, 191, 198
Allawi, Hassan, 164
al-Madaan tribe, 112
al-Masameer tribe, 113
al-Nawashi tribe, 183
al-Obediat tribes, 7, 16, 23, 25, 31, 33–4, 94–5
  Arab Spring and, 73, 75, 76
  Haftar and, 115, 116
  response to al-Obeidi's killing, 89
  Revolutionaries, 90
al-Qadisiyyah, 186–7
al-Qaeda, 208–10, 211, 212, 213
al-Qurnah Battalion, 216
al-Rubaya tribe, 85
al-Sadadah, 55
al-Senussi, Idris King, 16, 26
  fate of his supporters, 26–7
al-Shams (newspaper), 58
al-Suwayhilis, 82
Al-Thawra (newspaper), 185, 186–7
Al-Umma party, 97
al-Zuwalem tribe, 233
Amarah (now Meesan), 142, 181
Amiriyat al-Fallujah, 243
Anbar, 197, 209, 211, 213, 227, 243
Ansar al-Sharia, 91, 125

INDEX

anti-Americanism, 202
anti-feudalism, 146
anti-imperialism, 32, 137
Aqeel Hussein Aqeel, 46
Arab nationalism, 15–16, 26, 44, 145, 158
Arab nationalist ideals, 16, 20, 23, 26, 137
Arab Socialist Union of Iraq, 155
Arab Spring in Libya (2011) and aftermath
  civil war, 83
  counter-demonstrations, 73–4
  'Day of Rage', 69–70, 73, 78
  eastern tribes, 76–8, 87–92
  economic reforms, failure of, 70–1
  housing shortages, 70
  NATO's entry, 79–80
  new powerhouses, 81–7
  revolutionaries, 83–4
  self-preservation interests, 74–5
  spread of, 68, 69–73
  transition, 81, 104
  tribal militias took over key strategic sites, 89–90
  tribal revenge, 75, 83–6
  tribal society, 68–9
  tribes and politics, 92–101
  tribes response to, 10–11, 68–9, 73–81
  western and southern tribes, 78–9
  'Yellow Hats', 74
Arab Summit (Baghdad, 1990), 57–8
Araibi, Mohamed, 115
Aref, Abdulsalam, 145, 153, 154–5
Assaba, 105
Attir, Mustafa, 59

Attiya, Sheikh Hussein, 129
Aujailat, 105
Awakening Councils (Libya), 118
Awakening Councils (Sahwat) (Iraq), 212–13, 239–40
Awlad Abul Hul tribe, 82
Awlad Dweib tribe, 82
Awlad Suleiman tribe, 19, 39, 44, 48, 53, 74, 86
  Haftar and, 131
Awlia' Aldam Brigade, 90
Ayad, Suleiman, 73

Ba'ath party, 165
  de-Ba'athification, 195
  high-ranking members, killing of, 175
  international sanctions, 187
  leadership, 154, 161
  membership, 171
  party offices, 171
  power of Ba'athist officials, 171–3
  Saddam's dominance over, 175
  sheikhs acknowledged the leadership of, 186, 187
  sheikhs support during Iran–Iraq War, 179
  sons of sheikhs in, 173–4
  transformation, 160–1
Ba'athification, 185
  de-Ba'athification, 194, 195
Ba'athism, 56
Ba'athist regime, 155, 156, 157–90
  after the fall (2003), 195–207
  Agrarian Reform Law No. 117 (1970), 169–71
  anti-tribal rhetoric, 158–60
  al-Bakr leadership, 157
  bureau for tribal affairs, 187, 188

313

INDEX

categorisation of sheikhs, 187–8
collapse of, 192–3, 194, 195, 213
communiqué of 1968, 158
de-Ba'athification, 194, 195
eliminated the manifestation of feudal rule, 174
invasion of Kuwait (1990), 181, 187
"Law 90", 170
al-Majoun's arrest and release, 169
peasant co-operatives and associations, 171
Republican Guard, 165, 175, 184
're-tribalisation', 179–80, 185, 255
Saddam Hussein years, 175–84
sheikhs' power, end of, 170–5
'Sheikhs of the Nineties', 188–9
sheikhs' oath of allegiance to, 184–90
Shi'ite tribes threat, 166–8
strike against the 'feudalists', 166–8
tribal engagement, 184–90
tribal networks, 153, 159, 160–6
tribal surnames usage, banning of, 165–6
tribal vengeance, 192
tribes and the early years (1968 to 1979), 4–5, 11, 166–75
uprising (Mar 1991), 181–4
war against a Shi'ite power (Iran), 177
weapons supply to Kurdish tribes, 178
Ba'athists. See Ba'athist regime
kinship alliances, 154–5
return to power (1968), 157

uprising (Mar 1991) records, 183
views on tribalism, 158
al-Baddawy, Riyadh, 234
Badeen, Abduljawad, 73, 86, 95–6, 121, 123
al-Badrani, Sheikh Barazan, 241
al-Badri, Sheikh Ahmed Salal Abdulaziz, 196
Baghdad, 141, 168, 177, 221
Abdulmehdi meeting with sheikhs, 249–50
Arab Summit (1990), 57–8
ethnic cleansing, 208
'General Conference of the Sheikhs of Iraqi Tribes and Clans', 226–7
landowning sheikhs link with, 143
October protests (2019), 249
population, 145, 148
sheikhs and heads of clans towards, 186
sheikhs settlement in, 139
tribal conferences (Babylon Hotel), 226–7
Baghdad Radio, 147
Baghdad University, 165
al-Baghdadi, Abu Bakr, 242
al-Baidani, Sheikh Yousef, 179
Bakkar, Ibrahim, 33
al-Bakr and Saddam. See Ba'athist regime
from Beijat clan, 163, 164
meeting with sheikhs after the coup (Baghdad), 168
tribal networks, 153, 159, 160–6
al-Bakr, Ahmed Hassan, 153, 154, 155, 160
Ballam, Ziyad, 117
Bamyeh, Mohammed, 77

INDEX

Bani Arid tribe, 183
Bani Assad tribe, 252
Bani Lam tribe, 142, 245
Bani Malik tribe, 217
Bani Said tribe, 142
Bani Tamim tribe, 215, 216, 217, 250–1
Bani Walid plot (1993), 52–6, 62, 84
   collective punishment, 64
Bani Walid, 37, 62, 107
   Misratan forces attack, 84–5
Baragatha tribe, 91
Baram, A, 4–5
Barassa tribes, 7, 16, 24, 33, 87, 90, 116
Barce Office, 28
al-Bargathi, Mehdi, 50, 76, 89–90, 92, 114, 118, 127, 128, 130
Barqa Transitional Council, 94
Barzani, Mustafa, 160
Basic People's Congresses, 41, 42, 51, 63
Basra, 141, 148, 181, 189, 198, 221, 222, 234, 238, 245, 247, 249, 250
   claiming sheikhdoms, 230
   intra-tribal fighting, 253
   Operation Saulat al-Fursan (Charge of the Knights), 213–14, 215, 216, 217–18
Batatu, H, 140, 161
Battle of al-Qadisiyyah, 177
Bedouin tribes, 4, 59, 65, 122, 141, 154
   as security brigades, 40
   Tikrit, 162, 164
Beijat clan, 163, 164
Ben Ali, Zinabedinne, 70
Ben Jawad town, Libya, 60
Ben Nayal, 46
Ben Taha, Mohamed, 58

Benghazi, 16, 80, 94, 115, 126
   'Day of Rage', 69–70, 73–4, 75
   'First Gathering to Support Islamic Sharia' (Jun 2012), 91–2
   foreign oil workers, 20–1
   former regime officials returns, 130
   Islamist forces control over, 89, 90, 91
   Land Registration offices, 28
   LNA's control over, 118
   Misratans settled in, 49
   Operation Dignity campaign, 106, 107–9, 113, 114, 116, 117–18
   'Operation Snake Bite', 118
   population, 20–1
   Qadhafi loyalists, execution of, 87
   Sabri town, 20–1
   targeted assassinations and kidnappings, 104
   tribal affiliation, 59
   tribal associations in, 58
   US bombing raids on, 52
   US Mission in, 92
   Wisemen's council, 100
Benghazi Revolutionaries Shura Council, 118
Benghazi University, 24
Benjdiriya, Sheikh Mohamed Omar, 42, 54, 55, 57, 60, 78, 80
Bidour tribe, 251, 252–3
Bin Hamid, Wissam, 115, 117
Bin Sweilem tribe, 176
'Black Saturday', 115
Bouaira, Abu Bakr, 95
al-Breiki, Aisha Bint Abu Neran, 72, 79
"Brigade 28", 84

315

INDEX

"Brigade 604", 126
British mandate, 140–2
British rule, revolt against (Iraq, 1920), 192, 200
Bu Alwan tribe, 243
Bu Daraj tribe, 142
Bu Haliqa, Saleh, 125
Bu Issa tribe, 243
Bu Katef, Fawzi, 88, 117
Bu Kelal, Sheikh Subhi, 230
Bu Mahal tribe, 243
Bu Mohamed tribe, 142, 146
Bu Nimmer, 197
Bu Zaid tribe, 230
Buamid, Khalid, 109
Buamid, Sheikh Mabrouk, 79, 85–6, 110, 111
Bufahad tribe, 243
Buhaji Shahab tribe, 162
Buhalaq, Yousef, 62
Buheleq, Sheikh al-Senussi, 40, 49, 73, 92, 113, 116, 133
Buhulouma, Sheikh Suleiman, 86
bureau for tribal affairs, 187, 188
Bush, George W., 226

Calderoli, Roberto, 70
'Charter of Honour', 63–4, 65
Christian Science Monitor, 204–5
CIA (Central Intelligence Agency), 54
Coalition Provisional Authority (CPA), 194, 195, 201, 202, 209
    contracts, 203–4
    initial transition plan, 238
    Nasseriyah conference (15 Apr 2003), 197–8, 200
collective punishment, 63–5, 180–1
colonialism, 2, 16, 153, 158
Command of the National Defence Battalions, 221

Communists, 26, 150, 161, 167
constitutional referendum (Iraq, Oct 2005), 207, 239
coup d'état (attempted, Libya, 1975), 35–6
CPA. *See* Coalition Provisional Authority (CPA)
Crocker, Ryan, 199, 200, 201, 239
'cultural tribalism', 8, 256
Cyrenaica
    Arab Spring events in, 77
    Jawazi expelled from, 49–50
Cyrenaica Defence Force (CYDF), 27
Cyrenaican Transitional Council, 120
Cyrenaican tribes, 7, 33
    LNA and, 116
    and success of Haftar, 106
    See also al-Awaqir tribes; al-Obediat tribes; Barassa tribes

al-Danbous, Sheikh Adnan, 167, 174, 192, 196, 215, 224, 260

Dawa Party, 178, 202, 208, 214, 219, 220–1, 227
'Day of Rage' (Libya, 2011), 69–70, 73, 78
al-Deeb, Fathi, 24, 31
degga, 235
democracy, 39, 41, 42, 68, 91, 260
Democratic Patriotic Alliance of Kurdistan, 207
Derna, 75, 124, 131
Dersa tribe, 126
Dhi Qar, 174, 186, 248–9, 251, 252, 253
Diwaniyah, 169, 191, 198, 200, 249

INDEX

tribal conference (2018), 247
Dulaim tribe, 175, 180–1, 203, 204
Dulaimi, Sheikh Nawaf, 240
al-Dulaimi, Mohamed Mazlum, 181

eastern tribes (Libya), 76–8, 87–92
  Islamist forces, 87–9, 90, 95, 96, 100
  politics, 94–5
  Haftar's relations with, 105, 112–18
  See also Haftar, Khalifa; Islamist forces and Misratan allies
Egypt, 15, 56, 60, 68, 110, 154–5
election law (Libya, 2012), 92–4, 97
elections (Libya, Jun 2014), 110
electoral system (Iraq), 231
Escape to Hell (Qadhafi), 65

Fadhila militia, 195
Fadhila Party, 202
Faisal I, King, 140, 141
al-Faitouri, Ali, 62
Fallujah, 213, 240
Farhan, Abdulkarim, 153–4
al-Farhoud, Sheikh Abdelila Farhim, 226–7
Farkash, Safiya (wife of Qadhafi), 33
al-Faysi, Uyad, 90
federalist project (Libya), 95–7
Ferjan tribe, 51, 107, 112, 113–14, 125, 126
Fernea, Robert, 143
'feudalists', 166–8
Free Officers' Central Committee (Iraq), 145–6
Free Officers' coup (Iraq, 1958), 137–8, 145

Free Unionist Officers (Libya), 9, 11, 20, 21, 23, 34, 39
  Arab nationalist ideals, 16, 20, 23, 26
  as co-ordinator of SPLs, 62
  dismantling of, 38
  member selection, 21–3, 22t, 25
  Warfalla in, 44
al-Freiji, Sheikh Raed, 228–9, 231

al-Gaoud, Sheikh Fasal, 227
General Authority of Labour Forces, 59–60
'General Conference of the Sheikhs of Iraqi Tribes and Clans' (Baghdad), 226–7
General National Congress (GNC), 62, 92, 94, 96–7, 101, 107, 109, 112
  elections (2012), 92, 96–9
  political isolation law, 99–100
  revolutionaries stormed, 99–100
  suspension of, 106
General People's Committee, 39, 42, 59, 63
General People's Congress, 39
General Union of Iraqi Women, 183
al-Gharianni, Grand Mufti, 95
Ghayran, 18, 45, 58, 59, 131
Ghroum, Muftah, 53
Ghulam Ali, Sheikh Sadoun, 245
GNA. *See* Government of National Accord (GNA)
GNC. *See* General National Congress (GNC)
Government of National Accord (GNA), 119, 122, 127, 129–30, 131, 134
Green Book, The (Qadhafi), 34, 93

317

INDEX

H'neish, Khalifa, 44–5, 46, 51, 72, 134
al-Ha'iri, Ayatollah Sayid Kadhem, 235, 236
Hadideen tribe, 243
Hadithiya tribe, 163
Haftar, Khalifa, 103, 258
  al-Arabiya television appearance, 106, 107
  background, 106–7
  Benghazi victory, 130
  domination of Benghazi, 119
  eastern tribes relations with, 105, 112–18
  expanding control, southwards and westwards, 119–26
  export terminals control, 119–20
  Martyrs' Hall meeting (Tripoli), 107
  military council plan, 107
  oil ports attack, 122–3
  Operation Dignity campaign, 103, 105, 106, 107–9, 113, 114, 116, 117–18
  'Operation Snake Bite', 118
  political agreement (Skhirat, Morocco), 119
  Qasr Libya gathering (Green Mountains), 113
  relations between Jedhran and, 121–3
  success of, 106, 118
  tribal support for, 104–6
  use of patronage, 106
  See also Libyan National Army (LNA)
al-Hakim family, 202, 214
al-Hakim, Ammar, 214
al-Hakim, Mehsen, Grand Ayatollah 220
al-Hamdani, Sheikh Ra'ad Ouda, 197

Hamza, Awadh, 36
Hamza, Karim, 176
Hasawna tribe, 39, 44, 48
  Arab Spring and, 79–80
  vs. Magarha, 50–1
  Qadhafi's punishment to, 64–5
Hashd al-Atabat (Mobilisation of the Shrines), 245–6
Hashd al-Wilayee, 246, 247
Hasnawi, Abdulmonem Salim Khalifa, 64
Hasnawi, Sheikh Mohamed Aujail, 27, 30, 48, 61, 62–3, 64–5, 78
al-Hassan, Sheikh Malek, 205
al-Hassouni, Nasser, 37, 65, 73
al-Hatem, Sheikh Ali, 209, 210, 211, 212
Hawas, Adam, 31, 36
al-Hdhal, Sheikh Abduljabbar, 186
al-Heiss, Sheikh Hamid, 210–11
'hinterland culture', 4, 8
Hiraysha, Jamal, 96
Hmeidat tribe, 148
Hmoud, Hadeeb al-Haj, 148
al-Houni, Abdulmonem, 36
al-Houni, Abdulmotaleb, 72, 75, 83
House of Representatives (Libya), 112, 119, 127
  elections (Jun 2014), 110
Humaidi, Khweildi, 21
Hussein Juwaifi Brigade, 40, 90
Hussein, Saddam, 4, 175–84
  assassination plot (1989), 180–1
  as al-Bakr's deputy, 160
  betrayal, 181
  consolidation of power, 175
  as de facto leader of Iraq, 175
  dropped the al-Tikriti name, 165
  from Beijat clan, 163–4
  meeting with Shi'ite tribal sheikhs, 186–7

318

INDEX

relationship with sheikhs, 176–7
relying on kinship networks, 175
tribal committee, 165
tribal environment, 162–3
tribal politics, revived, 2, 159, 190
uprising (Mar 1991), 181–4
visibility of tribalism, 180
See also Ba'athist regime
Hussein, Sheikh Nada, 163
Huwaidi, Bashir, 36

Ibada tribe, 174
Ibn Faysal, Sheikh Mish'an, 142
Ibn Khaldoun's cyclical theory, 7–8
Ibrahim, Saleh, 37, 38, 54
Iranian revolution, 178
Iran–Iraq War (1980), 177–9, 180
Iraq
Americans views on, 194
constitutional referendum (Oct 2005), 207, 239
dismantling the old elites, 139
ethno-sectarian divisions, 193–4
independence in 1932, 141
intra-tribal fighting, 253–4
land tenure, 141–2
landowning sheikhs, 141–4, 149–50, 170
list-based electoral system, 231
mass tribal mobilisation (2014), 225, 239–46
oil prices (after 1973), 157
population, 141, 171
protests (Dec 2012), 228
revolt against British rule (1920), 192, 200
rural-to-urban migration, 138–9, 144–5
Tishreen (October) Movement (2019), 247–53

tribal conferences, 193
under British mandate, 140–2
Iraq political parties and tribes, 223–34
claiming sheikhdoms, 229–30
competition, 233–4
elections (Jan 2009), 223
loyal sheikhs, creating, 230
new political bargains, 230–1
parliamentary elections (2018), 232–3, 246
protests (Dec 2012), 228
tribal support, efforts to win over, 223–4, 228–9
Iraq, occupied
Ba'athist regime fall and aftermath, 195–207
coalition forces entry, 191
constitution drafting committee, 206–7
invasion of (Mar 2003), 191, 236–7
Iraqi tribes during, 191–5
Islamists and constitution, 206–7
Maliki engagement with the southern tribes, 213–22
militias, rise of, 195
National Assembly elections (Jan 2005), 205, 206
parliamentary elections (2005), 207–8
political parties and their own militias, 202–3
security providers role of tribes, 195–7
sheikhs' resentment, 199–201
sheikhs' struggles in political arena, 201–2
Shi'ite tribes support for, 191–2
short-sightedness of Americans, 201

319

INDEX

Sunni tribes countering US forces, 197
Sunni tribes' resistance, 191, 197
tribal appointments, 205
tribal blocs, failure of, 205
tribal engagement of Americans, 203–5
tribal sheikhs appointment to local governance, 198, 201
tribes under Maliki, 207–13
Iraqi Accord Front, 207
Iraqi Communist Party, 150, 160
Iraqi Islamic Party, 207
Iraqi nationalism, 177
Iraqi Republic, 137–56
Agrarian Reform Law (1958), 147–50
Aref regime's anti-tribal posture, 155
Communist elements, 148, 151
coup (14 Jul 1958), 137–8, 145
coup (1968), 155, 160
coup 1958 and decline of the tribes, 138, 155–5
establishment, 137
kinship role, 139, 140, 149, 153–6
landowner and peasant relationship, 149–50
military coup (1963), 137, 153–4
sheikhs during Aref's rule, 155
sheikhs' political power, reduction of, 146–7
tribal bloc and revolt (Sep 1959), 151–2
tribes and monarchy, 138, 139, 140–5
Iraqi Security Forces, 214, 215
Ishkal, Barani, 39–40
Ishkal, Omar, 44, 73, 74

ISIS (Islamic State of Iraq and the Levant), 11, 225
allegiance of sheikhs, 241–2, 243
detainees in Al-Hoot prison (Nasseriyah), 252
expansion of, 239
Maliki's response to, 243–4
Marja'iya's mass tribal mobilisation (2014), 225, 239–40, 244–6, 247
propaganda video, 242–3
Qadhadhfah and, 125
Sirte under, 124–5
Takfiri ideology, 241
Islamic Republic of Iran, 177, 198, 209, 215, 221, 244, 246, 247, 255
embassy attack (Karbala), 249
al-Sadr (Mohamed Baqir) support, 178
See also Iran–Iraq War (1980)
Islamic Supreme Council of Iraq (ISCI), 202, 208, 220
Islamism, 9, 60, 178, 207
Islamist forces, 11, 60–1, 71, 87–9, 90, 95, 96, 100
Abu Sleem prison massacre (1996), 71
Benghazi authorities co-operation with, 115
Benghazi Revolutionaries Shura Council, 118
elections (Libya, 2012), 92, 96–9
See also al-Qaeda; ISIS (Islamic State of Iraq and the Levant)
Islamist forces and Misratan allies dominating in the west, 119
eastern tribes aversion towards, 114–15
elections result (Libya, Jun 2014), 110

INDEX

Operation Dignity campaign, 106, 107–9, 113, 114, 116, 117–18

Operation Libya Dawn (July 2014), 110–12

Operation Sunrise (Dec 2014), 121–2

political agreement (Skhirat, Morocco), 119

isnads (Tribal Support Councils), 217–21

Israel, 16

Italians, 32, 259

Ja'afara tribe, 59

Jabar, F A, 8, 138, 153, 55, 212, 241, 138, 153, 155

Jabber, Salim, 122

Jaber, Abu Bakr Younis, 21
Jagayfa tribe, 243

Jalloud, Abdulsalam, 21, 23, 24, 31, 44
on Bani Walid plot (1993), 52–3, 54, 56
on coup (Libya, 1975), 37
on Free Officers dismissal, 38
on intercommunal rifts, 48, 50
on tribal engagement, 31, 33
on Tribal Laws and Wells law, 28, 29
tribal links, 33

Jamahiriyah system, 39, 42–3, 52, 56, 71

Janabi, Sheikh Adnan, 205

al-Jaroushi, Saqr, 127

Jawazi tribe, 49–50, 73

Jedhran, Ibrahim, 96, 119, 120–1, 122–3, 124

Jedhran, Salim, 122

al-Jerbi, Sheikh Fawaz, 222

Jibbour tribe, 175

Jibril, Mahmoud, 98

Jihad/jihadists, 123, 209, 211, 212, 259
against foreign invaders, 32
Libyans in Afghanistan, 60
al-Sistani call for, 244–6, 247
See also al-Qaeda; ISIS (Islamic State of Iraq and the Levant)

al-Jubouri, Sattam Ghanem, 180

al-Judai, Sheikh Taher, 78

Jumail, Libya, 46

Jumailat tribe, 155

al-Juroushi, Suqour, 122

Justice and Construction Party (JCP), 96, 98

Juwaili, Osama, 82–3

al-Kadhem, Mousa, 57

Karaghala, 81

Karamanli dynasty, 49

Karbala, 149, 181, 200, 221, 237, 249

Karbalai, Sheikh Abdulmehdi, 244, 248

al-Kassid, Sheikh Kadhem Risaan, 182

al-Keib, Abdulrahman, 83, 94

al-Kezza, Sheikh Abdulhameed, 120, 130, 256

al-Kezza, Sheikh Abdulsalam, 33

Kharbit, Sheikh Mazhar, 197, 199–200

'Khout al-jed' ('brothers of the grandfathers'), 43–7, 51, 53, 56, 85

kidnappings, 104, 213

kinship, 3, 6, 69, 153–6, 255
part in voting patterns, 97
Qadhafi on, 19, 30, 32, 38–40, 56
role of kinship in Iraqi Republic, 139, 140, 149, 153–6, 175

INDEX

Kurdish parties, 221–2
Kurdish rebellion, 184
Kurdish revolt (1975), 170
Kurdish tribes, 7, 10, 151, 178
Kuwait, invasion of (1990), 181, 187

landowning sheikhs, 141–4, 149–50, 170
Lattioush, Sheikh Salah, 113
Lempert, Yael, 200, 201
Lévy, Bernard-Henri, 80
Libya Shield 1 Brigade, 115
Libya Shield 2 Brigade, 115
Libya Shield Brigades, 90
Libya. *See* Qadhafi regime; Qadhafi, Muammar; post-2014 order (Libya)
    GDP, 20
    migration, 20
    oil discovery (1959), 20, 58
    'revolutionary legitimacy', 81
    statelessness image of, 3–4
Libyan Iron and Steel Company (LISCO), 37
Libyan Islamic Fighting Group (LIFG), 60–1
Libyan National Army (LNA), 11, 105, 116, 118, 119, 123–4, 126, 128, 132, 260
    al-Kaniat merge, 132
    attempted to detain al-Bargathi, 127
    formation of, 108
    Jedhran's forces and, 122
    military machine, strength of, 130
    Operation Dignity campaign, 106, 107–9, 113, 114, 116, 117–18
    al-Qaim's arrest, 129
    took control of Gharyan, 131

Tripoli attack, 131–3
al-Lwatti, Sheikh Breiq, 128

al-Ma'arafi, Giuma, 79
Maadan tribe, 82
Madkhalist forces, 106
Magarha tribe, 21, 22, 23, 33, 37, 38, 39, 59
    Arab Spring and, 78–9
    disengaged with electoral process, 93
    vs. Hasawna, 50–1
    vs. Mashashiya, 50
    in post-2014 order, 104
    subjected to revenge attacks, 86
al-Magariaf, Mohamed, 21–2, 32–3, 62
Magharba tribes, 42, 94–5, 117
    and Haftar, 123–4
    oil ports under, 119–20, 121
al-Magri, Abdulwahab, 132
Mahameed tribe, 21
Mahawar, Sheikh Karim, 251
al-Mahjdoub, Mohamed, 39
Mahmoudi, Baghdadi, 46, 47, 70
Majabra tribe, 21
Majberi, Fathi, 127
al-Majid, Ali Hassan, 181
al-Majid, Saddam Kamel Hassan, 181
al-Majoun, Sheikh Sami, 144, 149, 150, 197, 198, 226, 238–9
    on Maliki, 214–15
    as a member of the constitution committee, 206, 207
    on Saddam, 164
    tribal bloc and revolt (Sep 1959), 151–2
Maliki, Nouri, 239
    criticised the British army, 213–14
    elections (2010), 227, 231–2

322

INDEX

engagement with the southern
tribes, 213–22, 226
isnads (Tribal Support
Councils), 217–21
local election victory (2009),
226
Operation Saulat al-Fursan
(Charge of the Knights),
214–17
response to ISIS's growing
power, 243–4
response to Sunni protest
movement (2012), 240
took power, 208
tribal conferences (Babylon
Hotel, Baghdad), 226–7
tribes under, 207–13
Maliki, Sheikh Sabah, 217
Maliki, Sheikh Salam, 217
al-Mangoush, Yousef, 115
Marja'iya, 5, 11, 253
Ashura killings (2004), 237–8
constitution, 207
intervention in constitution, 239
during invasion of Iraq, 236–7
ISCI and, 220
khums payment, 234–5
mass tribal mobilisation (2014),
225, 239–40, 244–7
norms and customs, 235
role in Iran–Iraq War (1980),
178
role of *Marja'iya*, 234–5, 236
Shi'ite tribes and, 166, 225
Al-Sistani influence, 235, 236–
8
support to tribal bloc, 151
tribes and, 225, 234–47
Martyrs of al-Jazeera Brigade, 121
Mashashiya tribe, 50, 85, 86
Matouq, Mohamed, 54
Meesan Provincial Council, 198

Mehdi Army, 195, 202, 213, 214,
215, 216
al-Mehishi affair (1975), 35–8, 44,
52
al-Mehishi, Omar, 22, 35, 36, 37
Men and the City (Saddam), 162–3
Menfa tribe, 33
military coup (Iraqi Republic,
1958), 138, 155–5
military coup (Iraqi Republic,
1963), 137, 153–4
military coup (Iraqi Republic,
1968), 155, 160
military coup (Libya, Sep 1969),
15, 21, 23–4
al-Minshed, Sheikh Mohamed,
143, 155
al-Minshed, Sheikh Takleef, 167,
168, 170, 172, 173, 179, 182,
183, 186, 218, 232
as governor of Dhi Qar, 198
on *Marja'iya* and tribes bond,
234
on Sadrists, 236
al-Mismari, Abu Bakr Bu Nuwar,
113
Misrata tribes, 6–7, 22, 49, 94,
100, 106
as new powerhouse, 81–2, 84–
5
settled in Benghazi neighbourhoods, 88
See also Islamist forces and
Misratan allies; revolutionaries (Libya)
Misrata, 36–7, 45
anti-Misratan sentiment, 117–18
government posts, 83
as 'Masareet', 117
military council, 82
tribal associations in, 58
tribal identity, 81–2

INDEX

tribal revenge, 84
modern state creation, 25–30
modernisation, 2, 30, 43, 69, 255, 256
Mohamed al-Magariaf Brigade, 39–40
Mohsen, Abduljabbar, 185
Mosul, 141, 150–1, 239, 241
under ISIS control, 241–2
al-Mukhtar, Omar, 33
Muntassars (family), 82
Muslah, Rashid, 154
Muthanna, 169, 183, 219, 220, 230, 232–3

al-Nada, Sheikh Ali, 164
nahwa, 235
Najaf, 181, 200
Najm, Mohamed, 22
Naker, Abdullah, 83
Nalut, 83
al-Nasser, Mohamed Saif, 19
Nasseriyah, 166, 167, 169, 179, 181, 182, 184, 188, 189, 218, 236
Al-Hoot prison (Nasseriyah), 252
protests, 225–6, 249, 250, 251, 253
National Assembly elections (Iraq, Jan 2005), 205, 206
National Conference for the Sheikhs of Libya's Tribes (Tripoli), 80
National Forces Alliance (NFA), 98
National Front for the Salvation of Libya (NFSL), 49, 53, 54
National Islamic Front, 60
National Reconciliation Conference I (10 Dec 2011), 93
National Transitional Council (NTC), 80, 81, 84, 89, 92

draft constitutional declaration (2011), 97
resolution 192 of 2011, 93
nationalism, 153, 261
nationalist period, 4, 5
dawn of, 21
NATO (North Atlantic Treaty Organisation), 79–80
Nawayal tribe, 46–7, 86, 105
Nineveh tribes, 242, 243
Noman, Sheikh Aziz Saleh, 186
NTC. *See* National Transitional Council (NTC)
Nuwairi, Ahmed, 47

Obeid tribe, 243
Obeidi, A, 3
al-Obeidi, Abdulati, 25
al-Obeidi, Abdulfattah Younis, 33, 76, 89, 107, 116
al-Obeidi, Hamid, 25
al-Obeidi, Sadique al-Gaithi, 95
al-Obeidi, Sheikh Mustafa, 242
al-Obeidi, Suleiman Mahmoud, 33, 76, 89
oil
boom (Libya), 20, 30
discovery (Libya, 1959), 20, 58
fall in prices, 52, 157
Libyan ports, 119–20, 121
nationalisation of oil sector, 32
Oil Crescent, 119, 120, 124, 133, 258
Operation Dignity campaign, 106, 107–9, 113, 114, 116, 117–18
Othman, Abdullah, 23, 33–4, 38, 58, 63, 79–80
Othman, Kamila, 34, 45
Ottoman rule, 32, 140, 141

PanAm 103 flight bombing (Lockerbie, 1988), 52, 67

324

INDEX

Petraeus, David, 211–12
Petroleum Facilities Guard (PFG), 119, 120, 122, 123
PFG. *See* Petroleum Facilities Guard (PFG)
PMF. *See* Popular Mobilisation Forces (PMF)
Popular Army, 286n82
Popular Mobilisation Committee, 247
Popular Mobilisation Directorate, 244
Popular Mobilisation Forces (PMF), 243–4, 245–7, 249
Popular Mobilisation Units, 225
post-2014 order (Libya), 103–34
  Haftar and the eastern tribes, 112–18
  new divisions, 106–11
  Operation Dignity campaign, 106, 107–9, 113, 114, 116, 117–18
  Operation Libya Dawn (July 2014), 110–12
  'Operation Snake Bite', 118
  Operation Sunrise (Dec 2014), 121–2
  tribal relationships management, 126–34
  See also Haftar, Khalifa
post-Qadhafi period, 69
  eastern region in, 87–92
  new powerhouses, 81–7
  tribal identity in, 8–9
Presidency Council, 119, 127
Proclamation of the Republic, 16

al-Qa'ud, Abdulmajid, 46
Qadhadhfah tribe, 18–19, 72
  Arab Spring and, 73, 74, 84
  as ashraf, 57
  as Awlad Mousa, 57–8

  Barassa revenge against, 87
  electoral process, disengaged with, 93
  on Haftar, 134
  Haftar meeting with, 112
  in post-2014 order, 104
  Qadhafi's initiatives, 32
  as security brigades, 39–40
  tribal alliances, 43–7
  tribal revenge against, 86
  and Warfalla tribal alliance, 44
Qadhaf al-Dam, Mohamed, 19
Qadhaf al-Dam, Sayid, 40, 62, 74
Qadhaf al-Dam, Sidi Omar, 18, 19
Qadhafi and revolutionaries. *See* Free Unionist Officers (Libya)
  military academy (Benghazi), 19–20
  reliance on tribal sheikhs, 16, 34
  seized power, 15, 21
  as 'the sons of the country's tribes', 23
Qadhafi regime
  fall of, 68, 81
  foreign policy, 52
  modern state creation, 25–30
  as a 'pariah state', 43, 52, 67
  political activity, intolerance to, 56–7, 60
  political parties, banning of, 34–5
  security brigades, 39–40
  state-tribe relationship, 9, 43, 257
  tribal engagement, 30–40
  tribal role in, 3, 10, 16–18
  US unilateral sanctions, 52
Qadhafi, Abdulkader Said, 40
Qadhafi, Khamis, 72
Qadhafi, Moatassim, 70, 72
Qadhafi, Muammar
  buying loyalty, 60

325

INDEX

children of, 70–3
education, 19–20
end of, 80–1
on kinship and descent, 19
link with eastern tribes, 33
military academy (Benghazi), 19–20
military coup (Sep 1969), 15, 21, 23–4
multi-layered security apparatus, 56
rebellion against, 35–8
'revitalised tribalism', 17, 57
'stateless state', 3–4
tribal alliances, crafting, 10, 41, 47
tribal balance, maintaining, 47–52
his tribal identity, 18–24
tribal symbolism, employed, 2, 3, 17, 57
Tripoli University address, 16–17, 26
views on kinship relations, 30, 32
See also Qadhadhfah tribe; Qadhafi and revolutionaries; Qadhafi regime
Qadhafi, Saif al-Islam, 70–1, 72, 76, 87, 88, 108
Qahsat tribe, 46
al-Qaim, Faraj, 128–9, 130
Qassim, Abdulkarim, 137, 140, 145
Agrarian Reform Law (1958), 147–50
Shawaf on, 150
Qussay (Saddam's son), 181
Qwayfiya, Benghazi, 89, 91, 97, 115
al-Qzeeri, Tareq, 117

Rafa'i, Rafa (Mufti of Iraq), 244

Rajban tribe, 51
Ramadi, 155, 167, 168, 181, 195–6, 213, 227
Sunni protest movement (2012), 240
Rashidun army, 177
Republican Guard (Iraq), 161, 165, 175, 184
Republican Guard (Libya), 36, 38
retribalisation
in Iraq, 179–80, 185, 255
in Libya, 30–40, 95
revolutionaries (Libya), 81–7
dominance of, 103–4
elections (2012), 92, 96–9
Operation Dignity campaign, 106, 107–9, 113, 114, 116, 117–18
rise of, 81–7
tribal revenge, 75, 83–7, 92
See also Arab Spring in Libya (2011) and aftermath
Revolutionaries Brigades' Gathering, 88, 95
Revolutionary Command Council (RCC) (Iraq), 160, 161, 165, 167
Revolutionary Command Council (RCC) (Libya), 21, 36, 39
land ownership laws, 27–9
members and their tribes, 21–3, 22t, 25
redrawing of administrative boundaries, 29–30
supported by Barassa tribe, 24
tribal engagement, 31, 32
Revolutionary Committees, 39, 48
revolutionary new order (Libya), 81–7
al-Ribat, Sheikh Hussein, 183
al-Ribat, Sheikh Kadhem, 186
al-Rubai, Najib, 151–2

INDEX

al-Rumaid, Nadhem Faris, 246
al-Rumaidha, Sheikh Sabah Faris, 246
Rumaila, Mousa, 29, 45
Rumaitha, 238
rural-to-urban migration
Iraq, 138–9, 144–5
Libya, 58–9

Saba'a tribe, 59
Sadoun, Sheikh Sabri, 186
Sadr City, Baghdad, 196
al-Sadr, Ayatollah Mohamed Sadiq, 235–6
al-Sadr, Mohamed Baqir, 178
al-Sadr, Moqtada, 202, 216, 236, 246
Sadrists, 202, 208, 233, 235–6
Safa'ah, Majed, 139, 168, 252
Saff al-Fawqi, 19
al-Safi, Safa, 216
Safi, Tayib, 76–7, 130
Sahban Brigade, 59
Saif al-Nasr family, 48
Saif al-Nasr, Ghaith Abdulmajid, 36
Salaamla tribe, 59
Salabi, Ismail, 117
Samawah, 238
Saraya Salam Brigades, 246
Sarkasli, Mustafa, 88
Sasanian Empire, 177
Sayan tribe, 86
Sebha, 36, 37, 50, 74, 86, 97
sectarianism, 9, 158, 199, 208, 226
al-Senussi, Abdullah, 33, 53
Senussi, Saleh al-Ghazail, 47
al-Sha'alan, Hazem, 198
al-Sha'alan, Sheikh Hussein Ali, 182, 183, 198, 221
Shabana tribe, 143

Shabiya (province) system, 59
Shalgam, Abdulrahman, 45, 62, 70
al-Shamakh, Embarak, 33, 76
Shammar tribes, 142, 143, 151, 205, 222
Qassim's general pardon to, 151
Shanafiya, 183
Sharefan officers, 141, 145
Sharif, Sheikh Tayib, 116, 116
Shatt al-Arab Battalion, 216, 217
Shawaf, Abdulwahab, 150–1
'Sheikhs of the Millennium' ('4x4 Sheikhs'), 204
'Sheikhs of the Nineties', 188–9
Shi'ite political parties, 195, 209, 224
mistrust between Sunni tribal sheikhs and, 212
See also Iraq political parties and tribes
Shi'ite tribes of Iraq, 5, 7, 10, 11, 161
Islamism, 178
Maliki engagement with, 213–22
parliamentary elections (2005), 207
relationship with the parties, 234
sympathetic to the Islamic Republic, 177–9
Tishreen (October) Movement (2019), 247–53
uprising (Mar 1991), 182
See also Marja'iya
Shimmeri, Jameel, 251
Shirshab, Adel, 196
Showka, Sheikh Hamid, 204
Shyasha tribe, 162
Sidi Khalifa, 97, 128
Sirte Revolutionaries Brigade, 124–5

INDEX

Sirte Supreme Security Council (SSC), 124–5

Sirte, Libya, 18–19, 74, 84, 112, 124
  LNA forces takeover of, 126
  Misrata retook control of, 125–6
  under ISIS, 124–5

al-Sistani, Grand Ayatollah Ali, 206, 235, 236–8
  fatwa, 244–6, 247

Social People's Leaderships (SPL), 17, 61–3, 71, 79

'social tribalism', 8, 254

Social Youth Associations, 71–2

Soudan tribe, 227

Souq al-Shayouk, 182

State of the Law Alliance, 221, 227, 231, 232

'stateless state', 3–4

Stevens, Chris, Ambassador, 92

Suff al-Fawqi, 19, 44

Sulouq, Libya, 48

Sultan, Naji, 2, 234

Sunni tribes of Iraq, 5, 7, 10, 137, 161, 176, 180
  al-Qaeda and, 208–10
  Ashura killings (2004), 237–8
  co-ordination with US, 211–12
  joined ISIS, 240–1, 243
  kinship alliances, 154
  parliamentary elections (2005), 207
  protests (Dec 2012), 228, 239–40
  sent their sons to Istanbul, 141

Supreme Council of Tribes, 109

Supreme Security Committees (SSCs), 90–1

Surman, 105

al-Suwayhili, Faraj, 85

al-Suwayhili, Ramadan, 37, 85

Tamimi, Sheikh Kenan, 186

al-Tamimi, Sheikh Mansour, 189–90, 192, 199, 213, 215, 216, 250–1, 256
  on PMF, 247

tapu (land tenure), 141–2

targeted assassinations, 115, 117, 118

targeted killings, 115

Tarhouna tribes, 6–7, 62, 131, 105

Tarhouna, 45, 79, 82, 107, 113, 131–2

Tarkarta tribes, 163

Tayib al-Safi, 33

Tebu tribes, 86, 131

Tehran. *See* Islamic Republic of Iran

Tikrit tribes, 154, 161–2

Tikrit, 162, 163, 164, 284n20
  al-Awja village, 162, 163

al-Tikriti, Hardan, 154, 161–2

Tikritisation, 165

Tishreen (October) Movement (2019), 247–53

tribal affiliation, 17, 59
  Qadhafi's stern warning against, 42

tribal *asabiya*, 148, 155, 159, 162, 174

tribal associations, 58, 71

tribal bloc and revolt (Iraq, Sep 1959), 151–2

tribal committee, 165, 215

tribal conferences, 193
  al-Aziziya tribal conference (25 May 2014), 109–10
  Diwaniyah conference (2018), 247
  'General Conference of the Sheikhs of Iraqi Tribes and Clans' (Baghdad), 226–7
  Nasseriyah conference (15 Apr 2003), 197–8, 200

INDEX

National Conference for the Sheikhs of Libya's Tribes (Tripoli), 80
National Reconciliation Conference I (10 Dec 2011), 93
Tribal Criminal and Civil Disputes Regulation (1918), 141–2, 146
tribal culture
  degga, 235
  'Khout al-jed' ('brothers of the grandfathers'), 43–7, 51, 53, 56, 85
  nahwa, 235

tribal identity, 6–9
  Qadhafi and, 3
tribal land ownership, 27–9
  land tenure, 141–2
  landowning sheikhs, 141–4, 149–50, 170
Tribal Lands and Wells Laws, 27–9
tribal militias
  Arab Spring in Libya and, 89–90
  dominance and control, 1
  Iraqi political parties and their own, 202–3
  rise of militias in Iraq, 195
  Tripoli under the control of, 86, 91
  See also individual tribal militias by their names
tribal mobilisation
  mass tribal mobilisation (2014), 225, 239–40, 244–7
  Tishreen (October) Movement (2019), 247–53
tribal revenge, 75, 83–7, 92, 210, 237
  degga, 235
tribalism

elimination of, 138, 139–40
Iraq's post-1958 regimes and, 153
patronage and corruption, 16–17
Qadhafi 'revived', 17
Qadhafi on, 26
reduction of, 34
with feudalism, 138, 146, 149
tribes
  alternative centres of power, 42–3, 47–52
  codes of behaviour, 210
  Green Book on, 34
  inter-tribal conflict, 259
  literature on, 1–3
  Qadhafi as 'master manipulator', 42–3, 47–52
  as revolutionary toolkit of Qadhafi, 41–65
  structural transformation, 256–7
  term, 6
  tools of legitimacy, 56–65
Tripoli, 73, 74, 79
  fall of, 80–1
  new government in (2015), 119
  Operation Libya Dawn (July 2014), 110–12
  tribal associations in, 58
  under militias control, 86, 91
  US bombing raids on, 52
Tuareg tribes, 86
Tulfah, Khairallah, 163, 164, 169
Tulfah, Sajida Khairallah, 163
Tunisia, 60, 68, 70, 110
Turkoman tribes, 7

Uday (Saddam's son), 164, 181
UN (United Nations)
  air and arms embargo on Libya, 52

329

INDEX

peace process, 103, 119
political agreement (Skhirat, Morocco), 119
UN Food and Agriculture Organisation, 28
United Iraqi Alliance, 207, 208
urbanisation, 2, 20, 30, 69, 255
US (United States)
  bombing raids on Benghazi, 52
  Mission in Benghazi, 92
  tribal engagement and fight against al-Qaeda, 211–12
  tribal engagement of Americans, 203–5
  unilateral sanctions on Libya, 52
  US military personnel meeting with the sheikhs, 197

Wadi Ahmar, 94
Wadi al-Mardoom, Bani Walid, 29
Wagner Group, 132
Wakwak, Ezzadine, 89
War on Terror, 67
Warfalla tribe, 37, 38, 39, 42
  Arab Spring and, 73, 74, 78, 80
  disengaged with electoral process, 93
  khout al-jed with Zintan, 85, 111
  plot against Qadhafi, 52–6, 64
  in post-2014 order, 104, 117
  senior posts in the military, 53–4
  Social Council, 84
al-Warfalli, Muftah Matouq, 80
Warshefana tribe, 34, 79, 85–6, 105, 110
  support to Zintan, 111
Warshefana (area), 45

al-Waziri, al-Senussi S, 76
Wisemen's council, 100
WMD programmes, 67

al-Yawar, Sheikh Ahmed Ajil, 150–1, 153–4
al-Yawar, Sheikh Ahmed, 143
al-Yawar, Sheikh Ajil, 143
al-Yawar, Sheikh Ghazi, 205, 290n50
'Yellow Hats', 74

Zadma family, 48
al-Zarqawi, Abu Musab, 209
Zawiya Martyrs' Brigade, 125
Zawiya town, 30, 58, 82, 83, 101
Zawiya tribes, 6–7, 85–6, 105
Zayidi, Mustafa, 130
Zeidawi, Sheikh Mohamed, 214, 230, 245
Zidan Ali, 99
Zintan, 78, 82, 107, 108
  Bani Walid attack refusal, 85
  government posts, 83
  military council, 82–3
  Operation Libya Dawn (July 2014), 110–12
  tribal gathering (Jul 2013), 101
Zintani tribes, 6–7, 51, 64, 94, 98, 105
  attack on Mashashiya, 85
  Haftar and, 108, 109, 132
  as new powerhouse, 81–4
  Qadhafi address, 272–3n97
Zobah tribe, 197
Zuwiy, Salah Ghazal, 77
Zuwiya tribe, 3, 36, 42, 73, 77, 116, 121, 274n37
  Haftar and, 131, 133
Zwai, Mohamed Belqassim, 46